Light upon the River

HYMN TEXTS
BY CHRISTOPHER M IDLE

*Dedicated to the memory of three
Godfearing teachers of English:
J S M Thompson; C A A Parkinson; R E C Houghton*

Light upon the River

HYMN TEXTS
BY CHRISTOPHER M IDLE

ST MATTHIAS PRESS
Hope Publishing Company

© Copyright Christopher M Idle

see permissions and copyrights on page xiii for exceptions.

Published by
St Matthias Press,
P.O.Box 665,
London SW20 8RU,
UK

in association with

Hope Publishing Company
380 South Main Place,
Carol Stream, IL 60188,
USA

Hope Code no: 8012

ISBN: 1-873166-72-9

Printed in the UK by Print in Black

Cover photography: Jonathan Mark
Design: Tim Thornborough

FOREWORD

Few of the many sermons which I heard in my school days have lodged in my memory. This may be the fault of the preachers or of the listener. Perhaps certain sermons do their work even when they are forgotten, just as we cannot remember the meals we ate a month ago though they nourished us at the time. But I do recall quite vividly, more than fifty years later, one preacher solemnly advising us 'not to rush into print before the age of thirty-five'. As far as the hymn writer is concerned, this is good advice, however unsuitable for that occasion. And as one who for some years now has been urging Christopher Idle to publish a collection of his hymn texts (even if not quite since his thirty-fifth birthday) I have good reason for welcoming this definitive collection.

Within these covers you will find a voice which is characterized by much that is best in contemporary Christian hymnody. These texts are rooted, to begin with, in the pastoral ministry, the nurturing of faith and the leading of worship among congregations typical of those which line the Thames in south or east London, or which gather, sometimes in single figures, in the ancient churches of the East Anglian countryside. They spring from a practical understanding of the needs of a congregation.

But to render the highest service to a worshipping church, the hymn writer must first be a servant of the Word. John Stott has familiarized us with the idea of 'double listening', attending both to the world's agenda and to the voice of God in Scripture; and, as the Biblical references attached to these texts bear witness, the writer belongs to those who find in Scripture both the starting place, and the authenticating touchstone, of Christian song.

Charles Wesley's hymns have been described as containing 'the Bible in solution' and as being 'filled to saturation with Bible words, Bible similes, Bible metaphors, Bible stories, Bible themes'. By contrast, Christopher Idle has demonstrated elsewhere how in some modern worship songs 'even within the music the gospel, may be dissolved—slowly, sweetly and almost imperceptibly, but so decisively as to deceive if possible the elect.' This is the same metaphor used in two opposite senses. In the first, Wesley's hymns, the word of Scripture is so held in solution as to be communicated whenever they are read or sung. In the second, the gospel is being leached out and lost. The most casual reading of these texts will show to which of these categories they belong.

But I would not want to encourage merely a casual reading. One of the characteristics of this author is a lively mind, original, 'quirky' even, certainly thought-provoking. It has become over recent years steeped in the study and craft of hymnology, and by an understanding of our inheritance which sees further than most in interpreting the contemporary scene. Consider this, from the paper quoted above, as part of a perceptive analysis of the way words are used by differing schools of hymn writers:

> The Sydney Carter of the 1960s, though in some ways unique, certainly influenced others. So in *Lord of the dance* and *When I needed a neighbour,* 'holy' and 'creed' respectively are used in a pejorative sense. With this latter still a school favourite, in the absence of anything more convincing, generations of children grow up knowing nothing whatever about the creed except that it doesn't matter.

It is a weighty responsibility to put words into the mouths of worshippers, and the texts that comprise this book set out to be considered in what they say and (as befits a graduate in English) carefully crafted in how they say it. That is why they repay careful reading, and should withstand the repetition by which a hymn becomes a means of grace to the worshipper as well as an expression of praise to Almighty God. Just as John Wesley could say of his famous *A Collection of Hymns for the Use of the People called Methodists* (1779) that there was 'no doggerel, no botches, nothing put in to patch up the rhyme, no feeble expletives... no words without meaning', so you will not find in this collection what the author has boldly called 'drivel'. This is very different from the merit of simplicity; it is what the dictionary defines as 'idiotic utterance', a plain description of what most of us, on occasion, have been invited to sing from chorus sheet or OHP.

And to the pastoral heart, the Scriptural foundation, the original and imaginative cast of mind, the reading and study in literature and hymnology, one can add a musical ear. These are not texts only; they are *hymns*. Because the author, I suspect, hears them with an inward ear, they need to be sung as well as read upon the page. Unlike some texts which read well, they will then not disappoint.

And will they last? Perhaps that is not a question we should be asking. Paul, you remember, preaching at the synagogue at Antioch, spoke of King David as 'one who served the purpose of God in his own generation' (Acts 13.26), which is an aspiration high enough for any believer. T S Eliot, who brought a Christian mind to bear upon his art, had this to say of such unprofitable speculations:

> With our contemporaries, we oughtn't to be so busy enquiring whether they are great or not; we ought to stick to the question: 'Are they *genuine*?' and leave the question whether they are great to the only tribunal which can decide: *time*.
> ('On Poetry and Poets', London, Faber & Faber 1957)

We must surely agree that the lasting quality of greatness is not one to be claimed for contemporary hymns. It is as impossible as it is unnecessary for us to say. But of the *genuineness* of the texts that follow, no understanding reader can long be in doubt.

Timothy Dudley-Smith
April 1998

CONTENTS

Foreword v
by Bishop Timothy Dudley-Smith

Biographical note viii

Introduction ix

Permissions and Copyrights xiii

Hymn texts and notes:
    Nos. 1-200   Hymns through the Bible, except Psalms 16

    Nos. 201-264   From the Book of Psalms: versions and selections 217

    Nos. 265-279   Local and special: for particular congregations 286

Index of Scripture texts 310

Index of tunes 318

Index of selected themes 320

Index of hymn texts 323

BIOGRAPHICAL NOTE

Christopher Martin Idle was born at Bromley, Kent on September 11th 1938. After schooling at Eltham College he worked in an office, shop and hospital before studying English at St Peter's College Oxford and Theology at Clifton Theological College, Bristol. He married Marjorie Rycroft, who was then nursing, in 1963, and he was ordained in 1965. Following curacies at Barrow in Furness (Cumbria) and Peckham (SE London) he moved across the Thames to spend the next eighteen years in the London Borough of Tower Hamlets, at Poplar and Limehouse. In 1989 he became Rector of seven Suffolk villages joined as the Benefice of North Hartismere, resigning in 1995 and returning to inner London. In 1997 he was appointed Associate Minister of Christ Church, Old Kent Road, where he had earlier been curate.

Christopher and Marjorie have four much-travelled sons, all at present in England. Marjorie is also a writer and is the author of *Joy in the City* about their Limehouse years. They both enjoy books, music, family and friends. Christopher has written and spoken widely about hymns and served on several hymnal committees. His own texts appear in over a hundred hymn books world wide; among other writing was a weekly column in the East London Advertiser, editing the quarterly *News of Hymnody*, and three series on the Theology of Winnie-the-Pooh. He had a weekly slot on BBC Radio Suffolk; other concerns include the peace movement, issues of justice and development, and sharing the Christian gospel. Football and jogging are among his recreations.

Christopher Idle has also written:

The Lion Book of Favourite Hymns (Lion 1980; also *The Lion Book of Famous Hymns*, 1991)
Hymns in Today's Language? (Grove Books 1982)
The Journal of John Wesley (edited and abridged, Lion 1986)
Christmas Carols and their Stories (Lion 1988)
What shall we sing? (Fellowship of Word and Spirit 1996)
The Word we preach, the words we sing (Reform 1998)

He has contributed to more than a dozen other books, and provided a regular column for the monthly *New Directions* entitled 'Idle Curiosity: Highways and Byways of Hymns'.

INTRODUCTION

Nothing can adequately replace a Christian hymn. Is that a controversial claim? Even more arguably, I believe that nothing can adequately replace a Christian hymn book!

I do not want here to join the multitude who have tried to define a hymn. This collection includes some verses which look, and sound, more like songs, and one whole section intended for use as a resource for versions of the Biblical Psalms. True, the hymn as commonly understood in English is a relatively recent creature, and the hymnal even more so. But we have inherited some of the finest fruit from a wonderfully varied tree whose roots go deep into the Hebrew and Greek Scriptures which Christians receive as the word of God. In that sense all our hymns are 'modern', and those who dislike new things should, to be consistent, go back not just to singing metrical Psalms, but to using only the words of Scripture in the most accurate translation available.

But before we yield to the demands of the computer revolution, and present everything on a service sheet, an overhead projector screen, or even some vast electronic display, I hope we think long and hard about the many advantages of arranging, choosing, and singing hymns from the pages of a hymnal—not as the only available option but at least as one that is expected and familiar. I cannot believe that Christians who work daily with complex technology, whether on a car dashboard or a supermarket checkout, will really go to pieces in finding their way round a hymn book, or (of far greater significance) a Bible.

To arrange hymn texts alphabetically may be appropriate for a supplement, a mission booklet, a personal collection, or some other specialist production. But it hardly makes a hymnal fit for the congregation; hymn-choosing may easily become either an exhausting business or a random one. We faithfully plough through the indexes (if any) or we simply see what catches the eye on the opposite page; it is easy to get stuck in a favourite rut. A hymn book, as distinct from a mere assortment, expresses the mind of the Christian community on the patterns and proportions of its faith.

Whether the texts are arranged in terms of what believers experience (as John Wesley's choices famously were), or of the Christian calendar (however wide-ranging some items may be), or in a simple but systematic credal scheme (with suitable cross-referencing), the plan of the book is a constant reminder that 'worship' did not start with us, or even the day before yesterday. It brings together the best of what many generations, even centuries, have found to be true about the incarnation, or believed to be important about the cross, or asserted about the resurrection in the face of a mocking, persecuting, or indifferent world. It is a ready-made teaching aid in which the beginner can learn to delight, and the veteran explore the heights and depths of doctrine and devotion. Whatever mysteries still hide the origin of some of the Psalms, that book too has a shape to it; those 150 Hebrew songs were not thrown together at random, nor seen, heard or sung in isolation from one another. To use your church's hymnal, and to get to know and love it, is to experience the communion of saints, and to taste some of the joys of Hebrews 11 and 12.

Anyone picking up this book and reading thus far will presumably have some sympathy with these paragraphs. You are at this moment reading a printed page rather than pressing switches for a screen! But you will be aware of the resistance to hymns which in a few years has moved away from Quakers and Roman Catholics, and is now found in many churches where this year's songs are the main course; not, please notice, last year's, and not the main course of the music but the main course of the whole gathering.

In one of the finest works on hymns written in this century or any other, Professor J R Watson of Durham University concludes by hoping that his book may help 'to preserve the serious appreciation of hymns as literary texts and as aids to worship', and that it will have been worth while 'if it manages to slow down their disappearance in an age of neglect from outside the Church and from within it' (*The English Hymn*, Clarendon Press 1997). His words are chosen with care; his literary approach is robust, fascinating and distinctive, but it seldom loses sight of the singers on their feet on Sunday morning—or indeed, evening. He is aware of the later twentieth century form of the flight from faith and reason towards instinct and emotion. A wholesale distrust of what is perceived as cerebral makes hymns an easy target in a satirical age. The years, the centuries and the millennia are on the turn, and those of us who love hymns, and would support any of the various campaigns for real ones, must do our best to make sure that such treasures are not lost to our children's children.

So what am I doing about it, and what use is yet another collection of contemporary texts to what some might see as a dying cause and others as an already vast mountain of material, rivalled only by the Victorians at their hymn-writing peak? I count myself rich to have grown up on a diet of John Mason Neale in church on Sundays, and Isaac Watts at school assembly every weekday. Only later did I discover the wealth of Wesley, which of course I am still exploring; let alone the range of evangelical writers on both sides of the Atlantic. As a student in the Oxford Inter-Collegiate Christian Union (OICCU), I counted it the chief and most contentious action of our year on the 'exec' to steer through the replacement of 'Golden Bells' with 'Christian Praise'—one of those smaller, quality productions which still has much to teach the editors of fuller congregational books.

I have enjoyed writing almost since I can remember; verse or prose, comic or serious, short or long. When making for the nearest bus-stop, I always check that I have paper and pen somewhere about me. But although I ventured to edit gently one of the traditional hymns we had chosen for our wedding, I wrote my first hymn texts in 1965. My fellow-curate David Griffiths must take some responsibility here; needing some new words for one of the Youth Services of those days, he was the first to prompt me, while Michael Baughen first used my words more widely. I owe a debt of continuing gratitude to them both.

Since then, most of my texts have been written for similar reasons and at similar times. The reason, even when linked to the outward opportunity, was an inward compulsion; for the moment, everything else had to stop. The time, consequently, was often when I should probably have been doing something else.

The 'something else' has usually been part of my work as Rector (or similar) of a Church of England parish. Sooner or later I had to stop writing and resume rectoring; but I have invariably found that the two ministries are interwoven—I trust from above, since they are both received 'by the mercy of God' (2 Corinthians 4.1). As without the unrivalled privilege of parish ministry there would be little raw material from which to fashion a hymn, so also the 'duty and delight' of writing has fed the other parts of my work.

For the record, the main places of writing have been, in order: 31 Fife Street, Barrow in Furness; 63 Asylum Road and 59 Kings Grove, both London SE15; St Matthias Vicarage Poplar, and Limehouse Rectory, both E14; Oakley Rectory, Suffolk; and our present address, 13 Unwin Close, SE15 again. A handful of other sites and settings are indicated in the notes.

Marjorie, my wife, has usually prevented the worst of my work from leaving the house. With uncanny instinct she has repeatedly spotted weak points or obscure lines in early drafts; the only criticism of hers which I have not always yielded to is the painfully fair one: 'It's a bit long!' With far better musical sensitivity than mine, she has also guided me patiently away from bad tunes and towards better ones; she is not to blame for the choices which follow, but can often take credit for decisions between rival candidates, as well as much wisdom and toil towards assembling this collection..

Among other generous mentors, the chief for many years was Michael Perry. The loss of his kind but sometimes devastating criticism, and his unfailing friendship, was not the least reason for grieving at his early death in 1996. Thankfully, he completed so much of his own writing, both widely used and warmly treasured, in time to see an eloquent body of it in print.

Among many others whose companionship among the hymns I have valued over many years have been Timothy Dudley-Smith, whose own hymns have justly achieved the rank of modern classics, and whose most generous Foreword adds so much to this book; Ruth Day; Annette Farrer; Tim Grass; Bunty Grundy; Chris Hayward; the late Mervyn, Lord Horder; David Preston; Michael Saward; George Shorney; Jim Thompson; and Richard Underwood. Each of their roles has been distinct and beyond price; they each deserve at least a page, and my family, a book.

Others mentioned in later pages have written some wonderful tunes for my words. For practical reasons this book has no music; the words must stand in their

Light upon the River

own right, but that does not mean that they can do without their tunes! Where a new tune is indicated, I hope that hymn-users will apply for a copy of the music, as suggested on p.*xiii* . Members of the Hymn Societies in Britain and North America have been hugely stimulating in person and in print. The churches I have belonged to in Suffolk, London, and Barrow in Furness, have all played a patient and constructively critical role in my writing, whether knowingly or not. And I am very grateful to Tim Thornborough of St Matthias Press and George Shorney of Hope Publishing for making this collection possible. What about its plan?

The Northamptonshire town of Olney produced its own hymnal in 1779, and the *Olney Hymns* of Newton and Cowper became world-famous. Many of its classic hymns are still in wide use. Book One of its three sections is arranged in Bible order, with 141 hymns in a span from Genesis to Revelation. While not working quite so literally, Erik Routley was using a similarly Scriptural plan for *Rejoice in the Lord*, a hymnal of more than six hundred items, published posthumously by Wm B Eerdmans in 1985. This is in no way a successor to such classics; nor have I looked for balanced coverage of the Bible, since many of its chapters do not lend themselves to singing, and others are richly covered by other writers. Clearly too, not all these hymns here are expositions of the Scriptures under which they appear. But I hope the arrangement may help to indicate that hymns are servants of the word of God. They must never contradict its message by their own, nor distract a congregation from the Scriptures. If a hymn does not commend the Gospel by its text and in the singing, it does not deserve to be sung.

And the title of this collection? *As the light upon the river* was adopted by the Southwark Diocese as a hymn for its 75th anniversary celebrations in 1980. It appears here as No.265; the river is primarily the Thames, which has flowed along within walking distance of our five varied inner-London homes. But the river Waveney (see No.270) has its own very different, quieter attractions, as our parish boundary for six and a half precious years. As there are other rivers (Nos. 28, 198 and more) so there is another Light—which I find is an image coming in my first published hymn and in many of those in most use since then. In the end, beyond all millennia, Christ is our Light, and our river is endlessly changing yet totally reliable, delightfully surprising and constantly refreshing, because it is the water of his own life. If it is allowable to mix such metaphors and combine such activities, may we splash freely and drink deeply as we sing!

CMI Easter 1998

Light upon the River

PERMISSIONS AND COPYRIGHT

As with much hymnwriting, some of these texts have been modified for a variety of reasons since they first appeared in print. Those who use them are asked to note that the version printed here is the definitive and authorised text from the date of this publication. Very occasionally, small variations are allowed for specific reasons; for example, 'grain' for 'corn' in American books. Except where such permission has been given, please reproduce the text as printed here.

This also embodies the author's preferred style of layout, capitals, punctuation and spelling; there has to be room for some flexibility here (again, for American readers, or a publisher's house style), but all these factors are designed chiefly for clarity of understanding and singing. Some may prefer the custom of representing the divine name, particularly in Psalm versions, by 'LORD' rather than 'Lord', while others opt for different spellings of 'Hallelujah'. I ask only that the first lines of Nos. 73 and 242 should remain as they are, for ease of locating in Indexes! If the suggested tune is not yet in print or readily available, a copy may usually be obtained from the author via Jubilate Hymns if two stamped envelopes are supplied.

For all texts except Nos. 5 and 25, copyright is held by the author and is administered in the UK by Jubilate Hymns Ltd, c/o Mrs M Williams, 4 Thorne Park Road, Chelston, Torquay TQ2 6RX, and in the USA by Hope Publishing Co., c/o Mr Scott Shorney, 380 South Main Place, Carol Stream, Il 60188. For all other territories, please contact Jubilate Hymns for advice. Although in certain circumstances no fee may be charged for copies, permission to use all texts should be sought from the appropriate administrator.

Members of the Christian Copyright Church or School Licensing Scheme may reproduce the words—applying the correct copyright ascription on each copy—and account for it in their annual return to CCL. The texts are also available under CCLI and LicenSing arrangements.

Hymn texts Nos. 5 and 25 are © Copyright 1991 Christopher Idle and Stainer & Bell Ltd (PO Box 110, Victoria House, 23 Gruneisen Road, Finchley, London N3 1DZ) for the world except USA and Canada, and reprinted by kind permission from 'Hymns and Congregational Songs' Vol 2 No.3.

The extracts from 'Ballad of the Goodly Fere' from *Collected shorter poems of Ezra Pound,* and 'On Poetry and Poets' by T S Eliot are both reproduced by kind permission of Faber & Faber Ltd.

Light upon the River

Hymnographer: lines, slightly revised, which have appeared in the Bulletin of the Hymn Society of Great Britain and Ireland (October 1996) and in 'Silver Threads', for the Silver Jubilee of the Association of Christian Writers (March 1997).

Sometimes I have to chisel at the rock
to find an adverb, never mind a line;
I toil at the unyielding granite block
and rise as one emerging from the mine.

But sometimes I just brush away the sand
and see a shape already firm and trim;
the mind is far too rapid for the hand -
here stands this couplet, stanza, this whole hymn.

More often yet, some mixture of the two,
when finding just the word, the very rhyme;
I know the verse which soon took wings and flew,
and those which struggled through their upward climb.

But when Christ's people stand, the music sings,
then we can thrill to more important things.

27 December 1995

HYMN TEXTS
AND NOTES

HYMNS THROUGH THE BIBLE
except Psalms

Genesis 1.1-5
Evening: darkness and light

1 INTO OUR DARKNESS ONCE YOU CAME

Into our darkness once you came,
Jesus, our never-fading light;
now as we come to bless your name
judge us and save us, Lord, tonight.

One further day of grace has gone,
joys to remember, sins to mourn,
gifts overflowing, work undone
for which the time will not return.

No age, no shadow now turns back;
one span of life is ours to live:
have mercy, Lord, for your name's sake -
help us redeem each hour you give.

Evening and morning you have joined
as in the first of measured days;
so let each dawn and sunset find
your people greeting you with praise.

Soon we shall see you as you are,
Jesus whom earth and angels bless,
our midnight Hope, our morning Star,
our glorious Sun of righteousness.

LM Tune: OMBERSLEY

Scriptures: Jn 8.12 Psa 134.1; 25.11; 113.3 2 Kgs 20.9-11 Heb 9.27-28 Eph 5.16 Gen 1.1-5 1 Jn 3.2 Matt 25.6 Rev 2.28 Mal 4.2

Written: Limehouse, Jan 1980

In 1980 *Symphony*, a magazine of Christian verse, invited entries for a new evening hymn. This was one of two which I offered, using several Bible references to day and night, light and darkness. But it was my other text which was chosen to be printed; see No. 96.

Light upon the River

Genesis 1.6-10
Caedmon sings his Creator's praise

2 NOW PRAISE THE PROTECTOR OF HEAVEN

Now praise the Protector of heaven,
the purpose and power of the Lord;
all praise for his work shall be given,
our Guide and Defender and Guard.

In God's wise and wonderful plan
was made every marvellous thing;
in God all our blessings began,
the Father of glory, the King.

He first made the sky's lofty dome,
our holy Creator and Guard;
then fashioned the earth for our home
Almighty, Eternal, the Lord.

88.88. anapaestic Tune: STEVENAJ by Agnes Tang; CELESTE; or ADORAMUS

Scriptures: Gen 1.6-10; 2.4-15 Psa 104.24 Jas 1.17

Written: Poplar, May 1976; revised 1987

First published (this version): *Hymns for Today's Church* (Hodder and Stoughton) 2nd Edn 1987

According to the Venerable Bede (*Ecclesiastical History Bk 4*) Caedmon received the gift of song in a dream at the monastery of Whitby. Instructed by the Abbess Hild, Caedmon became a monk, writing and composing many Christian verses. Bede lists several, implying that before then the (Old) English language had not been used for such purposes. Since his Hymn of Creation *Nu scylun hergan hefaenricaes Uard* is his only undisputed original, it can claim to be the first known English hymn, from around AD 670. As there seemed no singable version available, I tried three varied paraphrases, keeping some of Caedmon's alliteration; this one was eventually selected. By the time HTC was due for a 2nd edition we were more aware of inclusive language issues; this text is less masculine-sounding than the first, which can be found in the 1982 edition. That may be fairer to its first author; this, to our own generation. Agnes Tang's tune was written in Sept 1996; meanwhile in 1991 'News of Hymnody' No.38 published Stephen Horsfall's DCM text *May heaven's guardian be praised.*

Light upon the River

Genesis 1.20-28
Creator and creatures

3 CREATOR GOD, WITH WHOM WE SHARE

Creator God, with whom we share
the ruling of your world, we ask
as we are named creation's heirs
make us more willing for our task.

For you have blessed all things that live,
that run or fly or swim or crawl;
but we were destined to receive
our stewardship of care for all.

All creatures share your gift of breath;
on every kind our race depends;
like us, they move from birth to death,
our servants, helpers, and our friends.

So turn us back from acts of wrong,
from all unkindness and neglect;
reverse the abuses of the strong
to right control and true respect.

Though now we find your world decayed,
enslaved by fear and locked in pain,
in Christ creation is remade,
all things restored, set free again.

O Christ, you shared a cattle stall
and rode the path a donkey trod;
Redeemer, Servant, Lord of all,
all creatures praise you, Lamb of God!

LM Tune: SUMMERCOURT by Keith Landis;
or WINCHESTER NEW

Scriptures: Gen 1.20-28 Rom 8.17-28 Eph 1.9-10 Col 1.15-20 Lk 2.6-7; 19.35 Jn 1.29

Written: Limehouse, 1977

My friend and neighbour Eddy Stride, while Rector of Spitalfields, often commented that most of the newer hymns about creation focused on the vegetable and mineral worlds, from flowers to galaxies, taking little note of the animal kingdom. As he said, Genesis 1.22 has a distinctive blessing at least on the swimmers and flyers; here is a text to reflect this, and our rediscovered responsibility as stewards of creation. Originally 1.3 read 'as man is named creation's heir', which gave a truer rhyme with the opening line. As to many this generic use of 'man' is no longer acceptable, I revised the first stanza in 1994. Similar changes, not always listed here, have been made in several texts. One tune is the first of several by Keith Landis suggested in this book; while Rector of a Californian parish he met me in London, sharing some of his own words and music. Further adventures of his come in my 'Christmas Carols and their Stories' (Lion 1988).

Light upon the River

Genesis 1.25; 2.19-20
Living creatures, living God

4 LONG BEFORE THE REIGN OF KINGS

Long before the reign of kings,
when the sun first lit the shore,
earth was filled with living things
God was pleased with what he saw.
Jungle beasts which Adam named,
creatures of the sea and air,
animals his children tamed
found God's blessing and his care.

God delighted to create
and supply with home and food
mites and monsters, small and great,
safely carried through the flood.
Forest dwellers, prairie herds,
all with fur or scale or wing,
tell his glory without words
and their Maker's splendour sing.

For they all fulfil his plan
and shall know his perfect reign
free from cruelty of man,
free from spur and whip and chain,
when gazelles lie down to sleep
next to hunters of the wild -
wolf and lamb and bear and sheep
tended by a little child.

God who sees the sparrow fall,
King of earth and sea and sky;
Holy Spirit, Lord of all,
without you we fade and die;
Christ our Sacrifice who came
as a lamb to shed your blood:
all that lives shall praise your name,
Maker, Saviour, living God!

77.77.D Tune: LITTLE HEATH by David Wilson; or ST EDMUND

Scriptures: Gen 1.16-17, 20-25; 2.19-20; 6-8 Psa 104.29; 148.7,10 Isa 11.6-7 Matt 10.29 1 Pet 1.19
Written: Limehouse, 1977

This text has an origin similar to that of No.3 above. Animal-lover Eddy Stride prompted me to express God's concern for animals, in a hymn with Biblical echoes stretching from creation to paradise via flood and redemption. It was printed in 1977 in a leaflet of the Catholic Study Circle for Animal Welfare, and in 1983 in the periodical 'Word and Music'. In 1980 it was accepted for a hymnal which never reached publication, but which alerted me to a possible match with David Wilson's tune. Several churches have used the words in local collections. Verse 1 line 4 uses the repeated phrase from Genesis 1 in the Good News Bible, a version I was then using

Light upon the River

Genesis 11.1-9
Cities of earth and heaven

5 GOD OF THE WORLD'S GREAT CITIES

God of the world's great cities
with all their soaring towers
as commerce builds its empires
and multiplies its powers:
    this is the earth that Jesus trod;
    do not abandon us, O God!

God of the crushed and broken
whose burdens Jesus bore,
in park and street and subway
you seek the helpless poor:
    still come to find them, and to save,
    whose city is their lifelong grave.

God of the friends and neighbours
whose pleasures Jesus knew,
whose births and deaths and weddings
bring tangled thoughts of you:
    in you they live and grow and move:
    O let them taste your total love!

God of the proud and mighty,
when crime or folly rules
remove earth's vicious tyrants,
restrain its godless fools:
    grant those you keep in their high place
    to love your truth, and know your grace.

God of the struggling remnant
baptized to bear that name
which at the end of all things
shall stand alone, supreme:
    O help your church, by your strong hand,
    confessing Christ, in Christ to stand.

God of the dawning kingdom,
while human wealth decays
you build a different city
of pure and lasting praise:
    here let your people live, O Lord,
    in Christ refashioned and restored.

76.76.88 Tune: STALHAM by Mervyn Horder

Scriptures: Gen 11.1-9 Jer 29.7 Lk 1.51; 19.10 Acts 17.27-28 Psa 14.1; 48; 87.1-3 Jn 19.11 Heb 11.10

Written: Limehouse, Aug 1980

First published: *Hymns and Congregational Songs* vol 2 no.3 (Stainer & Bell) Dec 1991. See page xiii for copyright note.

The metre is rare but regular; the text expresses some urban realities from a time when the Limehouse landscape was rapidly changing. We were being promised some nearby towers soaring higher than anything else yet—a promise fulfilled by the main Canary Wharf tower (a modern Babel?) in 1990. The rich were moving in and getting richer; most of the usual inner-city needs remained. These verses were revised in 1986 and need careful use; I struggled to find the adjective, for instance, in 3.4. I had no music in mind; John Wilson (of Guildford) who disapproved of the hymn's second word, suggested HOMINUM AMATOR. But the ideal tune came in Nov 1988 from the then 78-year-old Mervyn Horder. In December he played STALHAM at our piano, adapted from a wedding march he had composed earlier but which had remained unpublished. Words and music appeared together in 1991; in 1997 they were included in a worship resource pack ('Sounds like a beauty treatment'—MH) issued by the Church Urban Fund.

Light upon the River

Genesis 12.1-9
Setting out: looking ahead

6   THE GOD WHO SPOKE AT HARAN

The God who spoke at Haran,
who gave us his decrees
at Moreh and at Bethel
and Mamre's mighty trees:
this is the One we worship,
the living God we serve,
the Father pouring blessings
on those who least deserve.

From Abraham's long journey
to Moses' desert road
a people learned to travel
obedient to their Lord;
God's covenant of mercy
in every path and place
makes us his own by promise,
gives us himself by grace.

The God who sent the prophets
a kingdom to proclaim
has in the end sent Jesus
who bears the saving name:
the eternal Lord of glory,
the King who rules by love,
the Son who at his weakest
brings power from above.

Let none despise the promise
nor take such gifts in vain,
but come to find the cleansing
that purges every stain;
the freedom of God's children,
the joy of sins forgiven,
the Holy Spirit's fulness,
the sweet foretaste of heaven.

Let Abraham's true offspring,
set right by grace through faith,
be steadfast in their purpose,
obedient till death.
God speaks, and we will trust him;
his coming we expect:
he calls us friends, he loves us,
his mercy we reflect.

To God who chose his people
before they were conceived;
to Christ whose cross means victory
for all who have believed:
all glory in the highest
to God the Three-in-One!
and in the Holy Spirit
our path has just begun.

76.76.D Tune: KING'S LYNN

Scriptures: Gen 12.1-9; 13.3-4; 18.1ff Ex 15.22 Heb 1.1-3   1 Cor 1.18-25   2 Cor 6.1 Rom 4.16 Jas 2.23 Jn 15.15 Jer 1.5

Written: Peckham, 3 Jan 1996

Sometimes one text grows from another. While I was working, by request, on a Baptism hymn rooted in the covenant with Abraham, some thoughts reached the paper but not the hymn, which appears here as No. 9. After Christmas 1995 I began to gather the fragments, and early in the new year formed them into these verses. Their length demands a vigorous tune such as KING'S LYNN; they could also benefit from a procession to enhance the 'journey' theme (note: hymns sometimes need processions, not vice versa!). The early stanzas pick up several points where Abraham encountered the presence and word of God; later ones reflect the patriarch's place in the larger plan of redemption.

Genesis 12.1-9
Faith working

7 TO WALK THE WAY OF ABRAHAM

To walk the way of Abraham:
should that make us afraid?
'Go to the land that I will show' -
God called, and he obeyed.

To have the faith of Abraham:
can such things be achieved?
'Father of nations you shall be' -
God spoke, and he believed.

To pray the prayer of Abraham
is to be called God's friend
'Will not the Judge of earth do right?'
On his word we depend.

To join the race of Abraham
we trust what God has said:
so things impossible shall be,
for God can raise the dead.

To know the God of Abraham:
that is to know the name
of him who truly said 'Before
Abraham was, I am!'

CM Tune: DUNFERMLINE; or LONDON NEW

Scriptures: Gen 12.1-9; 15.6; 17.4; 18.23-33 Jas 2.23 Rom 4.16-25 Heb 11.8-19 Jn 8.58

Written: Peckham, 8 Dec 1995

This is another text which came about 'by accident' while I was working on the Biblical material about Abraham—see No. 9—which bore fruit in other, longer hymns. This one came with greater fluency, with each stanza staying close to its 'framework' quotation. Though written in Common Metre, it needs a carefully-chosen tune to match the stresses in each third line.

Genesis 15.1-6
The faith of Abraham

8 ABRAHAM'S FAITH

Abraham's faith give us today;
Abraham's prayer teach us to pray:
so shall we walk Abraham's way -
   glory be to God!

Abraham's life shall never end;
Abraham's church guide and defend:
hope of the world, Abraham's Friend -
   glory be to God!

Abraham's shield and great reward;
Abraham's Christ, alive, adored:
praise to your name, Abraham's Lord -
   glory be to God!

888.5 Tune: ABRAHAM by Stephen James

Scriptures: Heb 11.8 Gen 15.1; 18.22-33; 24.12 Isa 41.8 Rom 4.16 Jas 2.23 Jn 8.56

Written: York, Jan 1983

This was the first of several 'Abraham' texts,; it was written at the home of John and Isabel Young (46 St John St) where I had gone to fulfil a speaking engagement at the college where John was chaplain, and to recover from a bizarre incident at Limehouse, involving jogging past a fight outside a Chinese restaurant, which had left me limping. Not many of the existing hymns about Abraham said much about his faith, which is his central significance in much of the Bible; this is my starting point here. Stephen James' tune, composed later that year, makes this more of a song than a hymn; I adapted some phrases to match the music better.

Light upon the River

Genesis 15.1-6
Abraham's covenant family

9 THE COUNTLESS STARS OF HEAVEN

The countless stars of heaven,
the sands beside the sea:
to Abraham God promised
'So shall your children be'.
The patriarch believed it,
for God could do no less;
that act of faith was counted
as perfect righteousness.

So they became his people
and he became their God;
his promise gave direction,
his presence lit their road.
Committed to his covenant,
marked by his chosen sign,
to cross unknown horizons
they walked the path divine.

Lord Jesus, we have heard you
affirming Abram's faith,
and found the life eternal
that follows from your death:
so all who humbly enter
the kingdom of your heaven
are children of the promise,
baptized, set right, forgiven.

O let the world believe it!
The promise is for all;
for us and for our children
the Lord our God will call:
and those marked out as holy,
saved by one Man alone,
are one in Christ for ever,
adopted as his own.

Praise God our first Beginning;
praise Christ, the firstborn Son;
praise Father, Saviour, Spirit,
all-glorious Three-in-One -
creating from all nations
one new, beloved race:
the people of the covenant
to serve the God of grace.

76.76.D Tune: WOLVERCOTE; or OFFERTORIUM

Scriptures: Gen 15.5-6; 17.7-11; 22.17 Rom 1.5; 4.3ff; 5.17; 8.15-29; 9.8 Gal 3.6-8; 4.28 Heb 11.8-19 Jn 8.39,56, 3.14-16 Col 1.15,18; 2.9-12 Acts 2.28-39 1 Cor 7.14 1 Pet 1.9-10; 5.10

Written: Peckham, 9 Dec 1995

Our first 'Peckham period' (1968-71) was a time of much writing, mainly for *Psalm Praise*; this text was the first one I wrote during our second spell, from 1995. Eddy Stride, formerly Rector of Spitalfields and by then retired, had often pleaded for a Baptism hymn reflecting the (Anglican) view of the sacrament as a sign of the covenant of God's grace initiated with Abraham, made new in Christ. Spurred on by reading James Packer and Michael Saward and by his own forthcoming sermon in December, he urged me to provide a hymn that month. It was posted on the 9th and duly sung at 11.0 am on Christmas Eve at St George's Stamford; the theme of the service was 'Roots'. I think that Eddy's only disappointment was that I had not managed to include the word 'circumcision'.

Light upon the River

Genesis 28.10-22
Jacob at the gate of heaven: one

10 AS JACOB TRAVELLED FAR

As Jacob travelled far along
  the stony desert ways,
a passing vision made him strong
and turned his sleep into a song
  and all his pain to praise.

And as he saw, that night alone,
  a stairway to the sky
with angels moving up and down,
he heard the mighty voice of One
  who stood supreme on high:

'I am your fathers' God, the Lord;
  I bring your tribes to birth;
I am with you to guide and guard,
to see your family spread abroad,
  a blessing for the earth.'

And by the grace of God we share
  the way that Jacob went:
the Lord from heaven to earth comes near;
the upward path is now made clear
  in Christ, our one Ascent.

So may my eyes and heart and mind
  awake to see that grace,
those steps before me and behind,
as in the barren tracks I find
  the Lord is in this place.

I carry with me all the way
  the promise Christ has given;
and at each resting-place I stay
the guest of Jacob's God, and say
  'This is the gate of heaven!'

86.886(6) Tune: REPTON

Scriptures: Gen 28.10-22 1 Cor 14.47 Jn 1.49-51

Written: Poplar, March 1976

'When Jacob reached a certain place, he stopped for the night because the sun had set.' So begins the account of an unforgettably vivid, personally crucial, and justly famous episode in the travels of the father of the twelve tribes. In the 18th century it prompted Philip Doddridge to write his much-loved classic hymn *O God of Bethel*. Though rich in Scriptural allusion, however, Doddridge leaves out much of the story; this was my first attempt to express more of the narrative in singable form, linking it with our Lord's own clues to its meaning in John's Gospel. Here I have concentrated less on Jacob's rather qualified 'vows and prayers' than on the divine assurance preceding them. If REPTON is the chosen tune each fifth line is repeated. I revised the text in 1987 and 1998; since it had received little approval, No.11 (below) was another approach.

Light upon the River

Genesis 28.10-22
Jacob at the gate of heaven: two

11 THE SUN WENT DOWN ON JACOB'S GRIEF

The sun went down on Jacob's grief
   and night found him alone;
his guilt and fear had no relief,
   his pillow was a stone:
but God in darkness came, and kept
   his word of grace supreme,
to give new courage while he slept,
   new wisdom in a dream.

For Jacob in his sleep was shown
   God's messengers on high -
the angels moving up and down
   a stairway to the sky;
he heard the voice he scarcely knew
   of One whom none can see:
'I will protect and be with you,
   and you must trust in me.'

Our fathers' God grants us to share
   the way that Jacob went;
the upward path is now made clear
   in Christ, our one ascent:
our eyes and heart and soul and mind
   awake to see his face,
as in the desert tracks we find
   the Lord is in this place.

God's love is our security,
   the past has been forgiven,
and every resting-place can be
   the very gate of heaven:
our Saviour's promise makes us strong
   to face the barren ways;
our bitterness is turned to song,
   our sorrow into praise.

DCM Tune: FLIGHT OF THE EARLS

Scriptures: Gen 28.10-22 Jn 1.49-51

Written: Limehouse, Sept 1981

The background to this is sketched in the notes above (No.10). It is hard to assess one's own texts, so others may judge which of the two is more useful. The tune was one of many suggested by musical friends as suitable for new words; a welcome hint, since effective DCM tunes are not common, except some which are wedded to classic texts. I adjusted the words in 1987, and again for this present book.

Light upon the River

Genesis 48.15-16
Family blessings, ancient and modern

12 LORD GOD WHO BLESSED OUR FATHERS HERE

Lord God who blessed our fathers here
until their journeys' end,
Jacob's Redeemer, Isaac's Fear
and Abraham's true Friend:

As you have blessed us in our turn
and brought us to this day,
so may our sons and daughters learn
to know their God, we pray.

As you have led us all life through,
so while our children grow
may they find confidence in you
whom it is life to know.

As you direct our changing years,
through trials make them strong;
still be their God through joys and tears,
their health, their strength and song.

Your love enriches every home
in every age the same:
let praise from every family come
and songs to bless your name.

CM Tune: BEATITUDO

Scriptures: Gen 31.42-43; 48.15-16 Isa 41.8; 49.26; 60.16 2 Chron 20.7 Jas 2.23
Written: Poplar, Feb 1976

'Bless the lads' was a favourite petition of William Kelly, vicar of St Mark's Barrow in Furness with whom I served as curate, as he prayed for our sons and his. He was quoting the familiar AV (King James) version of Jacob's family blessing in Genesis 48. When in 1976 Michael Perry prepared a list of Bible passages for possible use in hymns (see No.48 and others) this was my starting-point for a text which enlarges on some of the titles and concepts here. Twenty-one years on, in our second spell at Christ Church Old Kent Road, I preached a short series of sermons from the last part of Genesis; we reached this chapter on June 29 1997 when the hymn was sung for the first time.

Light upon the River

Exodus 15. 1-18
Moses' victory song; prelude to Easter

13 I WILL SING THE LORD'S HIGH TRIUMPH

I will sing the Lord's high triumph,
ruling earth and sky and sea;
God my strength, my song, my glory,
my salvation now is he.
   Through the waters
God has brought us liberty.

By the storm and at the mountain
grace and judgement both are shown;
all who planned his people's ruin
power divine has overthrown.
   Nations tremble;
God has made his mercy known.

Who is like the God of Israel,
faithful, holy, throned above?
Stretching out the arm of anger
yet he guides us by his love.
   To our homeland
God will see us safely move.

Praise our God who in the thunder
led a nation through the sea;
praise the one whose blood released us
from our deeper slavery.
   Hallelujah!
Christ is risen: we are free!

87.87.87 Tune: OAKLEY by William O Jones; CWM RHONDDA
or UNSER HERRSCHER

Scriptures: Ex 15.1-18 Rev 1.5

Written: Bishop Woodford House, Ely, Feb 1975

First published: *Psalms for Today* (Hodder & Stoughton) 1990.

This first 'Song of Moses' (see also Deut 32 and Rev 15) is traditionally used by Christians at Easter, recalling Israel's escape from slavery and crossing of the sea, and the far greater triumph of Christ's cross and resurrection. I wrote the first draft of this paraphrase while staying at the Ely Diocesan Centre on one of the regular clergy conferences for the Tower Hamlets Deanery. It was sung at Limehouse on June 10 1977, and thoroughly revised in 1987, from its earlier 'I will sing my Lord's high triumph... Risen with Jesus, praise the God of Calvary!'. It was written for CWM RHONDDA (with repeats); TYDDYN LYNN and WESTMINSTER ABBEY have also been used.

Light upon the River

The Book of Numbers
Struggling to the promised land

14 GOD OF ISRAEL'S NAMES AND NUMBERS

God of Israel's names and numbers,
tribes and titles fully known,
you are heard in words and wonders,
cloud and fire, your glory shown,
seen in earthquake, lightnings, thunders,
holy God, the Lord alone!

God whose praise the earth is singing,
vine and fig tree, grain and oil,
milk and honey, well new-springing,
heaven's gifts and human toil:
grant us seed and harvest, bringing
daily bread from sun and soil.

God who holds the powers of nature,
guide your people on their way;
priests or donkeys glimpse the future -
let the Scriptures speak today!
Covenant-Lord of every creature,
feed and lead your church, we pray!

God of Aaron, Miriam, Moses,
Caleb, Joshua son of Nun,
Lord whose mighty hand disposes
how the rebels are undone;
God whose law your love discloses,
point us to the coming One!

Star of Jacob, Israel's Sceptre,
Jesus, lifted up on high,
here foreseen in strangest spectre,
one bronze snake beneath the sky!
Cure for sin, divine Protector -
'Look and live! Why will you die?'

God of tents beside the waters,
river's peace or threatening wave,
lawless sons or faithful daughters,
violent death or mountain grave:
praise for all your book has taught us!
Praise to God who loves to save!

87.87.87 Tune: OAKLEY by William O Jones;
PARKSTONE by Donald Webster; or CHURCH TRIUMPHANT

Scriptures: Num 1-2; 9.15-23; 13.27; 22.21-35; 14.30,38; 16; 24.17; 21.4-9; Jn 3.14-15; Num 24.5-6; 27.1-11; 36.1-12; 25; 20.22-29;

Written: Peckham, 18 July 1997

Sometimes an editorial group looks at a hymn and asks 'When would we actually *sing* it? This is just such a text; here the answer is, whenever you have a series on the book of Numbers! So these words were written for, and used at, just such a series at St Andrew the Great, Cambridge in August 1997; one of Chris Hayward's final requests to me from there; see Nos 22, 23 and others. They pick up some of the book's dramatic highlights as well as (I hope) its overall theme. Five months later, and entirely unconnected, Hugh Balfour also preached a 'Numbers' series at Christ Church Old Kent Road, so the first time I sang the hymn was at Evening Prayer there on January 18 1998. Welshman Bill Jones and Yorkshireman Dr Donald Webster, whom I often met at conferences of the Hymn Society, have composed several tunes for my texts.

Light upon the River

Deuteronomy 10.12-21
The law of love

15 WHAT DOES THE LORD OUR GOD REQUIRE

What does the Lord our God require
from all his people here?
To make his glory our desire,
his name our love and fear;
to keep the laws his love designed,
walking in all his ways;
to serve with all our heart and mind
the God who is our praise.

To God belongs the earth and heaven,
his creatures they contain;
and yet to us his love is given,
in us he comes to reign.
Away then, stubborn thoughts and words -
every rebellious thing
opposing God, the Lord of lords,
the uncorrupted king!

The widow and the fatherless
his strong protection share;
a stranger's need, a world's distress
must be his people's care.
See what the Father's power has done,
yield to the Spirit's claim;
display the victories of the Son
and glorify his name!

DCM   Tune: KINGSFOLD

Scriptures: Deut 10.12-21   1 Cor 15.57   2 Cor 2.14   Col 2.15
Written: Poplar, Dec 1975.

In a late 20th century wave of self-imposed revisions, several writers tried to reduce or eliminate the masculine-weighted language of earlier texts. Here I have made the expressions more inclusive than they were, but realise that it leaves much that is unacceptable to some. It is a straight paraphrase of a notable OT chapter seen through NT eyes. God's law is a gift of his love.

Light upon the River

Deuteronomy 32.1-47
God's grace and providence: the second Song of Moses

16 ATTEND, ALL HEAVEN AND EARTH

Attend, all heaven and earth:
the Lord will speak with you!
His words are like refreshing rain,
his truth like early dew.
He is the faithful Rock
whose perfect works proclaim
the beauty of his steadfast love,
the glory of his name.

For earth became corrupt
and disobeyed his call;
so well did we repay our God
who made and loved us all!
Remember days of old,
the generations gone,
and ask your fathers to explain
what God Most High has done.

He gave the human race
its boundaries and lands;
his chosen people learned to find
rich blessings from his hands;
for they became his care
and he became their own:
he led them with a father's joy
and from a kingly throne.

For Jacob was his child,
a foundling in the storm
whom God had rescued, fed and clothed,
and healed from every harm:

as eagles on their wings
lift nestlings high above
so does the Lord lift up his young
and holds them by his love.

He met his people's need;
his gifts were always good:
from fertile hills and watered fields
he nourished them with food;
sweet honey from the rock,
pure milk and fruit and meat,
with blood-red wine from choicest grapes
and bread from finest wheat.

Yet still the people sinned,
the ransomed ones rebelled,
deserted and defied their Lord;
so all their land was spoiled.
They earned the Saviour's wrath,
they worshipped things of earth,
forgetting all the promises
of God who gave them birth.

When all our strength grows weak
and all our hope has passed,
then God the Lord will come in power
to bring an end at last!
The Lord alone is God
who brings us to our grave
but raises us to life again;
he judges - he will save!

DSM   Tune: NEARER HOME

Scriptures: Deut 32.1-47   Acts 17.26   Rom 1.25
Written: Limehouse 1981

'They are not just idle words for you'; so the aged Moses declares immediately after this song, just before the account of his death. That applies to all this book's teaching, not least to the unique 'hymn' dominating chapter 32. Not only is it, like some of the Psalms, an extended recitation of the people's 'story'; it is a teaching hymn to remind them of their permanent need of his grace. Not all Christian congregations have the singing stamina of Israel; some of those who do will want a different tune. But those who value the vivid poetry and the forceful message of this book may like to use the first and last stanzas and make their own choice of the rest. The text was revised in 1983.

Light upon the River

Joshua 1.1-9
Travelling with the Lord; going by the Book

17 ALL THE LAW YOUR GOD HAS GIVEN

All the law your God has given,
teaching, promise, song, command,
guide your steps from here to heaven,
light your pathway through the land.

It is written, God has spoken;
ours to listen, read, obey:
Scripture never can be broken;
do not close your hearts today!

Make this book your meditation,
speak its truth by day and night;
let no doubt, no deviation
turn your foot to left or right.

Has not God your Lord commanded?
Do not fear the road is long;
never fear, for he has granted
in his strength, we shall be strong.

Where God leads you, take possession;
what he gives, with joy receive!
Set your course by his commission;
learn from him, and you will live.

Best of all, our God is with us,
starting, travelling, nearing home;
never will he lose or leave us,
all his love in Christ has come!

87.87.D Tune: BROADHEATH by Donald Webster;
or ALL FOR JESUS

Scriptures: Josh 1.1-9   Jn 10.35   Matt 1.23; 28.20
Written: Cambridge (39 Castle St) 19 Oct 1995

The Church of England's view of the Bible as 'God's word written' (Article 20) accords well with the opening of the book of Joshua. To a straight paraphrase of these exciting lines I have added phrases from the lips of our Lord, who often clinched a debate with 'It is written', and a passing nod in 6.1 at the alleged nearly-last words of John Wesley. While in Cambridge in 1995, staying above Bell's Sandwich Bar, we were visited by Christopher and Helen Hayward, then of that city. Chris was looking for suitable hymns for a forthcoming series on Joshua.

Joshua 24.14-24
Serving the Lord

18 SERVE THE LORD GOD ONLY

Serve the Lord God only, serve the Lord with fear;
he will make you willing, faithful and sincere.
If you will not serve him, if you won't obey,
you can choose from all the gods around today.
But, said trusty Joshua, hear this promised word:
As for me and my house, we will serve the Lord!

65.65 triple   Tune: ARMAGEDDON

Scripture: Josh 24.14-24
Written: Peckham, Summer 1971

The point of Joshua's appeal at the end of his book was not to offer a choice, but to demand obedience. The only 'choice' was that between the hopeless options available to those rejecting the living God. Does this make a hymn? Hardly! But it is included here for the sake of completeness and variety; written originally for our own family, we sang it at Christ Church Old Kent Road at our last Family Service there in June 1971.

Light upon the River

1 Samuel 2.1-10
The Song of Hannah: Old Testament Magnificat

19 IN GOD THE LORD MY HEART IS STRONG

In God the Lord my heart is strong,
my joy in him is free;
he gives my mouth a triumph song,
he saves and rescues me.

Not one is holy like the Lord;
our God, no Rock like you:
you weigh each boastful deed
    and word,
our every thought you know.

Your strength can fashion or destroy,
can ruin or create;
you lift the poor to heights of joy
and judge the rich and great.

You break the bow and stop our strife;
the hungry starve no more,
while lonely homes are filled with life
and welcome marks the door.

You guard the faithful, guide their feet,
and bring the wicked down;
you end at last this world's deceit
and give your saints a crown.

May God who raised me from the dust
and governs all my ways
direct my heart in humble trust,
my voice in perfect praise.

O Christ my King, whose mighty plan
makes such a prayer come true,
as in your pain our hopes began
your power shall make them new.

CM   Tune: ST FULBERT

Scriptures: 1 Sam 2.1-10   Lk 1.46-55
Written: Poplar, 1976

Every hymn has its moment. Eleven years after I wrote this version of Hannah's song, we sang it at Limehouse as we gave thanks for the arrival of another Hannah, newborn daughter of Paul and Ruth Day. We sang it again when she was baptized by immersion, together with her brothers Thomas and Christopher, on Sept 4 that year, 1987. I had by then revised the earlier version, adding a final stanza to reflect the prophecy of a strong king. It fell to a reluctant Samuel to anoint Israel's first and second kings, and to show that the nation's true sovereign was the Lord. This version was sung for a third time in Oct 1996, when Hugh Balfour was preaching through the first book of Samuel at Christ Church Old Kent Road. See also No.20 below.

Light upon the River

1 Samuel 2.1-10
Hannah's joy in the living God

20 MY HEART REJOICES

My heart rejoices and my strength is kindled
in my victorious, living God who saved me:
there is none like you, none so strong, so holy,
none like the Lord, my God.

Speak no more proudly, stop your mouth from boasting!
God governs all things, God the Lord of knowledge:
strong bows are broken, feeble limbs find courage;
God rules in all we do.

Making, destroying, giving life and taking,
God lifts the needy from their dust and ashes,
makes them sit boldly in the seat of honour:
God rules in all the earth.

Safe are the footsteps of his faithful people;
rebels and traitors fall in silent darkness:
Thunder from heaven, Judge of earth's proud nations,
Crown of my life, my king!

11.11.11.6 Tune: CHRISTE SANCTORUM

Scriptures: 1 Sam 2.1-10 Lk 1.46-55

Written: Poplar 1976

In her song of praise at the birth of Samuel, Hannah shows a settled dependence on God, rather than on any temporary excitement. At a crucial moment for the nation, she also attacks idolatry; in expounding this, Ronald Wallace adds that like the great prophets, she 'was given a glimpse of a more distant and ultimate event in which God would bring in salvation, not simply for Israel, but for all the ends of the earth' (*Evangel* magazine Autumn 1988). This second attempt to paraphrase the 'Old Testament Magnificat' is one of my rare texts in Sapphic metre; see No.19. Its move from meditation through prayer to challenge of God's enemies reflects, I hope, the heightened emotion of the original.

2 Samuel 2.26-28
A cry for peace from Abner, the army commander

21 MUST THE SWORD DEVOUR FOR EVER

Must the sword devour for ever,
ancient quarrels still persist?
How long brother use on brother
bomb or bullet, knife or fist?

When will someone break the deadlock,
halt the carnage, stop the race,
blow the trumpet not for battle
but for pausing, then for peace?

Let the strongest know their frailty,
let the weakest find their power;
let us seize the time for turning:
could this be God's day, God's hour?

Christ who lives in each believer,
come to make these murders cease;
win in us this greatest triumph,
Christ our champion, Christ our peace!

87.87 Tune: CHELWOOD by Donald Webster; or SUSSEX

Scriptures: 2 Samuel 2.26-28 Matt 26.51-52 Eph 3.17 Jas 4.1-10 Eph 2.14
Written: Peckham, 12-13 Sept 1996

On my first rural Remembrance Sunday, I took these verses as my text at Stuston in 1989, and again at Burgate in 1990. Later I gave up the attempt to reconcile the Bible's message with the community's expectations. But on our return to Peckham, I also returned to this narrative of hope in the middle of civil war and slaughter; originally this text was written with St Andrew the Great Cambridge in view: see No. 29, *King David was a man of war.*

Light upon the River

2 Samuel 23.1-4
King David, and the Son of David

22 WHEN DAVID FOUND HIS REST

When David found his rest,
his rule, his warfare past,
his foes laid low, his sins confessed,
God gave him peace at last.
Shepherd of Israel's land,
singer of psalm and song,
the strength divine was in his hand,
God's word upon his tongue.

A prophet for his day,
a king and yet a child
of God, an artist skilled to play,
a wanderer reconciled.
At Zion was his court,
his music and his prayer,
and here the sacred ark was brought -
a sign that God was there.

And David's name lived on,
his house, his line, his throne;
for God had spoken of a son
to be his very own;
and when the time had come
palm branches lined the road
to wave the Son of David home,
the Son of David's God!

On high and holy ground
the living Ark arrives;
where Jesus is, there God is found
to fill our land, our lives.
Bring welcome for your Lord,
his name salute and sing!
Come, see his glory, hear his word
and serve our coming King!

DSM Tune: TWO SAMUEL by Christopher Hayward

Scriptures: 2 Sam 23.1-4; 6.12,17; 7.12-16 Jn 12.13-15 Mk 11.7-10
Written: Peckham, 12-13 Sept 1996

Our starting-point in a text arising from the invitation noted at No.23 (below) is the account of 'the last words of David'. We touch on earlier events involving the Ark of the covenant and the promise of the Messiah, and far future ones as that promise is fulfilled in the coming of Jesus, 'great David's greater Son'. The text was sung at St Andrew the Great Cambridge on 24 Nov 1996 and at other times in that Advent term. Its new tune ('with driving rhythm') was composed and introduced by Chris Hayward, who had originally asked for words from this part of the Bible.

Light upon the River

2 Samuel 23.3-6
Godly leadership

23 WHEN RULERS JUDGE IN RIGHTEOUSNESS

When rulers judge in righteousness
and lead with godly fear,
their land and nation God will bless
and bring salvation near.

For like the light of morning sun
across a cloudless sky,
so is the king, the chosen one,
who loves the Lord Most High.

Or as the brightness after rain
when grass has newly grown,
so is a people free again
with justice on the throne.

So let the enemies of peace
be thwarted or removed,
corruption and oppression cease,
and faith and truth be loved.

O Lord, put right in every part
this land we know as home;
make known your rule in every heart,
in us, your true Shalom.

CM Tune: ST STEPHEN

Scriptures: 2 Sam 23.3-6 Col 3.15
Written: Peckham, 12-13 Sept 1996

The second book of Samuel does not seem to have been much frequented by hymnwriters for paraphrase, nor perhaps by preachers for sermons. But it has its own lyrical and gospel riches, and when Christopher Hayward, Music Director at St Andrew the Great Cambridge, said that the teaching theme for Autumn 1996 included this book, I searched it again for possible springs of new writing. This was the first of three texts; see also Nos.21 and 22. The following Spring, Hugh Balfour was near the end of a series on 2 Samuel, so it was also sung there on April 20 at our small but enriching evening service. Its final word, 'Shalom' is Hebrew for peace, well-being, wholeness; a word which through Jewish and Christian tradition has almost entered the English language. As it appears in many dictionaries I judged it allowable here.

Light upon the River

1 Kings 8.27-30
The congregation prays to the Holy Trinity

24 GOD OUR FATHER AND CREATOR

God our Father and Creator
over all the earth you reign;
God of cities, nations, planets,
whom the heavens cannot contain:
   come among your children here,
   make of us a house of prayer.

Christ whose undefended body
human hands destroyed and killed,
three days buried, till the moment
God had chosen to rebuild:
   raise your people from the dead,
   we your body, you our Head.

Holy Spirit, wind of heaven.
breaking earthly barriers down,
pouring out your gifts and graces -
life the seed, and love the crown:
   fill us all, till all become
   your pure temple, your true home.

Living Lord of past and future,
now through us your word fulfil;
changing scenes and times of crisis
prove that you are with us still:
   from one church, all praises be,
   praise to God, one Trinity.

87.87.77 Tune: POPLAR by Ian Yates; ALL SAINTS; or ST LEONARD

Scriptures: 1 Kgs 8.27-30; 56-57 Jn 2.18-22 1 Cor 3.16-17; 6.19-20 2 Cor 6.16
Written: Poplar, 1976
First published: *Hymns for Today's Church* (Hodder & Stoughton) 1982

Poplar Methodist Mission owes its origins to John Wesley's preaching in that part of East London, where he writes in his Journal for Nov 1787, 'Even at Poplar I found a remarkable revival of the work of God'! Its former home was known as 'Lax's' after the notable pastor who served there for over forty years. In 1976 the final services were held in that building, and the minister then, Douglas Wollen, led the congregation the few hundred yards down the East India Dock Road to their new home, formerly Trinity Congregational, briefly URC, to be known as Trinity Methodist Church. So I wrote this Trinitarian hymn with our Methodist neighbours in mind, since we Anglicans were shortly due for a similar move, from Poplar to Limehouse, and appreciated some of their mixed feelings. But the hymn was not sung until June 10 1979 at the church's anniversary, when Conference President Donald English was the preacher. By then Ian Yates, Assistant Minister, had written his tune POPLAR (to be distinguished from others of that name) for these words. The text, which may be considered a stray from the final part of this book, echoes Solomon's Old Testament prayer at the consecration of the temple he built, and of the New Testament message that today's temple consists of believers in Christ. Methodists will also recognise the quotation from their founder in verse 4 reflecting 1 Kings 8.57: 'May the Lord our God be with us...' Our son Jonathan continued the link with 'Trinity' when he worked on its staff from 1992-94.

Light upon the River

1 Kings 8.35-36
The gift of rain

25 RAIN ON THE EARTH

Rain on the earth by heaven's blessing,
showers for the land from laden sky,
water for well and spring and river:
God grant us rain, or else we die!

Rain is your gift for wise or wicked,
humans and cattle, herb and tree;
praise for its promise and its warning,
showing your wisdom, flowing free!

Come to our world of drought and flooding
hold back their danger and their fear;
dwell in the lands of dearth or drowning,
help them and save them by our care.

Early or late, on hill and valley,
thunderous torrent, gentle mist:
visit in mercy, not in judgement;
this is our prayer, who pray in Christ.

God send us rain, to green our pastures,
feeding our flocks, our fields and grain;
God fill our streams in all due seasons:
God of all grace, grant us good rain!

98.98 Tune: LUDHAM by Mervyn Horder

Scriptures: 1 Kgs 8.35-36 2 Chron 6.26-27 Matt 5.45 Jas 5.7 Gen 2.4-6 Psa 104.10-16
Written: Bujumbura, Burundi, 13 June 1991
First published: *Hymns & Congregational Songs* vol 2 no.3 (Stainer & Bell) Dec 1991. See page xiii for copyright note.

For part of Britain's 'drought' in 1976, we were staying in Suffolk. By the next two, 1989 and 90, we were living there. The year after that saw my first visit to Tanzania, going with Jonathan to visit Timothy and his work with Habitat for Humanity, just as an exceptionally long rainy season ended; a severe drought would strike later, in 1997. Some peoples realise their need of rain more than others and are closer to the Biblical world where rain means blessing. Few English hymns put it that way; *We plough the fields* is an exception. A morning in Kigoma watching torrential rain almost obscure Lake Tanganyika sparked off thoughts of a 'rain' hymn; it was almost completed during our flight home. But the main work was done at Bujumbura Airport as we waited for a delayed plane, and I had reached 2 Chronicles 6 in my own reading; the phrase 'rain on the land' in Solomon's prayer (also in 1 Kings 8) seemed crucial. Within two hours of getting it, Mervyn Horder had written his tune LUDHAM; in less than six months we appeared together in print. This was the shortest gap so far between writing and publication. On Sept 5 1993 we sang the hymn at Holy Communion at Thrandeston (Suffolk), with Mervyn at the organ. I have since read in John V Taylor's 'The Primal Vision' (SCM 1963) that to one Transvaal tribe 'the ultimate good is rain'; and in Vincent Donovan's 'Christianity Rediscovered' (Orbis, NY, 1985) that for the Masai, 'their word for God means rain... the most beautiful description of God they can think of'.

Light upon the River

1 Kings 17-18
Elijah the prophet

26 THE LAND IS DRY

The land is dry; the prophet's word
is clearly spoken, rarely heard:
the ground is hard and groans for rain;
Lord, speak, that we may live again!

The people die; the voice divine
rejects our clamour for a sign;
yet, Lord, in sin and death we mourn;
let breath be given, let life return!

False gods abound, and rival cults;
our lying enemy exults:
come, sweep them, Lord, from heart and mind
and Satan's prisoners all unbind!

The churches drift; we lose our nerve,
forgetting who it is we serve;
Lord, judge and save us; burn, and bless
and do not leave us comfortless!

As patriarchs and prophets prayed,
teach us to follow undismayed:
teach us to stand for you today;
but first, our God, teach us to pray!

Our Father, let it here be known
whose is the word, the blood, the throne;
throughout this earth that Jesus trod
let nations know that you are God!

LM Tune: ELIJAH by CHRISTOPHER HAYWARD;
or WINCHESTER NEW

Scriptures: 1 Kgs 17-18 1 Sam 3.1 Mk 8.12 Lk 11.1,20-22 Acts 27.23 Jn 14.18

Written: Peckham 18 June 1997

1997-98 were good years for Elijah. This was another request from St Andrew the Great Cambridge, where Chris Hayward's music launched the text. It was also intended for the 1998 'Word Alive' week, to accompany Roy Clements' addresses, but not after all used there. Elijah also featured in our own church's Home Groups and the preaching classes at the Cornhill Training Course, though these gave less scope for singing; some verbal changes were made then. Despite appearances, this text has no connection with No. 25.

Light upon the River

1 Kings 19.11-13
The voice of the Lord

27 LORD, YOU SOMETIMES SPEAK IN WONDERS

Lord, you sometimes speak in wonders,
unmistakable and clear;
mighty signs to prove your presence,
overcoming doubt and fear.

Lord, you sometimes speak in whispers,
still and small and scarcely heard;
only those who want to listen
catch the all-important word.

Lord, you sometimes speak in silence
through our loud and noisy day;
we can know and trust you better
when we quietly wait and pray.

Lord, you often speak in Scripture:
words that summon from the page,
shown and taught us by your Spirit
with fresh light for every age.

Lord, you always speak in Jesus,
always new yet still the same:
teach us now more of our Saviour;
make our lives display his name.

87.87 Tune: STUTTGART

Scriptures: 1 Kgs 19.7-18 Rom 15.17-19 Heb 1.1-2; 2.1-4; 12.25-26
Written: Barrow in Furness, 1966
First published: *Youth Praise 2* (Falcon) 1969

Together with No.104, *Christ the Light who shines unfading,* this was the first of my texts to be published, having been sung at St Mark's Barrow for the Pathfinders' 8th Birthday Service (16 Oct 1966). Its continuing use has surprised and sometimes embarrassed me; verse 4 does not mean that there are parts of Scripture where God does not speak, but that (as Scripture itself shows) he also speaks in other ways. In view of the 'signs and wonders' debates arising in the 1980s, this text could almost be a pre-emptive comment on their true place! It was sung first to STUTTGART; Norman Warren, Judy Davies and Christopher Johnson have all written new tunes for it, the last of which requires textual changes.

Light upon the River

2 Kings 2.13
Elisha the prophet

28 JORDAN'S WATERS PART IN TWO

Jordan's waters part in two;
see Elisha passing through!
Look! he holds Elijah's cloak,
for this younger prophet spoke:
'As you leave, let me inherit
double of your living spirit!'

Waters parted, waters healed;
see the power of God revealed!
Loaves and oil are multiplied,
breath renewed in one who died;
words of judgement and salvation
spoken to a lawless nation.

Jordan's river, which has known
Israel saved and overthrown,
now receives the Syrian lord -
Naaman longs for health restored;
once the word of God is heeded
here is all the cleansing needed.

By that word is poison tamed,
iron from the stream reclaimed,
armies blinded, made to see,
kings made beggars, beggars free;
so Elisha serves his warning
on a world that longs for morning.

Yes! For Christ makes all things good:
greater healing, freedom, food,
better news for rich and poor
than the prophets ever saw,
starting from that same swift river,
bound for death, he lives for ever.

Jesus, dawn on us today!
Take our dirt, our sin away;
Living Stream, in mercy rise,
cleanse our hearts, our tongues, our eyes:
by your Spirit's true anointing
let us serve at your appointing.

77.77.88 Tune: ELISHA by Christopher Hayward

Scriptures: 2 Kgs 2.7-14, 19-22; 4; 5.1-14; 6 Mk 7.37 Matt 3.13-17; 13.17 Jn 4.10-14 Rev 1.18

Written: Peckham, June 1997

The background here is similar to that for No.26 above; I have tried to include some of the notable events in the ministry of the second of this pair of prophets. It was a time of concentrated miracles matched only by Moses before their time, and the Gospel period after them, to meet the crisis in the nation. I originally wrote, and marginally prefer, 'see the man of God pass through' as line 2, holding back his name until verse 4 and omitting Naaman's altogether. But I was persuaded that the subject should appear more clearly from the start, unless the hymn can be carefully introduced.

Light upon the River

1 Chronicles 22.5-10
Two men of blood

29 KING DAVID WAS A MAN OF WAR

King David was a man of war,
of battle and of blood,
whose warfare often came before
his quiet walk with God.

He had to learn he could not build
a temple for the Lord;
the cries of those he maimed and killed
might drown the heavenly word.

A house of peace, a place of prayer,
for sacrifice and praise;
how could he rest his conscience here
when blood had filled his days?

But David's Son in days to be
would gain a different throne;
another man of blood was he -
the blood was all his own.

It shouts against the human race,
it shows the depths of sin;
if offers welcome, pardon, grace,
God's kingdom bursting in!

And in this blood is all our hope
and in that cross, our peace;
and if we dare to share this cup,
Christ, make our wars to cease!

CM Tune: WESTMINSTER; or DUNDEE

Scriptures: 1 Chron 22.5-10; 28.2-3 Psa 23.1-3 Heb 9.12 Col 1.20 Mk 10.38-39

Written: Peckham, 12-16 Sept 1996

Is any criticism of David implied in the divine ban on his building the temple of his dreams, as uniquely revealed in 1 Chronicles? In his stimulating volume on these books in the 'Bible Speaks Today' series (IVP 1987) Michael Wilcock, a man of peace, believes not. To my mind, though, the negative tone and solemn judgement in the prohibition seem clear enough. The theme for the hymn arose out of my work on related chapters in 2 Samuel (see No.21 for example); the first draft went through many revisions including some sharpened language in verses 3, 5 and 6—where I hope the 'cup' has some powerful resonances. On Aug 24 1997 we reached this spot in an evening series on Chronicles at Christ Church Old Kent Road, and it was first sung there by the small group present.

Light upon the River

2 Chronicles 5.13-14
Music for the glory of the Lord

30 WITH ONE VOICE THEY JOINED THEIR PRAISE

With one voice they joined their praise,
words and music for their Lord,
instruments and voices raised
tuned in unison's accord:
'God endures for ever'.

With one heart they wove their psalm,
made his praise their sacrifice;
gathered by one mighty arm,
rescued by one fearsome price:
God is love for ever.

With one mind the people sang
God within, around, above;
walls and roof and doorways rang
with the echoes of that love:
God is good for ever.

With one voice and heart and mind,
thrilling quavers, thundering chord,
so we join them; so we find
grace and glory in our Lord:
God is ours for ever.

77.77.5 Tune: NASSAU (=WURTEMBURG)

Scriptures: 2 Chron 5.13-14; 6.32; 7.1-10 Heb 13.15 1 Cor 6.19-20; 1 Jn 4.8,16 Psa 48.14

Written: Oakley, 3 Aug 1993

With One Voice was the name given to the 1977 Australian Hymn Book when it was republished for wider use two years later. (The American Lutherans used the same title in 1995.) Its editor Lawrence Bartlett spoke at Winchester in 1993 about plans for new revision; back home, we found ourselves reading at breakfast from 2 Chronicles 5 where this phrase occurs as the Ark is brought to Solomon's temple. This is the stuff of which hymns are made; the tune WURTEMBURG enables us to echo the familiar refrain of that occasion, that the Lord 'is good; his love endures for ever.' In 1998 it was accepted for publication.

Light upon the River

2 Chronicles 33.10-20
Manasseh prays

31 ALMIGHTY GOD, THE FOUNTAIN HEAD

Almighty God, the Fountain-head
of earth and sea and skies,
you sway the ever-moving tide
the spinning galaxies;
but from your light we mortals hide
and turn away our eyes.

How mean our varied schemes have been
of head and heart and hand!
the multiplying germs of sin
outnumber all the sand;
where is the one who dares go in
where angels trembling stand?

The glory of your majesty
is more than we can bear:
your face and form we cannot see
and yet you make us fear,
until we find the only plea
to save us from despair.

Do not destroy us, God, we pray
with guilt upon our head;
for when our debts we could not pay
another paid instead:
Your mercy has made clear the way
by blood that has been shed.

You did not leave Christ in the grave
nor sinners in the tomb;
all that you are, in Christ you gave,
in Christ our God has come:
and in that gift, our life we have,
and in that love, our home.

86.86.86 Tune: BRUNSWICK

Scriptures: 2 Chron 33.10-20 Matt 18.23-27 Acts 2.29-32 2 Cor 5.19

Written: Poplar, 1976

Towards the end of a 55-year reign of terror, corruption and superstition, King Manasseh of Judah repented. This is related briefly, and solely, in 2 Chronicles, but an enlarged and eloquent 'Prayer of Manasseh' is included in the Apocrypha; and my text begins from there and leads into an expression of penitence in Christian terms. However genuine the change of heart may have been, it came too late to save the king's victims, or the nation. The two main revisions of this hymn, in 1978 and 1987, brought in 'Fountain-head' on the one hand and 'germs' on the other. Timothy Dudley-Smith has also been drawn to this prayer in his text *Almighty Lord Most High draw near*, from 1987; so has Carl Daw with *Sovereign Maker of all things* (1990).

Light upon the River

Job 28
Where can wisdom be found?

32 WHEN MINES ARE DUG FOR SILVER

When mines are dug for silver
and hills cut through for gold,
explorers hunt their treasures
in cruel heat or cold;
they trace untrodden valleys
and sink unfathomed shafts;
in darkness long-forgotten
they ply their secret crafts.
    Tunnelling through the mountains
    they delve into the night;
    the solid rock they shatter
    to bring its wealth to light.

But when we search for wisdom
how can we know the way?
And where is understanding?
Nor earth nor sea can say.
Is it so deeply buried
unseen by living eyes
that death itself hears only
a hint of such a prize?
    Wealth cannot buy wisdom,
    for gems it is not sold;
    more precious far than silver,
    more rare than finest gold.

The Lord who looks on all things
and set the worlds in space -
he knows the way to wisdom
and he points out its place;
when God made winds and waters
and measured out the sea,
the thunder and the lightning,
he gave as his decree:
    Turn away from evil,
    to God commit your ways;
    to fear the Lord and love him
    is wisdom, love and praise.

76.76.D.66.76 Tune: WIR PFLUGEN

Scriptures: Job 28 Deut 6.5,13 Psa 111.10 Prov 1.7; 9.10
Written: Poplar, 1975

Are there, or were there, women miners? When I first wrote 'Men dig their mines for silver' I was uncertain; or did I even give it a thought while working on this fun-version of a favourite chapter? Later I became aware that we had two kinds of minefield here; I tried 'They dig their mines...'; but who are 'they'? So I settled for the present text in 1981, happily joined as it was to the tune for *We plough the fields*. In 1988 the whole scene came alive in fresh ways when after some months in Bolivia, Timothy came home with some stunning pictures of Potosi, the largest silver mine the world has known. Its heyday, 1600; its death toll horrific, now often 'explosive-related'; its treasures still being dug out. The hymn made its debut at Stuston, Suffolk, at our Family Service on Feb 11 1990, after we had read this poetic chapter antiphonally.

Light upon the River

Job 38.1-38
Creation's beauty; the Creator's glory

33 THE WORKS OF THE LORD ARE CREATED IN WISDOM

The works of the Lord are created in wisdom;
we view the earth's wonders and call him to mind:
we hear what he says in the world we discover
and God shows his glory in all that we find.

Not even the angels have ever been granted
to tell the full story of nature and grace;
but open to God is all human perception,
the mysteries of time and the secrets of space.

The sun every morning lights up his creation,
the moon marks the rhythm of months in their turn;
the glittering stars are arrayed in his honour
adorning the years as they ceaselessly burn.

The wind is his breath and the clouds are his signal,
the rain and the snow are the robes of his choice;
the storm and the lightning, his watchmen and heralds,
the crash of the thunder, the sound of his voice.

The song is unfinished; how shall we complete it,
and where find the skill to perfect all God's praise?
At work in all places, he cares for all peoples -
how great is the Lord to the end of all days!

12.11.12.11 Tune: FRIARMERE VICARAGE by Simon Beckley;
STREETS OF LAREDO; KREMSER; or ST CATHERINE'S COURT

Scriptures: Job 38.1-38 Psa 104.1-4, 19-24; 106.2; 136.1-9; 148.1-6
1 Pet 1.12 Rom 11.33-36

Written: Limehouse, 1976

First published: *Hymns for Today's Church* (Hodder & Stoughton) 1982

Among the mixed contents of the Apocryphal books are some exalted poems of praise to the Creator of all. Here Ecclesiasticus 42-43 is my main source; these chapters echo some of the Scriptures noted above. My text was written during our first month at Limehouse; its original form appeared in the *All Souls Langham Place supplement* (1980). One American book has further changed the words, while Larry Mayfield has set some of them to his ASH GROVE arrangement. I had the tune STREETS OF LAREDO in mind, but was happy to see KREMSER used in *Sing we merrily*, the St Paul's Cathedral 1995 Choir Supplement.

Light upon the River

Job 38.7
Morning stars and shouting angels

34 THE DANCE OF THE STARS IN BURNING GLORY

>The dance of the stars in burning glory
>weaves through the years in the deepest heaven;
>meeting, dividing, circling and parting,
>each with the light that the Lord has given.
>
>The steps of the angels in their patterns
>tread through the leagues of the pathless skies;
>praising, adoring, listening, obeying,
>swifter than light, as the stars they rise.
>
>The joy of creation in the Godhead
>rings with the love of the Three-in-One;
>saving, redeeming, making, renewing,
>wisdom and light are in God alone.
>
>The songs of the saints in a million churches
>spring into glory from time and space;
>born to a kingdom everlasting,
>daughters of light and the sons of grace.

10.9.10.9
Tune: ASKHAM BRYAN by Donald Webster

Scriptures: Job 38.7 Gen 1.16 Jas 1.17 Heb 1.14 Lk 1.19 Dan 2.20-23 1 Tim 6.15-16 Rev 1.10

Written: Limehouse, March 1988

A hymn, a song, or a poem? Hoping that they might be sung I include these verses, the only ones of mine inspired by a computer, or likely to be. Marcus has tried to lead his parents gently into a software world, including our work on this book; a decade earlier he demonstrated on his own screen what happens when four stars approach each other, and begin a kind of stately dance together. Make that ten, or fifty, or a billion; add sound and colour; recognise that this is no mere programmed automation but the hand of the loving, involved Creator—and a small glimpse of the glory of God's universe peeps through. Limehouse has too many earthly lights for stars to be seen clearly; the night sky was one of our new delights in Suffolk, beginning on the day we moved. The Bible references open up some of the links between stars, angels and churches which hymns have sometimes expressed. Nearly ten years on, to my delight, Donald Webster (see No.14 and others) became the first musician to attempt a tune; he has named it after his home near York.

For texts from the Psalms, see the next section, page 217

Light upon the River

Proverbs 8
The Wisdom of God: one

35 LISTEN! WISDOM CRIES ALOUD

Listen! Wisdom cries aloud
making truth and justice heard,
calling to the careless crowd
with the strong, insistent word -
Turn from foolishness and lies:
come, and I will make you wise!

Not the finest diadems
crowning earth's most powerful kings,
not the purest gold or gems
match the wealth that wisdom brings;
those who rule by wisdom's law
wisdom's riches shall explore.

When the heavens lay dark and cold,
while the universe was young,
wisdom saw God's plans unfold
where no angel yet had sung;
but one night in Bethlehem
angels told the world his name.

Christ, before all time began
working at his Father's side,
Word of truth, becoming man,
Christ, our wisdom crucified;
wisdom for our scene of shame,
powerful from the dead he came.

Wisdom, still the angels' theme:
all that lives, take up the sound!
Wisdom, King of kings supreme,
reigning, glorified and crowned:
Christ our prize and great reward,
Christ our wisdom, Christ our Lord!

77.77.77 Tune: RATISBON

Scriptures: Prov 8 Lk 2.11 Jn 1.1-14 Rev 4.12; 7.11-12 Phil 3.14 1 Cor 1.24,30-31 Col 2.2-3

Written: Limehouse, 1977

In days of multiplying and ever-changing church calendars and lectionaries, this recalls a time when the theme for the 5th Sunday after Epiphany was 'The Wisdom of God'. Perhaps this theme is underplayed in hymnody; my starting-point here is one of the classic poetic chapters from the Bible's Wisdom literature, interpreted by the New Testament declaration of Christ our Wisdom. See also No.36, below.

Light upon the River

Proverbs 8.12-36
The Wisdom of God: two

36 WHO CAN MEASURE HEAVEN AND EARTH

Who can measure heaven and earth?
God was present at their birth.
Who can number seeds or sands?
Every grain is in his hands.
Through creation's countless days
every dawn sings out his praise.

Who can tell what wisdom brings,
first of all created things?
One alone is truly wise,
hidden from our earthbound eyes:
knowledge lies in him alone,
God, the Lord upon his throne.

Wisdom in his plans he laid,
planted her in all he made,
granted her to humankind,
sowed her truth in every mind;
but with richest wisdom blessed
those who love him first and best.

Wisdom gives the surest wealth,
brings her children life and health;
teaches us to fear the Lord,
marks a universe restored:
heaven and earth she will outlast -
happy those who hold her fast!

77.77.77 Tune: ALIREB by Agnes Tang;
LUCERNA LAUDONIAE; or NORICUM

Scriptures: Prov 8,12-36; 20.27 Psa 19 Jn 1.1-9 Job 28.12-28

Written: Poplar, 1976

First published: *Hymns for Today's Church* (Hodder & Stoughton) 1982

Like No.35 above, this text (which was written first) owes much to Proverbs 8 and other Scriptures, and would fit the former Epiphany 5 theme, the Wisdom of God. But its more precise origins lie in the Apocryphal book Ecclesiasticus, which I was reading in its NEB version at the time. Following a long tradition, I have retained the pronouns 'he' and 'she' for God and wisdom respectively. It was possibly sung first at Ealing Abbey at a united churches' service for Education Sunday, Feb 3 1980, and was taken up by American Roman Catholics.

Light upon the River

Ecclesiastes 12
Decay and deliverance

37 REMEMBER YOUR CREATOR NOW

Remember your Creator now
while days of youth remain,
before the joyless days shall grow
in darkness, fear and pain.

Desire shall fail and weakness come
to halt our stumbling feet;
we go to our eternal home
and mourners tread the street.

With dimming lamps and fading songs
the body sinks in death;
the dust returns where it belongs
as God recalls our breath.

As all beneath the sun stagnates
in bondage to decay,
in pains of birth God's world still waits,
in hope his people pray.

God's children soon shall be revealed,
from all frustration freed,
their travail ended, sickness healed,
and Christ their Lord indeed.

CM Tune: DUNDEE

Scriptures: Eccles 12.1-8 Rom 8.18-27,39
Written: Poplar, 1975

Some of the hymns of John Mason Neale are brief selections from his longer paraphrases of even longer medieval Latin verse, sometimes none too cheerful. On a smaller scale, these five stanzas come from a longer poem based more extensively on the solemn warnings in Ecclesiastes 12. Its theme of frustration due to meaninglessness or 'vanity' is taken up from earlier chapters and finally applied to dying and death, before the more succinct conclusion. But as the apostle Paul relates this theme to his Gospel of hope and renewal, notably in Romans 8, it seemed possible to unite the two Biblical passages here, which could (just) serve as a hymn, if carefully chosen. It needs a serious tune such as DUNDEE. These verses were printed in *Symphony* magazine No.14 (1982).

Song of Songs
2.10-13 Love song

38 COME, SEE THE WINTER IS PAST

Come, see the winter is past,
the rain is over and gone:
the flowers appear in the meadows at last,
the time of singing has come.

The fig tree bears the young fruit,
the vines are fragrant and full;
the voice of the dove can be heard in the wood:
arise, my love, for I call!

O come, my love, come away!
To you, my own, I belong;
O come to the mountains of spices with me,
the gift of love for our song.

7.7.11.7 Tune by Mark Kellner

Scriptures: Song 2.10-13; 8.14 Jn 13.1 Gal 2.20 1 Jn 4.10

Written: Cambridge, Oct 1995

First published: Song leaflet (Somerset Press, Hope USA) 1997

A rare excursion, for me, into the song world. Mervyn Horder had for some time been looking for a singable paraphrase of appropriate selections from the *Song of Songs*, for a wedding choir to sing while the registers were being signed. After much badgering I produced this text while on holiday in Cambridge; approximately faithful, approximately rhyming, but regular in rhythm. He then decided that what he really wanted was something closer to the Authorised (King James) Version, not omitting 'Many waters cannot quench love' (8.7); for which I thought he hardly needed my versification. So this remained on file until Mark Kellner of Old Hickory, Tennessee, discovered it, set it to his music for three or four parts, and sent it to Jack Schroder of Hope Publishing. It was duly printed, and recorded on a promotional cassette. The love song which is my starting-point has traditionally been seen as indicating a greater love, which is reflected in the other Scriptures noted here. I discovered too late that I had repeated the first line of a lovely song, from the same source, by Stephanie Mason; a misprint when hers was published led me to think that I was varying the opening words.

Light upon the River

Isaiah 1.3
Animals wiser than us: Bethlehem and Calvary

39 CATTLE KNOW THEIR MASTER'S MANGER

Cattle know their master's manger
oxen feel their owner's tread;
we alone, in mortal danger,
shall we feel no joy, no dread?

Shall our God be ever nearer
than he is this day, this night?
Can his love be closer, clearer,
than in Bethlehem's pure light?

Yes! In darkness we have found him,
nailed upon a cross of wood;
here is love, and earth around him
is transfigured by his blood.

Hear his first, his final calling;
sense his footstep, see his hand:
he alone keeps us from falling;
how long till we understand?

Call on God while he is near us,
seek him while he may be found!
Christ has come! and he will hear us,
earth again be holy ground.

87.87 Tune: HESLINGTON by Donald Webster;
or LOVE DIVINE

Scriptures: Isa 1.2-3 Mk 15.33 1 Jn 4.10 Jude 14 Mk 8.21; 9.19 Isa 55.6-7 Ex 3.5

Written: Peckham, 27 December 1995

Another hymn which grew from the draft of a different one; in this case No.61, *Dark is all the world below him*. They seemed to separate of their own accord, and I completed both on the same day, in the same metre. Here Isaiah prompts our first and last stanzas; if the fourth has more than meets the eye, so much the better.

Light upon the River

Isaiah 6.1-8
Glory, mercy and news

40 LORD OF THE HEIGHTS, WE SING YOUR GLORY

Lord of the heights, we sing your glory,
led by the light our eyes have seen;
creatures of fire and flame cry 'Holy',
circling the throne from which you reign:
so let the earth be filled with glory -
shine on our world, most holy One!

Lord of the depths, we praise your mercy,
drawn by the love our hearts have found;
once you embraced the tree of glory,
reaching our guilt with nail-pierced hand:
judgement for sin; for sinners, mercy -
speak to our world, great King enthroned!

Lord over all, we preach your glory,
roused by the truth our ears have heard;
news of a victory won so dearly,
news of a hope that must be shared:
Jesus our gospel, Christ our glory -
come to our world, triumphant Lord!

98.98.98 Tune: FRAGRANCE
(= BERGERS = QUELLE EST CETTE ODEUR)

Scriptures: Isa 6.1-8; 57.15 Eph 3.18 Acts 5.30-32 Rom 10.14-15
Written: Limehouse, 1979

No hymn can do full justice to Isaiah's vision of the Lord, and his own pardoning and commissioning, but I hope this text touches on its central themes. It also explores some sound patterns around the two great words 'glory' and 'mercy', using assonance after the manner of Michael Saward in *When things began to happen*. Stanza two quotes a prayer from a 20th century Communion liturgy ('the tree of shame was made the tree of glory'); the final line came from a suggestion from Michael Perry. The hymn appeared in the quarterly *Word and Music* for April/June 1983.

Isaiah 12
God is my salvation

41 PRAISE GOD TODAY: HIS GLORIES NEVER END

Praise God today: his glories never end;
our Judge becomes in Christ our greatest Friend.

God brings us comfort where his anger burned,
so judgement and fear to peace and trust are turned.
Praise God today: his mercies never end;
our Judge becomes in Christ our greatest Friend.

Wells of salvation streams of life will bring;
with joy we shall draw from this life-giving spring.
Praise God today: his blessings never end;
our Judge becomes in Christ our greatest Friend.

Songs shall be his for this victorious day;
give thanks to his name, and teach the world to say:
Praise God today: his triumphs never end;
our Judge becomes in Christ our greatest Friend.

Love lives among us, Israel's holy One
who comes to the rescue—see what God has done!
Praise God today: his wonders never end;
our Judge becomes in Christ our greatest Friend.

10.11.10.10 Tune: CRUCIFER

Scriptures: Isa 12 Num 23.23 2 Cor 5.18-19 Rom 5.9-11; 8.1

Written: Poplar, 1976

First published: *Church Family Worship* (Hodder & Stoughton) 1986

A powerful tune joins a powerful chapter to form this hymn. At one stage of our work for *Hymns for Today's Church* it was suggested that as we were not including *Lift high the cross*, it would be a pity to lose the tune. So I drafted these words for that music; but eventually Kitchin and Newbolt (revised) won the day, and mine appeared instead in the periodical *Music in Worship* in 1986. Later still Christopher Rolinson's new tune required a start with verse 1, not the refrain; so this text has also appeared under the title *God brings us comfort*. The twelfth chapter of Isaiah is traditionally chosen for reading in the Christmas season; it is the Incarnation which best fulfils the prophet's words, and brings comfort and joy to God's people.

Light upon the River

Isaiah 25.6-9
This is our God!

42 SEE THE FEAST OUR GOD PREPARES

See the feast our God prepares;
all who hunger, come to dine!
Jesus with his people shares
richest food and finest wine.

Here he suddenly removes
prisoners' shame and mourners' grief;
here the wanderers whom he loves
find their rest and their relief.

Now our tears are wiped away,
now for ever death undone;
he who rose on Easter day
ends our darkness like the sun.

Christ our God! with joy acclaim
all the glories of our King:
Christ the Lord! we love his name;
every tongue, his praises sing!

77.77 Tune: DARTMEET by David Peacock; SAVANNAH, ORIENTIS PARTIBUS or DROOPING SOULS

Scriptures: Isa 25.6-9 1 Cor 11.23-26 Rev 1.16-18 Phil 2.11

Written: Limehouse, April 1977

First published: *Church Family Worship* (Hodder & Stoughton) 1986

As Isaiah 12 suggests Christmas (see No.41 above) so chapter 25 suggests Easter. I wrote this text for our first Easter season at Limehouse, where we sang it at Holy Communion on April 24 (Easter 2) to SAVANNAH. It expresses an unashamedly Christian view of the original prophecy. In his commentary 'The Prophecy of Isaiah' (IVP 1993) Alec Motyer says that the prophet first 'looks back to the covenant banquet of Exodus 24.11', then forward to the day when 'covenant promise will have become covenant reality'.

Light upon the River

Isaiah 35.1-7
Thirsting for rain

43 ALL THE BROWN AND BARE HORIZONS

All the brown and bare horizons,
thirsty lands and dusty ground,
cry to God in silent longing,
plead their cause without a sound.

Distant grey or blinding yellow,
every cracked and crumbling scene,
will these dry and hardened furrows
ever see the promised green?

Ask the thorn-bush and the scrubland
gasping for the timely rain,
cattle seeking shade and coolness:
when will water flow again?

All the scorching months and seasons,
all the days of sun and glare,
morning heat and noontide stillness:
can the Lord be living here?

Stone and rock and ditch and roadside:
these are home for growing things!
Even now the rains are coming,
even here the desert sings!

All the world is dry without him,
every land awaits his voice;
Come, Creator, Word, and Spirit!
Rise, our earth, in God rejoice!

87.87 Tune: ERPINGHAM by Mervyn Horder; or LAUS DEO

Scriptures: Isa 35.1-7 Matt 5.5-6 Jn 7.37-39 Rev 22.1-3
Written: Dodoma and Peckham, June-July 1996

In 1996 the usual dry season came in Tanzania; on our other visits the rains had lasted longer, and next year the drought was severe. Had we come later we would have seen even more dryness and dust in Singida and Nkinga, Tabora and Manyoni. In Tim's house in Dodoma I began some stanzas with 'All the brown lands, all the bare lands'; back home they grew to eight verses, and with Marjorie's help slimmed back to these six. No sooner had I sent them to Mervyn Horder than ERPINGHAM was in the post. Drought does not always mean a land under judgement, though now there are more remedies available—for some. It can always speak to us of a world dying for lack of the Living Water.

Light upon the River

Isaiah 35
The Return of the King

44 WHEN THE KING SHALL COME AGAIN

When the King shall come again
all his power revealing,
splendour shall announce his reign,
life and joy and healing:
earth no longer in decay,
hope no more frustrated;
this is God's redemption-day
longingly awaited.

In the desert trees take root
fresh from his creation;
plants and flowers and sweetest fruit
join the celebration.
Rivers spring up from the earth,
barren lands adorning:
valleys, this is your new birth;
mountains, greet the morning!

Strengthen feeble hands and knees;
fainting hearts, be cheerful!
God who comes for such as these
seeks and saves the fearful.
Deaf ears hear the silent tongues
sing away their weeping;
blind eyes see the lifeless ones
walking, running, leaping.

There God's highway shall be seen
where no roaring lion,
nothing evil or unclean
walks the road to Zion:
ransomed people, homeward bound,
all your praises voicing,
see your Lord with glory crowned,
share in his rejoicing!

76.76.D trochaic   Tune: TEMPUS ADEST FLORIDUM;
or GAUDEAMUS PARITER (=AVE VIRGO)

Scriptures: Isa 35 Rom 8.19-23 Heb 2.9; 12.12-13 Lk 19.10 Matt 11.2-6 1 Pet 5.8 Heb 2.9

Written: Poplar, 1975

First published: *Hymns for Today's Church* (Hodder & Stoughton) 1982

Scene: the Vanderbilt Plaza Hotel, Nashville, Tennessee, 1987. I am sitting in on the large committee for a major new American hymnal. Hundreds of texts are being sifted, all anonymously. Suddenly this one emerges from the pile. The person in the corner with the computer says straight away 'This has been rejected'. The person on my right says, loudly, 'Good!', and we quickly move on. Even then, this hymn had undergone some verbal surgery; more was to come with my problem verse 3; we have lost a true rhyme, but gained in other kinds of correctness. Some have inserted the word 'Christ' or 'Jesus' to make the meaning clearer. It was written for the *Good King Wenceslas* tune TEMPUS ADEST FLORIDUM—originally for springtime. Those for whom the 'Feast of Stephen' associations are too strong have an alternative; several other American books have been more welcoming than my Nashville friends. Although not connected in the writing, I have now offered versions of Isaiah 12 for Christmas, ch. 25 for Easter, and here, ch. 35 for Advent. Chapter 53, for Good Friday, appears below.

Light upon the River

Isaiah 37.14-17
A blessing from earth to heaven

45 BLESS THE LORD, OUR FATHERS' GOD

Bless the Lord, our fathers' God,
bless the name of heaven's King;
bless him in his holy place,
tell his praise, his glories sing.

Bless the Lord who reigns on high
throned above the cherubim;
bless the Lord who knows the depths,
show his praise and worship him.

Bless the Lord for evermore,
bless the Holy Trinity;
bless the Father, Spirit, Son,
sing his praise eternally!

77.77 Tune: ORIENTIS PARTIBUS

Scriptures: Isa 37.14-17 Psa 60.1; 99.1; 103.1-2; 20-22

Written: Limehouse, 1978

First published: *Church Family Worship* (Hodder & Stoughton) 1986

With the latest revision of Church of England services, *Bless the Lord, the God of our fathers* was formally introduced in the 1970s. We felt the need of some metrical versions of the 'new' canticles, and this was written, and published, before 'fathers' became too sensitive a word to use. By 1987 I was experimenting with a freer and more inclusive approach, which ended as No.264, *Bless the Lord in Psalm and chorus*.

Light upon the River

Isaiah 52.1-10
Zion awakes

46 CITY OF GOD, JERUSALEM

City of God, Jerusalem, where he has set his love;
church of Christ that is one on earth with Jerusalem above:
here as we walk this changing world our joys are mixed with tears,
but the day will be soon when the Saviour returns
    and his voice will banish our fears.

Sing and be glad, Jerusalem, for God does not forget;
he who said he would come to save never failed his people yet.
Though we are tempted by despair and daunted by defeat,
our invincible Lord will be seen in his strength
    and his triumph will be complete.

Sorrow no more, Jerusalem; discard your rags of shame!
Take your crown as a gift from God
    who has called you by his name.
Put off your sin, and wear the robe of glory in its place;
you will shine in his light, you will share in his joy,
    you will praise his wonderful grace.

Look all around, Jerusalem, survey from west to east;
sons and daughters of God the King are invited to his feast.
Out of their exile far away his scattered family come,
and the streets will be full of the songs of the saints
    when the Saviour welcomes us home.

14.15.14.20 Tune: HELEPETE by Agnes Tang; BENSON; or PURPOSE

Scriptures: Isa 43.5-7; 52.1-10; 61.3-6, 10-11 Jer 31.7-14 Zeph 3.14-20 Gal 4.26 Heb 12.22-24; 13.5 1 Kgs 19.1-14 Lk 15.22-24 Rev 19.6-9; 21.2-4

Written: Limehouse, 1977

First published: *Hymns for Today's Church* (Hodder & Stoughton) 1982

The theme of Jerusalem, Zion, the City of God, runs all through Scripture as a haunting refrain, varying from security and strength to rejection and ruin, then forwards to hope and glory. The Psalms and prophets, Gospels and Revelation all have classic visits to this most famous city on its hill. This text takes the lesser known book of Baruch, from the Apocrypha, as its starting point, but includes some of the Bible's major variations on this theme. We sang it on Advent Sunday at Limehouse in 1977, to BENSON; the American *Worship 3* set it to Martin Shaw's PURPOSE, while Agnes Tang's tune was written for Peckham in 1996.

Isaiah 53
Pierced for our transgressions; the Suffering Servant of the Lord

47 WHO BELIEVES WHAT WE HAVE HEARD

Who believes what we have heard,
who has seen God's power
    made known? -
when the Servant of the Lord
grew unnoticed and alone;
undesired by those around
and unlovely in their eyes,
like a root in desert ground
which men trample and despise.

Yet for us the Servant grieved,
all our sorrows he endured;
his the torment unrelieved,
his the bruising from the Lord;
here is all our guilt engraved,
here are all our wrongs revealed;
by his suffering we are saved,
by his tortures we are healed.

Far away like sheep we strayed,
by our own desires misled,
but the Lord our God has laid
all our sins upon his head;
to the slaughter once he came -
see the willing victim stand
as a sacrificial lamb
silent at the killer's hand.

So he spent his final breath,
all his life for us he gave;
men of violence shared his death
and a rich man lent his grave;
target of his people's hate,
by oppression snatched away -
who was mindful of his fate,
who considered it that day?

But he now prolongs his days,
raised from darkness into light;
sees his children bring their praise,
vindicates and sets them right;
for the criminals he prayed,
for their crimes he bled and died;
now the sacrifice is made
and the Servant satisfied.

77.77.D Tune: CHARLES WESLEY by Bob Eagle;
or LITTLE HEATH by David Wilson

Scriptures: Isaiah 53 Lk 22.37; 23.32-46, 50-53 Acts 8.32-33
1 Pet 2.21-25

Written: Poplar, March 1976

The triumph of the Servant is the title given to this part of Isaiah, starting at 52.13, in Alec Motyer's IVP Commentary quoted earlier (No.42). Here is one example of tune preceding text, as David Wilson's music in *Youth Praise* (1966) seemed to match the mood of this prophecy, central to the Christian faith and the purpose of the coming of Jesus. It also seemed unlikely to supplant other tunes for *Jesu, Lover of my soul*, for which it was composed. Several other contemporary hymn writers have also drawn on this chapter; its theme is inexhaustible.

Light upon the River

Isaiah 60.1-6
The light and the glory: Epiphany

48 ARISE AND SHINE! YOUR LIGHT HAS COME

Arise and shine! Your light has come
   as Christ dispels the night:
all nations under heaven's dome
shall cast away their deepening gloom
   to seek the Lord's great light,
   God's sunrise beaming bright.

Lift up your eyes around, and see
   the people come from far:
and gladly crossing land and sea
wise men with tribute there shall be,
   for truly wise they are
   as those who saw the star.

Yet richer frankincense and gold
   affirm the Saviour's praise:
wherever Jesus' name is told
new treasures now replace the old:
   God's love explores new ways
   and sets new hope ablaze.

Some worshipped once the child divine
   and saw the human face;
some tasted water turned to wine,
believed the word that gave the sign,
   and grew in every place
   as firstfruits of his grace.

So those whom God in Israel blessed,
   the first in Christ reborn,
with joy shall welcome all the rest
who come from north, south, east and west,
   by shining splendour drawn
   to greet the rising dawn.

86.86.66 Tune: REPTON

Scriptures: Isa 60.1-6 Matt 2.1-12 Mk 2.21-22 Jn 2.1-11 Jas 1.17-18 Lk 13.29

Written: Poplar, 1975

In the 1970s the writers who formed the nucleus of what became *Jubilate Hymns* worked on a list of Scripture passages which might prove fruitful for new work; see No.12 above. This was my approach to one of them, sung at Limehouse on New Year's Eve 1978, when our morning service had readings from Isaiah 60 and Matthew 2. So this further text from Isaiah also illustrates another season, with its themes for Epiphany. Unlike No.10 in this collection (and *Dear Lord and Father of mankind*) it uses the final phrase of REPTON to provide a sixth line of text rather than repeating line five

Light upon the River

Isaiah 60.15-22
No more violence

49 IT WAS NO EMPTY DREAMER

It was no empty dreamer
foretelling our release;
our God, our great Redeemer,
has promised perfect peace.

No crime will curse the nation,
no warfare wreck your days;
your walls shall be salvation
and all your gates be praise.

No sun will shine before you
nor moon adorn the night;
your God will be your glory,
the Lord, your lasting light.

The tree that God has planted
will spread across the land,
the place that God has granted
the people of his hand.

The covenant he gave us
will bring that longed-for Day;
for Christ who comes to save us
we watch and work and pray.

The Lord our God has spoken,
his purpose must prevail;
our peace shall not be broken,
his word can never fail.

76.76 (or 76.76.D) Tune: KOCHER (or WOLVERCOTE)

Scriptures: Isa 60.15-22 Rev 21.23 2 Pet 3.1-13 Jn 14.27
Written: Peckham, 24 Sept 1997

This text began in the middle ('your God will be your glory', from v.19 of the chapter I was then reading) and grew in both directions. Later in the morning of its completion, we gave lunch to Robert and Sheila Emery; apart from my brother David, Robert has known me longer than anyone still living, as we attended Nettlestone School Bromley as rising fives. He is now a Reformed Church Minister in New South Wales; every Australian I meet seems to know him. I guessed he would ask, as many do, 'Are you still writing hymns?', so I was able to respond, 'Well, here's this morning's!' and present it to him. This text has an accidental echo of the almost forgotten 1759 original by Joseph Hart, *No prophet or dreamer of dreams*, known now from its final stanza 'This, this is the God we adore, our faithful, unchangeable Friend'. Dreams can guide us only if accompanied by God's words.

Light upon the River

Jeremiah 9.23-24
Boasting in the Lord: one

50 HOW SHALL THE WISE BE PROUD OF THEIR WISDOM

How shall the wise be proud of their wisdom,
how shall the strong be proud of their might?
How shall the rich be proud of their treasure?
These things shall fade like dreams in the night.

Who would be proud, let this be their boasting -
knowing the Lord, their Saviour and Guide;
not for themselves, but his be the honour:
God be their glory, Christ be their pride.

Boast in the Lord for his loving-kindness;
honour his name whose judgements are right:
all through the earth God rules by his wisdom -
love is his promise, truth his delight.

10.9.10.9 Tune needed

Scriptures: Jer 9.23-24 Jas 1.11 Eccles 1.17; 2.8-11 Psa 115.1
Written: Poplar, 1974

This prophetic appeal first hit me as a new student at Oxford in 1959, as preached (I think) by John Stott as the 'Freshers' Sermon'. Fifteen years on, and it seemed a fine theme for a hymn; another ten, and we were in trouble for such first lines as mine: 'How shall the wise man be proud of his wisdom'. In revising the text to its present form, I lost the more familiar metre which fitted such tunes as EPIPHANY HYMN (*Brightest and best*), and produced one which still awaits some music.

Light upon the River

Jeremiah 9.23-24
Boasting in the Lord: two

51 HOW CAN SCHOLARS BOAST OF WISDOM

How can scholars boast of wisdom
or the strong be proud of power,
or the wealthy vaunt their treasures
which shall perish in an hour?

Few of all the wise and mighty,
few with riches or high birth
God has chosen, but the humble,
counted nothing on this earth.

So by those the world despises
God has put its strength to shame;
non can glory in his presence,
none may boast but in his name.

God delights to keep his covenant;
all he does is just and right,
and his act of highest mercy
makes us holy in his sight.

So to know him is our glory
and the cross is all our pride,
where to all this world's inducements
we with Christ are crucified.

Christ our wisdom, power, and treasure!
Freed by him, with him made one,
all who love him, called his people,
boast of what the Lord has done!

87.87 Tune: MERTON

Scriptures: Jer 9.23-24 1 Cor 1.26-31 Gal 6.14
Written: Limehouse, 1977

A second try at expressing Jeremiah's heart-cry, now in a simpler metre, links it with two related New Testament letters, concerning wisdom and boasting respectively. John Stott had a hand in this too; in 1977 he was the visiting speaker at the Bishop of Stepney's Lent Lectures at the Royal Foundation of St Katharine, and in his series on evangelism he made the connection between these three Scriptures.

Light upon the River

Jeremiah 31.31-37
'I will make a new covenant'

52 OUR GOD HAS MADE HIS COVENANT NEW

Our God has made his covenant new -
the Lord himself has spoken -
not like the covenant made before
which human sin had broken.
He took his people by the hand
and led them through the desert land
by steadfast love and goodness.

But now God sets his law within—
on human hearts he writes it;
the people God has made his own,
one holy church, recites it.
So all alike their God will know
from least to greatest, high and low,
by steadfast love and goodness.

The Lord will count their sins no more -
their guilt shall be forgiven;
this promise comes from God who made
the sun, and earth, and heaven:
and Christ who brings us peace with God
has sealed this covenant with his blood
in steadfast love and goodness.

87.87.887 Tune: LUTHER'S HYMN; or LAUS DEO (Bach)

Scriptures: Jer 31.31-37 Heb 8.6-13; 9.11-15; 12.24 Rom 5.1 Lk 22.20

Written: Poplar, 1975

Since this part of the Bible is crucial to our understanding of the purpose of Jesus, especially of his dying, it is surprising that it has been comparatively neglected in hymns. This text was written partly to fill a gap, and sung at Poplar at the time. We also used it at Peckham in 1997, when Isaac Wuni, who was with us from Ghana for a year, preached on Jeremiah 31 as part of a series at Christ Church.

Jeremiah 31.33-34
God's law in our hearts

53 THE LORD HAS SAID THAT HE WILL BE OUR GOD

> The Lord has said that he will be our God
> and we shall be his people!
> For he writes on our hearts
> all the words of his law;
> he forgives all our sins
> and remembers them no more:
> and this is God's new covenant with us
> in Jesus Christ our Lord.
>
> Step out in faith that he will be our God
> and we shall be his people!
> For the lost are restored
> from the west and the east;
> we shall all know the Lord
> from the greatest to the least:
> and this is God's new covenant with us
> in Jesus Christ our Lord.

10.7.6666.10.6 Tune: COVENANT SONG by Norman Warren

Scriptures: Jer 31.33-34 Heb 12.1-2; 13.20

Written: Limehouse, 1980

First published: *Jesus Praise* (Scripture Union) 1982

In 1980 the Covenanters youth movement was looking for a song to help them celebrate a special anniversary; John Short (then Vicar of New Malden) asked me to supply a text on the 'covenant' theme, for which Norman Warren (then Rector of Morden) would write a tune. The resulting song was used at the celebrations and printed elsewhere, without ever becoming widely known.

Light upon the River

Ezekiel 1-2
The glory of the Lord

54 THE VISION OF THE LIVING GOD

The vision of the living God
    came once in blinding storm;
and glowing in its heart of flame,
their smooth unswerving course the same,
like swiftly-moving torches came
    four beasts in human form.

Each wore in front a human face,
    an eagle's head behind,
an ox and lion at each side,
as on they flew with wings spread wide,
God's Spirit as their constant guide,
    and lifted by the wind.

And moving with them, jewel-bright,
    four seeing, shining wheels;
a vault above, and there a throne
where radiance like the rainbow shone
on One in majesty alone
    whose voice all power reveals.

In God made flesh we see and hear
    true likeness, faithful word;
and though all hell should disobey,
no fear nor fainting shall dismay
the prophets sent to show today
    the glory of the Lord.

86.8886 Tune: REVELATION by Noel Tredinnick

Scriptures: Ezek 1-2 Rev 4 Jn 1.1,14 Heb 1.3 Col 1.15-19; 2.9 Isa 6.1-8; 40.30-31
Written: Poplar, 1975

'Here' says William Greenhill, 'you shall find more of God than you expect'! This 17th century Anglican and Puritan was beginning his great commentary on Ezekiel, itself a storehouse of treasure. The strange but majestic prophet has been much loved, he says, 'in troublesome and tumultuous times'. I confess an affection, too, for Mr Greenhill, who not only served in such times with graciousness among opponents, and moved from Suffolk to inner London; he was an honoured predecessor of mine as Rector of Oakley (though his house has gone) and in the Parish of Stepney including what is now Limehouse. Ezekiel himself is always well worth the textual wrestling; but apart from the old spiritual *Ezekiel saw a wheel*, as sung by Paul Robeson, hardly an obvious port of call for hymnwriters. In these verses I have tried to express some of the mystery as well as the glory, and to go beyond the vision to the work given to the prophet, and to the full expression of that glory in Christ.

Light upon the River

Daniel 2.20-23
God gives timely wisdom

55 THE GLORIOUS GOD OF HEAVEN

The glorious God of heaven,
the Lord who made the light,
who changes times and seasons
in majesty and might;
the only Judge of nations
whose counsel makes us wise:
that name be blessed for ever
with whom all wisdom lies.

Deep mysteries are opened,
God sees where darkness hides;
for what we ask is answered
and where we seek, God guides:
the Father of our fathers,
the strength of all our days,
the source of all our knowledge,
to God be all our praise!

If we will look for mercy
and, listening, learn to pray,
the King of kings is ready
to speak and save today:
with mind and heart illumined,
with sin and wrong forgiven,
from earth we praise the Father
and bless the God of heaven.

76.76.D Tune: PENLAN; or NYLAND

Scriptures: Dan 2.20-23 Rom 9.5 2 Cor 11.31 Psa 139.11-12 Matt 7.7-8 Eph 1.7,18

Written: Poplar, 1974

Sometimes, as for Daniel and his friends, and their modern counterparts in similar parts of the world, the gift of God's wisdom is a matter of life and death. Yet more important, it has eternal consequences. So it is vital to know, as they did, that the Lord is 'the God of heaven'—the phrase from Daniel 2 which begins and ends the hymn, and which must never be taken for granted. This text was originally accepted for publication, but was squeezed out by the wealth of material on this theme.

Light upon the River

Hosea 11.1-4
God's beloved child

56 WHEN ISRAEL WAS YOUNG, YOU LOVED HIM

When Israel was young, you loved him,
from Egypt you called your son;
but now all the more you call him
the further your child has gone:
    our God, you will not desert us
    for you are the Holy One!

As babes in your arms you brought us
before we could understand;
we grew—it was you who taught us,
we walked—and you held our hand:
    our God, you will not desert us;
    you seek us in every land.

The reins of your love have led us,
without you we could not move;
you bent down to help, and fed us,
you lifted us high above:
    our God, you will not desert us,
    your heart is ablaze with love!

Though once we refused to have you
and trusted deceit and lies,
and called to the empty shadows
that never could hear our cries:
    our God, you will not desert us;
    O Lord, in your love arise!

87.87.87 Tune: IN SILENCE MY SOUL IS WAITING by Christian Strover;
or HOSEA by Christopher Hayward

Scriptures: Hos 11.1-4, 8-9,12 Heb 12.7-10,25; 13.5 Eph 2.1-10
Written: Poplar, March 1976

Sometimes a text and tune, though making their entrance together, do not seem ideally matched. It is hard to find universal agreement on such delicate courtships, but I have felt that Christian Strover's lyrical tune, set in *Psalm Praise* (1973), needed words in a different mood from the explosiveness of Michael Saward's Psalm 62 version. These I tried to provide in this approach to a prophecy precious to Christians because of Matthew 2.15, but whose meaning is not exhausted by that fulfilment. The words had a further musical interpretation when Christopher Hayward at Cambridge, looking this time for hymns on Hosea, provided his own tune which was used at St Andrew the Great in 1997.

Light upon the River

Hosea 14.1-8
'I will love them freely': God gives repentance

57 RETURN TO FACE YOUR GOD

Return to face your God!
Your sin has made you fall;
return, and make your prayer to him:
'O God, forgive us all!'

Return to face your God!
Begin again to learn
the Lord alone can rescue those
with nowhere else to turn.

Return to face your God!
Give him your promised praise;
the Lord is just and merciful,
and true in all his ways.

'I bring my people back;
I lead them by the hand,
and I will be to them like rain
upon a barren land.

I bring my people back;
like trees they shall take root,
majestic, fragrant, fixed and firm,
and bearing sweetest fruit.

I bring my people back;
their idols they destroy,
and I will be their hope and strength,
their shelter and their joy.'

To God the Father, Son,
and Spirit, be all power,
dominion, worship, thanks and praise
henceforth for evermore!

SM Tune: CARLISLE

Scriptures: Hos 14.1-8 Acts 5.31; 11.18 1 Thess 1.9
Written: Limehouse, 1979

A hymn of two halves and a doxology. The first three verses take the voice of the prophet; the next three, the voice of the Lord. The doxology praises God who not only commands repentance (Acts 17.30), but in his grace provides it, to both Israel (5.31) and the Gentiles (11.18). The text is a straightforward paraphrase of God's message of love for a wayward, rebellious nation.

Light upon the River

Amos 4.13
The lion roars

58 THE LORD WHO MADE THE MOUNTAINS

The Lord who made the mountains
and fashioned humankind,
reveals his thought and shows to us
the purpose of his mind:
he turns the night to morning,
his breath is wind and flame;
he moves in power across the world
and holy is his name.

When thunder shakes the forest
whose spirit feels no fear?
When God declares his mighty word
who dares refuse to hear?
Do lions roar for nothing
when all the sky grows dark?
Does sudden ruin wreck our hopes
unless it is God's work?

The distant stars and planets
trace out a vast design;
the sun and moon obey the laws
of One who makes them shine:
he lifts the tossing waters
and pours them on the earth;
and God who saves and judges us
controls our death and birth.

He calls us to his kingdom,
reclaims us from our sin,
and guides our feet to find the way
that we may enter in:
our guilt is here forgiven,
and ruined lives restored;
for none who trust him shall be lost -
so speaks our sovereign Lord.

To God the Father, glory!
To God the Son be praise!
To God the Spirit, worship now
and through eternal days!
Let angels in the heavens
and those redeemed by blood
with songs of gratitude and love
adore the living God.

76.86.D Tune: ALFORD

Scriptures: Amos 4.13; 3.4-6; 5.8; 9.5-6 Job 9.1-10 Lk 1.68,77-79 Rev 5.9

Written: Limehouse, 1977

The book of Amos is rich in the imagery of a prophet, preacher and poet—but surprisingly little-used in hymns. This admittedly selective text originally began with what is now verse 2, keeping Amos's order; we sang it at Limehouse on Jan 15 1978. In a group discussion, some felt it strange to start with a series of questions; to confirm that, the *Eltham College Hymn Book*, (where it was first printed) left the verse out entirely. But some further revision led to the present form of the text in 1987.

Light upon the River

Micah 4.1-5
Swords into ploughshares

59 O WHERE SHALL PEACE BE FOUND

O where shall peace be found,
and where an end to slaughter -
all lands be holy ground,
all peoples free from murder?
   Where weapons are unmade
   the prophet's word comes true
   and none shall be afraid
   when God makes all things new.

The mountain of the Lord
shall rise above all others;
in Christ we are restored
as neighbours, sisters, brothers:
   our grey machines of death
   are turned to nobler use
   when over all the earth
   his kingdom is let loose.

We long to see the day
when love completes that vision!
But God who hears us pray
demands our clear decision:
   Lord, give us ears to hear,
   and wills to heed, your voice;
   to yield no more to fear,
   to make your path our choice.

67.67.66.66 Tune: SHONA by Agnes Tang;
ONE-O-ONE by Agnes Tang;
RINKART; NUN DANKET; or DARMSTADT

Scriptures: Mic 4.1-5 Isa 2.1-5 Rev 21.4-5 Gal 3.28 Col 3.11

Written: Limehouse, 3 July 1984

First published: *News of Hymnody No.31* (Grove Books) July 1989

The way of Christ is incompatible with reliance on weapons of mass destruction. Even Christians who agree with such a statement differ on what we should do about it; hence the final verse of this paraphrase of Micah and Isaiah. I wrote it in response to a BBC TV 'Songs of Praise' search for hymns about peace; unusually, I wrote it in one steady session. But it did not gain favour. Much later, in 1996, Agnes Tang wrote a tune (later named SHONA) for *Now thank we all our God*, which I thought ideal for this text; she did not agree, and came up instead with ONE-O-ONE.

Light upon the River

Haggai 1.6
Disappointments and remedies

60 IS YOUR HARVEST LESS THAN YOU HAD HOPED

Is your harvest less than you had hoped?   *(repeat)*
Lavish in your planting, gathering but little;
food and drink and wages never seem sufficient:
is your harvest less than you had hoped?

Work, for I am with you, says the Lord!
God is still among us, yearning in his Spirit;
why are we so busy, careless of his kingdom?
Work, for I am with you, says the Lord!

Be strong, all you people of the land!
All who lead the nation, set aside your comfort;
seek first heaven's treasure, nourishment eternal:
be strong, all you people of the land!

God will shake the heavens and the earth!
Skies and seas and cities, all shall yield their harvest;
more than gold or silver, their Redeemer's glory:
God will shake the heavens and the earth!

9(9).666.9 Tune: HAGGAI by Christopher Hayward

Scriptures: Hag 1.6; 2.4-9 Matt 6.31-33 Jn 6.27 Rev 21.22-26

Written: Cambridge (39 Castle St) 19 Oct 1995

Haggai's words were vital to his own generation. It is hard to think of any more relevant to our own. On a personal level, 'Work, for I am with you, says the Lord' (Hag 2.4) was a text I had on my student bedsit for encouragement; the original context is a bit wider than that. This was another request from St Andrew the Great, Cambridge, via Chris Hayward, who wrote his tune ('Cool jazz') the next April. This was just in time for the hymn's launch on the 21st, to accompany the sermon series on the book.

Light upon the River

Matthew 1.20-25
God with us: Emmanuel

61 DARK IS ALL THE WORLD BELOW HIM

Dark is all the world below him;
can the angels' news be true?
God is with us: we can know him,
found this night so small, so new.

Why the sky so dark above him?
Must he die, to make us free?
God is for us: we can love him
who is nailed upon the tree.

How can rebel earth deserve him?
He has made our hearts his own;
God is in us: we can serve him
by his Spirit's fire alone.

All the world is lost without him;
come to Christ—Emmanuel!
God has spoken: do not doubt him;
hear, believe, and sing Noel!

87.87 Tune: CROSS OF JESUS; or HALTON HOLGATE

Scriptures: Matt 1.20-25 Lk 2.4-16 1 Pet 2.24 Eph 3.16-17 1 Thess 4.13 Heb 1.1-2

Written: Peckham, 27 Dec 1995

'God is with us: we can know him!' The occasion, Carols by Candlelight, Christ Church Old Kent Road, 17 Dec 1995; our first Christmas in Peckham for 25 years. The preacher, James Russell, the Lay Assistant, soon to start training for ordination. With his wife Annabel he was then living in the lower part of 59 King's Grove, our own address in 1970-71. The words stayed with me over Christmas, prompting others which soon provided a framework for this text—though the four matching phrases were moved down, at Marjorie's prompting, to form the second lines rather than the first, for each verse. So we start with wistful questioning rather than bald assertion. For me, a rare Christmas text.

Light upon the River

Matthew 2.1-12
Wise men

62 WISE MEN, THEY CAME TO LOOK FOR WISDOM

Wise men, they came to look for wisdom,
finding one wiser than they knew;
rich men, they met with one yet richer -
King of the kings, they knelt to you:
    Jesus, our Wisdom from above,
    wealth and redemption, light and love.

Pilgrims they were, from unknown countries,
searching for one who knows the world;
lost are their names, and strange their journeys,
famed is their zeal to find the child:
    Jesus, in you the lost are claimed,
    aliens are found and known and named.

Magi, they stooped to see your splendour,
led by a star to light supreme;
promised Messiah, Lord eternal,
glory and peace are in your name:
    Joy of each day, our Song by night,
    shine on our path your holy light.

Guests of their God, they opened treasures,
incense and gold and solemn myrrh,
welcoming one too young to question
how came these gifts, and what they were:
    Gift beyond price of gold or gem,
    make among us your Bethlehem.

98.98.88 Tune: NEUMARK (= BREMEN)

Scriptures: Matt 2.1-12 1 Cor 1.30-31 Psa 77.6; 118.27 Job 35.10

Written: Limehouse, 1981

First published: *Hymns for Today's Church* (Hodder & Stoughton) 1982

While preparing an Epiphany sermon in Jan 1981 I realised afresh the treasures in this strange yet familiar narrative. I found much help in Prof R V G Tasker's 1961 'Tyndale' Commentary on Matthew—now superseded but a small and faithful landmark in its day. So my sermon outline was adapted to verse, which eventually became a hymn. Among small changes since the earliest draft were some resulting from comments by George Timms, hymnwriter and then my Archdeacon, at a clergy conference at Ely, where I introduced it soon after it was written. Since then it has been published in the UK, USA, Canada, Hong Kong and Australia; strange too are the journeys of hymns.

Light upon the River

Matthew 5.1-2; 7.28-29
Jesus the teacher

63 TEACH ME, LORD JESUS, ALL I NEED TO KNOW

Teach me, Lord Jesus, all I need to know:
   form within me your mind;
   let all the truth I find
make me more humble, more truly to grow.

Teach me, Lord Jesus, all I need to do:
   help me by love to live,
   suffer and work and give,
learning obedience, and learning from you.

Teach me, Lord Jesus, all I need to say:
   set my tongue free to speak
   true words, and pure and meek,
patterned on yours, which shall not pass away.

Teach me, Lord Jesus, all I need to be:
   train me and put me right
   till I reflect your light,
till you complete all your purpose for me.

10.6.6.10 Tune: LLAN by Stephen James

Scriptures: Matt 4.23; 5.1-2; 7.28-29; 28.20 Mk 1.21 Lk 4.31 Jn 7.46 Acts 1.1

Written: Limehouse, April 1981

My notes on this text show simply when it was written, that I sent it to Robin Leaver in July, and that it was slightly reshaped to adapt better to Stephen James' tune. Steve was then living near us, and working at St Helen's Bishopsgate in whose 1982 Song Book it was included. 'Jesus the Teacher' was the theme for the 9th Sunday before Easter in the Lectionary we were then using.

Light upon the River

Matthew 6
Daily bread

64 OUR GOD, SUPREME AND GOOD

Our God, supreme and good,
how richly you have loved!
But nations die for lack of food
and are we still unmoved?

While human lives are lost
in misery and fear,
shall we complain about the cost
of all our comforts here?

So many face their death
by famine, flood and war;
yet we, their neighbours,
 spend our breath
in crying out for more.

So keen to eat and drink,
so anxious what we wear!
Our God, reverse the way we think
and teach us how to share.

Show us we dare not wait
when desperate voices call;
save us from sending help too late,
too grudging, and too small.

You made your purpose known
by one rejected man;
the earth his bed, a cross his throne,
new life for all, his plan.

So for your world we pray
through Jesus Christ, your Son;
give us the bread we need each day:
on earth, your will be done.

SM Tune: EDWIN by Edgar M Deale; or ST GEORGE

Scriptures: Matt 6 Jas 2.14-17 1 Jn 3.16-18 Isa 53.3 Lk 9.57-58; 11.2-3 Jn 10.10
Written: Poplar, 1975
First published: TEAR Fund, 1976

Can God be both supreme and good? The Evangelical Alliance Relief Fund (TEAR Fund) was founded in Nov 1968; in 1976 its leadership was looking for a new hymn expressing concern for the world's needy people. This text, written a year before, was adopted as 'the TEAR Fund Hymn' in its publications, including services for TEAR Fund Sunday. Partly because the subject requires great sensitivity (hymns should rarely preach, and never nag, patronize, or suggest easy solutions) this became one of my most-revised texts. Most changes were small and date from 1981 or 1993, but the cumulative effect has been to leave intact only its opening and closing lines. It is one of the most requested texts of mine which does not appear in any hymnal. Whatever else we say or sing about a suffering world, our response must relate to Christ's cross and our lifestyle; this remains a hymn which cannot be sung by the truly poor. But it points to one way of answering that first question.

Matthew 7.24-27
Wise building

65 LORD, TEACH YOUR CHILDREN HOW TO BUILD

>Lord, teach your children how to build
>>by wood and nail,
>>brick, stone and tile:
>you learned such building as a child
>as hand and arm and eye were skilled,
>>here for a little while.
>
>Lord, show your children where to build
>>by word and deed
>>at neighbours' need:
>not on the sand our work be found
>but on the rock, the solid ground
>>where you have been obeyed.
>
>And Lord, be with us as we build,
>>not dust and bones
>>but living stones,
>a temple growing, Spirit-filled,
>just as the Father's heart has willed
>>for his beloved ones.

844.886 Tune needed

Scriptures: Mk 6.3 Lk 6.46-49 Matt 7.24-27 1 Cor 3.9-17 Eph 2.19-22 1 Pet 2.4-5
Written: Oakley, 4 June 1992

When our eldest was small, and we had read about the wise and foolish builders, he said 'Jesus told that story to show how we should build houses, didn't he, Dad?'. Trying to be honest, I said 'Well, not quite...', and tried to explain. As an adult working in Bolivia, Tim first encountered the home-building mission Habitat for Humanity International. From 1989 to 1996 he worked with Habitat in Tanzania, and then in London, employing what founder Millard Fuller calls 'the theology of the hammer'. After seeing something of his work in 1992, I wrote two texts with the mission in mind (see also No.100) and later gave them to HFHI. This one, in an unusual metre, needs a new tune. The word translated 'carpenter', used of Joseph and Jesus in the Gospels, includes joinery but also many other branches of the building trade. More important, I now think the young Tim had a point; there is always more to explore in Matthew 7, but whatever materials we use, the same wisdom and obedience are vital.

Light upon the River

Matthew 8.23-27
Saviour of the world

66 JESUS, SAVIOUR OF THE WORLD

Jesus, Saviour of the world,
you have bought your people's freedom
by your cross, your life laid down;
now bring in your glorious kingdom.
    Come to help us!

Christ, who once on Galilee
came to your disciples' rescue,
we, like them, cry out for help:
free us from our sins, we ask you.
    Come to save us!

Lord, make known your promised power,
show yourself our strong Deliverer;
so our prayer shall turn to praise,
hear us, stay with us for ever.
    Come to rule us!

When you come, Lord Jesus Christ,
filling earth and heaven with wonder,
come to make us one with you,
heirs of life, to reign in splendour.
    Hallelujah!

78.78.4 Tune: MOWSLEY by Cyril Taylor; or ST ALBINUS

Scriptures: Jn 4.42 1 Jn 4.14 Matt 8.23-27; 20.28 Mk 4.35-41; 10.45 Rev 5.9-10 Psa 140.7 Rom 11.26-27

Written: Limehouse, 1978

First published: *Church Family Worship* (Hodder & Stoughton) 1986

It was at Poplar in 1971 that I first began to use regularly the canticle with this first line—a translation of the Latin *Salvator Mundi*. It was soon to be incorporated into an official but 'experimental' Daily Office. Later I began to put some of these items into metrical versions to be sung to familiar hymn tunes. While this one has several Biblical echoes, its first tune suggests Easter; it uses assonance rather than rhyme, and is structured round the words 'Lord... Jesus... Christ'.

Light upon the River

Matthew 10.1-4
Twelve apostles, one God: a counting song

67 TWELVE FOR THE TWELVE APOSTLES

Twelve for the twelve apostles,
eleven for eleven with names in heaven and
ten for the ten commandments;
nine for the nine ungrateful men and
eight who were saved from drowning;
seven for the seven stars in God's hand and
six for the jars of water;
five for the loaves that Jesus shared and
four for the gospel writers;
three, three, for Easter Day;
two, two, the great commands -
love your God, your neighbour too:
God is one, and God alone has made you and can save you.

Tune: GREEN GROW THE RUSHES-O (refrain)

Scriptures: Matt 10.1-4 Lk 6.13; 10.20; 17.17 Ex 34.28 1 Pet 3.20 Rev 1.16 Jn 2.6; 6.9 Mk 8.31; 12.28-31
Written: Poplar, 1974

A fun-song for juniors that actually teaches something, written for a term of twelve weekly assemblies at St Matthias' School Poplar and also used at Stepney Greencoat School in Limehouse—both being C of E Aided Primary Schools where I was for some years Incumbent, governor and parent. Each line had its visual aid; we started at the end ('God is one...') and built it up backwards until the song was complete. The Bible verses referred to are only one selection; others may fit equally well. The origins of the song are part Hebrew, part pagan, part Christian; in Devon and Cornwall it is called 'The Dilly Song', as described in a leaflet from the English Folk Dance and Song Society.

Light upon the River

Matthew 24.29-46
The Advent hope

68 WHEN THE SUN IS DARKENED

When the sun is darkened and the
 moon gives no light
and the stars fall from the sky,
then in heaven will appear the
 long-promised sign
that proclaims the Son of Man.

All the peoples of the world will
 cry and lament
when they see the Son of Man
coming in great power and glory
 high on the clouds
with his angels serving him.

He will send his angels with a
 loud trumpet blast
from the farthest bounds of heaven;
from the four winds they will gather
 his chosen ones
who are ready for their Lord.

None on earth can prophesy the
 day or the hour
which the Father knows alone;
keep awake and well-prepared, for
 Jesus will come
at the time you least expect.

Happy is the servant who is
 found keeping faith
when the Master comes again;
heaven and earth will pass away, but
 never the words
of the Lord, the Son of Man.

84.78.47 Tune: ADVENT PSALM by Norman Warren

Scriptures: Matt 24.29-46; 25.13 Mk 13.24-37 Lk 21.27-33 Isa 13.10 Joel 2.10 Rev 1.5-7; 6.12-14

Written: Peckham, 1970

First published: *Psalm Praise* (Falcon) 1973

One aim of the group working on *Psalm Praise* was to produce selections of Scriptures similar to the Easter Anthems in the Book of Common Prayer, suited to other seasons of the year; I was delighted that Advent was one of those assigned to me. The line structure is regular, but the unusual metre (adapted to be close to the text of Matthew) and the absence of rhyme show it to be one of my earlier efforts. Norman Warren's much-acclaimed tune, which received its name ADVENT PSALM later, rapidly grew on me after initial doubts, and has been recorded with these words. Whatever recent changes have reshaped the church's year, Advent remains for many its solemn but exciting beginning.

Light upon the River

Matthew 25.1-10
Here is the Bridegroom!

69 WAKE, O WAKE, AND SLEEP NO LONGER

Wake, O wake, and sleep no longer,
for he who calls you is no stranger;
awake, God's own Jerusalem!
Hear the midnight bells are chiming
the signal for his royal coming;
let voice to voice announce his name!
  We feel his footstep near,
  the Bridegroom at the door:
  Hallelujah!
The lamps will shine with light divine
as Christ the Saviour comes to reign.

Zion hears the sound of singing;
her heart is filled with sudden longing:
she stirs, and wakes,
    and stands prepared.
Christ her Friend and Lord and Lover,
her Star and Sun and strong Redeemer:
at last his mighty voice is heard.
  The Son of God has come
  to make with us his home:
  sing Hosanna!
The fight is won, the feast begun;
we fix our eyes on Christ alone.

    Glory, glory, sing the angels
    while music sounds from strings and cymbals;
    all humankind, with songs arise!
    Twelve the gates into the city,
    each one a pearl of shining beauty;
    the streets of gold ring out with praise.
      All creatures round the throne
      adore the Holy One
      with rejoicing:
    Amen be sung by every tongue
    to crown their welcome to the King.

898D.664.88 Tune: WACHET AUF (= SLEEPERS, WAKE)

Scriptures: Isa 35.10; 52.1-2 Matt 25.1-10 Mk 13.32-37 Lk 12.35-37 Song 2.8; 4.16; 5.4,16 Prov 23.11 Rev 1.16; 2.28; 4.6-9; 5.8-14; 21.2-3, 10-21; 22.16 Psa 150.4-6

Written: Limehouse, Oct 1981

First published: *Hymns for Today's Church* (Hodder & Stoughton) 1982

Here is a new approach to Philipp Nicolai's classic German hymn (c.1597) *Wachet Auf.* In response to requests, I prepared my paraphrase from a basic translation provided by our son Jeremy. I made some changes to the kaleidoscope of Biblical imagery in the original, varying between true rhyme (in the penultimate lines) and assonance or 'chime', but I did not succeed in finding a new opening line to distinguish this from other versions. The text has been much-requested by American Roman Catholics; new tunes have been skilfully composed, but I still cling to the Nicolai/Bach masterpiece.

Light upon the River

Matthew 26.30
Hymn after Communion

70 AT THE SUPPER'S ENDING

At the supper's ending
faith seems firm and strong;
twelve the voices blending
in their Hebrew song

Lord, whose love has freed them,
can they as they sing
guess where night will lead them,
or what day may bring?

Now, as then, together
by one bread, one cup,
we are pledged for ever
to one kingdom's hope.

Lord, you need no grieving;
you have borne our sins:
teach us at our leaving,
worship now begins.

65.65 Tune: NORTH COATES

Scriptures: Matt 26.30 Mk 14.26 Jn 13.1 1 Cor 10.16-17 Lk 22.16 1 Pet 2.24 Rom 12.1

Written: Peckham, Jan 1996

A hymn for use after Communion; see the notes to No.80, *Before they leave the upper room*. The twelve who sing (verse 1) are Jesus and the eleven; Judas has gone. Their Hebrew song in is one of the 'Hallel' Psalms (114-118) used at Passover; the night of verse 2 is, first, that of Maundy Thursday, on which Jesus is betrayed; the day (Good Friday) brings crucifixion. In the New Testament, worship (verse 4) is not so much what happens 'in church' as the offering of ourselves to God at all times.

Light upon the River

Matthew 27.29
Crowned with thorns

71 MY LORD OF LIGHT

My Lord of light who made the worlds,
in wisdom you have spoken;
but those who heard your wise commands
your holy law have broken.

My Lord of love who knew no sin,
a sinner's death enduring,
for us you wore a crown of thorns,
a crown of life securing.

My Lord of life who came in fire
when Christ was high ascended,
your burning love is now released,
our days of fear are ended.

My Lord of lords, one Trinity,
to your pure name be given
all glory now and evermore,
all praise in earth and heaven.

87.87 iambic Tune: HA DVAR by Agnes Tang; THRICE BLEST by Roy Hopp; WILFORD by George Gardner; DOMINUS REGIT ME; or BARBARA ALLEN

Scriptures: Gen 1.1-3; 3.17 Matt 27.29 Mk 15.17 Jn 19.1-5 Jas 1.12 Rev 2.10 Acts 2.3 Rom 5.5 1 Jn 4.18

Written: Poplar, 1976

First published: *Songs of Worship* (Scripture Union) 1980

For once, the tune (BARBARA ALLEN) was suggested to me before the words were written; *The King of love* is a surprisingly rare example of a hymn in this metre. The text was printed in 'The Christian Herald' (7 June 1980) in a review of current writing. Although it is placed here with Passiontide references to the crown of thorns, it is a Trinitarian hymn which also touches on creation and Pentecost. In 1996 Agnes Tang wrote a new tune, which I prefer to pair with No.80.

Light upon the River

Matthew 27.50-61
Death and life at the cross

72 MASTER, WHAT LOVE IS HERE

Master, what love is here!
for you have dealt with sin;
the temple curtain tears apart
and we are welcomed in.

Master, what power is here!
for you have broken death;
the ground is shaken, tombs laid bare,
the dead are given breath.

Master, what grace is here!
for you have ended doubt;
your enemies have watched you die:
'This is God's son!' they shout.

Master, what hope is here!
for you bring faith to birth;
the infant church of two or three
will grow to span the earth.

Here at the cross I stand
to feel and hear and see
what you have felt and said and done
for ever, and for me.

SM Tune: DOMINICA

Scriptures: Matt 27.50-61 Mk 15.38-39 Matt 18.20; 28.18-20 Lk 24.44-49 Acts 1.8

Written: Peckham, April 1996

Good Friday evening 1996 found us at Christ Church Old Kent Road, after spending from noon to 4.30 at Limehouse. Hugh Balfour our Vicar led us in quiet meditations on the cross, based on Matthew 27. In the third of these (verses 50-61) he showed how sin and death were dealt with, faith was established, and the tiny church gathered in embryo in the small groups drawing near at the moments of dying and burial—and, most startlingly, resurrection. Over Easter I put together four verses starting with Hugh's main thought: 'Lord, you have dealt with sin'; later my four 'headlines' became second lines, I added a fourth stanza and 'O Lord' became 'Master'. The Short Metre requires a stressed note to start with.

Light upon the River

Matthew 28.1-10
Christ is risen: Hallelujah!

73 HALLELUJAH: CHRIST IS KING

Hallelujah: Christ is king! Hallelujah: let everyone sing.
Hallelujah, wherever you are, join in to praise the Lord—Hallelujah!

Hallelujah: Christ can save, Hallelujah, alive from the grave.
Hallelujah! now death is defeated, we live to praise the Lord—Hallelujah!

Hallelujah: Christ the light: Hallelujah, the end of the night!
Hallelujah, the day of salvation, the day to praise the Lord—Hallelujah!

Hallelujah, Christ shall reign: Hallelujah, he's coming again!
Hallelujah, to God be the glory, all nations, praise the Lord—Hallelujah!

Hallelujah, Christ is Lord! Hallelujah, his name be adored!
Hallelujah! we join with the angels who always praise the Lord—Hallelujah!

(repeat last line)

Tune: HALLELUJAH (as recorded by 'Milk and Honey' 1979)

Scriptures: Rev 19.1,4-6 Matt 28.1-10 2 Cor 6.2 Rom 14.12; 15.11 Heb 9.28 Psa 117; 148.2

Written: Limehouse, April 1979

Why should the Eurovision Song Contest have all the best tunes (and the worst)? This quotation, variously attributed, I took to heart in 1979 when an Israeli group 'Milk and Honey', reputedly formed solely for that year's event and disbanding afterwards, entered with their song *Hallelujah*. They duly won, though reaching only No.5 during their eight weeks in the charts. 'Top of the Pops' was then part of our sons' weekly TV viewing, some of which we shared. This seemed too good an opportunity to miss for reclaiming the Biblical, Hebrew word for 'Praise the Lord'; so I took it. It was sung at Limehouse and elsewhere while the tune remained popular; by starting on middle C (in the key of A flat) each verse can be raised by a semitone without going too high by the end.

Light upon the River

Matthew 28.18-20
The great commission

74 ALL AUTHORITY AND POWER

All authority and power,
every status and domain
now belongs to him who suffered
our redemption to obtain;
Angels, demons, kings and rulers -
over all shall Jesus reign!

All the nations owe him worship;
every tongue shall call him Lord.
How are they to call upon him
if his name they have not heard?
Therefore go and make disciples,
preach his gospel, spread his word.

All the clear commands of Jesus
must be heeded and obeyed;
full provision for our weakness
in his teaching he has made:
in the gospel words and symbols
saving truth to us conveyed.

All the time he will be with us,
always, to the end of days
with his own believing people
who keep steadfast in his ways.
God the Father, Son and Spirit
bless us—and to God be praise!

87.87.87 Tune: EXOUSIA by David Wilson;
or UNSER HERRSCHER (= NEANDER)

Scriptures: Matt 28.18-20 Heb 1.4; 9.12 Rom 10.13-14
Written: Peckham, 1971
First published: *Psalm Praise* (Falcon) 1973

As well as Advent, I was charged by the *Psalm Praise* team with writing an 'Ascension canticle'. Here too was a privilege, as I am an Ascension enthusiast; Christmas apart, these were the best attended midweek festivals of our Suffolk years. Unlike No.68 above (see notes) this is not a paraphrase but a hymn built on the four 'alls' of Matthew's text, which I have sometimes used as a Family Service framework. The 'gospel symbols' of verse 3 include Baptism, with the Trinitarian name of Matt 28.19. The hymn has been the most requested of all from our first 'Peckham period', not least for global mission events and publications. It is to Luke that we owe the ascension narratives; Matthew treats the great commission differently. But none of the gospels leaves us in any doubt about our priorities.

Light upon the River

Mark 1.1-13
Jesus is baptized

75 SEE CHRIST WHO ON THE RIVER'S SHORE

See Christ who on the river's shore
with John the Baptist stood,
his secret in the name he bore:
the holy Lamb of God.
> See all his body washed and wet
> baptized in Jordan's flow,
> as here his shame and glory meet,
> his pain and triumph show.

See, Christ submits himself to John,
the Lord bows to his slave!
See where he stoops, the sinless one,
to share a sinner's grave!
> See him arising from the stream
> where all the past now dies;
> from yet a colder tomb he came
> and now calls us to rise.

See Christ to whom the Father speaks
as his beloved Son;
Messiah's chosen task he takes,
the servant's work begun.
> See him on whom the Spirit fell
> descending like a dove,
> in whom we find a springing well
> of peace and joy and love.

See Christ through forty hungry days
with sand and stones for bed;
in lonely trials and desert ways
with him may we be led.
> See him, the anointed Lamb who died
> to whom all praise we bring;
> see Christ baptized, Christ crucified,
> and Christ our reigning King!

DCM Tune: ACLE by Mervyn Horder; or VOX DILECTI

Scriptures: Matt 3.13-4.11 Mk 1.1-13 Lk 3.21-22; 4.1-13; 12.50 Jn 1.29-36 Gal 5.22 Rev 5.12-14 Acts 10.36-43

Written: Poplar, 1975

When I wrote this there were few hymns about the Baptism of our Lord; such hymn-guides to the Lectionary as we had were hard-pressed to recommend much for this major Epiphany theme. Since then several new ones have appeared, from such writers as Bernard Braley, Carl Daw, Timothy Dudley-Smith, George Timms and others. My own is based on the gospel accounts, taking up some of the significance of this unique Baptism, and subsequent temptations, for our salvation. We sang it at Poplar in 1975 to VOX DILECTI; it then lay dormant for many years. Mervyn Horder wrote his tune for it around 1995; Chris Hayward then introduced it at Cambridge (to KINGSFOLD) in Jan 1997.

Light upon the River

Mark 1.14-20
'Follow me': first disciples

76 LORD, YOU CHOSE YOUR FIRST DISCIPLES

Lord, you chose your first disciples
from a group around the lake,
and they followed when you called them,
coming gladly for your sake.
Then they watched you as you travelled,
learned to trust in what you said,
saw you love and save the outcast,
reach the lost and raise the dead.

Lord, we long to make disciples
from the group for which we care;
sweet success or bitter failure,
joy or grief with you we share.
Let the lost be found and welcomed,
let the dead find life anew;
we have shared in their rebellion:
let them come to share in you.

When the pressures seem to crush us
you delight your power to prove;
when the barriers divide us
you bring harmony and love.
Your good news shall be our message
making us and others whole,
all your ways our perfect pattern
and yourself our glorious Goal.

87.87.D Tune: STENKA RAZIN (*Youth Praise* 247)

Scriptures: Matt 4.18-22 Mk 1.14-20; 3.13-19 Lk 5.1-11; 15.1-24; 19.10 Rom 10.1 Tit 3.3-8 2 Cor 4.8-10 Eph 2.14-17 1 Pet 2.21 Phil 3.14

Written: Herne Bay Court, Kent, 1970

Some hymns and songs are right for a single occasion and do not last beyond it; here may be one such, written at a Frontier Youth Trust Conference I attended in order to learn more of the skills of open youth work. I was then running an 'open' club in Peckham; at the conference I shared in planning an act of worship which drew together many of our common concerns. I liked the hymn enough to revise it in 1987; failure, trust, pressures, barriers are still with us; so is Christ's good news.

Light upon the River

Mark 1.32-39
The steps of Jesus

77 COME AND TREAD THE PATHWAY

Come and tread the pathway
walk this road again,
stone and step and valley,
city, hill and plain:
    this is where his feet have trod,
    here was found the way of God.

Come and see the people,
pressing at the door,
thronging on the hillside,
crowding by the shore:
    sights that once supremely moved
    him who came and saw and loved.

Come and hear the accents,
town and country talk,
cry and laugh and greeting;
listen as we walk:
    this is where his voice was heard,
    here God spoke one crowning word.

Walk and look and listen
in our streets today,
sharing in the story,
learning how to say,
    here among us Christ has come,
    God with us, our Friend, our Home.

65.65.77 Tune: ORMESBY by Mervyn Horder

Scriptures: Mk 1.32-39, 45; 2.1-2,13,23; 3.7,13,32; 4.1-2; 5.21,24; 6.1-4, 30-34 Jn 1.14 Mt 1.23 Heb 1.2

Written: Limehouse, 1988

Some time in 1988 Mervyn Horder supplied his tune ORMESBY for the text *First and Best-beloved* (No.188). It certainly fitted, but it also seemed to me to suggest words of more movement—perhaps the walking of footsteps...? I wrote these verses precisely for his music, to which he then added the direction 'At walking speed'; I took that as a mark of his approval.

Light upon the River

Mark 10.42-45
Jesus Christ: unique leader, sole redeemer

78 MY LORD, YOU WORE NO ROYAL CROWN

My Lord, you wore no royal crown;
you did not wield the powers of state,
nor did you need a scholar's gown
or priestly robe, to make you great.

You never used a killer's sword
to end an unjust tyranny;
your only weapon was your word
for truth alone could set us free.

You did not live a world away
in hermit's cell or desert cave,
but felt our pain and shared each day
with those you came to seek and save.

You made no mean or cunning move,
chose no unworthy compromise,
but carved a track of burning love
through tangles of deceit and lies.

You came unequalled, undeserved,
to be what we were meant to be;
to serve, instead of being served,
to pay for our perversity.

So when I stumble, set me right;
command my life as you require;
let all your gifts be my delight,
and you, my Lord, my one desire.

LM Tune: SPLENDOUR (cf PUER NOBIS NASCITUR)

Scriptures: Mk 10.42-45 Matt 20.25-28; 23.5-12; 26.51-52 Jn 8.32 Heb 2.14-16; 4.14-15 Lk 19.10

Written: Limehouse, Nov 1978

First published: *Hymns for Today's Church* (Hodder & Stoughton) 1982

My holiday reading in 1978 included Hans Kung's *On Being a Christian*, which I picked up from a station bookstall and opened on the train. I was moved by its fresh treatment of the person of Jesus, notably the description of four kinds of leader: in the king, the revolutionary, the hermit and the politician. These are the only categories, says Kung; Jesus Christ fits none of them! Back home, I began to write; the first four verses correspond to the four leadership-models, all transcended by Jesus whose uniqueness is set out in the last two. I had other tunes in mind, but the marriage to Michael Praetorius' tune, variously named and arranged, proved ideal; it was my own choice for the special events introducing *Hymns for Today's Church*, including a Westminster Abbey preview and a St Margaret's Westminster launch—robes and swords notwithstanding. In 1987 I revised verse 5 to improve the stress and bring it nearer to Mark 10.45. Since then the words have been set to more tunes, old and new; in 1992 they were sung at a Good Friday presentation in Nottingham Prison.

Light upon the River

Mark 11—16
Holy Week

79 SUNDAY WAS THE DAY

Sunday was the day when
   he came to Jerusalem,
Christ on a donkey,
   a strange sort of king!
But crowds came to meet him,
   with branches to greet him
and nobody was going to
   stop the children sing.

Monday he went among the
   crowds in the temple,
found it full of cattle as the
   cash flowed free;
he stood and faced them,
   made a whip and chased them:
'My Father's house is for prayer'
   said he.

Tuesday he was welcomed
   by Martha at Bethany;
Mary anointed him with rich perfume:
   some were there who grumbled,
soon they were humbled -
this day pointed to his cross and tomb.

Wednesday, a last chance of
   teaching in the city,
warning of danger and judgement day;
   stones would be crumbling,
   Jerusalem tumbling,
his words would never pass away.

Thursday in the upper room,
   twelve sitting with him,
master is a servant and
   washes their feet;
bread he is breaking,
   and the cup is taking —
'My blood, my body—drink, and eat!'

Friday he's a prisoner,
   dragged before the governor;
a travesty of justice—
   he's nailed to the wood:
there he was crucified—
   for our sins he died:
this is the Friday that we call Good.

Saturday's the Sabbath,
   day of rest and quietness;
his body lies in the dark, alone:
   every enemy and friend
   thinks this is the end;
   guarded is his grave,
   sealed with a stone.

Sunday morning early,
   first day in the week,
first day of everything—can it be true?
Death has lost control here—
   Hallelujahs everywhere;
Christ is alive—all the world is new!

Tune needed

Scriptures: selected from Matt 21-28; Mk 11-16; Lk 19.28-24.53; Jn 12-21
Written: Peckham, April 1996

In a conversation with Graham Corneck, who by 1996 had been a vicar in Deptford for 23 years, we reminded ourselves how little most people know even of an outline of Jesus' life. We were approaching Holy Week, during which Marjorie and I attended St Luke's Deptford for the first time since 1961, joining Graham, Sue and others for a memorable 'Christian Passover' celebration. That week I began to versify some of the main events of the days we were remembering. We cannot date them precisely, but the scheme I use has fair support in the Gospels. Many 'days of the week' songs are comic, and the rhythm of this one is risky. But other writers have sometimes put tentative verses into print, and it may be that a musician in the folk idiom can find a tune that makes the words work. The stresses are regular, but punctuation negotiable and text revisable.

Light upon the River

Mark 14.26
The last supper: after communion

80 BEFORE THEY LEAVE THE UPPER ROOM

Before they leave the upper room
disciples join in singing;
they cannot know the days to come
nor what the night is bringing.

So we, like them, can lift our song
to praise our God and Giver;
the Lord who calls us to belong
has made us his for ever.

The gifts of peace, the gifts of love
we have been handling, sharing;
God grant us wisdom from above
to show our faith by caring.

Although like them we cannot guess
our roads through joy or sorrow,
we trust the risen Christ to bless
and walk with us tomorrow.

67.67 iambic Tune: RIDLINGTON by Mervyn Horder;
MAKROLINE by Agnes Tang; or ST COLUMBA

Scriptures: Matt 26.30 Mk 14.26 Jas 2.18; 3.17 Lk 24.15
Written: Peckham, Jan 1996

On 22nd Jan 1996 Jonathan wrote from his flat in Bow, London E3: 'I wonder if you could turn your mind to a hymn to sing during/after communion... theologically sensible (not just clichéd banality), to the point, three verses rather than two to ensure you don't have to sing it twice, meditative but not soppy...' This was the first such request from within our family; by the end of the week I was able to send some suggestions of other hymns in this category, with three drafts of my own—this, and Nos. 70 and 132 (see notes for these texts). In March I sent them to Mervyn Horder; two tunes came back that week, and in April he and I made some mutual adjustments. The praise in verse 1 was a 'Hallel' Psalm for Passover; the night would bring betrayal. The gift of peace (verse 3) is often shared as a physical greeting; the gifts of love are the sacramental bread and wine. Christ 'hath instituted and ordained holy mysteries, as pledges of his love, and for a continual remembrance of his death, to our great and endless comfort' (Prayer Book service of the Lord's Supper). Jonathan's church was then St Mark's Old Ford (Victoria Park) where he and Rosie Deedes were married a few months earlier. But the hymn was first sung on Maundy Thursday, 9 Apr 1998, at Christ Church Old Kent Road.

Mark 15.25-37
Christ crucified

81 DOWNTRODDEN CHRIST

Downtrodden Christ, to you we pray
who at the third hour of the day
were led away and nailed up high
in naked shame beneath the sky:
show through the pain that scars your face
the love of God, and our disgrace.

Uplifted Christ, to you we pray
who at the sixth hour of the day
took all our guilt upon that tree
in darkness, blood, and agony:
look on our pride and unbelief;
grant us repentance and relief.

Outstretching Christ, to you we pray
who at the ninth hour of the day
alone dismissed your final breath
and opened heaven by your death:
come to our dying world and reign
that we with you may live again.

88.88.88 Tune: LONDON ROAD by Norman Warren;
MAUTBY by Mervyn Horder; MELITA;
or ST CHRYSOSTOM

Scriptures: Mk 15.25-37 Jn 3.14-16 1 Pet 2.24 Acts 5.31; 11.18 Jn 19.30 Rev 4.1

Written: Poplar, 1976

First published: *Hymns for Today's Church* (Hodder & Stoughton) 1982

According to Mark's gospel, Jesus spent six hours hanging nailed to a wooden cross. His three time-references form the structure of this text, written originally as the third, sixth and ninth hours 'of this day' (our 9, 12 and 3 o'clock) and sung accordingly at our final Good Friday service at St Matthias' Church Poplar in 1976. It was printed in the church magazine for Easter that year. In 1997 I was asked to suggest some contemporary hymn texts for the 'Banner of Truth' Youth Conference, where modern hymns had not featured before; this was one of the few accepted, and the most recently written. Verse 3 echoes the *Te Deum:* 'When thou hadst overcome the sharpness of death, thou didst open the kingdom of heaven to all believers'. If MELITA (the tune originally in mind) expresses the solemnity of this event, the newer tunes represent also its stark violence.

Light upon the River

Luke 1.26-35
Annunciation

82 GOD HAS BEEN GRACIOUS

God has been gracious; a Son he gives us;
Jesus is his name.
He will be great; he will bear the title,
Son of the Most High.

He will be King, on the throne of David
ruling without end;
born through the power of the Holy Spirit:
holy is this child.

He has been promised, and with the Father
promises come true.
God has been gracious; a Son he gives us;
Jesus is his name.

10.5.10.5 Tune: SCRIABIN by David Wilson

Scriptures: Lk 1.26-35 Rom 8.32 Heb 1.8 Matt 1.18-21 2 Cor 1.20

Written: London (Peckham or Poplar?), 1971

First published: *Psalm Praise* (Falcon) 1973

An Advent or Christmas contribution for *Psalm Praise* (see No.68, notes), which David Wilson's striking tune, used on recordings linked with the book, makes it more of a choir song than a congregational hymn. The text picks up some of the key announcements made by the angel to Mary in Luke's account. One of the few churches to request it has been Plumstead's 'People's Hall' (FIEC).

Light upon the River

Luke 1.46-55
Magnificat

83 MY SOUL PROCLAIMS THE GREATNESS OF THE LORD

My soul proclaims the greatness of the Lord,
and my spirit sings for joy to my Saviour God!
his lowly slave he looked upon in love;
they will call me happy now, for mighty are the works
he has done, and holy is his name.

In every age, for those who fear the Lord
come his mercy and the strength of his mighty arm:
he routs the proud, throws monarchs off their thrones,
while he lifts the lowly high, fills hungry ones with food,
and the rich sends empty away.

To Israel his servant he brings help
and the promise to our fathers is now fulfilled;
for Christ has come, according to his word,
and the mercy that he showed to Abraham is now
for his children's children evermore.

10.12.10.13.9 Tune: ANDREW MARK by Norman Warren

Scriptures: Lk 1.46-55 1 Sam 2.1-10 Jas 5.1-6 Acts 2.39
Written: Peckham, 1970
First published: *Psalm Praise* (Falcon) 1973

When Mary's *Magnificat* was more valued in the Church of England than it is now, it seemed useful to have several ways of singing it to add to the traditional chants. So this text, one of my first written for *Psalm Praise*, appeared alongside contrasting versions from Timothy Dudley-Smith, Michael Perry and Michael Saward. I sketched out my own rather cheerful tune to match the free speech-rhythms I had used; but Norman Warren's haunting melody proved the key to its mood and wider usefulness. It was soon published and recorded in the USA, and sung in Westminster Abbey in May 1987.

Light upon the River

Luke 2.4-7
Jesus: born to save

84 CHRISTMAS GREETINGS, CHRISTMAS JOY

Christmas greetings, Christmas joy
for the new-born baby boy!
And for Jesus now we sing
born a baby, born a king.

Born to laugh and born to cry,
born to live and born to die;
born to rise up from the grave,
born for sinners, born to save.

When the proper time had come
God gave us his only Son;
for the new-born baby boy,
Christmas greetings, Christmas joy!

77.77 Tune: CHRISTMAS GREETINGS by E M Stephenson; or MONKLAND

Scriptures: Lk 2.4-7 Matt 2.2 1 Tim 1.15 Gal 4.4-5 Jn 3.16 Rom 8.32
Written: Peckham, Dec 1969
First published: *Sing to God* (Scripture Union) 1971

When I led the Explorers group (7s to 11s) at Christ Church Old Kent Road, I wrote this for them, with a tune of my own. It was first sung by them, then at the Carol Service when our new Bishop of Woolwich, David Sheppard, was the preacher; Miriam Davis, (later to serve with OMF in Japan) wrote the harmony, and words and music were printed the next year in the Scripture Union teaching magazine. Elspeth Stephenson then improved on the tune for SU's new junior songbook, since when it has also appeared in a Latvian equivalent. In 1995 I found that Carey Baptist Church at Reading, scene of many hymn committees, had included it in its own children's supplement. At the other end of the scale, my little song shares with that greatest of all hymns, *Hark! the herald angels sing*, the device of the repeated 'born to...' lines, and a conviction that there is more to Christmas than babies.

Light upon the River

Luke 2.8-14
Good news of great joy: Christmas and other angels

85 ANGELS ARE BRINGING NEWS IN THE MORNING

Angels are bringing
news in the morning;
splendour from heaven
    lights up the sky.
Can we envisage
Bethlehem's baby
grown up to manhood,
    led out to die?

Angels are telling:
Now he is risen!
See where they laid him,
    empty it stands.
Can we believe it
till we have seen him,
till he has shown us
    marks on his hands?

Angels are calling:
Christ is returning!
Day of our judgement
    dawning at last.
Can we imagine
how we shall face him,
fearing the future,
    fleeing the past?

Lord of the angels,
baby no longer,
Star of our morning,
    shine on our way:
crucified Saviour,
risen Redeemer,
King of all glory,
    save us today!

5554.D Tune: MORNING by Michael Metcalf; or BUNESSAN.

Scriptures: Lk 2.8-14; 23.26; 24.1-8, 36-40 Mk 13.26-27 Num 24.17 Rev 22.16

Written: Poplar, 1972

First published: *Songs of Worship* (Scripture Union) 1980

When Brian Seaman was Chaplain of the Mayflower Family Centre in Canning Town (and so a neighbour of ours in the early 1970s) he felt the need of new words to the *Morning has broken* tune—more truly, the music of *Child in the manger*—with clearer Christian content and possibly a Christmas theme. My first draft started 'Once they were bringing...', and we sang it on Christmas Eve at St Matthias' Poplar in 1972; at that stage every line rhymed, on a pattern ABCDABCD. Later I decided that 'they' was too vague and the rhyming too clever; I added a verse and reduced the rhymes to one per stanza. Since that time many more texts have been written for BUNESSAN; one editorial group chose Michael Metcalf's MORNING for mine. For Christmas 1996 Ian and Fiona Enticott used verse 4 on their Christmas card from Morogoro, Tanzania, where they then served with Crosslinks (mission society), and where we had enjoyed some memorable meal-stops without ever meeting them.

Light upon the River

Luke 2.8-20
Angels, shepherds, Mary—and Christ!

86 PRAISE TO GOD AND PEACE ON EARTH

Praise to God and peace on earth!
Hear what heaven's angels say;
fear shall die at glory's birth -
Jesus is alive today!

Shepherds have no time to lose,
come to worship, go their way,
bursting with the latest news -
Jesus is alive today!

Mary wonders at her child,
keeps in mind as well she may
promises in him fulfilled -
Jesus is alive today!

Angels' music, shepherds' word,
we may sing as well as they;
Mary's Son is Christ the Lord -
Jesus is alive today!

77.77 Tune: PRAISE TO GOD by Cyril Tennant;
ANELLEN by Roger Mayor; MELLING; or SAVANNAH

Scriptures: Lk 2.8-20, 33, 51 2 Cor 1.20 Acts 25.19 Rev 1.18
Written: Poplar, 1974
First published: *Carol Praise* (Marshall Pickering) 1987

In the early 1970s the American-born 'Jesus movement' overflowed briefly but joyfully into Britain, with songs, shouts, and badges with such slogans as 'Jesus is alive today'. Cyril Tennant, then Vicar of Christ Church Gipsy Hill, asked if I could write a text with that phrase as a repeated 4th line, to a tune he had written. So it was sung on Christmas morning at Poplar in 1974, and presumably at Gipsy Hill; a revised text appeared in the periodical *Word and Music* in Oct 1985. When first formally published, it carried an alternative reading in a footnote: 'Jesus Christ is born today'.

Light upon the River

Luke 2.25-38
Glory of Israel, Light for the world:

87 MERCY AND PEACE FROM HEAVEN'S KING

Mercy and peace from heaven's king
to those who waited long!
Angels on high were first to sing
on earth Messiah's song.
Lift up your eyes! See dawn at last,
the morning has begun!
This weary world's long night is past;
to us is born a Son.

People of every tongue and race
find Israel's dreams come true;
God's covenant of saving grace
makes all creation new.
Nations, arise! Acclaim the light,
in gloom no longer stay;
Gentile and Jew, receive your sight,
and darkened souls, the day!.

Jesus the child of Bethlehem,
the man from Galilee,
comes to redeem Jerusalem
and make all cities free.
Trust in the ancient promises,
obey the present word:
life from the dead in Christ our peace,
our glory and our Lord.

DCM Tune: NORWOOD by Sara Brown

Scriptures: Lk 2.13-14; 25-38 Rom 13.11-12 Isa 9.6; 60.1-3 Lk 18.42 Rom 11.15 Eph 2.14 Mic 5.5

Written: Poplar 1976, Limehouse 1988

The first form of this text was a version of the 'Song of Simeon', *Nunc Dimittis*, starting 'For Israel's peace and Judah's King their land had waited long'; after some revision it was sung to ELLACOMBE at our 'Carols by Candlelight' at Limehouse in 1978. Then in July 1988, on a visit to St Luke's West Norwood, I heard Sara Veacock (as she then was) and others sing *O little town of Bethlehem* to her own tune, as used in that church. With her agreement, I adapted my words (which had the same metre) to her music, which she named NORWOOD and arranged in parts. The only surviving lines from the original are 1.4 and 2.6.

Light upon the River

Luke 2.41-42
Son of the Father

88 HIS FATHER'S HOUSE

His Father's house
is where the Son must be;
let those who find him, learn whose Son is he.

His Father's love -
by this the Son has come;
pure glory focused in a virgin's womb.

His Father's grace -
in this the Son will grow;
great favour granted us, his strength to know.

His Father's plan -
by this the Son reveals
true wisdom, which his perfect life fulfils.

His Father's world
is where the Son must die,
whose new-built temple rises to the sky.

4.6.10 Tune: ERLESTOKE by John Barnard;
or SONG 46

Scriptures: Lk 2.21-52 Jn 1.10-14; 2.18-22; 6.38-40 Eph 2.19-22 Rev 21-22

Written: Limehouse, May 1991

First published: *Evangelicals Now*, Nov 1993

This text arose from study of the first recorded words of Jesus, characteristically questioning, enigmatic, purposeful ('I must be...') and concerning his heavenly Father. They link a story unique to Luke with one unique to John, and an enigmatic prophecy about the temple which was twisted into false evidence against Jesus at his trial, and into mockery at his crucifixion. SONG 46 was the tune in mind until John Barnard wrote ERLESTOKE, with which the words were first published.

Light upon the River

Luke 4.16-21
The Kingdom manifesto: freedom song

89 IF THE SPIRIT OF GOD IS MOVING US NOW

If the Spirit of God is moving us now
(Holy Holy Holy, cry the seraphim)
then the kingdom of Christ is present in power
(Glory, glory, glory to God!).
If the gospel of Christ means sight for the blind...
then Lord Jesus, I pray, don't leave me behind...

O Spirit, come... O Spirit, come...
Tell the truth of freedom for the prisoners:
set them free, let them see, make them all they need to be,
open up the prison for the Lord!

If the Christians have good news for the poor...
then show us what our money is for...
And if this is still the year of the Lord...
the slavery's one thing we can't afford...

O Spirit, come...

The anointed King won't leave us in doubt...
for he welcomes us in and sends us all out...
So who will go for freedom today?...
Save us and seal us and send us we pray...

O Spirit, come...

Irregular Tune: HAND ME DOWN MY
    SILVER TRUMPET, GABRIEL

Scriptures: Isa 61.1-2 Lk 4.16-21; 10.1-4 Matt 9.38; 10.1-10; 12.28 Heb 13.21

Written: Kigoma/Tabora/Dodoma, Tanzania, 3-4 June 1994

Several established hymns were apparently written on trains; this is my small contribution to the genre, admittedly more song than hymn as it uses a tune long associated with gospel singer Mahalia Jackson (available in *Alleluya*, A & C Black 1980). Marjorie, Tim and I were travelling by overnight train from Kigoma to Dodoma; the tune in my mind had to compete with the train rhythm and the music on the cassette of a fellow-passenger on an opposite bunk-seat. The Gospel source sets out the purpose of Jesus, as he applies Isaiah's prophecy to his own coming.

Light upon the River

Luke 7.11-17
Raising the dead at Nain

90 LIFE-GIVING CHRIST, OUR HOPE AND HEAD

Life-giving Christ, our hope and head,
who met the sad and raised the dead;
new miracles of love begin
for mourners, and the dead in sin.

Draw near to homes of double death
where stirs no sign of pulse or breath:
confront this last of enemies:
command the dead, that they arise!

By the compassion of your heart,
your Spirit given, your hand stretched out,
by costly power and kingly word
bring life to lifeless ones, O Lord!

So shall they rise and breathe and speak;
death's powers dissolve, its shackles break:
old wounds are healed, old wrongs put right;
on ancient darkness shine your light!

Then filled with praise and holy fear
let all in wondering faith draw near
and know that Christ our hope, our home,
our prophet and our God, has come.

Praise Christ who raised a widow's son;
in Christ the Father's will be done:
Christ with the Spirit's fulness came;
all glory to the Saviour's name!

LM Tune: GONFALON ROYAL

Scriptures: Lk 4.1,14; 7.11-17; 8.46 Eph 2.1 1 Cor 15.26 Jn 6.38
Written: Oakley, 1989

Many hymns deal with resurrection, physical or spiritual. But in our first year in Suffolk, I struggled to find a hymn directly relevant to the village funeral at Nain and the raising of the widow's son. This text needs both sensitive use and a vigorous tune; when Matthew Roberts preached at Christ Church Old Kent Road (8 Mar 1998) on this miracle, Agnes Brough accompanied our first singing of it.

Light upon the River

Luke 10.28-36
Transfiguration

91 WHEN JESUS LED HIS CHOSEN THREE

When Jesus led his chosen three,
to lift the shadow from their sight;
and on the mountain let them see
his face transfigured, crowned with light:
what grace that day to them was given!
To men on earth, a glimpse of heaven.

There Moses and Elijah stood
and spoke about his exodus:
their freedom purchased by his blood,
a Passover fulfilled for us.
The law and prophets meet their Lord,
see God revealed, and man restored.

Then from the cloud there came a voice,
'This is my own beloved Son':
the Scriptures' theme, the Father's choice,
their Master stood supreme, alone;
they saw his glory, and they heard
the one eternal, living Word.

So may we see and know this grace:
the truth which, like a burning light
illuminates the darkest place
till Christ himself shall end the night,
when to his people's longing eyes
God's day shall dawn, his sun shall rise.

88.88.88 Tune: ST MATTHIAS

Scriptures: Matt 5.17; 17.1-8 Mk 9.2-8 Lk 9.28-36 Jn 1.1,14 1 Jn 1.1-3 2 Pet 1.16-19
Written: Limehouse, 1977
First published: *Hymns for Today's Church* (Hodder & Stoughton) 1982

The Transfiguration of our Lord is a theme immensely rich for theology, worship, prayer and hymnody. Not all the older hymns on the subject have lasted well; an encouragement of recent years has been a wealth of new material including texts by Michael Hewlett, Brian Wren, Timothy Dudley-Smith, Keith Landis, Thomas Troeger, Carl Daw and Alan Gaunt. This might come third in that approximately chronological order; how many we now need is a moot point, but at least the church calendar changes allow us to celebrate the Feast more than once! My text uses Luke's unique reference to the 'exodus' of Jesus, with all that suggests for freedom, its cost and its future. Some may prefer to sing 'hope' as the penultimate word of verse 2; as with many such 'inclusive' changes, something is lost as well as gained.

Light upon the River

Luke 10.38-42
Christ in our home; Christ our Home

92 COME, LORD, TO MAKE YOURSELF AT HOME

Come, Lord, to make yourself at home
and take your rightful place;
let glory shine from every room,
a dwelling filled with grace.

Your wisdom touched the early plans
before they came to be;
your strength was in the builders' hands
with seasoned carpentry.

You gave the wood, the brick, the stone,
you loved us long before;
so grant your light to everyone
who enters at our door.

The bread we break, the cup we drink,
you share among us still;
let all we do and say and think
reflect your perfect will.

Our going out, our coming in
be governed by your care;
each task we finish or begin
shall find you with us here.

So stay with us, much-travelled Friend,
with us receive and give;
at dawn or noon or journey's end
in you, our Lord, we live.

CM Tune: ABRIDGE

Scriptures: Matt 2.23 Lk 2.39, 51-52; 10.38-42; 19.5-6; 24.28-31 Prov 9.1; 15.6,15,17; 17.1 Mic 4.4 Zech 4.4; 8.4-5 Rom 12.2 Psa 121.8
Written: Oakley, Jan 1992
First Published: *Peculiar Honours* (Stainer & Bell: Congregational Union) 1998

Though located here with Martha and Mary, the text is not based on that occasion. It began life as another hymn for 'Habitat for Humanity' (see Nos. 65 and 100), but changed in the writing to one about all our homes, and in 1998 was accepted for publication. Martha's home is one of many where Jesus was welcomed, and which he did not leave quite as he found it. No single Scripture deals with this topic, but many bring wisdom to bear on it.

Light upon the River

Luke 15.17-21
Repentance

93 WE HAVE DONE WRONG, AND ONLY GOD CAN SAVE US

We have done wrong, and only God can save us;
we have done wrong, and only Christ puts right.
We need to change and use the gifts he gave us;
we need to change and walk into his light.

We have been lost, and only God can hear us;
we have been lost, and only Christ can find.
We need to call, to know that he is near us;
we need to call and leave our fears behind.

We are not right, and only God can heal us;
we are not right, and only Christ can mend.
We need to come; disguise will not conceal us;
we need to come to find a lasting Friend.

We look to God and looking, learn to praise him;
we look to God and praising, learn to pray.
Christ walks with us and those who love, obey him;
we walk with Christ to live for him today.

11.10.11.10 (47.46.D) Tune: O STRENGTH AND STAY

Scriptures: Psa 34.4-6; 51.1-4, 14-15; 103.1-4 Lk 15. 1-2, 17-21; 19.10 Rom 10.13-14 Col 2.6
Written: Peckham, Jan 1996

It is hard to find a contemporary text serving the same purpose as Charlotte Elliott's *Just as I am*. Some would question the need of such hymns, but where there is still room for enquirers or 'seekers' at church services, these verses express the desire to repent and believe in Christ. They took this form in early 1996, based on lines drafted a year or so before; they aim to be gentle but searching, with a variety of blending images, and simple repeats broken and therefore sharpened in the last stanza. I hope they can be used with integrity by established believers; they certainly express something of what I feel, and want sometimes to say or sing. The music needs to be strong and flowing; not every tune in this metre will do.

Light upon the River

Luke 22.39-44
Trees: Gethsemane, Golgotha and beyond

94 WHEN YOU PRAYED BENEATH THE TREES

When you prayed beneath the trees, it was for me, O Lord;
when you cried upon your knees, how could it be, O Lord?
  When in blood and sweat and tears
  you dismissed your final fears,
when you faced the soldiers' spears, you stood for me, O Lord.

When their triumph looked complete, it was for me, O Lord;
when it seemed like your defeat, they could not see, O Lord.
  When you faced the mob alone
  you were silent as a stone,
and a tree became your throne; you came for me, O Lord.

When you stumbled up the road, you walked for me, O Lord;
when you took your deadly load, that heavy tree, O Lord,
  when they lifted you on high
  and they nailed you up to die,
and when darkness filled the sky, it was for me, O Lord.

When you spoke with kingly power, it was for me, O Lord
in that dread and destined hour you made me free, O Lord.
  Earth and heaven heard you shout;
  death and hell were put to rout,
for the grave could not hold out; you are for me, O Lord.

Tune: KELVINGROVE

Scriptures: selected from Matt 26.36—28.10 Mk 14.32—16.8 Lk 22.39—24.8 Jn 17.1—20.18 Acts 5.30; 10.19; 13.29 Gal 3.13 1 Pet 2.24

Written: Oakley, July 1990

First published: *Worship Songs Ancient and Modern* (Canterbury Press Norwich) 1992

The opening lines grew from seeing our Lord's prayers in the garden of Gethsemane, described in the first three Gospels, in the light of John 17.20. The text weaves around the 'tree' theme found in many Scriptures about the cross, including the earliest Christian preaching and teaching. Paul Wigmore was looking for new words to a traditional Scots tune, as well as for new hymns about the cross. Opinions have varied on whether they match here, but this was one of those accepted for the collection he edited; it became my first to appear in an 'Ancient and Modern' publication.

Light upon the River

Luke 24.1-10
The garden, the tomb and the Lord

95 SEE YOUR HANDS OVERFLOWING WITH FLOWERS

See your hands overflowing with flowers:
let me ask you, who are your flowers for?
They are flowers I had gathered for Jesus;
empty is the tomb—he is there no more!
Hallelujah, hallelujah, hallelujah, hallelujah!

Hear your voice overflowing with singing:
tell me, have you known such delight for long?
O, my Lord from the grave has arisen;
all the earth will ring with an Easter song!
Hallelujah...(etc)

Look, your eyes overflowing with laughter:
say what makes them shine with a light so rare?
It is Jesus the Lord—he is living;
every day is radiant, for he is there!
Hallelujah...(etc)

Now you need no more wreaths for his body:
in our risen Lord are his people raised.
So with eye, heart and hand we shall serve him,
and our voices sing, Jesus Christ be praised!
Hallelujah...(etc)

10.10.10.10 Tune: DINE HENDER ER FULLE
AV BLOMSTER by M Marcello Giombini

Scriptures: Lk 24.1-10 Jn 20.1-18 Col 3.1

Written: Oakley, 1989

First published: *News of Hymnody* (Grove Books) No.34, April 1990

This Scandinavian Easter carol expresses something of the women's joy at meeting the risen Christ. Like its Christmas equivalents, it is a song of the spirit rather than the letter—they were initially carrying spices, and filled with dread—but gardens had flowers in that Jerusalem springtime, and fear was soon overwhelmed by gladness. The theme travelled from the Italian of Marcello Giombini (1970) via the Swedish of Lars Lundberg (1973) and the Norwegian of Svein Ellingsen (1976) to the English paraphrase of Kenneth Sagar (1988) who encouraged my own version: see also No.151.

Light upon the River

Luke 24.13-35
Evening: on the road to Emmaus

96 O LORD WHOSE LOVE DESIGNED THIS DAY

O Lord whose love designed this day,
you walked with us along the road;
so as the daylight fades away
stay with us when we rest our load.

Our stumbling steps were known to you
before we recognised your face;
you loved us long before we knew
your covenant of saving grace.

You spoke your word of truth to us,
bringing us gladness when we grieved;
we found forgiveness at your cross,
and yet how slowly we believed!

But now we see our wounded hands;
you share with us the broken bread:
these are your pledges, your commands,
our living Lord, who once was dead!

So through the darkness, we our light,
O Lord whose love designed this day;
we praise and bless your name tonight
for love that never fades away.

LM Tune: ANGELS' SONG; or MELCOMBE

Scriptures: Lk 24.13-35 Hos 11.3-4   1 Cor 11.23-26; 13.8,13
2 Cor 6.7 Eph 1.7 Col 1.13 Rev 1.18 Psa 134.1

Written: Limehouse, Jan 1980

The Emmaus road is one which many of us love to walk again 'in heart and mind' every Easter, as a reminder of the historic resurrection and as a model of Christian experience and discovery. In 1980 *Symphony* magazine, for Christian verse, invited entries for an evening hymn. This contribution was printed in Issue No.9, for Spring/Summer that year: see also No.1 of this collection. Verse 3 reflects the value of Christ's gospel sacraments which 'he hath instituted and ordained... as pledges of his love' (Book of Common Prayer).

Light upon the River

Luke 24.42
The Easter honeycomb; a ballad for the Lord Jesus

97 O WHEN JESUS LAY THERE IN THE MANGER

O when Jesus lay there in the manger
then his head was as soft as thistledown;
but how could we know that this tiny little child
would have thistles and thorns for his crown (O yes!),
would have thistles and thorns for his crown?

O when Jesus laboured in the village
people said that their carpenter was good;
but how could we know that to finish off his work
he'd be nailed to a great trunk of wood (O yes!)...?

O when Jesus rode into the city
then it seemed that he couldn't go wrong;
but how could we know that by Friday nine o'clock
they would sing quite a new kind of song (O yes!)...?

O when Jesus hung there in the darkness
we all heard when he shouted out loud;
but how could we know he was hanging there for us
who were only a part of the crowd (O yes!)...?

O when Jesus drained the cup of horror
then they laid him inside the quiet tomb;
but how could we know on the first day of the week
he would eat from the sweet honeycomb (O yes!)...?

Tune: JOHN HENRY

Scriptures: Lk 2.7; 24.40-43 Mk 6.3; 11.7-10; 14.36; 15.15,17,25,34,46 Jn 19.18,30
Written: Poplar, 1976

While still with the Chris Barber Jazz Band, Lonnie Donegan recorded in 1954 a lively song about John Henry, a larger-than-life steel-worker on the American railroad as the pioneers moved west. The 'skiffle' treatment of the previous century's ballads and work-songs enjoyed a new wave of popularity on both sides of the Atlantic. They are not often adaptable for Christian use, but in 1976 I finalised a text which had been in note-form for ten years; the fourth verse and the start of the fifth could be taken more slowly that the rest. According to legend and song, John Henry died 'with his hammer in his hand'. The Lord Jesus Christ died with nails in his—driven there by an earlier hammer. My song shows some stark contrasts from the Gospels, and ends with a disputed but triumphant text. Luke 24.42 (AV) includes honeycomb as well as broiled fish; a detail which Ezra Pound noted in his 'Ballad of the Goodly Fere' (fere = companion):

A Master of men was the Goodly Fere,
A mate of the wind and the sea.
If they think they ha' slain our Goodly Fere
They are fools eternally.
I ha' seen him eat o' the honeycomb
'Sin' they nailed him to the tree.

Light upon the River

Luke 24.45-49
One gospel for all nations

98 GOD'S WORD TO GOD'S WORLD

God's word to God's world! In one name alone
the truth must be told, the Saviour made known;
since Jesus has suffered and died for our sin,
God's kingdom is offered for all to come in.

Since God first loved us, we grow by his love;
the word of the cross shows mountains can move:
it links every nation, it leads to one song;
in Christ our salvation the weak are made strong.

Encircling the earth by prayer and in praise
we witness new birth, new hope and new ways;
where churches are sowing the seed of God's word
his kingdom is growing, his harvest assured.

Each language and land, each culture and race -
for all, God has planned a pathway of grace;
to wait or to travel, not ours but his choice,
to silence the devil and tune to God's voice.

One Father of light, one Saviour for all,
one Spirit, ignite your church by your call;
in faith and repentance our hearts are your throne;
your word makes the entrance, your love is the crown:
      Lord Jesus, come!

10.10.11.11 Tune: LAUDATE DOMINUM

Scriptures: Lk 8,11,15; 24.44-49 I Jn 4.19 1 Cor 1.18 Matt 17.20; 21.21 Mk 11.23 Jas 1.17 Acts 4.12; 20.21 Rev 22.20
Written: Oakley, 1995

The opening five words became the motto of Crosslinks (founded in 1928 as BCMS, the Bible Churchmen's Missionary Society) in the 1980s; this text was written for the society in 1995 and revised at Peckham towards the end of that year—see No.121. When sung to the recommended tune, the final three words fit the Coda designed for 'Amen, amen', as in the 1965 *Anglican Hymn Book*. In verse 2 the 'cross' and the 'links' are woven into some New Testament phrases, but a hint of the society's former slogan 'BCMS is on the move!' had to be dropped. Change and diversity in method are meant here to blend with the authentic Biblical gospel, and the message of salvation through Jesus Christ alone. We have many friends among Crosslinks mission partners, and while unemployed I was able to do some voluntary work at the Lewisham Way offices, within walking distance from home.

Light upon the River

John 1.1-14
The Incarnation: John and Athanasius speak of their Lord

99 THE WORD WAS VERY GOD

The Word was very God
before creation came;
in the beginning was the Word
and Jesus is his name.
That Word which some deny
and others make a joke:
he is the Word whom we adore,
the Word the Father spoke.

The love we owe to him
above all things on earth
will be the greater, since as man
he seemed so little worth.
The more his name is scorned
and unbelievers jest,
so much the brighter shines his truth,
the Godhead manifest.

What some revile as lies,
impossible, malign,
he plainly shows is possible,
most certain, and divine;
and on the cross, his shame,
his utter nothingness,
is that which overcomes the world
and all the world shall bless.

DSM Tune: RE'EMI by Agnes Tang; or ST GEORGE (SM)

Scriptures: Jn 1.1-14; 16.33; 19.1-5 1 Cor 1.18,27 Acts 17.32-34 1 Jn 1.1-2; 5.5 Psa 73.25
Written: Peckham, 5 May 1996

Among my Easter holiday reading at Cambridge in 1996 was the slim paperback *St Athanasius on the Incarnation*, translated with characteristic self-effacement by 'A religious of the CSMV' (at Wantage) and provided with a stimulating Preface by C S Lewis dated 1944. I had never read this before—which amply vindicates Lewis's pointed comments on our reading habits—and was immediately struck by the sheer poetry of the opening pages, arising directly from its theology. Neither Athanasius nor his translator can be blamed for the verses I began later; but the foundation for them (after John's own Scriptures) is theirs. I had begun with what is now the fifth line; to avoid a negative opening, I then wrote a new 'verse 1' in Short Metre, with the tune ST GEORGE in mind. Then in September our Christ Church organist Agnes Tang brought us some new tunes, including one written for *Teach me, my God and King;* this seemed ideal, and after we had agreed to arrange the words and music in three 8-line stanzas, the hymn was first sung at Carols by Candlelight on 15 December.

Light upon the River

John 1.10-14
The old, old story: no room (a Habitat hymn)

100　AS ONCE FOR YOU, LORD CHRIST, THERE WAS NO ROOM

As once for you, Lord Christ, there was no room,
the doors were shut, the welcome never came;
so, Maker, Builder, Friend, we pray you, come
for those today who find things just the same.

Look, Lord, upon our wandering, straying world;
without you all are homeless, lost indeed;
and as you made your home with us of old,
by us, your body, meet this human need.

And grant that we who know a heavenly birth,
with you our home, here and eternally,
may build to make this lovely, needy earth
fit habitat for all humanity.

10.10.10.10　Tune: MUNSLOW by John Barnard;
or SURSUM CORDA

Scriptures: Jn 1.10-14 Lk 2.7-8; 4.28-30; 9.51-53; 23.18-25 Matt 9.36 Mk 6.30-34 1 Jn 5.1-2 Psa 90.1

Written: Oakley, 4 June 1992

The last line of this text carries the clue to its purpose. In 1992 Tim was home briefly before starting a second 3-year term with Habitat for Humanity (International) in Tanzania—see Nos. 25, 43, 65, and 92. Here is one unsolicited attempt to express something of the home-building mission's underlying belief and practice. John Barnard composed the tune for what is not an easy metre; words and music were later passed on to HFHI at Americus, Georgia.

Light upon the River

John 2.1-11
The first sign of glory: a wedding at Cana

101 JESUS, COME, FOR WE INVITE YOU

Jesus, come, for we invite you,
Guest and Master, Friend and Lord;
now, as once at Cana's wedding,
speak, and let us hear your word:
lead us through our need or doubting,
hope be born and joy restored.

Jesus, come! transform our pleasures,
guide us into paths unknown;
bring your gifts, command your servants,
let us trust in you alone:
though your hand may work in secret,
all shall see what you have done.

Jesus, come in new creation,
heaven brought near by power divine;
give your unexpected glory
changing water into wine:
rouse the faith of your disciples -
come, our first and greatest Sign!

Jesus, come! surprise our dulness;
make us willing to receive
more than we can yet imagine
all the best you have to give:
let us find your hidden riches,
taste your love, believe, and live!

87.87.87 Tune: BEST GIFT by Ronald F Krisman; WORTHAM by William O Jones; NIDDELDALE by Donald Webster; ST NICHOLAS by William Ellis; or REGENT SQUARE

Scriptures: Jn 2.1-11 Eph 3.20 Psa 34.8 1 Pet 2.3

Written: Limehouse, Epiphany 1979

First published: *Hymns with the New Lectionary* (Grove Books) 1980

The Marriage Service in the Book of Common Prayer begins by speaking of 'holy Matrimony... which holy estate Christ adorned and beautified with his presence, and first miracle that he wrought, in Cana of Galilee'. Several hymns refer briefly to this 'Sign' of his glory, but I knew of none taking it as a central theme. This text was written to fill the gap—not a wedding hymn as such (though it appeared in *The Wedding Book*, Marshall Pickering 1979), but trying to reflect some of the wonder of this unique event and draw out its implications. Many varied tunes, some specially composed, have been published with these words; among my favourites is BEST GIFT by the Texan liturgist Ronald Krisman, used in Fort Worth on my visit to the American Hymn Society's conference in 1987. Seven years later, the British equivalent event at Newcastle used NEANDER. Dan Damon, Alistair Goude, Agnes Tang and Norman Warren have also written tunes.

Light upon the River

John 7.37
'Come to me!': the gospel invitation

102 CHRIST IS ALL THE WORLD'S GOOD NEWS

Christ is all the world's good news;
Christ commands the world to choose,
heaven to find and hell to lose,
    turn and come to him!

Love into this world was sent;
love's full measure here was spent;
love to death and burial went:
    look, and come to him!

Come, but counting first the cost;
come to bury every boast;
come to one who loves the lost:
    think, and come to him!

If this great desire you have,
self must sink into the grave;
lose your life, and Christ will save:
    die, and come to him!

But unless God draws us on
none can come to know his Son;
yet his love refuses none:
    all may come to him!

Christ makes heavy burdens light;
Christ turns blindness into sight,
fills our hunger, sets us right,
    trust, and come to him!

Christ the path, the light, the door;
come to him whose word is sure;
come, you need no reasons more:
    come, O come to him!

777.5 Tune: CHARITY

Scriptures: Jn 3.21; 6.37, 65; 7.37; 8.12; 10.7-9; 13.1; 14.6 Lk 14.28-30 Matt 11.25-30; 16.24-26 Mk 8.34-37 Rom 3.27 Rev 22.17

Written: Poplar, 1975

First published: *Songs of Worship* (Scripture Union) 1980

In early 1975 Scripture Union was planning a new hymn and song book, which was eventually published in 1980. Helen Smart (later Hazlewood) belonged like us to St Matthias' Church Poplar, and worked at that time as an SU Editor; one evening she came home with an urgent request for more evangelistic hymns—as well as more on the Bible: see Nos.169 and 171. The Wesleys used many hymns 'Exhorting and beseeching to return to God' (*Come ye sinners, poor and needy,* and so on); whether they are still useful may be less certain. But I drafted this text in some haste, trying to urge repentance while avoiding heresy; like many others it was revised more than once. With John Blanchard I believe that 'Christ calls us not to choose but to change'; I hope the language here is in line with that of the Gospels. All are summoned there, not to pick and choose as they please, but to come to Christ and follow him. Of the churches using the hymn in their own supplements, half have been Baptist and half have been Church of England.

Light upon the River

John 7.46
The words of Jesus Christ

103 MASTER, BY YOUR WORD OF WELCOME

Master, by your word of welcome
all who hear are called to come;
by your free forgiveness draw us,
raise us up and bring us home.
   By your word of mighty healing
   we shall find your power to save;
   keep us from those wasting evils
   which bring terror to the grave.

Master, by your word of wisdom
teach our minds and meet our needs;
make us apt and ready pupils
on the path where learning leads.
   By your word of gentle patience
   help us when we feel afraid;
   stretch our faith by hard endurance,
   strengthen us for whom you prayed.

Master, by your word of warning
straighten out our rebel ways;
rid our minds of all pretences,
free our wills of all delays.
   By your word of holy anger
   kill our self-deceit and pride;
   all that contradicts your purpose,
   let it all be crucified!

Master, by your word of mercy
you have made us all your own;
mercy chose and called and found us,
mercy brings us to your throne.
   By your word of free adoption
   let us sons and daughters prove,
   praising you in words of worship,
   serving you in lives of love.

87.87.D Tune: LLANSANNAN

Scriptures: Jn 6.63,68; 7.46; 12.47-50; 17.8 Mk 4.1-20; 8.38 Matt 12.37 Eph 2.4-5 Tit 3.3-8 Hos 14.2

Written: Limehouse, 1981

A prayer arising from meditation on the words of our Lord Jesus Christ. The Gospels have examples on almost every page; together they cover all these categories and more. The Scriptures referred to here include examples of such words, claims about them, and our words of response.

Light upon the River

John 8.12
The light of the world

104 CHRIST THE LIGHT WHO SHINES UNFADING

Christ the Light who shines unfading
in the sad, sin-darkened mind,
guiding those who stray in error,
opening eyes that sin made blind,
shows himself the Lord of glory,
shining for a lost mankind.

Christ the Bread who came from heaven
hungry souls to satisfy:
just as loaves must first be broken,
our Life-giver had to die,
made himself a generous Offering,
gave himself for our supply.

Christ the Life who rose in splendour
from the cold and dismal cave
on the resurrection morning,
conquered death and burst his grave,
showed himself the mighty Champion,
filled with love and strong to save.

Christ the King to earth returning
surely will not long delay;
Christ the Son of God requires us
now to trust him and obey;
stands himself as Lord and Saviour,
asking our response today.

87.87.87 Tune: CHRIST THE LIGHT by Norman Warren;
or REGENT SQUARE

Scriptures: Jn 8.12; 9.5 1 Cor 2.8 Jn 6.35,41; 11.25-26 Matt 25.31 Mk 1.1 2 Pet 3.18

Written: Barrow in Furness, 1966

First published: *Youth Praise 2* (Falcon) 1969

This is one of the first hymns I wrote and one of the first two to be published. Like No.27, *Lord, you sometimes speak in wonders,* it was sung at the Pathfinders' 8th Birthday service at St Mark's Barrow in Furness where I was a Curate—16 Oct 1966. When I first saw Norman Warren's tune I marginally adapted the words to the music, but the changes were overlooked; other small ones have been made since. Among churches using this in their supplements have been those at Northwood, Bishopsgate and Langham Place. The text does not present a full array of our Lord's titles, or even those in John's gospel, but aims (as the original service did) to set out some of his achievements, claims and demands.

Light upon the River

John 11.25-26
Christ risen, ascended, returning

105 COME TO A WORLD OF NEED

Come to a world of need,
Lord Christ, our risen Head;
make known your power in word and deed
to raise the living dead!
Our days are but a breath
and earth exhausts its span;
you break the vicious rule of death
and give new life to man.

Come, and stretch out your hand
to take away our fears;
despair shall fade at your command
and songs replace our tears.
The victory has been won,
the grave has met defeat;
at last its power to hurt has gone -
your triumph is complete.

Come, and our death is gain,
our faith and hope secure,
our bodies rescued from their pain,
our resurrection sure.
In you we live and die
who died and rose again;
Lord Jesus Christ, ascended high,
come in your power and reign!

DSM Tune: DIADEMATA

Scriptures: Jn 5.21-25; 11.25-26 Jas 4.15 Rom 5.12-17; 6.8-9 1 Cor 15.42-43, 54-57 Eph 2.4-6; 4.8-9 Phil 1.21

Written: Limehouse, 1977

'I am the resurrection and the life, saith the Lord...' If there is a better way than that to start a funeral, I have yet to find it. But Jesus raised not only a tiny number of the physically dead; he gave life to very many who were 'dead in sin'—to use language adopted by the apostles from their Lord's own words. Even 'Leave the dead to bury their dead' (Lk 9.60), harsh as it sounds, contains seeds of hope if the Life-giver is here. The hymn, written for Easter to Ascension, is not limited to that season.

Light upon the River

John 14.2
Heaven; a place prepared

106 CHRIST HAS PREPARED FOR US A PLACE

Christ has prepared for us a place
of joy as yet unseen, unheard,
of glory promised by his grace
to all who take him at his word:

A place where no disease is found,
no sin, no sickness, no despair;
where light and life and love abound,
for Love himself is dwelling there:

A place where through eternity
the sounds of praise bring sweet delight;
where every voice in harmony
combines in worship day and night:

A place where splendour meets the eye -
a flowing river, fruitful trees,
the holy city towering high,
and yet more glorious sights than these:

A place where we shall see at last
the Lamb of God upon his throne;
his wounds are healed, his pain is past,
his people free, his victory won!

Lord, stir our hope, and give us grace
that day when all things are made new
to find the wonder of that place,
to see and know and worship you.

LM Tune: SOLOTHURN

Scriptures: Jn 14.2 Rev 5.6,11-14; 21.4-5; 22.1-4
1 Jn 3.2 Lk 10.20; 12.32 Phil 2.23

Written: Barrow in Furness, 1968

Whether through failure of imagination, loss of confidence, distrust of the imagery or sheer unbelief in the promises, contemporary hymns about heaven are rare. Are we content to leave the topic to our medieval or Victorian predecessors? 'Secular' writers are often ready to explore an ideal future. And C S Lewis pointed out, notably in his essay *Weight of Glory*, that Jesus rebukes us, not because our desires for heaven are too strong, but because they are too feeble (Matt 6.19-21 etc). In this 'Barrow' hymn, lightly revised since, I try to face the challenge while confining myself to what Scripture reveals.

Light upon the River

John 14.26
The promised Holy Spirit

107 SPIRIT OF HOLINESS

Spirit of holiness, wisdom and faithfulness,
Wind of the Lord, blowing strongly and free;
strength of our serving and joy of our worshipping,
Spirit of God, bring your fulness to me.

You came to interpret and teach us effectively
all that the Saviour has spoken and done;
to glorify Jesus is all your activity,
Promise and Gift of the Father and Son: *(chorus)*

You came with your gifts to supply all our poverty,
pouring your love on the church in her need;
you came with your fruit for our growth to maturity,
richly refreshing the souls that you feed: *(chorus)*

You came to the world in its pride and futility,
warning of dangers, directing us home;
now with us and in us, we welcome your company:
Spirit of Christ, in his name you have come: *(chorus)*

13.10.13.10 and chorus Tune: SPIRIT OF HOLINESS by Keith Landis;
or BLOW THE WIND SOUTHERLY

Scriptures: Jn 14.26; 15.16,26; 16.7-15; 20.19-23 Rom 1.4 Lk 24.49 Acts 1.4-8 1 Cor 12.4-13 Gal 5.22-25

Written: Poplar, Spring 1975

First published: *Hymns for Today's Church* (Hodder & Stoughton) 1982

In the 1950s the contralto Kathleen Ferrier recorded the folk-song *Blow the wind southerly* as an unaccompanied solo which soon achieved classic status. Following a long tradition, I ventured to model this text on that music, bearing in mind that the words for 'spirit' in the Biblical languages also mean 'breath' or 'wind'. It was sung at St Matthias' Poplar at our Whitsunday evening Communion service, 8th May 1975. Twenty years later it had become one of the most-requested of my texts, taking its 'Englishness' to many countries. Two of the three Michaels of *Jubilate Hymns* (without whom the enterprise would never have started, or persevered) had an indirect hand in it. Michael Baughen commented that we had many 'Come, Holy Spirit' hymns, but few which declared that the Spirit has come. So my text led up to a climax at the end of verse 3. But when it was sung at Ealing Abbey in 1980 (see No.36) Michael Saward, who chose it, commented afterwards 'It did seem to go on a bit...' Most editors have agreed, and ironically omitted the stanza which first prompted its writing. I am content with this, but print the full version here to show why I wrote it, and what you may be missing!

Light upon the River

John 16.28
Going to the Father

108 CHRIST IS GOING TO THE FATHER

Christ is going to the Father;	Christ is going to the Father,
heaven and hell and earth, attend!	from the world he came to save,
Marked by blood, in death made perfect,	bringing life to those who listen,
see the Man to God ascend.	raised in wonder from their grave.
Love was captured, cursed and murdered;	Eldest of a new creation,
in the losing, love has won;	Head of all, he leads the way,
in the dying, love has risen;	calling, drawing all who follow,
by its ruin, gained a throne.	sharing his ascension day.

Christ is going to the Father;
hear a newborn nation cry -
earth made new by heaven's music:
Glory be to God on high!
Sing Hosanna, all believers;
Hallelujah, shout his name!
Jesus, universal Saviour,
all the universe proclaim!

87.87.D Tune: ASCENDED by Stephen James;
EBENEZER (=TON-Y-BOTEL); or TANYMARIAN

Scriptures: Jn 5.21-25; 6.62; 16.28 Lk 2.14; 24.36-52 Col 1.15-20 Eph 1.10, 19-23 1 Pet 3.22

Written: Limehouse, 1981

First published: *New Songs of Praise 5* (Oxford University Press) 1990

For some years the clergy of Tower Hamlets (Deanery and London Borough) met each February at Ely; I wrote this after an address there by Rowan Williams, then at nearby Cambridge. He spoke of 'the one coming of Christ, to the Father'; my original opening used the word 'coming', until I had to agree from an earthly angle this was a 'going'—see Jn 16.28 in particular. Stephen James, living near us and on the St Helen's Bishopsgate staff, provided a tune; it was included in the St Helen's songbook (1982) and sung at Limehouse next year on the Sunday before Ascension Day, when our theme was 'Going to the Father'. Then in 1989 OUP's Julian Elloway, while rejecting the tune and one verse, accepted the remaining words for a new series of hymn booklets. So I revised the whole text, including a new second verse, and it was published in that form to EBENEZER; alternative, TANYMARIAN. Alan Luff has pertinent comments on both tunes in *Welsh Hymns and their Tunes* (Stainer & Bell 1990, pp.193, 211); Alan Gaunt's review of the OUP collection (*News of Hymnody*, Oct 1990) judged that the text was 'rather dragged down and partially submerged by EBENEZER'! He suggested 'WURZBURG or something new'; in *Hymns for the People* David Peacock opted for the traditional RUSSIAN AIR. I still think that the original Stephen James tune takes some beating.

Light upon the River

John 18.19—19.30
On trial

109 HE STOOD BEFORE THE COURT

He stood before the court
on trial instead of us;
he met its power to hurt,
condemned to face the cross:
    our King, accused
    of treachery;
    our God, abused
    for blasphemy!

Those are the crimes that tell
the tale of human guilt;
our sins, our death, our hell -
on these the case is built:
    to this world's powers
    their Lord stays dumb;
    the guilt is ours,
    no answers come.

The sentence must be passed,
the unknown prisoner killed;
the price is paid at last,
the law of God fulfilled:
    he takes the blame,
    and from that day
    the accuser's claim
    is wiped away.

Shall we be judged and tried?
in Christ our trial is done;
we live, for he has died,
our condemnation gone.
    In Christ are we
    both dead and raised,
    alive and free:
    his name be praised!

6666.4444 Tune: CLARLI by Agnes Tang;
MARLEE by Leland B Sateren; or ST JOHN

Scriptures: Jn 18.19—19.30 Matt 26.57ff Mk 14.53ff Lk 22.66ff 1 Jn 2.2; 4.9-10 Rev 12.10 Rom 3.19-26; 6.4-6; 8.1-2 Col 2.13-15 1 Pet 2.24

Written: Limehouse, June 1980

First published: *Hymns for Today's Church* (Hodder & Stoughton) 1982

Good Friday 1980 at the East London Tabernacle, Mile End; I had persuaded Gordon Fyles (formerly of BCMS, see No.98; then at St Mary's Islington) to speak at a meeting of several local churches whose ministers prayed together regularly. His theme: that Jesus Christ not only suffered and died as the substitute for sinners, but that in our place he was also interrogated, tried and sentenced. Gordon took us through the day's events in the light of Romans 8.1 and similar texts. I put this interpretation into these verses, starting with the almost anonymous prisoner (He stood...) and ending as the preacher had done with Romans 8. Other lines also reflect his address, including the silence; Jesus had nothing to say because we were, and are, indefensible (cf. Jn 18.19-21). The hymn was sung at Nottingham Prison on Good Friday 1992, and printed in full in Michael Perry's *Preparing for Worship* (Marshall Pickering 1995) among samples of contemporary writing. The chosen metre has both demands and rewards; tunes must be chosen with care, particularly noting the flow of the second half of each stanza. Both the modern tunes listed succeed admirably.

Light upon the River

John 20.1-18
Easter morning

110 THE LORD IS HERE, THE DARKNESS GONE

The Lord is here, the darkness gone;
the Easter victory now is won:
his church resounds with ringing praise,
this brightest, best, and first of days.
   Hallelujah! for Christ is King
   his resurrection now we sing.

Good news began this glorious week
when mourners heard the angel speak:
'Why look for him among the dead?
for he is risen, as he said'.
   Hallelujah! he lives today;
   see where his wounded body lay.

While some were dazed by doubt and gloom
still Mary lingered by the tomb;
she stood perplexed and freely cried
for her dear Master crucified.
   Hallelujah! he died to save;
   now he has left an empty grave.

But she was found by her lost Lord
and 'Mary!' was his startling word.
They met with joy; she went with speed
to gasp, 'The Lord is risen indeed!'
   Hallelujah! With this new dawn
   death is destroyed and hope is born.

This passing world may yet refuse
to see the signs or hear the news;
but by the life and love he gives
we know today that Jesus lives:
   Hallelujah! Redeemed by blood
   in Christ we live to serve our God.

LM with chorus Tune: THE FIRST NOWELL

Scriptures: Matt 28.1-10 Mk 16.1-8 Lk 24.1-10 Jn 3.19; 15.18-19; 20.1-18, 30-31 1 Cor 15.1-4 2 Tim 1.10 1 Pet 1.3, 18-19
Written: Poplar, 1976

Is it allowable to borrow one season's tune for another? Some music may for a time seem untransferable; but if Easter tunes have been taken for Christmas, may we not borrow one back? Other tunes may also fit, but we are used to a narrative text to THE FIRST NOWELL, which can be varied by its descant. This uses parts of the resurrection story from all the Gospels, with John's account prominent in verses 3 and 4.

Light upon the River

Acts 1.12-26
Matthias is chosen: one

111 WHERE IS THE ONE OUR GOD WILL CHOOSE

Where is the one our God will choose?
Judas had gone; he died in shame,
but Peter counselled: Christ can use
another to declare his name:

One who with us has shared and talked
since John baptized and led the way,
along the paths that Jesus walked
until the Lord's ascension day:

A witness who will give his word:
'Jesus who died now lives again!';
whose eyes have seen the risen Lord,
whose lips can preach his coming reign:

A man prepared to give his hand
to service in the humblest place;
yet also take a leader's stand,
equipped with apostolic grace.

So he who at that mighty start
sent out Matthias with good news
still knows today the human heart:
where is the one our God will choose?

LM Tune: ANGELS' SONG

Scriptures: Acts 1.12-26 1 Cor 9.1 Matt 20.25-26 Mk 10.42-44 Jn 15.16

Written: Poplar, 1974

It may only be someone who has served in a 'St Matthias' Church' who would wish to write even once on this theme; or someone wanting to cover every saint's day, in the style of some older Anglican hymnals. Only the first applies to me; since the hymns relevant to our Patronal Festival in Poplar were all about Judas, I tried to reflect here the only evidence we have about Matthias and his qualifications for the job. This was completed in St Matthias' Vicarage about half way through our five years there; St Matthias' Day was 24 Feb, though even that has now been moved. Twenty four years on, our publisher's name is also appropriate! Originally it began 'Where is the man...', as it was a man for whom the other eleven were looking; a change here may make it more useful. No.112 below came about when I was not satisfied with this one, but it was the first which almost reached publication.

Acts 1.12-26
Matthias is chosen; two

112 TO KNOW GOD'S MIND AND DO HIS WILL

To know God's mind and do his will
disciples sought his face;
with Judas gone, they now must fill
the twelfth and vacant place.

They looked for one prepared to lead
and witness by his word:
'Though Jesus died, he lives indeed,
for I have seen the Lord!'

One who has followed in the way
since John at first baptized,
and walked with them until the day
they saw the ascending Christ.

Matthias then was set apart,
apostle of good news;
and God who knows the human heart
still calls those he will use.

Lord, make your battle-line complete;
make known your sovereign choice,
that we may serve with willing feet
and Christ-uplifting voice.

CM Tune: ST BERNARD

Scriptures: Acts 1.12-26; 10.36-43 Mk 10.52 Isa 52.7

Written: Poplar, March 1976

This hymn was born at St Matthias' Vicarage; see the notes to No.110. St Matthias' Church (the people) moved with us to Limehouse that year; the building and the vicarage now have other names and functions, as does St Matthias' School in Bullivant Street, once attended by all our sons and the first school for Jeremy and Marcus. During our weekly assemblies there I introduced another song which hardly merits a formal number; it was sung merrily as a 'round' to the tune LONDON'S BURNING'. In its defence I claim that this too is faithful to Acts chapter 1:

*Saint Matthias joined the others
as a witness with a message
Jesus Christ is alive!
Hear the news from Saint Matthias!*

Light upon the River

Acts 2.1-11
Every nation under heaven, at Pentecost

113 GOD OF EVERY TRIBE AND NATION

God of every tribe and nation
Lord of continents and seas,
Architect of earth's salvation
to its furthest boundaries:
come, renew your whole creation,
come to heal this world's disease.

Christ whose cross and resurrection
gives new hope to every race,
let us see your own reflection
shining out from every face;
every colour and complexion
consecrated by your grace.

Holy Spirit, life-creating,
turning silence into song,
all our deep desires translating
into prayers in every tongue:
speak with fervour unabating
truths that make your people strong.

Father, Son and Holy Spirit,
bring an end to earth's despair!
by your grace let us inherit
peace beyond our boldest prayer;
worlds remade shall sing your merit,
heavens renewed your praise declare.

87.87.87 Tune: BUSHILL by Agnes Tang;
ST HELEN; or LINGWOOD

Scriptures: Acts 2.1-11;10.34-41;18.23 Rom 8.18-27 Eph 1.9-10;3.20-21 Col 1.19-20 Phil 4.7 Rev 21.1

Written: Limehouse, 1977

First published: *Hymns with the New Lectionary* (Grove Books) 1980

My more closely 'Pentecostal' text is *Holy Spirit, heaven's breath*, placed at No.274 because of its specific origins. This one is a Trinitarian hymn expressing the international scope of the Spirit's coming, dating in its present form from 1977 but drawing on an earlier version. The 'Commonwealth and Continental Church Society' (later renamed 'Intercon') was looking in 1973 for a new hymn embodying its work, mainly among Britons overseas. The Society accepted and printed *God who guides the ceaseless movements*; verse 2 included the lines: 'Christ whose cross and resurrection saved men near and far away / in the city, snow or sunshine, save our countrymen today'—referring to its holiday chaplaincies in Europe and elsewhere. In 1981 it helped to launch a Wycliffe Hall (Oxford) mission. Agnes Tang's tune, written for No.101 (above) may prove more useful than a traditional one.

Acts 4.2
Proclaiming in Jesus the resurrection of the dead

114 SING GLORY, GLORY, HALLELUJAH! (version)

Chorus: *Sing glory glory, Hallelujah; glory, glory to the King!*
Sing glory glory, Hallelujah; he is risen, so let us sing.

Thank you, Jesus, thank you, Jesus, that you laid your body down;
you have given us life eternal; by your cross we gain a crown. *(chorus...)*

By your mighty resurrection death and hell have met defeat;
you have conquered, Lord and Saviour; all creation is at your feet. *(chorus...)*

Christ is risen; Christ is risen! and in Christ we shall arise;
Hallelujah, he is coming! raise your voices and lift your eyes!. *(chorus...)*

Tune: SING GLORY, GLORY

Scriptures: Acts 2.23-24; 3.15; 4.2,10; 5.30; 17.18 etc 1 Jn 5.11 1 Tim 4.8 Heb 2.5-9 1 Cor 15.20-26, 54-57 Rev 20.6 Col 3.1 Lk 21.28

Written: Poplar, 1975

First published: *Church Family Worship* (Hodder & Stoughton) 1988

From the 1970s onwards Garth Hewitt has been a leading Christian singer and songwriter. Many of his songs were and are, both original and searching; he visited Poplar in 1975. One of his simplest and liveliest songs was based on the traditional chorus given here; he has recorded the first line as above, with varied repeats. My own additions were intended to add more content to the rousing rhythm while keeping it simple (?); we sang it in Limehouse at Easter 1977 and Peckham at Easter 1998.

Light upon the River

Acts 4.7-20
Salvation found in no-one else

115 THROUGH ALL THE WORLD LET CHRIST BE KNOWN

Through all the world let Christ be known;
   his name and power be praised today!
   The stone the builders threw away
has now become our cornerstone.

For Jesus Christ of Nazareth
   by violent hands was crucified;
   rejected and disowned, he died,
but God has raised him up from death.

His Spirit like a fountain poured
   instils in us such power and peace
   that, moved by love, we cannot cease
to share what we have seen and heard.

Salvation comes by Christ alone;
   no other name on earth is given
   to bring us life, to give us heaven;
through all the world let Christ be known!

LM Tune: CHURCH TRIUMPHANT

Scriptures: Psa 118.22-24 Lk 20.9-18; 24.44-49 Acts 4.1-31 Jn 7.37-39

Written: Poplar, 1976

This text is built around the apostle Peter's statement in court (the Sanhedrin) in Acts chapter 4, including the reference to Psalm 118 which he evidently learned from his Master's own teaching. Its final revision was made at Oakley in 1993.

Light upon the River

Acts 9.1-31
The conversion of Saul of Tarsus

116 SAUL OF TARSUS PLANNED IT

Saul of Tarsus planned it:
break the church by force!
till the Lord of glory
met him in mid-course;
blinding him at noonday
Christ confronts his foe,
all his pride and passion
suddenly brought low.
    Christ is with his people
    when their blood is shed;
    those who wound the body
    wound the body's Head.

That Damascus journey
showed the man his Lord;
brought a brother's welcome,
sacrament and word.
When the Lord's opponent
calls upon his name
all the past is over,
all its sin and shame.
    Christ is with his people,
    flooding them with light,
    in his love baptizing,
    giving back their sight.

Paul the new apostle
preaches now with joy
truth which he had fiercely
laboured to destroy.
God the Father's purpose
in the Son is shown;
from the Holy Spirit,
power to make it known.
    Christ is with his people
    as they all make plain
    his renewing mercy,
    his dynamic reign.

Some from every city
now with opened eyes
turn from death and Satan
and in Christ arise.
In his church advancing
let us serve today;
those who see the vision
dare not disobey.
    Christ is with his people,
    hope of every race,
    Lord in every language,
    King in every place.

65.65 triple Tune: ARMAGEDDON; HERMAS; or ST GERTRUDE

Scriptures: Acts 9.1-31; 15.36; 22.1-21; 26.1-23 1 Cor 2.8 Eph 1.11-12; 4.15-16 Col 1.18; 2.19 2 Cor 5.17

Written: Poplar, 1976

The apostle Paul was often under attack in his lifetime; much of his writing is also dismissed today by one group or another, even within the church. His 'wonderful conversion', however, is still celebrated in the calendar and collects; in the tradition of John Ellerton's *We sing the glorious conquest* I wrote this especially for Jan 25 1976. In 1987 I was invited on that date to St Paul's Shadwell; as Julian Scharf, the minister, asked if I had a hymn to suggest, I revised it and we sang it to ST GERTRUDE. Ten years later still Noël Tredinnick arranged that tune for the All Souls Orchestra and introduced it at St Paul's Beckenham (Kent) for a festival in September, soon after which it was accepted for publication. On this theme Michael Saward has also written *Lord of glory, in our darkness*, originally for St Paul's Cathedral. My own text is built around the refrain 'Christ is with his people'; Acts 9.5 may have been one crucial seed for the later flowering of this great New Testament doctrine.

Light upon the River

Acts 13.38-52
Mighty Redeemer: mixed response

117 JESUS WHOSE GLORY, NAME AND PRAISE

Jesus whose glory, name and praise
resound from every shore,
the King who reigns in righteousness,
enthroned for evermore!
    This we believe and sing and know,
    for by this faith we live;
    and yet our flame burns small and low,
    so few his grace receive!

Where are the Saviour's just rewards,
why is our fire so dim?
So loud our praise of lesser lords,
so faint our songs for him!
    And if I search into my heart
    to find some signs of grace,
    with idols I have filled each part,
    proud self in every place.

Jesus! on earth you found that few
would follow and obey;
our world attacked and murdered you,
or simply turned away.
    Heaven may have no tears for us,
    no pain or loss to bear;
    but your deep wounds at one grim cross
    have won our welcome there.

Glorious, though scarred by nail and thorn,
once low, now high above;
our King who suffered curse and scorn,
whose kingdom is your love:
    Jesus whose praise is in your death,
    whose blood your name displays,
    grant us to sound in every breath
    your glory, name and praise.

DCM Tune: NATIVITY (double)

Scriptures: Acts 13.38-52; 17.32-34 1 Cor 1.26-31; 8.5-6 Isa 32.1
Jer 23.5 Heb 1.8 Lk 12.32 Jn 6.66 Rev 21.4 Eph 1.3-8; 4.9-10 Phil
2.5-11

Written: Oakley, 1989

'His glory, name and praise'; that subtitle on the Contents page of at least two hymnals ('Christian Praise' 1957; 'Hymns of Faith' 1964) was the starting-point for this text, which after earlier jottings began to take shape during our first month at Oakley. The Lord Jesus Christ is the subject of those phrases, and mine; this was my first Suffolk hymn. It is an attempt to relate the claims we often make when we sing, to the sometimes discouraging realities which were also known in the earliest days. As Gerald Bray has written 'Jesus showed his disciples his wounds because he wanted them to see that they were still there; the resurrection body had not been healed of its scars, which meant that the ascended body would continue to have them' (*Churchman* 101.2, 1987; cf 'those wounds yet visible above, in beauty glorified' from *Crown him with many crowns*). That is the only path to glory.

Light upon the River

Acts 14.17
Singing in and for the rain

118 SING WHEN THE RAIN IS COMING

Sing when the rain is coming,
sing when the clouds are grey,
sing when the birds are homing
under the darkening day;
> Saviour and Lord confessing
> children of heavenly birth,
> for the rain will provide a blessing
> for the earth.

Sing when the rain is falling,
not knowing what shall be;
sing when the streams are calling,
rushing and full and free.
> Sing through the midnight sorrows,
> sing in the day serene,
> till the dawning of new tomorrows
> fresh and green.

Sing when the rain is over,
sing when the sun shines clear;
sing of the Lord's good favour,
goodness and mercy here.
> Sing out the ancient story,
> sing till we see his face,
> praising Jesus, the Lord of glory
> and of grace.

Tune needed

Scriptures: Acts 14.17 1 Kgs 18.41-46 Gen 8.1-5 Song 2.10-13 Psa 23.6 Rev 22.4

Written: Peckham, 26 June 1997

Though much of 1997 was dry in England, June was a rainy month. Londoners seem to complain more than Suffolk people about the weather; Christians in either place have a better option—to sing! The rhythm of these lines resembles *Wonderful grace of Jesus*; can any musician offer a modern tune?

Light upon the River

Acts 15.25-26
Risk

119 AND DID YOU RISK YOURSELF, O CHRIST

And did you risk yourself, O Christ,
for such a world as ours,
into its hands to yield your life,
your name, your gifts and powers?
    So few had seen and touched and heard,
    so few received your love! -
    but now your Spirit and your word
    have set us on the move.

What stories fill those early days
of saints whose names we know,
who risked their lives to speak your praise
and saw your kingdom grow!
    What news escapes to reach us now
    and shames our little faith -
    believers risking all for you
    through prison, pain and death.

Lord, help us to release our grasp
on all that chokes the seed,
on all that undermines our task
or contradicts our creed;
    to find the new security
    of launching into space
    when you baptize us, set us free
    and give the opening grace!

No status, goods or power of choice,
no right and no renown
can matter when we hear your voice
or glimpse your thorny crown;
    when we are least in human eyes
    in you we are most strong;
    can this be risk, to die, to rise
    with you, our Glory Song?

DCM Tune: KINGSFOLD

Scriptures: 1 Jn 1.1 Lk 12.32 Acts 15.25-26 Phil 2.25-30 Matt 6.30 Mk 4.7,19 2 Cor 12.9-10 Rom 6.1-14 2 Tim 2.11 Ex 15.2

Written: Peckham, 3 Feb 1997

First published: *Baptist Times*, 1 May 1997

Does God take risks? Did Jesus take risks? I faced such questions afresh in early 1997, on receiving David Peacock's request; could I 'quickly put together' a hymn for that year's Baptist Union Assembly to be held at Westminster in April? 'Taking the Risk' was the chosen theme of its incoming President, Sri Lankan Frederick George. Clearly, Baptists took risks; so I gave the subject some thought, prayer and work. I thought that divine risks, if any, were of a different order from human ones; were they part of our Saviour's humanity? It seemed right to begin and end with questions, without prejudging the answers. On reading Paul Helm's account of 'no-risk' theology in *The Providence of God* (IVP 1993) I wondered if I had got it right, and was relieved at his reassurance; certainly, as Frederick George said, 'much of the teaching of Jesus has this theme'. Both the New Testament and news of Christians round the globe provide much supporting evidence. At any rate, the text was completed on Feb 3rd, printed in the Assembly's 'Worship Book' and sung at Westminster. John Capon published it in his *Baptist Times* editorial in May, with some comments based on my own notes. That issue also featured an interview with the President, and his Assembly address. Together with Mohan and Sarah Seevaratnam I was later to meet him, and discover that one of my school RE teachers had been his Pastor in Colombo—BMS missionary Eric Sutton-Smith. I am not sure that I fully engaged with the theme as he saw it (including the church's institutionalised racism), but I hope the text still stands. My fuller notes touch on the Father's omniscience, the Son's temptations, the believer's assurance, and a positive use of 'creed' in a hymn. Like 'risk' itself, there is more than one meaning to 'world', 'move', 'space', 'grace', and 'Glory Song'.

Light upon the River

Acts 16.5-15
The Gospel reaches Philippi

120 THE SPIRIT LED BY DAY

The Spirit led by day;
God spoke the word by night:
so Paul's companions found their way—
their Lord was all their light.

The miles across the sea,
the struggles overland -
so one small group reached Philippi,
by grace to break new ground.

One quiet riverside,
one Sabbath space for prayer:
God's chosen moment to provide
life for his people there.

They worship Israel's God,
and Abr'am's Lord they fear;
but now from travellers on the road
the missing news they hear.

Christ's servants speak the word,
and open ears they find,
they see afresh the living Lord
who opens heart and mind.

So Lydia believes
and finds her Christ has come;
the truth into her heart receives,
the church into her home.

One household is baptized
in this strategic place;
one open door for Jesus Christ,
the firstfruits of his grace.

God raise us from the dead
the risen Christ to know;
his name be praised, his gospel spread
by churches born to grow.

SM Tune: ST THOMAS; or (if DSM) JERICHO or ISHMAEL

Scriptures: Acts 16.5-15 2 Cor 11.26-27 Phil 1.1-6
Written: Clermiston, Edinburgh, 26 July 1993

The arrival of Paul, Silas, Luke and Timothy at Philippi is an attractive, vivid story in itself, and a strategic step forward for the Gospel, following the vision at Troas across the Aegean Sea. The church they planted that day was later to receive one of the happiest letters in the New Testament. Having provided several texts on Philippians from our holiday locum in Scotland (see notes to No.152), I heard from Bob Horn that hymns based on Acts 16-20 were needed too. This was my contribution in Short Metre which I hope matches the narrative style; I did not at first plan an eight-stanza text, and DSM tunes may be more appropriate.

Light upon the River

Acts 16.6-10
The kingdom advances, the mission extends

121 GLORY TO GOD, THE SOURCE OF ALL OUR MISSION

Glory to God, the Source of all our mission;
Jesus be praised, the Saviour, Lord and Son!
Praise to the Spirit who confirms the vision;
in all the world the will of God be done!

Proud in our wealth, or destitute and broken,
we cannot live by earthly bread alone;
but by the word that God himself has spoken
we are set free to make our Master known.

Eastward or westward, northward, southward moving,
finding new fields, new patterns and new role,
Christ's fellow-workers, all his goodness proving,
see how our God is making people whole!

Linked by the cross at which we are forgiven,
joined by the love that came to find and save,
one in the hope of God's new earth and heaven,
we love and give since he first loved and gave.

Send us, Lord Christ, to serve at your direction,
dying and living, yours in loss and gain,
true to the Gospel of your resurrection,
working and praying till you come to reign.

11.10.11.10 Tune: HIGHWOOD

Scriptures: Acts 16.6-10 Jn 3.16; 6.38-40 Deut 8.3 Matt 4.4 Lk 4.4; 19.10 2 Cor 6.1 Eph 1.7 Rev 21.1; 22.20 1 Jn 4.9-19 Isa 6.8ff Phil 1.20-24; 3.7-11
Written: Oakley, July 1995

It is hard, but necessary, to write contemporary hymns about the church's worldwide evangelistic mission. We can get beyond *From Greenland's icy mountains;* Frank Houghton's earlier 20th century missionary poems are still fervently sung, as are Jim Seddon's more recent ones. Margaret Clarkson has sustained the genre in Canada. These writers share the sense of divine love, world need, Christian obedience and personal urgency which led to the birth of Crosslinks (formerly BCMS; see No.98). In June 1995 I had a letter from Sue Knight, then Crosslinks Editorial Secretary, asking me to try to write a hymn for the society. So together with *God's word to God's world*, this was the first I wrote that year but the last at Oakley; and one of the last to receive a thoroughgoing but wittily merciful critique from Michael Perry, who visited us in August. He liked verse 4; not simply because 'Crosslinks' appears there in code. I wanted a strong tune, but not one inseparably wedded to another hymn. Line 1 originally had 'the Maker of all mission'; then 'the Spring of all our mission' (which I preferred); the hymnal committee who first accepted it for future publication opted for the version printed here. It did not gain favour with Crosslinks, but I hope may still prove useful elsewhere.

Light upon the River

Acts 17.24-29
The unknown God revealed

122 LORD, YOU NEED NO HOUSE

Lord, you need no house,
no manger now, nor tomb;
yet come, I pray, to make
my heart your home.

Lord, you need no gift,
for all things come from you;
receive what you have given -
my heart renew.

Lord, you need no skill
to make your likeness known;
create your image here -
my heart your throne.

56.64 Tune: TENHEAD by John Barnard; EVINGTON by David Preston; PLATT'S LANE by Evelyn Sharpe; or SOMMERLEID

Scriptures: Acts 17. 24-29 Lk 2.7; 23.53 Eph 3.17 1 Chron 29.14 1 Cor 4.7 Ezek 11.19; 36.26 Rom 8.29 2 Cor 3.18 Col 3.10

Written: Limehouse, 1978

First published: *Hymns for Today's Church* (Hodder & Stoughton) 1982

Paul, it appears, never planned to linger in Athens; he was simply waiting for Silas and Timothy to catch up after his hurried exit from Berea. But he lost no opportunity to explain the Gospel, in synagogue, market-place, and then more formally and famously at the sophisticated Areopagus. Starting on familiar ground, he boldly moved to commend the living God who needs none of the provisions of paganism to house him, help him, or represent him; and from there, to Christ. I was working on my own sermon to this effect when the powerful simplicity of it all struck me afresh. Short hymns are often the hardest to write, but here the structure of the text seemed to slot into place. It was written with SOMMERLEID in mind; other tunes have since been preferred, or composed.

Light upon the River

Acts 17.30-31
The Advent judgement

123 TO EVERYONE WHOM GOD HAS MADE

To everyone whom God has made
he now commands repentance:
his day of judgement has been fixed;
his chosen Judge has been made known
by Jesus' resurrection.

As we are destined once to die,
and after death comes judgement;
for many sinners Christ once died,
and will appear a second time
to save those watching for him.

With angel-shout and trumpet-call
the Lord will come from heaven;
the dead in Christ will first arise,
then those still living meet the Lord
and be with him for ever.

So since the world will be laid bare
and since the Lord is coming,
what sort of people should we be -
what holy readiness display
to hasten his arrival?

We do not know when he will come:
it may be in the morning,
or yet at midnight, dusk or dawn;
will Jesus find us unprepared
or wise, alert and faithful?

87.887 Tune: CHOSEN JUDGE by Norman Warren

Scriptures: Acts 17.30-31 Heb 9.27-28 1 Thess 4.16-17 2 Pet 3.10-12 Mk 13.32-37
Written: Peckham, 1970
First published: *Psalm Praise* (Falcon) 1973

The Advent season was one of those assigned to me in 1969, as a small group worked on some 'New Testament canticles' as an addition to the then unnamed book of new Psalm versions (see No.68 and others). We were encouraged to write in speech rhythms, without rhyme; the musicians would then work on our texts. This one takes a different Scripture for each of its five verses, which are arranged in logical (rather than chronological or Biblical) order. The metre is unusual but consistent; Norman Warren improved on the tune I had sketched out, while Stephen Layfield has also recorded his own music to these words. Verse 5 was revised again just before publication; the final three adjectives match the qualities required respectively in our Lord's parables of the bridesmaids, the householder, and the servants with the 'talents'—using Matthew 25 as well.

Romans 1.1-7; 16.25-27
The Trinitarian Gospel

124 HOLY LORD AND FATHER

Holy Lord and Father
for the love you give
to your name be glory;
in your life we live.

Holy Lord and Saviour,
love uplifted high,
to your name be glory,
in your death we die.

Holy Lord and Spirit,
make your love our prize,
to your name be glory,
in your power we rise.

Holy, holy, holy!
Songs of love unite,
heaven flames with glory,
earth reflects your light.

To the Triune Godhead
love, all love, be given;
Glory, glory, glory,
fills all earth and heaven.

65.65 Tune: NORTH COATES

Scriptures: Rom 1.1-7; 16.25-27 Isa 6.3 Eph 1.17-23; 4.1-6 Rev 4.8
Written: Limehouse, March 1979.

This is a distillation of earlier drafts in a metre requiring special discipline. The word-patterns I was exploring give 'glory' in each third line, 'love' in each second line, and 'holy' in each first one until the final stanza which unites the three Persons in the Triune God. Its location here in Romans may seem arbitrary; but prayerful devotion and missionary action can never be separated. This great epistle, brimful of both, provides all the elements needed for the text of the hymn.

Light upon the River

Romans 6.1-14
Baptized into Christ, alive to God

125 BAPTIZED INTO CHRIST JESUS

Baptized into Christ Jesus,
baptized into his dying,
buried with him in the grave,
we have died with Christ.
Then just as he was truly
raised by the Father's power,
so God raises us to live from now in Christ.

Sin must no longer rule us,
self must not be the master,
Satan must control no more
mind or mouth or hand.
Brought back to life and freedom,
gladly we now surrender
thoughts, words, deeds to him who governs them by grace.

Not by the body's washing,
not words and water only,
but from conscience and in faith
we have made our vows.
With Christ and all his people
this holy baptism sharing,
we now praise the risen, reigning, coming Lord!

7775.77.11 Tune: DEVA by Michael Baughen

Scriptures: Rom 6.1-14 1 Pet 3.21-22 Gal 3.27 Eph 1.19-20 Col 2.12; 3.1-10 Tit 3.5

Written: Poplar, 1974

Two factors prompting this were a song without words, and a subject needing work. When Richard Bewes wrote *God is our strength and refuge* from Psalm 46, it proved impossible to print it with Eric Coates' 'Dambusters' music to which it was written and always sung. So Michael Baughen wrote his tune in order to complete the page—which left it unused unless new words could match it. We also saw the need for some fresh baptismal hymns; surprisingly few Baptists had written any, and most of the extant Anglican ones were about babies (and 'the sign of the cross') rather than baptism—or even water! Things have now improved, but here I use two classic NT paragraphs and incidentally give the almost unsingable word 'baptism' its correct number of syllables: two and a half. Text and tune were initially accepted for publication, but both then fell out of favour and others took their place.

Light upon the River

Romans 10.9-11
Not ashamed; not shamed

126 MAKE US, O GOD, ASHAMED OF SIN

Make us, O God, ashamed of sin,
and give its power no place;
but not ashamed that we have been
adopted by your grace.

Make us ashamed of every flaw
in hearts which you lay bare;
but not ashamed, if your pure law
is clearly written there:

Ashamed of all our loveless words
which hurt or wound or maim,
but not ashamed to be the Lord's
and speak your holy name.

Make us ashamed to use our hands
as selfish tools of greed;
but not ashamed of your commands
to serve our neighbour's need

So when our God is fully known
and all his power acclaimed,
when heaven and earth and hell bow down
we shall not be ashamed.

CM Tune: CREDITON; or ST FLAVIAN

Scriptures: Rom 1.16; 6.19-22; 9.33; 10.9-11 Psa 119.6,46,78,80 Mk 8.38 Phil 1.20 2 Tim 1.8-12; 2.15 1 Pet 4.14-16 1 Jn 2.28
Written: Limehouse, Dec 1976

A Concordance contains far more entries than those shown here, for a topic given greater prominence in the Bible than we might imagine. 'Shame' also features strongly in Ecclesiasticus chs. 41-42, which first suggested this hymn soon after we moved to Limehouse. It may prove suitable for Lent or for other penitential occasions, so long as we, like the text, end on a practical and positive note.

Light upon the River

Romans 11.33-36
The glorious God: one

127 FAR GREATER THAN GREAT

Far greater than great and more loving than love,
much closer than close is our God on the move;
far higher than high and much deeper than deep,
far louder than tempests, more silent than sleep.

More glorious than glory, far better than good,
more homely **than clothes** and more filling than food;
more lovely than starlight, more needful than milk,
more massive than mountains yet softer than silk.

If we are not up to it, what does that prove?
Our God has come down to it, such is his love!
For down to our world he has come in his grace,
down for us, to meet us and speak to our face.

And nearer than seeing and hearing is he,
for with us and in us we find him to be,
and over and under, around and beside,
more living than life is the Lord who has died.

But how shall we know if these things can be true?
For some lean on old gods and some run to new.
It's only the Spirit whose power can reveal
that God is our Father and Jesus is real.

Lord Jesus, we want to be part of your scene!
We pray it, then find that we always have been;
before we existed, you called us your own,
and when it's all over, we've hardly begun.

11.11.11.11 (65.65.D) Tune: RESTORATION by Ronald Watson; or ST DENIO

Scriptures: Rom 8.15-21; 11.33-36 Psa 36.5-9 Isa 40.12-31; 57.15 Acts 17.24-31 Jn 14.16-17; 16.13-15 Eph 3.20 1 Tim 6.13-16 Jer 1.4-10 Gal 1.16   **Written:** Peckham, Dec 1995

'A rediscovery of God: rescuing the individual from individualisation, marginalisation and the market'; such was the snappy title of the Cecilia Goodenough Lecture at St Giles' Camberwell, Sept 17 1995, at which I was not present. Browsing among the leaflets after a service there in December, I saw the lecturer's name and picked up a copy of the address. The speaker was David Jenkins, then retired from the bishopric of Durham, whose earlier utterances had prompted No.135 below. Here he provided more positive food for thought; as well as some typical Jenkins politics, he declared with passion and poetry that God is much greater than great, Jesus much closer than close, the Holy Spirit more loving than love. And that if we are not up to it, the good news is that God has come down to it; and much more. The bishop's very phrases lent themselves to verse, suiting the mood and feel of ST DENIO (*Immortal, invisible*); later I found Rusty Edwards in *The Yes of the Heart* (Hope, 1993) enthusing over RESTORATION, set there to his *Rejoice and prepare now*. My own text touches on many Scriptures, but is as close to the Romans 11 doxology as to any; see also No.128 following.

Light upon the River

Romans 11.33-36
The glorious God: two

128   ONE BEYOND ALL

One beyond all, you
   love us to call you;
what name will reach you,
   what voice can teach you?
Hand cannot clasp you,
   mind cannot grasp you:
where can we find you,
   lost humankind?

No thought without you,
   all words about you;
none were before you,
   all things adore you,
silent or speaking,
   circling or seeking,
groaning and longing
   make you their song.

One sign has shown you,
   one heart has known you;
one way was pointed,
   one Son anointed:
crowds gathered near him
   eager to hear him;
who has received him,
   who will believe?

Manger-wood held him,
   tree timber killed him;
when metal nailed him,
   iron impaled him:
stone has concealed him,
   garden revealed him;
God has upraised him,
   all heavens praise!

Here is our ending,
   outcasts befriending;
here our beginning,
   losers are winning:
now we shall name him,
   love and proclaim him;
end our disorder
   Jesus our Lord!

55.55.55.54 Tune: HARROW WEALD by John Barnard

Scriptures: Rom 8.22; 10.9; 11.33-36 Eph 3.20 Psa 148.1-6; 150.6 Matt 11.27; 12.38-40 1 Tim 2.5; 3.16; 6.15-16 Lk 2.7; 4.14-15; 23.33 Acts 10.38-40 Jn 1.12; 19.41-42; 20.1 Isa 53.1 Phil 2.6-11 **Written:** Peckham, 17 Sept 1996

Another neighbouring church and a different written source produced this second hymn to our glorious God, touching many Scriptures but best linked with some of Paul's wondering doxologies. I had known Graham Corneck since 1962; he moved to Deptford as Vicar in 1976, and was still confronting his friends with new discoveries of God. Over the phone in 1996 he read from Gregory Nazianzen's 4th century 'Dogmatic Poems': 'O thou who art beyond all, how came thou to be called by another name? What hymn can sing of thee? No name describes thee. What mind can grasp thee?' etc. These profound meditations, he suggested, could form the basis of a new hymn; would I kindly oblige? I did my best, veering off from this immediate source to speak of Jesus (named only in the final line) as the sole clue to knowing the unknowable God. The metre is unusual but not unknown, being used for D T Niles' translated text *Father in heaven, grant to your children*, as set to John Barnard's tune in HTC.

Light upon the River

Romans 12
Worship, love and blessing: a wedding hymn

129 NOW IN VIEW OF ALL GOD'S MERCIES

Now in view of all God's mercies,
love that rescues, makes us whole,
let us offer up in worship
mind and body, heart and soul,
to the Lord whose hand has formed us,
blood has cleansed and word sustained:
Jesus Christ whose cross redeemed us,
earth renewed and heaven gained.

Let our varied gifts be ready,
burning zeal with love sincere,
hope rejoicing, patience steady,
open door and listening ear;
laugh and cry with one another
through the joy or pain God sends;
welcome neighbour, sister, brother,
giving time and making friends.

Let us bury greed and grudging,
find how meekness is most strong,
leave to God the place of judging,
not repaying wrong with wrong.
See the rule of Christ advancing,
let his will be understood;
praying, working, peace-enhancing,
evil overcome with good.

Fill these two, we pray, with blessings,
faith in marriage. church and home,
hopes ahead beyond our guessing,
love's surprises yet to come:
let no wealth or want oppress them
as they build their lives on you;
Father, Son and Spirit, bless them
now in truth made one, made new.

87.87.D Tune: BLAENWERN

Scriptures: Rom 12; 14.19 1 Jn 1.7 1 Pet 4.8-11 Phil 4.11-13 Matt 5.5,9 Prov 30.7-9 Gen 2.24

Written: Peckham, Aug 1997

In June 1997 we had supper with Alistair Bell, of Christ Church Old Kent Road. The other guest was a newer member, Rebecca Cruickshanks; over the meal three things emerged. One, they planned to marry next May; no great surprise. Two, would I conduct the service? Three, could I write a hymn for the occasion?—for me, the first request of its kind. BLAENWERN and Rom 12.9ff were specified; the latter needed some prefacing, since it depends on verse 1 ff., which itself depends on chs.1-11. So here is a metrical summary of Romans, focusing on chapter 12 and a bride and groom. 'Love' comes deliberately in three stanzas; faith, hope and love in the fourth, which leads from 'two' (line 1) to 'one' (line 8). After consultation with the couple my text was adjusted, and ready with some ten months to spare. Alistair and Rebecca had sung together both at Peckham, and in the choir for *Prom Praise*.

Light upon the River

1 Corinthians 5.7-8
Let us keep the Feast: Easter Anthems

130 CHRIST ONCE WAS SACRIFICED

Christ once was sacrificed,
Passover Lamb for us,
so let us keep the Feast this day;
purged from all stain of sin,
filled with his truth and love,
let us to Christ all homage pay.

Christ has been raised from death,
never to die again;
death has no power to mock his word.
We too have died to sin
to live to God alone,
raised up in Jesus Christ our Lord.

Christ has been raised to life,
Firstfruits of all the dead;
so all who sleep in death are raised.
Though Adam's family die
Christ's family comes alive;
for this new life his name be praised!

To God the Father, praise!
Praise Jesus Christ the Son!
Praise to the Spirit changelessly!
Glory to God be given
as it has ever been,
glory that evermore shall be!

668.668 Tune: ASCALON

Scriptures: 1 Cor 5.7-8 Rom 6.10-11   1 Cor 15.20-22
Written: Limehouse, 1978

Before the Book of Common Prayer Collect, Epistle and Gospel of Easter Day are printed the Easter Anthems, drawn by Thomas Cranmer from these three Scriptures, with the Gloria. They are appointed to be used instead of the Venite (Psalm 95) on that occasion. When some of us were looking at ways of varying the canticles then used, before other versions became available, I arranged this one in 1978.

Light upon the River

1 Corinthians 11.23-26
The Lord's Supper: one

131 CHRIST THE LORD WHO CALLS US

Christ the Lord who calls us
by his loving grace
meets us at his table,
gives to each a place;
everyone who trusts him
here becomes his guest
at this meal most costly,
holiest, and best.

Once he gave his body
on a cross of wood;
now he lives to bless us
with his precious food:
'Do this' he commanded
'to remember me';
let us taste his goodness,
his salvation see.

By this loaf now broken,
by this cup of wine,
Christ provides his people
with his gracious sign;
joining in one body,
all may take one bread,
sharing in one Spirit,
governed by one Head.

All the host of heaven
join our thankful song;
saints, apostles, prophets,
all the martyr throng;
with the holy angels
let his church proclaim
his atoning mercy,
his unrivalled name.

Christ be all our glory
till he comes again;
by his death we conquer,
by his life we reign:
Christ who made us welcome,
Christ who calls us friends,
shall receive our worship,
praise that never ends.

65.65.D Tune: EVELYNS; KING'S WESTON

Scriptures: Matt 26.26-28 Mk 14.22-25 Lk 22.14-20 1 Cor 10.16-17; 11.23-26; 12.12-13 Psa 34.8 Eph 4.15-16 Rev 5.9-14; 12.11 Rom 5.17 Jn 15.15

Written: Poplar, 1975

When not so many new hymns for Holy Communion were available as there are now, this was first sung on Maundy Thursday at St Matthias' Poplar, March 27 1975, in an earlier form 'Jesus who invites us'. It appeared in several local church supplements including those of All Souls' Langham Place and St Helen's Bishopsgate; of all my unpublished texts to date, this has been in most demand and (in response to group comments) one of the most revised. As well as references to the New Testament accounts of the Last Supper, it draws on the Prayer Book liturgy (verse 4) and *Te Deum Laudamus*.

Light upon the River

1 Corinthians 11.23-28
The Lord's Supper: two

132 WE HEARD CHRIST'S WORD, AND LOOKING BACK

We heard Christ's word, and looking back
recalled the road behind us;
at every turning of the track
he came to seek and find us.

We searched our hearts and looked within
and cried to God to cleanse us;
we found the One who bore our sin
now lives, and still befriends us.

We raised our eyes to look above
and praised the mighty Giver
for every blessing of his love,
and words that last for ever.

So now in hope we look ahead
where earth's new dawn is breaking;
for Christ is coming, as he said,
and heaven is in the making.

87.87 Iambic Tune: RIDLINGTON by Mervyn Horder;
or DOMINUS REGIT ME

Scriptures: 1 Cor 11.23-32 Deut 8.2 Lk 19.10; 21.33; 24.15,32 1 Pet 2.24 Rom 13.11-12

Written: Peckham, Jan 1996

As a teenager I recall learning what I have often passed on in Confirmation groups since; that at Holy Communion we look in four directions. 1 Cor 11 has them all: back in remembrance, upwards in gratitude, inwards in self-examination, and forward in hope, 'till he come' (the words on the grave of the maternal grandfather I never knew). They govern these four stanzas, written for St Mark's Old Ford at Jonathan's request—see No.80. In a first draft lines 2 and 4 of the final verse read 'to where the Son still rises... to bring still new surprises'. When he visited us in Peckham, laden with music and flowers, Mervyn Horder insisted that line 2 was horrible and line 4 untrue; I duly rewrote them.

Light upon the River

1 Corinthians 11.23-32
The Lord's Supper: three

133 TO CHRIST WHO ONCE THIS SUPPER MADE

To Christ who once this supper made
the night on which he was betrayed,
in confidence we now draw near;
the Lord is risen! the Lord is here!

As in that room he took the bread,
gave thanks, and broke, and gave, and said
'This is my body, given for you';
so may the Lord this gift renew.

As then, we drink this cup of wine,
the newest, sweetest covenant-sign,
declaring how his precious blood
has won and sealed our peace with God.

Let us who this Communion share
approach with praise and love and fear;
first judge ourselves, seek what is good,
then by his Spirit taste this food.

For as these holy gifts we take
till Christ returns, and for his sake,
joined in our Lord's triumphant name
his saving death we here proclaim.

LM Tune: BRESLAU

Scriptures: 1 Cor 11.23-32 Matt 26.26-28; 28.6-7 Mk 14.22-25 Lk 22.14-20; 24.6-7 Heb 4.16 Rom 5.1 1 Pet 3.11

Written: Poplar, 1974

First published: *Hymns for Praise & Worship* (Evangel Press, Indiana, USA) 1984

The third in this trio of Communion hymns (see the two texts above, also Nos.70 and 80) was the first to be written. It is placed here because it reflects the warnings towards the end of 1 Cor 11, which gives us the earliest written account of the Last Supper, and of the Lord's Supper. This too appeared in the All Souls' Langham Place supplementary hymn book in 1980 and was requested for others; so far it has been formally published only in America. It has some liturgical echoes; maybe 'The Lord is here' is better sung than said? But some form of 'on the night he was betrayed' (1 Cor 11.23) is rightly repeated at every Communion service.

Light upon the River

1 Corinthians 15.1-28
Known Gospel: unknown future

134 WE MEET TOGETHER IN THE NAME

We meet together in the name
of Christ the resurrected,
whose truth for ever stands the same
yet prompts the unexpected.
We find assurance in the Lord
whose mercy never changes
but who confronts us with the word
that hurts, and rearranges.

The gospel's truth securely stands:
Christ suffered, died, was buried,
raised up; all power is in his hands
whose grace is ever varied.
So let us build upon the rock
of Christ our resurrection,
but never fear the bracing shock
of his unguessed direction.

Supreme, the holy Scriptures speak,
the Spirit's word unbroken,
to face alike the strong, the weak,
and tell us: God has spoken.
We cannot change what God alone
has given for our obedience,
but gladly face the paths unknown
and pledge him our allegiance.

87.87.D iambic Tune: DUMPTON GAP

Scriptures: 1 Cor 15.1-28 Heb 1.1-2; 4.12-13 Matt 7.24-25; 28.18 1 Pet 4.10 Jn 10.35; 11.25-26 2 Tim 3.15-17 Jas 4.14-15

Written: Peckham, 27 Jan 1996

Apart from the date I have no note or recollection of writing this text. But by then we had lived in our Peckham flat for over four months, and apart from one funeral back in Suffolk I had neither led a service nor preached a sermon since moving—a strange experience, and the first such gap for more than thirty years. So the tension we felt in adapting to a new lifestyle may have been in my mind; but we did not intend to revise our fundamental confidence in the Gospel of Jesus Christ, as revealed in the Bible. Two years later I tidied up a phrase or two, but the tension expressed here may speak for others besides ourselves. Some of us are tempted to avoid reality by falling back on traditional formulae; others spread confusion by bending to the latest fashion. We all need a more positive, sane Christian mind to maintain a true equilibrium.

Light upon the River

1 Corinthians 15.12-20
Now is Christ risen from the dead

135 IF CHRIST HAD NOT BEEN RAISED FROM DEATH

If Christ had not been raised from death
our faith would be in vain,
our preaching but a waste of breath,
our sin and guilt remain.
    But now the Lord is risen indeed;
    he rules in earth and heaven:
    his Gospel meets a world of need -
    in Christ we are forgiven.

If Christ still lay within the tomb
then death would be the end,
and we should face our final doom
with neither guide nor friend.
    But now the Saviour is raised up,
    so when a Christian dies
    we mourn, yet look to God in hope—
    in Christ the saints arise!

If Christ had not been truly raised
his church would live a lie;
his name should never more be praised,
his words deserve to die.
    But now our great Redeemer lives;
    through this we are restored:
    his word endures, his church revives
    in Christ, our risen Lord. (Hallelujah!)

DCM Tune: VOX DILECTI

Scriptures: 1 Cor 15.12-20 Lk 21.33; 24.34 Matt 28.18 1 Thess 4.13-14 Acts 8.2 Job 19.25 Psa 119.89 Isa 40.6-8 1 Pet 1.25

Written: Limehouse, May 1984

First published: *Church of England Newspaper,* March 29 1985.

In the 1980s the resurrection of Christ was often headline news, after some controversial Easter broadcasts. David Jenkins (then Bishop of Durham) claimed he believed in it; but a 'resurrection' where the tomb may still house a corpse is hardly resurrection at all, in Biblical or even credal terms. The unambiguous statements in 1 Corinthians moved me to write this text, suited (by the contrasts in each stanza) to a Victorian tune which has been variously condemned or highly praised. We sang it the following Easter at our Sunrise Service in the garden of Christ Church Spitalfields—a shared event with Limehouse; it was also sung at Crowborough, and appeared in the quarterly *Word and Music* as well as the *CEN.* The first books to include it were *Anglican Praise* (OUP 1987) and *Hymns for the People* (Marshall Pickering 1993). Michael Perry suggested a final 'Hallelujah!', which in 1988 John Wilson supplied (triple) in time for the Hymn Society's 'Act of Praise' at Bristol that summer.

Light upon the River

2 Corinthians 4.4
Testimony

136 I NEVER LOOKED FOR JESUS

I never looked for Jesus;
praise God, he looked for me!
By the blinding sin that held me in
I could never truly see.

I paid no heed to Jesus;
he paid in full for me.
To release a slave his life he gave
and he bought my liberty.

I spent no love on Jesus;
he spent his blood for me:
for the source of love is God above
and it meant his agony.

I had no time for Jesus;
he made the time for me:
and he shows me how to serve him now
and enjoy eternity.

I have no claims on Jesus
but he has claims on me;
and his greatest claim is still the same
as it was on Calvary.

76.97 Tune: SANDOWN by Anne Hills

Scriptures: 2 Cor 4.4; 6.19-20; 7.22-23 Lk 15.4,8 1 Pet 1.18-19 1 Jn 4.7-10

Written: Barrow in Furness, 1967

This informal 'borderline' text was among the first I wrote. Russell Eves from Barrow, whose family emigrated to Australia, wrote a tune which we used at St Mark's YCF (youth group). In 1972 the text was accepted for a Scripture Union songbook which did not materialise. I tidied up the words in 1998.

Light upon the River

2 Corinthians 4.4-6
Christ the image of God

137 WHERE IS THE GLORY OF OUR GOD

Where is the glory of our God,
   the trace of his pure light?
Each day, each night we read his lines;
from earth to sky his rainbow shines
   and faith illumines sight.

Where is the image of the Lord,
   the likeness of his face?
In human heart and mortal mind
is where we may most surely find
   the mysteries of his grace.

Where is the message of the Christ,
   the echo of his voice?
In words from hill and lake and tree,
and stone and road, he reaches me;
   and hearing, I rejoice.

86.886 Tune: BINNEY'S

Scriptures: 2 Cor 3.18; 4.4-6 Psa 19.1-3 Gen 1.26-27; 9.12-17 Rom 8.29 Jas 3.9 Matt 5.3; 9.22; 13.3; 27.46; 28.1-10

Written: Dodoma and Peckham, June-August 1996

Our 1996 visit to Tanzania started gently. Tim had been away and had some catching up to do; Marjorie and I enjoyed walking, reading and writing. The question-and-answer form dates from that week; the full text from when we returned home. Verse 3 lines 3-4 are Gospel references, not hints of Wordsworth. The choice of tune makes it possible to avoid resorting again to REPTON.

Light upon the River

2 Corinthians 6.1-2
The day of salvation: new beginnings

138 NOW IS THE TIME, THE TIME OF GOD'S FAVOUR

Now is the time, the time of God's favour,
promise and hope for a people restored;
listen, repent, and turn back to the Saviour,
truly to welcome the year of our Lord!

This is the day of Jesus' arrival;
here in the desert, the threshold of home.
After earth's longings comes heaven's revival;
God, make us ready this day as you come!

Here is the hour, the hour of salvation;
learn the new song for new people to sing:
risen from death is the Source of creation;
lift up your heads for the hour of the King!

Do not delay, but come now to meet him,
Sabbath and Jubilee joining in one;
Christmas and Easter and Advent will greet him;
see a fresh universe rise to the Son!

10.10.11.10 Tune: ADVENT by Christopher Hayward

Scriptures: 2 Cor 6.1-2 Mk 1.15; 13.32-37 Rom 8.18-22 Rev 5.9; 14.3 Lk 21.28,36 Heb 4.6-9 Lev 25.8-55; 27.17-24
Written: Peckham, 27 June 1997

By 1997, 'millennium fever' ran high as the year AD 2000 approached. This was intensified in the nearby London Borough of Greenwich, from where time was historically measured; by Christians anxious that 'Jesus might not be invited his own party'; and among them, by some wanting suitable millennium hymns. Competitions and booklets were being planned as I wrote this, avoiding the potentially overworked 'two thousand years', already used memorably by E H Sears in 1849 (*It came upon the midnight clear*) and Richard Bewes in 1964 (*It was just two thousand years ago*). This text uses a basic sequence of time/year/day/hour, without building one item into each stanza; the rhythm is regular but probably needs a new tune. Its Biblical soundings include the Jubilee Year when all debts were cancelled, an international goal much canvassed in the 1990s, not least by church leaders.

Light upon the River

2 Corinthians 6.3-10
Servants of God; Paul outlines his workload

139   PREACHERS OF THE GOD OF GRACE

Preachers of the God of grace,
heralds of the dawning day -
fit them, Lord, for all they face,
prove their calling, guide their way.
Meeting failure or success,
keep their faith and vision sure,
agents of your righteousness,
trained for unremitting war.

Undeterred by praise or blame,
dear to God, on earth unknown,
zealous for your holy name,
making known what you have done:
constant testing they endure,
persecution, pain and blood;
by your Spirit keep them pure,
fill them with the love of God.

In their weakness, Lord, be strong,
Satan's claims let them destroy;
in their sorrows let their song
be of Christ, their hope and joy.
Fools for you—yet make them wise,
though on them all spite is poured
by a world that crucifies
faithful prophets of the Lord.

Dying daily, let them live;
fainting, make their spirits bold;
empty, teach them still to give;
poor, they shall enrich the world.
Triumph, Lord, when we despair,
honour those whom kings despise:
make their work your church's prayer,
grant your glory as their prize.

77.77.D Tune: ST GEORGE'S WINDSOR

Scriptures: 2 Cor 4.7-11; 5.13; 6.3-10; 11.16-30; 12.5-10 1 Pet 5.10 Eph 3.17-19 Matt 23.34 Acts 26.28 Col 4.2-4

Written: Poplar, 1976

In days when we are rediscovering shared ministry and exploring new patterns for mission, is it unhelpful to mark out preachers or 'full-time workers' for special treatment, in hymns or elsewhere? The New Testament clearly shows the distinctive work of church leaders, whatever their titles; we may be strangers to their pioneering struggles and sufferings, but many in the world are not. Near the end of our time in Poplar I based these verses on the apostle Paul's account of himself (which he wanted the churches to know) notably in 2 Cor 6. They aim to be in the same tradition as classics by Wesley, Montgomery and others; they could be used at an ordination, commissioning, farewell or anniversary, or (as at their debut on 7 Dec 1997 at Christ Church Old Kent Road) for a series on 2 Corinthians.

Light upon the River

2 Corinthians 8.9
The lifestyle of Christ

140 JESUS, MOST GENEROUS LORD

Jesus, most generous Lord,
whose nature is to give,
direct your searching word
upon the way we live.
    The hungry cry
    with none to heal;
    so make us feel
    their agony.

Once rich, becoming poor,
you filled us by your grace;
move us to care much more
about your starving race:
    by love may we
    bring hope to birth
    and learn on earth
    simplicity.

You fasted forty days,
fed thousands in their need;
so touch our meals with praise
and set us free from greed.
    You travelled light
    on roads of dust,
    and pilgrims must
    keep you in sight.

No palace for your home,
no gracious dwelling there;
let us in every room
show you are welcome here.
    To death you came
    in nakedness;
    the way we dress
    is costlier shame.

Help us serve you alone,
to follow where you lead,
renouncing gods of stone
and wealth and power and speed;
    to share abroad
    your rich supplies,
    most humble, wise
    and generous Lord.

6666.4444 Tune: SOMERTON A by Mervyn Horder; or LOVE UNKNOWN

Scriptures: 2 Cor 8.9 Jas 2.15-16 1 Jn 3.16-18 Lk 4.1-2; 6.20-21, 27-38; 8.1-3; 9.12-17, 57-58; 23.33-34

Written: Poplar, 1975

First published: *The Hymn* (Hymn Society in the United States and Canada) Vol.7 No.3, July 1996

Samuel Crossman's *My song is love unknown* says: 'In life no house, no home, my Lord on earth might have; in death, no friendly tomb but what a stranger gave'. Topic and tune may have come together in this text, which I entered for two different searches for 'lifestyle' hymns, which both came to nothing. It was revised, as so often with Michael Perry's comments in mind, in 1981; two years later it appeared in a hymn booklet of the Hambledon Valley group of churches in Oxfordshire, and then in *The Hymn*. Further textual adjustments came in 1987, and Mervyn Horder's tune the year after.

Galatians 2.20
Christ loved me, and gave himself for me

141 LORD MOST HIGH

Lord most high, how can I
thank you for all you gave me?
Your dear Son left his throne,
gave up heaven to save me.
> Over and over I did you wrong,
> spurned your grace and favour;
now I find I was blind
till you showed me my Saviour.

I shall sing of my King
though he reigns far above me;
tell how he pardoned me,
how he's promised to love me.
> Over and over I'll spread the news -
> there's no greater story -
once he came bearing shame;
soon he'll come in his glory!

Tune: EDELWEISS by Richard Rogers

Scriptures: Gal 2.20 Psa 45.1; 47.2 Jn 9.25 Heb 9.28 Rev 22.20

Written: Barrow in Furness, 1966

A tune from the sixties from a record-breaking show, *The Sound of Music*. I set these words to it for Pathfinders and YCF (later CYFA) youth groups at St Mark's Barrow, where it was often sung. Not all such pairings are convincing; the titles to Psalms such as 22 and 45 suggest they are worth trying.

Light upon the River

Galatians 5.1
The freedom of a Christian

142 FREEDOM AND LIFE ARE OURS

Freedom and life are ours,
for Christ has set us free!
Never again submit to powers
that lead to slavery:
> Christ is the Lord who breaks
> our chains, our bondage ends;
> Christ is the Rescuer who makes
> the helpless slaves his friends.

Called by the Lord to use
our freedom and be strong,
not letting liberty excuse
a life of blatant wrong:
> freed from the law's stern hand
> God's gift of grace to prove,
> know that the law's entire demand
> is gladly met by love.

Spirit of God, come, fill,
emancipate us all!
speak to us, Word of truth, until
before your feet we fall:
> glory and liberty
> our Father has decreed,
> and if the Son shall make us free
> we shall be free indeed.

DSM Tune: FROM STRENGTH TO STRENGTH

Scriptures: Gal 5.1, 13-14 Jn 8.31-36; 15.15 1 Pet 2.16 Rom 13.6-10 Eph 5.18 Lk 4.18
Written: Poplar, 1975
First published: *Hymns for Today's Church* (Hodder & Stoughton) 1982

'The Liberty of a Christian Man' (1520) was one of Martin Luther's Reformation challenges. If he were writing today, he might re-word his title; so have I (in 1987) revised the earlier version of this text from the masculine language of verses 1 and 3 as first printed. But I hope it stands in the true tradition of freedom hymns, rooted here in that letter of Paul's which is most concerned with liberty. The subject was one requested by Scripture Union; see Nos.102, 169 and 171. Though not used by SU, the text appeared in the All Souls Langham Place and Hildenborough Hall supplements (1980, 81); Richard Bewes also quotes it in *The Church Marches On* (Mowbray 1985). It was written for the distinctive FROM STRENGTH TO STRENGTH; many DSM tunes do not match the rhythm.

Light upon the River

Ephesians 1
All blessings in Christ: one

143 FATHER OF OUR LORD JESUS CHRIST

Father of our Lord Jesus Christ,
the God of grace and peace -
we bless his name whose blessings still
to earth and heaven increase.

Destined in love to be his own
and all his plans fulfil,
who more than we should celebrate
the purpose of his will?

Freed by the blood of Christ, who once
stood trial in our place,
spurred on by love, should we not tell
the riches of his grace?

Raised by our life-creating God,
our hope, our rock and tower,
believers find by surging strength
the greatness of his power.

Stamped with the Holy Spirit's seal,
our owner's mark and claim,
by one ambition we are moved:
the glory of his name.

God who in Christ poured out his heart,
to us his mind made known -
he will in Christ, creation's Lord,
bring all things into one.

CM Tune: NATIVITY

Scriptures: Eph 1; 4.30; 6.23-24 Col 1.9-19 1 Pet 1.1-5 Prov 18.10 2 Cor 1.22

Written: Poplar, 1974

This hymn began with the text from Ephesians 1.3 (appearing as well in other Epistles) which formed a natural opening line, together with the fourth lines of stanzas 2 to 5, derived from the exalted language of the same chapter. The rhythm requires the recommended tune or one with similar emphasis.

Light upon the River

Ephesians 1.3-8
All blessings in Christ: two

144 THE WONDER OF SALVATION

The wonder of salvation
beyond our words to speak,
beyond our minds to fathom
or even hearts to seek;
when we were lost and helpless,
enslaved, infected, dead,
all we could never dream of
God made good in our stead.

How close corruption held us,
since that was sin's reward!
How bleak for one to perish,
created by the Lord!
How could the law be cancelled
till all had been fulfilled?
How could the race be pardoned
when sinners should be killed?

All this was seen in heaven
by God's eternal Son;
moved by untold compassion
the rescue was begun;
shall death enjoy its triumph
and sin retain its crown
while those who bear God's image
must fall in ruin down?

The Word assumed a body
and took it for his own;
born of a chosen virgin,
as Man the Word was known.
He died the death of sinners
that we in him should die;
the name this world has trampled
in heaven is lifted high.

Such grace, such love for sinners,
such mercy through such pain!
It calls us to repentance
and love for him again.
How can we now ignore him?
How can we turn away?
Christ, be our God for ever,
Jesus, our Lord today!

76.76.D Tune: CRUGER; or PENLAN

Scriptures: Eph 1.3-8; 2.1-10   1 Tim 3.14-16 Rom 3.19-26; 5.6-8; 11.33-36   2 Pet 3.9 Gen 1.26-27 Jn 1.14; 21.28 Matt 1.20-25 Lk 1.26-35   2 Tim 2.11-13 Phil 2.5-11 Tit 2.13

Written: Peckham, 1996

This companion to *The Word was very God* (see notes to No.98), also arose from reading Athanasius in April 1996. 'De Incarnatione' (c.AD 318) in translation, was one of the shortest of the Haywards' books, and one of the greatest. This is not a close paraphrase, but a selected verse adaptation.

Light upon the River

Ephesians 1.18
Learning, loving, growing, standing: in Christ

145 NOW LET US LEARN OF CHRIST

Now let us learn of Christ:
he speaks, and we shall find
he lightens our dark mind,
so let us learn of Christ.

Now let us love in Christ
as he has first loved us;
as he endured the cross
so let us love in Christ.

Now let us grow in Christ
and look to things above
and speak the truth in love;
so let us grow in Christ.

Now let us stand in Christ
in every trial we meet,
in all his strength complete:
so let us stand in Christ.

66.66 Tune: EPHESIANS by Christopher Hayward;
GRIDLEY by Keith Landis; GROWING by Robin Sheldon;
PARKSTONE by David Peacock; or IBSTONE

Scriptures: Eph 1.17-18; 4.13-15; 5.1-2; 6.10-13 1 Jn 4.19 Heb 12.2 Col 3.1-2

Written: Poplar, Aug 1976

First published: *Songs of Worship* (Scripture Union) 1980

The simplest hymns sometimes require most time and care. One of the last I wrote in Poplar, this text takes four themes from Ephesians, not quite in order, and uses a word pattern where 'Christ' is clearly prominent. The fourfold 'now' reflects the Christian's new life and status as characteristically set out by the apostle Paul; the fourfold 'so', the equally typical consequences. The words were first sung to IBSTONE and published to GROWING; several other tunes have been composed for them.

Light upon the River

Ephesians 3.14-21
Paul prays to the Father

146 FATHER AND GOD, FROM WHOM OUR WORLD DERIVES

Father and God, from whom our world derives
all fatherhood in every family,
we bow our knees for power to fill our lives,
your mighty grace, your Spirit's energy.

For Christ to make his home in every heart;
to plant and build us in his love's pure strength;
to help his church to grasp in every part
love's boundless height and depth, and breadth and length.

With all God's fulness let us now be filled
and know the splendour of his love unknown;
expect the gifts a father gives his child,
and share the trophies that our king has won.

To God be praise! His power in us can do
far more than we can ask or understand
through Jesus Christ, who by his church makes new
for every age the glories God has planned.

10.10.10.10 Tune: LAVENDON by Paul Edwards;
WILLARD by Keith Landis; or WOODLANDS

Scriptures: Eph 3.14-21; 4.12-13 Col 1.4-12 Matt 6.9; 7.9-11 Lk 11.2, 11-13 Jas 2.5   1 Pet 1.3-4

Written: Poplar, 1974

First published: *Hymns for Today's Church* (Hodder & Stoughton) 1982

Paul's great prayer in Ephesians 3 was the reading, and preacher's text, at our wedding in 1963. Years later it was surprising to find how few hymns had drawn on it. This was an early paraphrase submitted to (though not written for) what became the Jubilate group, who helped to improve it; it became 'N1' on our initial list of possibles. In those days WOODLANDS was not so much in demand as it later became; more tunes in this metre are needed, but for these words ELLERS should be avoided.

Ephesians 4.4-16
The gifts and the Giver

147 GIVE THANKS FOR THE GIFTS AND GIVE PRAISE TO THE GIVER

Give thanks for the gifts and give praise to the Giver!
One body, one Spirit, one hope in God's call;
one Lord and one faith and one baptismal washing,
one Father of all, over all and in all.

But all of the members receive by God's goodness
equipment for service, the blessings of love;
for Christ who came down is now raised and ascended,
and freely apportions his gifts from above.

So some are apostles and some are his prophets;
evangelists, pastors and teachers he gives
to build up a body mature in its stature,
in Christ new-created, in Christ the church lives.

No longer as children, we grow to completeness;
convinced, we no longer uncertainly move:
with Christ as the Head and his people one body
we all work together, made strong in his love.

12.11.12.11 Tune: STREETS OF LAREDO

Scriptures: Eph 1.22-23; 4.4-16; 5.29-30 Rom 12.4-8 1 Cor 12.4-7, 12-13 Col 1.18

Written: Poplar, 1975

'Past and present, near and far, praise the gifts and Giver! Floreat Elthamia: stand and flourish ever!' So runs the chorus of what, for its time, was a very fine school song. From 1946 to 1956 I attended Eltham College in SE London, where for some years I learned English from its author whose name appears in my dedication: C A A Parkinson. His words echoed for me as I began to write on God's varied gifts of grace, at a time when some preferred to find them only in 1 Cor 12. We sang it on Ascension Day 1975 at St Matthias' Poplar; inevitably it was later revised. Holy Trinity Wealdstone and St Andrew the Great Cambridge have both used it; among those recognising its personal resonances was Old Elthamian hymnwriter Michael Saward.

Light upon the River

Ephesians 4.7-16
Our ascended Lord

148 ASCENDED CHRIST

Ascended Christ, who gained
the glory that we sing,
anointed and ordained
our prophet, priest and king:
   by many tongues
   the church displays
   your power and praise
   in all her songs.

No titles, thrones or powers
can ever rival yours;
no passing mood of ours
can turn aside your laws:
   you reign above
   each other name
   of power or fame,
   the Lord of love.

Now from the Father's side
you make your people new;
since for our sins you died
our lives belong to you:
   from our distress
   you set us free
   for purity
   and holiness.

You call us to belong
within one body here;
in weakness we are strong
and all your gifts we share:
   in you alone
   we are complete
   and at your feet
   with joy bow down.

All strength is in your hand,
all power to you is given;
all wisdom to command
in earth and hell and heaven:
   beyond all words
   creation sings
   the King of kings
   and Lord of lords.

6666.4444 Tune: TRIMINGHAM by Mervyn Horder; or DARWALL'S 148th

Scriptures: Eph 4.7-16; 5.30 Col 1.18; 2.9-10; 4.12 1 Cor 6.19-20 Rom 6.19-22; 12.4-8 2 Cor 12.9-10 Matt 28.18 Rev 17.14; 19.16

Written: Limehouse, 1977

First published: *Hymns for Today's Church* (Hodder & Stoughton) 1982

The Ascension has many fine hymns, and usually only one specific Thursday and Sunday on which to sing them! I have risked adding yet another to one of my favourite seasons (see No.74 etc.) as they can after all be sung at other times. From Isaac Watts onwards, this metre has also attracted many writers, made strict demands on them, and brought corresponding rewards in congregational music.

Ephesians 5.8-14
Christ will shine on you!

149 LIGHT OF GLADNESS, LORD OF GLORY

Light of gladness, Lord of glory,
Jesus Christ our King most holy,
shine upon us in your mercy:
earth and heaven join their hymn.

Let us sing at sun's descending
as we see the lights of evening,
Father, Son and Spirit praising
with the holy seraphim.

Son of God, through all the ages
worthy of our holiest praises,
yours the life that never ceases,
light which never shall grow dim.

888.7 Tune: FARRANCE STREET by Lyn Kendrick;
or QUEM PASTORES

Scriptures: Eph 5.8-14 Jn 1.4-9; 8.12 1 Cor 2.8 2 Cor 4.6 Heb 1.3 1 Tim 6.15-16 Isa 6.1-3 Acts 20.7-8 Mk 1.1 Rom 1.4 Rev 5.9,12

Written: Limehouse, 1978

First published: *Hymns for Today's Church* (Hodder & Stoughton) 1982

'Phos hilaron', the Greek evening hymn from the 3rd or 4th century, seems to be the most ancient Christian hymn still regularly sung, except those from the Scriptures. It is also the earliest whose complete text we have; 20th century hymnals often have versions by Keble (*Hail, gladdening light*) or Bridges (*O gladsome light*). When in the 1960s the Church of England began the official revision of its Prayer Book services, it curiously inserted these in 'alternative' liturgies which discarded most other archaic language. Noting that Julian's 'Dictionary of Hymnology' listed 21 English versions even before Bridges, I felt the need of a contemporary text for this ancient source; it proved to be one of the few to be published as I first wrote it. In 1991 it appeared in 'A Musical Companion to the Service of Light' (RSCM); a new tune was written in 1988 by Lyn Kendrick who was organist (subsequently, licensed lay Reader) at Limehouse, and one of our oldest friends. Writing in 'The Hymn' (Hymn Society of America) April 1989, M Eleanor Irwin traces the historical appeal of the original, listing two older versions not in 'Julian' and ten (including this) published since; she also sees the second word ('hilaron', cheerful) as its most distinctive. The seraphim, the 'fiery ones', are seen and heard in the Bible only in Isaiah's vision (ch 6), and their very uniqueness makes them much discussed. 'Holiness' comes in each of my three verses as it is the context of their appearance and the theme of their cry.

Ephesians 5.15-17
Redeeming the time

150 LORD OF OUR TIME

Lord of our time, help us, we pray,
to prize the joy each moment brings;
to squander no good gift today
nor waste our lives on useless things.

Direct our minds, our lips, our hands,
make straight the pathways for our feet;
show us which tasks are your commands
to be pursued until complete.

Without your power all schemes shall fall;
inspire our wills, our strength renew,
O Lord, the source and guide and goal
of all we think and say and do.

In all things waiting to be done,
in private hope and public fame,
our aim and purpose in each one
shall be the glory of your name.

LM Tune: SIMEON

Scriptures: Eph 5.15-17 Col 3.17; 4.5 1 Thess 4.11-12 2 Thess 3.6-13 Psa 31.15; 34.1; 62.8 Eccles 3.1-8 Rom 11.36

Written: Limehouse, 1978

'God never hurries;' wrote A W Tozer; 'there are no deadlines against which he must work. Only to know this is to quiet our spirits and relax our nerves.' Max Warren (in *The Master of Time*) and Michel Quoist (in *Prayers of Life*) are among other recent writers who take their cue from such Biblical sources as are sampled here. Jesus had a sense of time but not of rush; he often warned of his coming 'hour'. But few hymnwriters since Thomas Ken have helped us to sing about it. My chief source, however, is Samuel Johnson's prayer from 1752; he felt more guilty than most of 'sloth', and was scrupulously sensitive over 'lavishing' time on 'useless trifles'.

Light upon the River

Ephesians 5.19-20
Trinitarian thanksgiving

151   MOON AND BRIGHT SUN

Moon and bright sun, wind and white cloud,
and blossom and babes, God made them all;
sky and good earth, all these are yours:
Father, Creator, we thank you!

Thank you, our Lord, our God,
thank you, our Love, our Life,
thank you, our holy and wonderful Friend.

Nailed to a tree, Jesus the Son -
for sinners he died; God raised him up!
Yes, you are King; yes, you are here,
Saviour and Lord, Hallelujah!

Thank you, our Lord...

Living and warm Spirit of God,
and holy and true Wisdom and Strength:
carry us through new every day,
Voice of the Lord, we will trust you.

Thank you, our Lord...

Tune: MANE OG SOL by M Egil Hovland

Scriptures: Eph 1.17; 5.19-20 Gen 1.6-26 Acts 5.30-32; 10.36-43 Isa 11.2 Jn 14.16-17; 15.26

Written: Oakley, 1989

Kenneth Sagar is both organist and engineer; we met through a church link between Limehouse and Lindfield, near his home in Sussex. During our opening months in Suffolk, he sent some Scandinavian hymns with his own prose translation, to see if they would transfer to English verse (see also No.95). This began in 1973 in the Swedish of Britt Gerda Hallqvist, with a tune from Egil Hovland of Oslo in 1974, and a 1977 Norwegian translation by Arve Brunvoll. As with *See your hands overflowing with flowers*, the Norwegian version appears in *Norske Salme Bok* (1985) the official hymnal of the Norwegian Lutheran Church. The main theme of this lyrical verse is clearly gratitude to the Father, Son and Holy Spirit; one God as Creator, Redeemer, Helper, as shown in the Scriptures.

Light upon the River

Philippians 1-2
The church, warts and all

152 LORD, YOU HAVE SEEN YOUR CHURCH'S NEEDS

Lord, you have seen your church's needs;
our clamour you have heard:
at every point make known your mind;
apply to us your word.

When leaders argue, workers fail,
and faithful saints lose heart,
grant to us all your peace, your strength;
your love to us impart.

When illness strikes or loss invades
or ranks are thinned by death,
then come among us with new hope
and with reviving breath.

When Christians are in rival groups
and churches torn by strife,
make us repent, be reconciled,
and so restored to life.

We plead, O Christ, that when you come
you will find faith on earth;
one church awakened by one truth,
alive by one new birth.

CM Tune: ST HUGH; or ST FRANCIS XAVIER

Scriptures: Phil 1-2; 3.8; 4.2,7,13 Lk 18.8 Psa 85.6 1 Pet 1.3
Written: Clermiston, Edinburgh, 15 July 1993
First published: *Spring Harvest Praise 1994* (Spring Harvest) 1994

In June 1993 Bob Horn, former editor of *Evangelicals Now* and then General Secretary of UCCF (Universities and Colleges Christian Fellowship), wrote to several writers appealing for some hymn and song texts for the next year's 'Spring Harvest'. He was involved in the 'Word Alive' week which shared the venue, planning, and song book with this large teaching and holiday gathering; like others, he wanted more Biblical content to the singing. One theme that year was the Letter to the Philippians, where Paul deals with several church problems which are all too contemporary. The next month we took a holiday locum at Emmanuel Church at Clermiston, living in the home of Peter Warren, its pastor. Like other texts to follow, based on the epistle, I wrote this during our stay; it was the only one which proved acceptable, but appeared with a less than ideal tune. No doubt Paul could have dealt with that problem, too.

Light upon the River

Philippians 1-2
In Christ: for Christ

153 THE SAINTS IN CHRIST

The saints in Christ are one in every place
to serve the gospel of his costly grace;
from those first days to this, our hope the same:
the love of Christ, one Lord, one saving name.

In chains for Christ! his prisoners love to sing,
for slaves and free rejoice to praise our King;
what though the church on earth still suffers wrong?
The cross of Christ remains our pilgrim song.

To live is Christ, for us, to die is gain;
where then shall be our hunger, danger, pain?
Our joy to preach good news to rich and poor,
then be with Christ, to live for evermore.

Lord Jesus Christ! heaven's praise let earth repeat;
the work that you began, you will complete:
your enemies by grace become your friends;
the day of Christ shall dawn, and never ends.

10.10.10.10 Tune: SAINTS IN CHRIST by Eric Lewis;
or YANWORTH by John Barnard

Scriptures: Phil 1-2; 3.18-20; 4.21-22 Acts 16.12-15,22-25 1 Cor 7.22 Gal 3.28 Rom 5.10 2 Cor 5.14-20

Written: Clermiston, Edinburgh, 19 July 1993

First published: *News of Hymnody No.57* (Grove Books) Jan 1996

One of a clutch of texts written for 'Word Alive' but not used there (see No.152 above); the second of them to be published. I hoped that John Barnard would let me link it to his fine tune, for which they were written. Philippians is a most Christ-centred letter; the hymn is intended to reflect this by using many of Paul's phrases about Christ—with a reminder in verse 2 of his mixed reception in Philippi.

Philippians 1.5-6
Living the Gospel: church and ministry

154 PARTNERS IN THE GOSPEL

Partners in the Gospel
may our title be
from that day, Lord Jesus,
when we first could see
> why from heaven to death you came,
> how you won the highest name.

Worthy of the Gospel?
May it shape our life,
filled with loving boldness,
freed from fear and strife,
> finding joy in pain and loss
> by the pattern of your cross.

Working for the Gospel,
may your church defend,
preach it and confirm it,
suffer and contend,
> till at last our prayers give way
> to the glories of your Day.

65.65.77 Tune: ORMESBY by Mervyn Horder

Scriptures: Phil 1.5-6,12-14,27; 2.5-11; 3.10; 4.3   1 Thess 1.5-10; 2.2 Eph 6.19-20 Jude 3 Tit 2.13

Written: Peterborough—Norwich, 20 July 1993

Travelling home to Suffolk from Edinburgh (see No.152 above), required three trains. During the middle part of our journey I wrote these words, as the final hymn of the 'Philippians' batch. It is built around the 'Gospel' phrases in 1.5, 1.27 and 4.3 and also touches the letter at other points. The tune, written five years before (see No.77) came to mind as the text took shape. From Edinburgh to Peterborough I had been tidying up the other holiday writing; that first train, I saw as we alighted, had a hymn-loving engine impressively named 'Charles Wesley'.

Light upon the River

Philippians 1.12-14
In chains for Christ

155 WHEN PRISON WALLS EXTEND THEIR REACH

When prison walls extend their reach
and captives are not freed,
hear us, our Father, and outstretch
your arm to meet our need.
   When shadows lengthen in the days
   of danger, lies and death,
   grant to your church the will to pray
   with clear, persistent faith.

When Christians fear that earthly power
will quench their liberty,
grant them the steadfast mind to know
your word runs swift and free.
   When brothers, sisters come to die
   by fire or rope or gun,
   grant them the grace to fix their eyes
   on Christ, your risen Son.

For prison's secret miracles,
for witness borne through shame,
letters and books from lonely cells -
all glory to your name!
   For converts won in high-walled yard,
   for songs outlasting pain,
   martyrs who gained their hope's reward -
   our hearts give thanks again.

For love replacing cruel hate,
for enemies made friends -
Father, as all your deeds are great,
your praise shall never end.
   Yours are the walls, the lock, the key,
   and Christ the open door;
   our justice, mercy, life and joy,
   our freedom evermore.

DCM Tune needed; or BEATITUDO (CM)

Scriptures: Phil 1.12-14 Gen 39.20-23; 41.14 Psa 105.16-22; 107.10-16 Jer 37-38 Mk 6.14-29 Jn 10.7,9 Acts 12.1-19; 16.16-40 Col 4.18 2 Thess 3.1 2 Tim 2.9 Heb 12.2; 13.3 Rev 2.10; 3.7

Written: Oakley and Stepney, June 1993

Prison is found more often in our Bibles than in our hymn books. Some hymns (such as *Who would true valour see*) were written in prison, but not about it. Marjorie and I have both been inside in various capacities, and it seemed natural for this to be my first response to Bob Horn's request for hymns in 1993: see No.152 etc. It began at Oakley, continued on the train, and was completed when I stayed with Jonathan in London, where I had gone for the Evangelical Ministry Assembly of the Proclamation Trust. One surprise guest that year was a bishop from the Sudan where Christians had suffered (as in my second verse) well away from any public view or concern but on a massive scale. The next month's *News of Hymnody* happened to include *Christ the prisoner, Christ the victim* by prison chaplain Keith Pound. My own text applies to many other Scriptural references to prison. It is printed for a DCM tune; whatever is chosen needs a strong beat beginning its third and seventh lines.

Light upon the River

Philippians 1.20-21
Trusting Christ whatever happens next

156 IN LIFE OR DEATH, LORD JESUS CHRIST

In life or death, Lord Jesus Christ,
be all in all, I pray;
your life, your death make known in me
on earth, till heaven's day.

In sun or shadow be my help;
your voice shall guide my feet:
teach me by your incisive word;
your work in me complete.

In calm or crisis, be my hope
and take my mind in hand;
so shall I trust you, even where
I cannot understand.

In loss or profit, be my joy;
my hours for you be spent:
I can do all things in your strength;
so shall I be content.

In risk or safety, be my friend;
I place my hand in yours,
with you to rest, or wait, or walk,
or run with all my powers.

O Christ my help, my hope, my joy,
my all-enduring Friend,
all that I am belongs to you
who loved me to the end.

CM Tune: WESTMINSTER or THIS ENDRIS NYGHT

Scriptures: Phil 1.6,10,14,20-21; 2.4-8,13-17,24,27,30; 3.7-8,12,16,18; 4.4-8,11-13,18 Heb 4.12-13 Lk 5.5 Jn 13.1; 21.6 Isa 40.30-31 1 Cor 3.22; 6.19-20 Gal 2.20

Written: Clermiston, Edinburgh, 16 July 1993

While staying in Edinburgh, which for eight years was Jeremy's academic home (see also No.152), we were visited by friends from Glasgow; we walked with them on nearby Costorphine Hill overlooking the city and the firth of Forth. Their daughter Felicity, who was born with perfect eyesight, had been completely blind for 18 months; now she was nearly ten. But with her hand safely in her father's, she waited, walked, or ran along the hill with perfect confidence. Verse five of my text aims to express this kind of trust. The stanza originally belonged to another draft, which became No.157 below, but it spread too far and this was the cutting I took from it. The final stanza brings together help, hope, joy, friend, from the earlier ones: each is an aspect of Christ's relationship with me. The tunes named are possibles until a more suitable one is found, or composed.

Light upon the River

Philippians 2.4-5
The Christian mind

157　LORD, TEACH US TO REJOICE IN YOU

Lord, teach us to rejoice in you
in chains or liberty;
but not to rest one hour too long
while others are not free.

Grant us your patience, gentle Christ,
if hunger stalks our path;
but when our sisters have no bread
lend us your righteous wrath.

Help us, strong Christ, to know your grace
wherever we may live;
but for our brothers' homelessness
divine impatience give.

Give us a peaceful, quiet mind
for all we lack or need;
but zeal to help when neighbours cry,
to heal where nations bleed.

Lord Christ, you came not for yourself;
for us you faced the worst:
for your sake let us serve your world;
for their sake, put you first.

CM Tune: THRANDESTON by Mervyn Horder; MENDIP; or BRISTOL

Scriptures: Phil 1.7; 2.2-5,11,21; 3.8; 4.10-14, 23 Jas 2.15-16
1 Jn 3.17

Written: Clermiston, Edinburgh, 15 July 1993

The key word is 'but' in each third line, until verse five. Often in Philippians, Paul the apostle and prisoner shows personal contentment combined with discontent with the status quo; he urges 'the mind of Christ' which looks to the interests of others. For its writing, see No.152. Mervyn Horder called his tune SOUTHWELL until finding two more of that name. It then became THRANDESTON; in that village the hymn was first sung, at Holy Communion on 5 Sept 1993. Mervyn was our weekend guest at Oakley; we introduced the hymn together, and he then accompanied us all on the organ.

Light upon the River

Philippians 3.4-14
Rewards and comparisons: one

158 THIS WORLD HAS GREAT REWARDS TO GIVE

This world has great rewards to give
and counts achievements high,
but all its honours and delights
can never satisfy

For love of God I count as loss
my profit and my pride;
there's greater gain in knowing Christ
than all the world beside.

For Christ has made me right with God,
his merit now is mine;
and faith alone joins me to Christ
by his supreme design.

His is the strength by which I live,
his risen life I share;
and if I want to rise with him
I suffer with him here.

I have not yet obtained the prize,
complete in heart and soul,
but turn my back on what is past
and reach for Christ, my Goal.

CM Tune: ST STEPHEN

Scriptures: Phil 3.4-14 Eccles 1-2 Heb 12.1-2
Written: Barrow in Furness, autumn 1966
First published: *Psalm Praise* (Falcon) 1973

The New Testament reading for Sunday evening 6 Oct 1966 was Phil 3.4-14. That became the theme for our St Mark's Barrow Pathfinders' 8th Birthday service on that day, on which I based this text. It was revised in 1971-2 by myself and others; the new first line may sing better than the original 'This world has many tempting things', but is less true (since the world has ultimately nothing to give) and has made me want to drop the text quietly. However, Jesus spoke of the empty 'reward' which we may receive if we aim for it, and the eternal joy in God by way of contrast (as in Matthew 6.1-21). Since I hope that the hymn also makes that clear, and because it is still being requested, it is included here.

Light upon the River

Philippians 3.4-14
Rewards and comparisons: two

159 HOW GOOD IS LIFE, AND LENGTH OF DAYS

How good is life, and length of days!
Far happier, when we learn God's praise.
Though strength or skills may bring us fame
our best rewards are in his name.

To work and rest can both be sweet;
in Christ alone are both complete.
We learn to run, to ride, to swim,
but better far, to walk with him.

Designs and colours please our eyes;
God's wisdom brings a richer prize.
Fine music makes the heart rejoice
but better far, to hear God's voice.

What joy are friends, and health restored!
What greater joy, to love the Lord!
To govern is a noble thing,
but better far, to serve the King.

Our birth and death are times of tears,
but Jesus lives, and rules the years.
As generations rise and fall,
to live in Christ is best of all.

LM Tune: ASHLAND by Keith Landis; or MORNING HYMN

Scriptures: Phil 3.4-14 Psa 4.7; 21.4; 73.23-26 Prov 3.1-18 Lk 10.38-42 Col 1.10; 2.6 Matt 6.33; 22.37-38 Jn 6.27; 12.26; 14.15,21; 21.15-17   1 Jn 2.15-17

Written: Poplar, 1975

According to the Apocryphal book Ecclesiasticus (ch.40), 'Wine and music gladden the heart, but better still is the love of wisdom... Wealth and strength make for confidence, but better still is the fear of the Lord.' The good/better contrasts here, which I was reading in 1975, do not always carry 'religious' morals; but the chapter suggested this text, which draws on many Scriptural themes. It aims to express delight in God's natural world rather than indifference to it, and a reaching beyond it rather than contentment with it.

Light upon the River

Philippians 4.4-9
Food for thought

160 WHATEVER THINGS ARE LOVELY

Whatever things are lovely,
whatever things are right,
all that is pure and noble:
make these things your delight.
Whatever is praiseworthy
and beautiful and true,
all excellence and virtue
shall form Christ's mind in you.

In all things, make thanksgiving;
for all things, join in prayer:
the peace of God will guard you -
rejoice—the Lord is near!
Let nothing make you anxious;
what you have learned, obey:
the God of peace be with you
and Christ be all your way.

76.76.D Tune: CHRISTIAN by Mervyn Horder; AURELIA; or CRUGER

Scriptures: Phil 2.5; 4.4-9 Prov 3.5-6; 23.7 Rom 12.2 Col 3.2
1 Pet 1.13-15; 4.7 Jn 14.6

Written: Clermiston, Edinburgh, 19 July 1993

I hope it is not arrogant to try to paraphrase these exquisite words near the end of the epistle; it may be better than passing them by in our hymns. This was the shortest and last of the 'Edinburgh' texts (No. 152 etc); I wrote it in the early morning of 19 July, after a final jog round the hilly streets of Clerwood and Costorphine, from where the river Forth can be glimpsed. All the lines except the last in each stanza come from Phil 4. The words were sung first in 1995 to AURELIA (at St Andrew the Great, Cambridge); if that or CRUGER seem too grand, and if CHRISTIAN (written earlier) does not quite match, then the field is open.

Light upon the River

Philippians 4.11-13, 19-20
Christian contentment

161 WHEN WE ARE IN WANT

When we are in want
or we have more than all we need,
then let us learn of God in Christ
    to be well content.

Hungry or well-fed
and living freely or in chains,
we can do everything in Christ
    who provides our strength.

God will meet our needs
according to his glorious wealth,
so let us give to God in Christ
    honour, glory, praise.

Glory be to God
the Father, Son, and Spirit: praise
from all creation evermore,
    and from God, all grace.

Tune: WHEN I FEEL THE TOUCH by Keri Jones and Dave Matthews

Scriptures: Phil 1.2,7,11; 4.11-13, 19-20, 23 Psa 23.1 Matt 6.33
2 Cor 8.9-15; 9.8-15

Written: Clermiston, Edinburgh, 10 July 1993

This final text in the series introduced at No.152 was the first I wrote at 127 Clermiston Road, four miles west of the centre of Edinburgh. I hopefully annexed a *Mission Praise* tune for another comparatively rare theme in hymnody; this too was used at St Andrew the Great Cambridge, but not at 'Word Alive'. The earlier draft started 'When I am in want' but soon moved to the plural; it ended with 'praise from all the church for evermore', but later included all creation. There is a case for both.

Light upon the River

Colossians 1.12-20
Christ the Firstborn over all creation

162 PRAISE TO GOD THE FATHER

Praise to God the Father!
God who saves his people,
rescues us from darkest powers
and tyrannies of night;
brings us liberation
by the Son, Christ Jesus,
who bears the likeness
of immortal light.

Forces seen and unseen
made in the beginning,
depths of spirit, heights of mind,
and worlds in time and space:
all in Christ created,
by and through and for him,
in Christ existing
find in him their place.

Origin and Firstborn
of the church, his body,
raised from death to be its Head
in sovereignty alone;
God's full nature sharing,
universe reclaiming,
peacemaking Saviour,
praise to Christ the Son!

66.76.66.55 (12.13.12.10) Tune: TERSANCTUS; or ST HELENS

Scriptures: Col 1.12-20; 2.9-10,15 Jn 1.1-9 Heb 1.3 1 Tim 6.15-16 Eph 1.9-10, 19-23; 2.14-17 Phil 2.6

Written: Poplar, 1974

First published: *Carol Praise* (Marshall Pickering) 1987

A sermon by A W Rainsbury at St Peter's College Oxford (for OICCU, the Christian Union) first opened up for me the glory of Christ as seen through this first chapter of Colossians. That was Jan 1961; thirteen years later a hymn began to take shape, and after thirteen more it reached publication. I had TERSANCTUS in mind, but Kenneth Coates' fine tune ST HELENS is also appropriate. From a different St Helen's (see No.237) Dick Lucas has written on this part of the epistle: 'If it was a spiritual song along the lines of 3.16 it would make the teaching hymns of even a Charles Wesley appear lightweight' (*Fulness and Freedom*, IVP 1980). Like others, he makes the point that 'within three decades of the crucifixion, language like this was in normal circulation among the churches to describe Jesus of Nazareth... There never was a time, from the beginning of the church's life, when the highest honours of the Godhead were not given to his name'.

Light upon the River

Colossians 3.1-14
The risen life: Easter epistle

163 IF WE ARE RAISED TO LIFE WITH CHRIST

If we are raised to life with Christ,
no more to creep along the ground,
we fix our minds on things above
where Christ is King at God's right hand.

If we are raised to life with Christ
we put to death our fatal greed
and all abuse of hand or brain,
for God will judge each godless deed.

If we are raised to life with Christ,
daily renewed in every part,
we join with all who know our God,
one image stamped on every heart.

If we are raised to life with Christ
who loved and chose us for his own,
we walk his way, reflect his light,
and share his love which makes us one.

LM Tune: PASSONS By Keith Landis; FESTUS; or FULDA

Scriptures: Col 3.1-14 Heb 1.3 1 Pet 1 1-5; 3.22 Rom 2.12,16; 8.13,29-34 2 Tim 4.1 Rev 20.12-13 2 Cor 3.18 Eph 1.4,11,19-20; 4.21-32; 5.8-14

Written: Poplar, 1974

Dick Lucas again (see No.162 above): 'The imperatives of the New Testament are always well supported with incentives.' And again, on this page of Colossians: 'In a letter that has superlative things to say about Christ, it is no surprise to find superlative things said about his church'. Following the welcome given in 1973 to many of the New Testament paraphrases in *Psalm Praise*, it was natural to look for other potential 'Christian canticles'. Next year the start of Colossians 3 struck me with refreshing force, and seemed to be one such possibility. For many of us, its special power is permanently connected with its place in the Book of Common Prayer as the Epistle of Easter Day.

1 Thessalonians 1
A church is planted

164 GRACE AND PEACE BE OURS FOR EVER

Grace and peace be ours for ever
from the Father and the Son;
faith, love, hope combine together:
so God's churches are begun.

See what faith in God can offer! -
born in preaching, fed by prayer,
taught to serve and trained to suffer,
working, growing everywhere.

Look how love has learned to labour! -
God who chose, who first loved us
reaches friend and foe and neighbour
by the scandal of the cross.

Watch where hope inspires endurance! -
takes with joy what God has given,
turns from idols, finds assurance,
waits for Christ, his Son from heaven.

Spirit's power and heart's conviction
mark his plans in every place;
Saviour's word and resurrection
crown his church with peace and grace!

87.87 Tune: LAUS DEO; or HALTON HOLGATE

Scriptures: 1 Thess 1   1 Cor 1.23; 13.13   Rom 10.17   1 Jn 4.19; 5.21 Gal 5.11 Phil 3.20

Written: Cambridge, 20 Oct 1995

This was another fruit of some days in Cambridge, and a visit by Chris and Helen Hayward to our holiday flat at 39 Castle Street (see No.14 and others). One of Chris's requests was for new texts based on the first Epistle to the Thessalonians; the main draft was written that week, starting with the greeting ('Grace and peace') characteristic of the apostle Paul. Like both 1 and 2 Thessalonians, it also ends with 'grace', and is structured around the familiar NT triad of faith, hope, love (1 Thess 1.3).

1 Thessalonians 5.4-11
Sleeping or waking: Evening

165 ALMIGHTY LORD, THE HOLY ONE

Almighty Lord, the Holy One
whose reign in glory we await,
look down from your eternal throne
and our dark world illuminate:
from sons and daughters of the light
dispel the shameful deeds of night.

Defend us from all evil powers;
our weakness and fatigue replace
through all the silent sleeping hours
with sweet refreshing by your grace:
forgive our sins, our hope renew,
that we may rest and rise with you.

88.88.88 Tune: SURREY

Scriptures: 1 Thess 5.4-11 Jn 3.19 Rom 13.11-12 Eph 5.6-13 Isa 40.29-31 Psa 4.8; 121.3-7; 127.2 Acts 3.19 Matt 6.12; 11.28-30 Lk 11.4

Written: Limehouse, 1978

First published: *Hymns for Today's Church* (Hodder & Stoughton) 1982

Not everything said in prayer transfers readily for singing. Since writing this short evening hymn I have reacted against the habit of setting everything in sight to music; most Collects are better left as they are. But in working towards *Hymns for Today's Church* we were keen to explore old and new sources, and this version of two ancient texts was accepted. The prayers from the Gelasian and Leonine Sacramentaries (from around the 8th and 7th centuries respectively) on which its two stanzas are based, became familiar to many through the late night service of Compline. But the New Testament, notably its epistles, has much to say about many kinds of sleeping and waking.

Light upon the River

1 Thessalonians 5.5-24
Brothers and sisters in Christ

166 AS SONS OF THE DAY AND DAUGHTERS OF LIGHT

As sons of the day and daughters of light
no longer we sleep like creatures of night:
for Jesus has died that with him we may live;
by all he has given, we learn how to give.

One body in Christ, let all play their part;
the lazy be warned, the timid take heart:
let those who are hurt never pay back with wrong,
but serve one another—together be strong!

Be constant in prayer, at all times rejoice,
in all things give thanks; let God hear your voice!
Alive to the Spirit, alert to his word,
test all things, and hold to what pleases the Lord.

May God who first called, gave peace and made whole,
preserve us from fault in body and soul;
our Lord Jesus Christ keep us firm in his grace
until at his coming we meet face to face.

10.10.11.11 (55.55.65.65) Tune: LAUDATE DOMINUM;
or HOUGHTON

Scriptures: 1 Thess 5.5-24 Rom 12.5,17; 13.11-12 Eph 5.8-14 Jn 12.36 2 Cor 9.11 1 Cor 12.12-13,27 2 Thess 3.6-13 Matt 5.38-39 1 Pet 2.24; 3.8-9 Gal 5.13 Phil 4.4-5 1 Jn 4.1 Jude 24-25

Written: Poplar, 1975

First published: *Hymns for Today's Church* (Hodder & Stoughton) 1982

In a poll of inner-London clergy in the early 1970s, one strongly-expressed need was for more hymns about relationships between Christians, rather than those concerned only with our relationship with God. The pendulum soon appeared to swing the other way, but that response resulted in this basic paraphrase of just such a passage in Paul's writing. Some lines, notably the opening ones, were much chewed over in group discussion before settling on their published form. The hymn was sung first at Poplar, and at the service at Limehouse when I was Instituted as Rector—26 Oct 1976.

Light upon the River

1 Timothy 3.16
Doctrine that sings

167 GREAT THE WONDER, GREAT THE MYSTERY

Great the wonder, great the mystery
which appeared in human body:
by the Spirit vindicated,
seen by angels, heard by nations,
in this world believed in, lifted
high in clouds of heaven's glory.

Here is truth and found trustworthy:
suffering with him and dying,
with him we shall rise and triumph;
if we scorn him, he will scorn us;
faithless, we shall find him faithful
who cannot deny his glory.

One we bless, above all blessing,
Name of names, Wonder of wonders,
Power and love and breath immortal
deep in light we cannot fathom,
God beyond all earthly vision,
whom to know is all our glory.

88.88.88 trochaic Tune needed

Scriptures: 1 Tim 3.16; 6.15-16 2 Tim 2.11-13 Acts 1.9 Rom 6.5 Phil 3.10-11 Matt 10.33 Lk 12.9 Isa 9.6 Jn 1.18
Written: Cambridge, 19 Oct 1995

Woven into the text of the New Testament there are phrases from several early Christian hymns. So at least it seems to scholars who pay careful attention to the vocabulary, rhythm, style and subject of the Greek language in such places. Eph 5.14 and Phil 2.6-11 are striking examples; so, possibly, are at least three extracts from the letters to Timothy which I have used here, though not in order. Here I have returned to regular but non-rhyming verse in order to stay as close as I can to Paul's meaning, or to his quotations if such they are. This was written at 39 Castle Street; see Nos.17 and others above.

Light upon the River

1 Timothy 6.13-16
Eternal Lord and Light

168 ETERNAL LIGHT, SHINE IN MY HEART

Eternal light, shine in my heart,
eternal hope, lift up my eyes;
eternal power, be my support,
eternal wisdom, make me wise.

Eternal life, raise me from death,
eternal brightness, make me see;
eternal Spirit, give me breath,
eternal Saviour, come to me:

Until by your most costly grace,
invited by your holy word,
at last I come before your face
to know you, my eternal God

LM Tune: JACOB by Jane Marshall; FRY by Keith Landis; SARAH RACHEL by Norman Warren; MERRITT by John David Petersen; SEVEN SEAS by David Peacock; GRANBY by Roy Hopp; BEN LOMOND by Keith Landis; OMBERSLEY; or HERONGATE

Scriptures: 1 Tim 6.13-16 2 Cor 4.6 Heb 6.19 1 Pet 1.3-4 Prov 8 Jn 1.4-5; 5.21-25 Ezek 37.1-14 Rev 3.20; 22.4 Phil 3.8-10 Deut 33.27
Written: Limehouse, 1977
First published: *Hymns for Today's Church* (Hodder & Stoughton) 1982

Alcuin (properly Ealhwine) was an 8th century scholar from York who became leader of the cultural and intellectual renaissance under Charlemagne, and Abbot of Tours from 796 until his death eight years later. Among much of his surviving Latin writing is a simple prayer included in *Daily Prayer* (ed. Milner-White and Briggs, OUP 1941) on which this hymn is mainly based; it includes many echoes of the Bible, and the phrase 'your most costly grace' which we owe to Dietrich Bonhoeffer. As well as the newer tunes listed, many of which are American and written for this text, Bruce Saylor composed an anthem from his own tune, used in 1986 in the American Cathedral in Paris. The words were sung at Michael Saward's Institution as Vicar of Ealing (1978), and at Grace Episcopal Church in Anniston, Alabama, on my first Sunday in America (May 1987); it is my one text in *The Hymnal 1982* for American Anglicans. That summer it also featured in the British Hymn Society's 'Act of Praise' at Leeds, while in 1997 it broke new ground for me by appearing in the hymnal of the United Church of Christ in Japan, where in translation it had somehow acquired two more stanzas. The tune ACH BLEIB BEI UNS also looked rather different there from its western arrangements. Verse 2 line 2 is correct as above, since our spiritual blindness needs more than 'help' (as is sometimes printed). It is also useful to quote the first line in full to avoid confusion with Binney's *Eternal light, eternal light*.

2 Timothy 3.15-17
The Bible: one

169 POWERFUL IN MAKING US WISE TO SALVATION

Powerful in making us wise to salvation,
witness to faith in Christ Jesus the Word;
breathed out for all by the life-giving Father:
these are the Scriptures, and thus speaks the Lord.

Hammer for action and compass for travel,
map in the desert and lamp in the dark;
teaching, rebuking, correcting and training:
these are the Scriptures, and this is their work.

Prophecy, history, song and commandment,
gospel and letter and dream from on high,
words of the wise who were steered by the Spirit:
these are the Scriptures; on these we rely.

Gift for God's servants to fit them completely,
fully equipping to walk in his ways;
guide to good work and effective believing:
these are the Scriptures: for these we give praise.

11.10.11.10 dactylic Tune: YVONNE by Norman Warren; LIVING WORD by Simon Beckley; GUDS ORD by Donald Hustad; HOLIFIELD by Agnes Tang; EPIPHANY HYMN; or LIEBSTER IMMANUEL

Scriptures: 2 Tim 3.15-17 Jn 1.14 Rev 19.13 Jer 23.29 Psa 119.105 Eccles 12.11 2 Pet 1.21 Deut 8.6

Written: Poplar and Limehouse, 1974 and 1977

First published: *Songs of Worship* (Scripture Union) 1980

In writing to Timothy about the Hebrew Scriptures, the apostle Paul says that they are 'able (Gk *dunamena*) to make you wise for salvation through faith in Jesus Christ'. This was the starting point for a hymn about the Bible, drafted in response to a Scripture Union request: see No.102. If such things are true of the Old Testament, then we may surely apply them to the complete volume; each genre of writing (as sketched out in verse 3) is equally the inspired word, as the Church of England's foundation documents assert. The hymn was revised at Limehouse in time for the SU book, and again in 1994 in response to comments on v. 2 l.1 and v.3 l. 3. Some unauthorised changes have been made on both sides of the Atlantic; this is now the authentic version. It was sung at the 'Islington Conference' in central London in 1977 and again in 1981. It has been richly supplied with tunes, including one which Don Hustad played to us on a visit to Oakley in 1991, before it appeared in print.

Light upon the River

2 Timothy 3.16
The Bible: two

170 WHEN AT FIRST THE WORD WAS SPOKEN

When at first the word was spoken
God's good Spirit gave it voice,
breathed it out through faithful servants,
named and called by sovereign choice.

When the word was heard and written,
copied by each ready scribe,
sacred text became the treasure
prized by every Hebrew tribe.

When the word was learned and pondered
priest and prophet found its power,
as the Spirit winged its message
for a nation's crisis hour.

When the word was scorned and flouted,
God's agreement thrown aside,
Jesus Christ fulfilled its purpose,
spoke and suffered, lived and died.

When the word was sown and planted
by the friends the Master chose,
news of hope reached every people:
'For our sins he died, and rose!'

When the word is preached among us,
spoken loud and clear today,
Judge and Saviour, help us listen,
hear, repent, believe, obey!

87.87 Tune: KIEV or MARCHING

Scriptures: 2 Tim 3.16 Ex 3.1-17 Isa 6.8ff Jer 1.4-10; 45 Ezek 3.1-9 Ezra 7.10 Matt 5.17 Mk 4.1-2 Lk 24.44-49 Acts 8.4; 10.33

Written: Barrow in Furness, 1967

The excuse for one more hymn about the Bible is that relatively few speak of obeying the word of God. This one began life in Barrow, being sung there as 'When God's word at first was spoken'; in that form it was accepted for one hymnal that never appeared. Since then it has been much revised in the interests of colour, inclusiveness and fluency (1979, 1987, 1998) and, I hope, improved.

Light upon the River

Hebrews 4.12-13
The Bible: three

171 HOW SURE THE SCRIPTURES ARE

How sure the Scriptures are!
God's vital, urgent word,
as true as steel, and far
more sharp than any sword.
    So deep and fine
    at his control
    they pierce where soul
    and spirit join.

They test each human thought
refining like a fire;
they measure what we ought
to do and to desire.
    For God knows all;
    exposed it lies
    before his eyes
    to whom we call.

Let those who hear his voice
confronting them today
reject the tempting choice
of doubting or delay.
    For God speaks still;
    his word is clear
    so let us hear
    and do his will.

6666.4444 Tune: DARWALL'S 148th

Scriptures: Heb 3.7,15; 4.7,12-13 Psa 95.7-8 Phil 2.13

Written: Poplar, 1976

First published: *Hymns for Today's Church* (Hodder & Stoughton) 1982

Though based on a different Epistle, this hymn text has the same subject as the two previous ones, and arose from the same situation as No.169 etc. Helen Hazlewood, a member of St Matthias' Poplar until her wedding there to David in 1974, was a Scripture Union editor and had passed on a request for more 'Bible' hymns. Among early adjustments was a re-drafted opening line, which now clearly sets the agenda for what follows. Early appearances included the Limehouse Pathfinders' 3rd Birthday service (23 Sep 1979), All Souls' Langham Place Supplementary Hymn Book (1980), and the Islington Conference in 1981. DARWALL'S 148th is more suitable than most tunes, as the flow of the words is designed to match it; if this is already over-subscribed, the invitation to composers is again open.

Light upon the River

Hebrews 4.14-16
Christ our High Priest

172 SINCE OUR GREAT HIGH PRIEST, CHRIST JESUS

Since our great High Priest, Christ Jesus
bears the name above all names,
reigning Son of God, surpassing
other titles, powers and claims -
    since to heaven our Lord has passed,
    let us hold our witness fast!

Since we have a Priest who suffered,
knowing weakness, tears and pain,
who like us was tried and tempted,
unlike us, without a stain -
    Since he shared our lowly place,
    let us boldly seek his grace.

Sacrifice and suffering over,
now he sits at God's right hand,
crowned with praise, no more an outcast,
his pre-eminence long-planned;
    such a great High Priest we have,
    strong to help, supreme to save.

Love's example, hope's attraction,
faith's beginning and its end,
pioneer of our salvation,
mighty advocate and friend;
    Jesus, high in glory raised,
    our ascended Lord be praised!

87.87.77 Tune: OUR GREAT HIGH PRIEST by Norman Warren;
or ALL SAINTS

Scriptures: Heb 1.3; 4.14-16; 6.18-20; 7.25; 12.2 Phil 2.9 Mk 1.12-13; 14.32-39 1 Pet 2.22 1 Jn 2.1; 3.4 Col 1.18 Eph 4.10

Written: Peckham, 1971

First published: *Psalm Praise* (Falcon) 1973

This was one of my Ascension commitments on the *Psalm Praise* team: see No.74. Originally it had three stanzas; following comments by the group I rewrote the third verse and added a fourth. It was sung first on Ascension Day 1973 (31 May) at our evening Communion Service at St Matthias' Poplar.

Light upon the River

Hebrews 11
Faith's portrait gallery: one

173 STRONG IN CHRIST, OUR GREAT SALVATION

Strong in Christ, our great salvation,
called to be his new creation,
Christians, sing in celebration,
living by our faith.
Saints of old were led and guarded,
famous names or unrecorded
all alike in God rewarded,
living by their faith.
   All who love and fear him
   learn by faith to hear him;
   in distress his name confess,
   believing it an honour to be near him.
All those choosing this world's bruising
know that in Christ they're never losing,
gaining more than they're refusing,
living by their faith.

Abraham inspired a nation,
searching for a sure foundation;
made his God his destination,
living by his faith.
Moses left his power and pleasure,
Egypt's wealth that none could measure,
finding God a greater treasure,
living by his faith.
   Many more were hated,
   driven out, ill-treated;
   facing death, they kept the faith
   and sang about the glory that awaited.
No derision, pain or prison,
ever destroyed their heavenly vision;
we with them say 'Christ is risen!',
living by our faith.

Tune: MEN OF HARLECH

Scriptures: Hebrews 11; 12.1-3 2 Cor 5.17 Hab 2.4 Rom 8.18 Phil 3.7-11 Gen 12.1-9 Ex 2-4 Acts 7.1-38 1 Cor 15.20

Written: Peckham, May 1971

First published: *Church Family Worship* (Hodder & Stoughton) 1986

This text began as a question, was seen as a challenge, and remains a problem. It can be dangerous to ask a writer if there are any Christian words to a particular tune; Michael Lumgair (at that time a Curate in Attenborough, Notts) asked me this about a famous Welsh song, and this was the result. It seemed to fit the strength of mood in Hebrews 11, which gives prominence to Abraham and Moses but also mentions the 'noble army of martyrs', which grows terribly day by day, most of whom remain unknown on earth. It was sung at Limehouse in 1977 (20 Nov), and in 1980 appeared in print in the *Eltham College Hymn Book* and in *Pathfinder News*. Finally in 1998, against the odds, its language was made gender-inclusive. Some Welsh patriots may feel it does disservice to a national song; at the other end of the scale, it may stir memories of the Scout classic about Woad whose lines stick in the memory: 'Romans came across the channel, all dressed up in tin and flannel...' But for those who can get away with it, here is the answer to Michael's question: there are now.

Light upon the River

Hebrews 11
Faith's portrait gallery: two

174 GIVE PRAISE FOR FAMOUS MEN

Give praise for famous men
from history's open page,
by whom our God unfolds his plan
for each succeeding age.

Some wore a kingdom's crown
and made themselves a name;
some by God's word
   brought kingdoms down
and with his judgement came.

Some fashioned wisest laws
to guard our liberty;
some champions of a lonely cause
set slaves and prisoners free.

Some gave their land its songs
of love and hope and faith;
some fought against malignant wrongs
unceasingly till death.

Some preached to courts and kings
a Saviour's sovereign claim;
some paid the price his service brings
through torture, blood and flame.

Let us pursue the prize
and praise their deeds and words;
the life is theirs that never dies,
the glory is their Lord's

SM Tune: VENICE; or ST ETHELWALD

Scriptures: Heb 11 2 Sam 8.13 Isa 6.8ff Jer 1.9-10 Ezek 3.1-9
2 Sam 12.1-14; 23.1 1 Kgs 4.32; 17.1; 18.16-21; 21.17-29
2 Kgs 1.15-17 Dan 2.24-47; 3.8-30; 5.13-31; 6 Mk 6.14-29 Acts 26

Written: Limehouse, 1977

First published: *Hymns for Today's Church* (Hodder & Stoughton) 1982

Unlike the previous and following texts 173 and 175, this one proved resistant to attempts to remove the limitations imposed by its first line. The clue is a purple passage from the book Ecclesiasticus, ch 44, which sometimes features at stately memorial services. I began with that in mind, recalling also the many possible illustrations for every stanza of which the Bible texts above are only a sample, and by no means rule out other historical figures, or contemporary ones. The Islington Conference featured it in 1979, and the *Eltham College Hymn Book* in 1980. My best attempt to rephrase verse one ran 'Give praise for all the saints from history's open page, the church's God-sent militants...'; this got no further than an unimpressed Michael Perry. So my only 'improvement' on the Apocrypha is to transfer the 'praise' at the beginning and end from the 'famous men' to God who sent them.

Hebrews 12.1-2
Eyes fixed on Jesus

175 FRIENDS OF GOD WHOSE FAITH ABOUNDED

Friends of God whose faith abounded
have their victories told aloud;
by such witnesses surrounded,
Christ's unseen, uncounted crowd,
    we take up the unfinished race,
    chosen, trained, inspired by grace.

Confident and persevering,
firmly let us run to win,
stripped of all the interfering
rags and shreds of stubborn sin;
    still on Jesus fix our eyes,
    faith's foundation and its prize.

Jesus, for the joy before him
made a crown of thorns his own,
seated now where we adore him,
high upon his Father's throne;
    see the shame which he endured,
    share the triumph he secured.

87.87.77 Tune: ST LEONARD

Scriptures: Heb 12.1-2 Jas 2.23 Rev 7.9 1 Cor 9.24-27 2 Tim 4.6-8 Phil 3.12-14 Matt 27.29 Mk 15.17 Jn 19.1,5

Written: Poplar, 1975

First published: *Songs of Worship* (Scripture Union) 1980; as *Men of God whose faith abounded*. Though this is rooted in Hebrews 12, we cannot understand 'Therefore...' without first hearing chapter 11; many of the 'victories' were won through torture and death rather than by avoiding such things. I wrote it before 'men' became almost unusable as referring to both sexes; in 1987 I grasped the nettle of the first word and settled on the simplest possible change, remembering Abraham, 'God's friend'. He features strongly in Hebrews 11; by grace and in faith, all Christian believers are his children.

Light upon the River

Hebrews 13.8
Yesterday, today, for ever

176 GOD OF ALL HUMAN HISTORY

God of all human history,
of time long fled and faded,
yours is the secret mastery
by which the years are guided;
King of unchanging glory
from ages unrecorded.

God of the hidden future
unfolding life for ever,
hope of each ransomed creature
as time speeds ever faster:
raise us to our full stature
in Christ, our one Redeemer!

God of this present moment
requiring our decision,
now is the hour of judgement
for ruin or salvation:
grant us complete commitment
to your most urgent mission!

77.77.77 (distinctive) Tune: UNFOLDING by Noël Tredinnick

Scriptures: Heb 13.8 Psa 21.4; 90.1-2; 133.3 2 Tim 1.10 Eph 4.13-15 Jn 12.31 2 Cor 6.2

Written: Gorsley, nr Ross on Wye, April 1978

While pondering the wonder of God's hand on past, present and future, I wrote these verses at 'Sunnyside', home of Patrick and Beryl Goodland. Pat was the Baptist minister in Gorsley, where the 'Jubilate' words group had some days of intensive work on *Hymns for Today's Church*. The syllable count may suggest a familiar metre, but the rhythm needs special treatment such as Noël Tredinnick's new tune provides. The text appeared in the 1980 supplement at All Souls' Langham Place, where Noël became Music Director in 1971; eventually in 1998 it was accepted for publication in a hymnal.

James 5.1-6
Our planet earth; an early green hymn

177 LORD, SHOW US HOW TO LIVE

Lord, show us how to live
set free from waste or greed,
content with what you give,
concerned for all in need.

Our choking seas and soil,
our fields diseased and sore -
what we so quickly spoil
you only can restore.

But we were brought to birth
creation to subdue,
to tend your teeming earth,
co-workers, Lord, with you.

By learning how to share,
your faithfulness we prove;
by discipline and care
our lives reflect your love.

O Father, come to heal
where your good gifts decay;
O Spirit, give us zeal,
O Saviour, show the way!

Our shame is to destroy
or leave your work undone;
our duty and our joy
to make your goodness known.

66.66 Tune: ST CECILIA ; or GRIDLEY

Scriptures: Jas 1.17-18; 5.1-6 Gen 1.28; 2.15; 3.17-19; 9.1-7 Phil 4.10-11 Psa 145.7 Rom 2.4
Written: Poplar, March 1976

Even the visible needs of planet earth are not met by charities, appeals, emergency funds, pressure groups or governments. We still need all these; but this text expresses a conviction that although God has shown us how to live, we must also show a healthy sense of our own ignorance (as well as failure), our dependence on God (as well as action) and reverence for God (as well as for life). And that we have all been far too slow to simplify our lifestyles. 'Our duty and our joy' in the penultimate line echoes a prayer from Holy Communion; that service also reminds us how God values his creation.

Light upon the River

James 5.13-16
Health and healing

178 GOD OF HOPE AND LORD OF HEALING

God of hope and Lord of healing, we come to you in prayer;
in our living, in our dying, you promise to be there.
For the weak we ask your courage, and your patience for the strong;
stay with those whose pain is sharpest and those enduring long:
and provide for all the weary your precious gift of sleep;
with the glad let us be joyful, and weep with those who weep.

By the grace of your forgiveness, by virtue of your word,
by the sacrament which brings us the comfort of our Lord;
by the life he freely gave us, and the cross to which he came,
by the glory of his kingdom, the power of his name:
come to meet your praying people, be with us as we kneel;
come to help us, God our Saviour, for you alone can heal.

14.14.15.14.14.14 Tune: THAXTED

Scriptures: Jas 5.13-16 Rom 12.15; 15.13 Psa 103.1-4; 107.20; 127.2 2 Cor 1.3-4 Matt 6.13 Ex 15.26

Written: Limehouse, 1977

Most Christians feel strongly about healing; what we believe about it affects most of us regularly. In this text I have put some of my own understanding of the Bible's teaching, in days when it is easy to overbalance into either unrealistic credulity or unbelieving scepticism. It has a chequered history, starting with the invitation from *Jubilate* musicians to find new words to THAXTED, joined with the need for contemporary hymns on this theme. Its original three stanzas were reduced to two; after much group discussion, revision, rejection and reinstatement it failed to reach the final list. Michael Perry's justly acclaimed *O God beyond all praising* proved a far better match for the music, and Mervyn Horder's new tune did not seem quite right. For some, the reference to the sacrament may seem strange; for others, entirely natural. If to misuse the Holy Communion may damage our health (1 Cor 11.30) it need not surprise us if to partake in true penitence and faith should enhance it.

Light upon the River

1 Peter 1.2
Sovereign God: Father, Son and Holy Spirit

179 IN GOD THE FATHER'S PLAN

In God the Father's plan
his children are secure;
the work he once began
is certain to endure.
    All-sovereign King by whom we live,
    all thanks we give, all praises bring.

The living Lord who died
has sprinkled with his blood,
redeemed and purified
his church to serve her God.
    Lord Jesus Christ, our world you shared,
    our heaven prepared, supreme High Priest!

The Spirit's power sustains
this royal, priestly race;
by him the Saviour reigns,
through him we learn God's grace.
    Most holy One, your gifts equip
    Christ's fellowship, neglecting none.

To God the Father's throne
eternal songs we raise:
all praise to God the Son;
to God the Spirit, praise!
    We sing again, all glory be.
    great Trinity, to you: Amen!

66.66.88 (6666.4444) Tune: TERRYL by Jeffrey Rickard; or CROFT'S 136th

Scriptures: 1 Pet 1.2; 2.4-5 Phil 1.6 Eph 5.25-27 Heb 3.1   1 Cor 12.4-7
Written: Limehouse, 1977

When Isaac Watts published his *Psalms of David* in 1719, he ended his epoch-making collection with a set of Doxologies—single stanzas ascribing glory to God the Holy Trinity, in varied metres to match his Psalm versions. The last of them begins 'To God the Father's throne...'; I could not recall ever singing it, or many of the others. But these are noble lines which formed the basis of verse 4 above, then growing backwards into this full text, with considerable help from Peter's first Epistle. While looking for fresh language in which to praise God, as Watts notably did, we cannot wholly avoid the concept of kingly, omnipotent rule which undergirds the assurance and security of the people of God. As with most hymns in this metre, the words need to be sung through before a tune is chosen.

Light upon the River

1 Peter 2.9-10

Chosen people, royal priesthood, holy nation

180 IF GOD HAS CHOSEN A NATION

If God has chosen a nation
in his purposes of love,
and the only ones who are native sons
are those born from above:

If God has chosen a priesthood
for the service of the King,
and if we believe, we may all receive
the same commissioning:

If God has chosen a people
to belong to him by grace,
and if faith alone makes us all his own,
among his holy race:

Then we can be God's possession,
in the priesthood we may share,
being called from night to his Son's clear light
God's glories we'll declare.

8.7.10.6.D Tune: SHOREHAM by Michael Baughen

Scriptures: 1 Peter 1.3,23; 2.9-10 Ex 19.1-6 Jn 3.3-8 Rom 4.16

Written: Peckham, 1970

First published: *Psalm Praise* (Falcon) 1973

After beginning life as a hymn suggested by 1 Peter 2.9-10, this single-sentence text reached its later form during our early work on *Psalm Praise*. On finding that there was room for items other than straightforward paraphrases I submitted these verses, which after some revision were duly accepted as 'A Psalm of Commitment' alongside Michael Baughen's new 'double' tune. I had originally based the unusual rhythm on a 3rd-line phrase, 'for Jesus Christ, once sacrificed'; eventually the words went while the metre stayed. In Scripture, 'sons' are not only male; for Peter, the 'priesthood' is not only clergy.

Light upon the River

1 Peter 2.21-25
Christ our unique sin-bearer and nonviolent example

181 TO THIS WE HAVE BEEN CALLED

To this we have been called,
for Christ has suffered this for us
and spelled a pattern out for us
that we should follow in his steps.

For he did nothing wrong;
he spoke no lie; through curse and pain
he gave no threats nor curses back,
but trusted in the righteous Judge.

He took our sins himself
in his own body on the cross,
that we should end our life to sins
and start a life to righteousness.

His wounds have made us whole;
like sheep we strayed, but we have now
turned back to him who guards our souls,
our Leader, Rescuer and Guide.

6888 Tune: OUR CALLING by Norman Warren

Scriptures: 1 Pet 2.21-25; 3.13-18 Isa 53.7-9 Matt 5.38-48; 16.24-26; 26.52 Lk 6.27-38

Written: Peckham, 1970

First published: *Psalm Praise* (Falcon) 1973

We are better at making exceptions to the nonviolence of Jesus than we are at applying it. Not so Simon Peter, who was disarmed by his Master before watching the events he was later to write about. For him as for Paul, the meaning of the cross is not exhausted by its primary purpose of redemption; here Jesus is both Saviour and Example, Propitiation and Pattern. The hymn is a kind of twin to its predecessor above; both were written at the same place, around the same time, from the same Epistle and in the same freer style of the *Psalm Praise* team. But this one stays closer to the New Testament text than No.180; we sang it at St Matthias' Poplar for our 6.30 Communion service on 25 March 1973, and with Norman Warren's new tune it appeared in the book as a 'Passiontide Psalm'. The final line aims to represent the functions of the 'Shepherd and Bishop of your souls'.

Light upon the River

1 Peter 2.21-25
Strangest victory

182 IN SILENT PAIN THE ETERNAL SON

In silent pain the eternal Son
hangs derelict and still:
in darkened day his work is done;
fulfilled, his Father's will.
   Uplifted for the world to see
   he hangs in strangest victory,
   for in his body on the tree
he carries all our ill.

He died that we might die to sin
and live for righteousness;
the earth was stained, to make us clean
and bring us into peace.
   For peace he came, and met its cost;
   himself he gave, to save the lost;
   he loved us to the uttermost
and paid for our release.

For strife he came, to bring a sword,
the truth to end all lies,
to rule in us, our patient Lord,
until all evil dies:
   for in his hand he holds the stars;
   his voice shall speak to end our wars,
   and those who love him see his scars
and look into his eyes.

86.86.8886 Tune: REALITY by John Bell;
or IN SILENT PAIN by David Peacock

Scriptures: 1 Pet 2.21-25; 3.18 Isa 53.7 1 Jn 1.1-3,7 Jn 3.14-15; 6.38; 13.1; 19.30 Matt 10.34; 20.28; 27.45-50 Rom 5.1 Col 1.20 Rev 1.7,15-16; 2.1; 22.4 Lk 24.38
Written: Oakley, April 1989 and July 1990
First published: *Worship Songs Ancient and Modern* (Canterbury Press Norwich) 1992

Do we really need them?' asked Hymn Society Chairman Alan Luff at a Westminster Abbey 'Come and Sing' in May 1989, as he introduced some new hymns. I had written this in the previous month, and saw the force of his question, as ever. This one has a double origin; at the 'Jubilate' Annual Meeting the day before the Abbey event, Michael Saward had commented how few modern hymns concerned the atonement. Themes of the day were Christ's reign, triumph, majesty, power... but rarely his cross; to find 20th century items for Good Friday he had to go back to fifty year old CSSM choruses. I returned to our new home at Oakley and worked on a first version of this text; six CM stanzas set to BANGOR. A year later, Paul Wigmore was also searching for Passiontide hymns for a new A & M book, and one tune he wanted to use was John Bell's REALITY. I redrafted my earlier lines for the new demands of rhyme and rhythm. This version was accepted; a 1990 treatment of the theme taken 20 years before in No.181. David Peacock's tune came later in *Hymns for the People*.

Light upon the River

1 Peter 5.6-11
Songs of Praise

183 WHEN WE ARE DOWN YOU RAISE US UP

When we are down you raise us up,
when we are weak you make us strong;
when we are lost you bring us hope,
our Strength, our Saviour and our Song:
to God be glory all our days!

When we are bound you set us free,
when we are wrong you put us right;
when we are blind you let us see
our world's Redeemer and our Light:
in Christ we come with songs of praise!

88.88.8 Tune: SONGS OF PRAISE by Robert Prizeman

Scriptures: 1 Peter 5.6,10,11 Job 22.29 2 Cor 7.6; 12.9-10 Isa 12.2; 40.29-31 Lk 4.18 Psa 19.14 Prov 23.11

Written: Oakley, 10 August 1990

First published: *Worship Songs Ancient and Modern* (Canterbury Press Norwich) 1992

In unplanned juxtaposition, this text was written around the same time as the last one; they were required for the same purpose, draw on the same Epistle, and appeared together in the same book. In August 1990 I heard from Robert Prizeman, composer of the BBC TV *Songs of Praise* signature tune, who wanted to adapt a text of mine to his music. As the one in question already had seven specially composed tunes, and I was not keen to change verses which in any case expressed a rather different mood, I offered instead to write some new words. Robert sent me the melody line and a tape from the programme; this two-stanza song was the result, after some minor adjustments had been agreed. It was included when the book (as above) was launched at St Margaret's Westminster in May 1992, and on the corresponding tape by the St Alban's Cathedral Singers. With different accompaniment (a village church organ) it also proved singable in Thrandeston, Wortham, and other Suffolk settings. The words start in a low-key singalong style, work through some Biblical and musical ups and downs towards a clear Christian acclamation, and end with the 'songs of praise' of the programme's title. One irony was that, as I was originally assured and the introduction at Westminster asserted, 'everyone will know the tune'. The only exception seemed to be me, as I had never heard it before.

Light upon the River

2 Peter 1. 1-19

A taste of glory; transformation and transfiguration

184 COME, PRAISE THE NAME OF JESUS

Come, praise the name of Jesus
for all his gracious powers,
our only God and Saviour
who makes his goodness ours;
he calls us to his kingdom,
the Lord of life and death,
to see his face in glory
and know him now by faith.

His virtue and his wisdom,
endurance, self-control,
his godliness and kindness,
his love which crowns them all:
this is his royal nature
that we are called to share,
his robe of perfect beauty
that we are given to wear.

To see his shining splendour
in every sunless place
where Christ, the light of nations,
appears in truth and grace:
transfigured by his likeness
we make the vision known,
reflecting in our faces
the radiance of his own.

The King of grace inspires us
to love him more and more,
to grasp our hope more firmly
and make our calling sure;
Christ Jesus, Lord and Saviour,
to this dark world you came,
and for the dawn of heaven
we praise your holy name.

76.76.D Tune: COME PRAISE THE NAME by Stephen James;
or TEDCRICK by Agnes Tang

Scriptures: 2 Pet 1.1-19; 3.18 Tit 2.13 Rom 13.14; 14.9 Col 3.9-14 Matt 17.1-8 Mk 9.2-8 Lk 2.32;9.28-36 Jn 1.4-5,14-18; 3.19; 12.46 2 Cor 3.18 1 Jn 3.2-3

Written: Limehouse, 1977

First published: *Hymns for Today's Church* (Hodder & Stoughton) 1982

The transfiguration of Christ is being rediscovered, it seems, by hymnwriters among others: see No.91. This text paraphrases the opening of 2 Peter where it is seen as both authentic history ('we saw...we heard...we were with him') and spiritual reality ('partakers of the divine nature'). Several tunes have been used; my own favourites are those named above. Stephen James' music was used at Limehouse and at St Helen's Bishopsgate; that from Agnes Tang, organist at Christ Church Old Kent Road, came later. MORNING LIGHT was used for the Morning Service on BBC Radio 4 on 18 April 1993, the Sunday after Easter, broadcast from Mansfield Road Baptist Church, Nottingham. The words were mine; the music was played by Audrey Axford, the church organist, who is my sister.

Light upon the River

2 Peter 1.21
Men spoke from God

185 WHEN HOLY MEN OF OLD ANNOUNCED THE WILL OF GOD TO MAN

When holy men of old announced the will of God to man
they spoke of sin and sacrifice and how the world began,
but Jesus Christ the Saviour was the centre of the plan
   by the promise of his word.
      God has given us a Saviour; all the world sing Hallelujah!
      God has given us a Saviour, and his name is Jesus Christ.

When Christ was born in Bethlehem no crowds were there to see;
the love of God had brought him down from heaven for you and me;
from guilt and greed and selfishness he came to set us free,
   by the promise of his word.   *God has given us...*

The Scriptures that were written, Jesus said he would fulfil;
he healed the sick and stilled the storm and taught his Father's will;
he met the power of evil and remained unbeaten still
   by the promise of his word.   *God has given us...*

When Christ was led to Calvary, they killed God's only Son,
and he became the Sacrifice for sin, though he had none;
he took the Father's punishment for all that we had done
   by the promise of his word.   *God has given us...*

When Christ on Easter morning from the graveyard rose again
the power of God was shown on earth, and heaven sang Amen;
today the life may come to us that came to Jesus then
   by the promise of his word.   *God has given us...*

Tune: BATTLE HYMN OF THE REPUBLIC

Scriptures: 2 Pet 1.21 Matt 2.1; 8.14-27 Jn 6.38 Lk 4.21; 23.33; 24.1-8 Heb 9.26; 10.12 Isa 53.4-6 Rom 8.11

Written: Barrow in Furness, August 1965

This opening line from 1965, one of the first hymn texts I wrote, may not pass muster today. One of several revisions began 'God's messengers of long ago...', but after trying various emendations I have left it largely as it was first sung at St Mark's Barrow on 5 Sept 1965. The event was 'The Greatest Story Ever Told: Jesus Christ Today', a youth service planned and led by my fellow-curate David Griffiths. He had asked me to write some words for the tune he wanted to include, in days when little else suitable existed for that rousing music. It was used for a while in Barrow and elsewhere; David introduced it at the national Pathfinder Rally (for 11s to 14s) in Westminster Central Hall. In those days verse 2 line 2 ran 'from sin and spite and selfishness...', and the chorus lacked 'all the world sing Hallelujah'. The Scriptures used above are only a sample of the well-known Gospel stories referred to; it is located under 2 Peter for its first line only. The hymn had a late flowering in the Philippines, thanks again to the near-veteran but still youthful missionary David Griffiths, serving (with his wife June, another former Barrow colleague) with the Overseas Missionary Fellowship: OMF International. He wanted to use it at a youth event in Manila; the text, with annotations, reached him just in time. One suggestion for those still singing it would be to take verse 4 at a slower and more thoughtful pace.

1 John 1.5-7
God is light: walk in light

186 TRUE LIGHT, BLAZING IN THE DARKEST PLACE

True light, blazing in the darkest place;
true light, shining out from Jesus' face:
true light, chasing all the dark away;
true light, burning in our hearts today:
True light, shadows cannot make it dim;
God is light: darkness cannot hide from him.
So let us walk in his clear shining by day and night:
in Christ we live in light.

Irregular Tune: A GAELIC BLESSING by John Rutter

Scriptures: 1 Jn 1.5-7; 2.8 Gen 1.3-5 2 Cor 4.6 Jn 1.5,9; 8.12; 9.5; 12.35-36,46 Lk 24.32 Acts 26.18 Jas 1.17 Psa 27.1; 139.11-12 Eph 5.8,14 1 Pet 2.9

Written: Peckham, 21 Sept 1996

'Deep peace of the running wave to you'; I had known that ancient Celtic prayer since boyhood. Its imagery and rhythm made an impact then, and still do. The flowing air, quiet earth, shining stars and gentle night have all had special appeal along the Suffolk lanes from 1989 to 1995. Not all are similarly moved; one year on from Oakley, in Sept 1996, Christopher Hayward asked for a revision of the 'blessing' for a choir piece at St Andrew the Great Cambridge. But to 'revise' would surely be to wreck it; I would have to hear John Rutter's music afresh and see if a different text was conceivable. It seemed to need two long monosyllables corresponding to 'Deep peace'; Biblical roots; and rhyme—if I was not to close each line with the same words, as in 'to you'. I turned to the first Letter of John, starting a draft 'We know...' which did not rhyme well and sounded too self-satisfied. Should there be a second, balancing stanza? No, said Chris; one was enough. With further critical help from Marjorie, this was the eventual result, as completed in Peckham and sung at Cambridge.

Light upon the River

Revelation 1.4-20
Easter song of praise: Exultet!

187 EXULT, CREATION ROUND GOD'S THRONE

Exult, creation round God's throne!
All heaven, rejoice! All angels, sing!
Salvation's trumpet sound aloud
for Jesus Christ, our risen King.

Exult, O earth, in radiant hope;
in Christ's majestic splendour shine!
The Lord is here, the victory won,
the darkness drowned in light divine.

Exult, all Christians, one in praise
with our Jerusalem above!
This roof shall ring with Easter songs
that echo Christ's redeeming love.

Exult in God, pure well of truth;
in Christ, fresh Fountainhead of grace;
in Spirit, flowing stream of life,
eternal joy our hearts embrace.

LM Tune: WINTERTON by Mervyn Horder;
FENNY STRATFORD by Paul Edwards; or GONFALON ROYAL

Scriptures: Rev 1.4-20; 4.2-8; 5.11-14; 11.15; 21.2 Psa 103.20-21; 148.1-2 1 Cor 15.54-57 Gal 4.26 Isa 12; 35.10 Jn 4.10-14; 7.37-39
Written: Limehouse, 9 July 1987
First published: *Come, Rejoice* (Marshall Pickering / Hope) 1989

A letter from Michael Perry in 1987 enclosed the text of this ancient hymn, translated from the Latin into rhythmic English prose; a fully metrical version could be useful, he suggested. I had at that time not written any hymns for some three years; but thus spurred on, I worked at it from around 11.30 to noon that day. My first draft had three stanzas; 'Exult' seemed a more striking opening than 'Rejoice', and the 'Jerusalem above...which is the mother of us all' (Gal 4.26) more appropriate than 'Mother Church' in the version in front of me. In March, Michael sent Mervyn Horder some texts in search of tunes; Mervyn provided WINTERTON, saying it needed four verses. So I added a doxology and adjusted the rest; Paul Edwards then came up with FENNY STRATFORD, and enthusiasts for this tune considered three verses quite enough! Paul's tune was published (and recorded) first, starting on top E (for choirs) or D (for the rest of us). My climactic verse has been either labelled optional, or omitted. Since then, other versions have appeared as the Canticle has been revived in Easter liturgies.

Light upon the River

Revelation 1.5-6
First, and Last, and Only One

188 FIRST AND BEST BELOVED

First and Best-beloved,
Source and Fountain-head;
eldest child of Mary,
Firstborn from the dead:
>you have taken on the worst;
>take us now, to put you first.

Last of priests and prophets,
wiser than the wise,
Gift beyond all others,
mercy's final Prize:
>footsore Stranger, now our Friend,
>stand for us at journey's end.

Only Son and Saviour,
lonely, dying Lord,
name of love unrivalled,
treasure unexplored;
>sole Resource for humankind,
>form in us your single mind.

Ending and Beginning,
making all things new,
all our past and future
find their point in you:
>Amen! at your feet we fall,
>sovereign Christ, our All-in-all!

65.65.77 Tune: ORMESBY by Mervyn Horder;
or SUMMERVILLE by Bob Moore

Scriptures: Rev 1.5-6,17-18; 2.8; 3.14 Lk 2.7,23 Rom 8.29 Col 1.15-19 Heb 5.1-10 Mk 6.4 Acts 3.17-26 Jn 3.16-18; 4.6,19; 15.15 Phil 2.2,5; 3.14 Eph 1.10

Written: Limehouse, 1984

First published: *NewSong* (Hope Publishing, USA) Jan 1994

Brian Wren's hymn on the Transfiguration *Christ upon the mountain peak* has the line 'First and Last and only One'. Pondering these three Biblical concepts or roles of Christ I wrote five verses in 1983 starting 'Best-beloved and first Begotten', to explore the priority, finality and uniqueness of Jesus Christ—whose actual name was held back until the final stanza. Feeling it to be a bit wordy, I then aimed at a briefer version and produced this text. I kept both on file; this one received more severe treatment from Michael Perry, but since it attracted two tunes and a publisher, it replaced its predecessor. In 1988 Mervyn Horder first asked to see some of my unpublished texts, and this attracted his tune (19 Oct) for which I later wrote Nos.77 and 154. Brian Wren picked up these words without knowing what prompted them, and with his notes and Bob Moore's tune included them in his American periodical.

Light upon the River

Revelation 1.10,18
Sunday morning song

189 IT WAS ON SUNDAY MORNING

It was on Sunday morning
that the great King of glory
who had been dead and buried
rose to life again:

So on this Sunday morning
we will sing to the Saviour;
he's alive now for ever -
Jesus Christ our Lord!

777.5 (distinctive) Tune: HE CAN BREAK EVERY FETTER by Philip E Jessop

Scriptures: Rev 1.10,18 Psa 118.22-24 Matt 28.1 Mk 16.2 Lk 24.1 Jn 20.1,19 Acts 20.7 1 Cor 16.2

Written: Peckham, 1969

The Tustin Estate beside the Old Kent Road in SE London is dominated by three tower blocks and includes shops, a community hall, and Pilgrim's Way Primary School where Timothy and Jonathan started during my time as Curate at Christ Church. To extend our children's work, Miriam Davis and I (see also No.84) began 'The Tustin Sunday Morning Club' in the hall; after clearing up the debris of the previous night's celebrations, we started each Sunday with this theme song. The tune was No.48 in *CSSM Choruses* (1921; subsequently, *Scripture Union Choruses*), *He can break every fetter*. It came, appropriately, from 'Pilgrim Choruses' (Pickering and Inglis); a rousing song but short on information. My text aimed to convey something to remember about Christ, and why we were there at all.

Revelation 4-5
Glory in Excelsis: one

190 ALL GLORY BE TO GOD ON HIGH

All glory be to God on high;
upon this earth his peace be given!
we bless and celebrate your name
for your great glory, God of heaven:
   our thanks in festival we bring,
   almighty Father, God and King!

O Lord of love and Lamb of God,
O Christ, the Father's only Son,
you take away a world of sin:
have mercy from your Father's throne:
   at God's right hand his reign you share;
   accept our praise, receive our prayer.

For you alone, the Holy One,
you are the Lord, Most High alone;
one with the Holy Spirit's life,
with all the Father's glory one:
   as all your church her prayer outpours,
   Lord Jesus Christ, all praise be yours!

88.88.88 Tune: FARMBOROUGH

Scriptures: Rev 4-5 Lk 2.14 Dan 2.19 Jn 1.18,29,36 Heb 1.3; 8.1; 10.12; 12.2 Acts 7.48

Written: Poplar, 1975

In Neil and Willoughby's *The Tutorial Prayer Book* (Church Book Room Press, 1912, 1959) a plea was expressed for more flexibility in singing 'Glory be to God on high', the ancient Biblically-based canticle *Gloria in Excelsis* which triumphantly concludes the Communion service in the Book of Common Prayer. 'It is, perhaps, a matter for regret that no single musical setting of this hymn has been composed, at the same time worthy of the hymn and not needing a choir to render it' (p.353). In some ways things have moved on. The Gloria has varied its text, music, and position in the service; since mine was written, metrical versions have appeared from Michael Perry, Carl Daw, Timothy Dudley-Smith (two), Kevin Mayhew (five!) and No.191 below. Where churches have strong musical traditions, few of these may be needed; the rhythms of the BCP version remain supreme. But for some, the rapid and recent growth in Glorias suggests that Messrs Neil and Willoughby were well ahead of their time.

Light upon the River

Revelation 4-5
Gloria in Excelsis: two

191 GLORY IN THE HIGHEST TO THE GOD OF HEAVEN

Glory in the highest to the God of heaven!
Peace to all your people through the earth be given!
Mighty God and Father, thanks and praise we bring,
singing Hallelujah to our heavenly King.

Jesus Christ is risen, God the Father's Son!
With the Holy Spirit, you are Lord alone:
Lamb once killed for sinners, all our guilt to bear,
show us now your mercy, now receive our prayer.

Christ the world's true Saviour, high and holy One,
seated now and reigning from your Father's throne:
Lord and God, we praise you! Highest heaven adores;
in the Father's glory, all the praise be yours!

11.11.11.11 Tune: CUDDESDON; or LAND OF HOPE AND GLORY

Scriptures: Rev 4-5 Lk 2.14 Dan 2.19 Jn 1.29,36; 4.42 Isa 57.15 Heb 1.3; 8.1; 10.12; 12.2

Written: Poplar, 1976

First published: *Hymns for Today's Church* (Hodder & Stoughton) 1982

Partly to improve on No.190 (see notes, above) and partly to redeem a magnificent tune, I wrote this next version of the Gloria. When Dame Clara Butt heard Elgar's first 'Pomp and Circumstance' march, she decided (they say) that she was born to sing it; 'Write me a song with that refrain!' she said to the composer. He did, and with A C Benson's words, 'Land of hope and glory' arrived. Elgar then allowed no other lyric to go with his music. But why not give the glory where it belongs? This was the tune for which I wrote, and which launched the words at Limehouse on Whitsunday evening 1979. Next year they appeared in the All Souls Langham Place supplementary hymn book and from 1988 onwards featured frequently at 'Prom Praise' at the Royal Albert Hall and elsewhere. In Nov 1995 they were sung (with only one misprint) at the Westminster Abbey inauguration of the Church of England's new General Synod—just after I had resigned from my position as a licensed clergyman. But that time, as in more decorous books such as the 'New English Hymnal' (edited by my former Archdeacon George Timms, himself a hymnwriter), a tune without the Elgar associations was chosen. The Canticle extends more widely than Rev 4-5, but depends on these chapters more than any others.

Light upon the River

Revelation 7.9-17
The song of the great multitude

192 HERE FROM ALL NATIONS

Here from all nations, all tongues and all peoples,
countless the crowd, but their voices are one;
vast is the sight and majestic their singing:
'God has the victory; he reigns from the throne.'

These have come out of the hardest oppression,
now they may stand in the presence of God,
serving their Lord day and night in his temple,
ransomed and cleansed by the Lamb's precious blood.

Gone is their thirst and no more shall they hunger,
God is their shelter, his power at their side:
sun shall not pain them, no burning will torture;
Jesus the Lamb is their Shepherd and Guide.

He will go with them to clear living water
flowing from springs which his mercy supplies;
gone is their grief and their trials are over,
God wipes away every tear from their eyes.

Blessing and glory and wisdom and power
be to the Saviour again and again;
might and thanksgiving and honour for ever
be to our God: Hallelujah! Amen.

11.10.11.10 Tune: NEW CROSS by Agnes Tang; MORNING STAR by James P Harding; CRUDWELL by W K Stanton; or O QUANTA QUALIA

Scriptures: Rev 5.12-14; 7.9-17; 19.1,4 Matt 24.21 Mk 13.19 Jn 1.29 1 Pet 1.19 1 Jn 1.7 Psa 23.1-3 Isa 25.8; 49.10 Ezek 34.23
Written: Poplar, 1972
First published: *Psalm Praise* (Falcon) 1973

Together with all the *Psalm Praise* team in the stimulation of working together, Eddie Shirras and Richard Bewes deserve thanks here. Our book was well advanced when Eddie (then on the CPAS staff) suggested exploring the wealth of material in Revelation; when I wrote this text, reverting by now to rhyme, Richard (then Vicar of Harold Wood) suggested the tune O QUANTA QUALIA. As to the music, being acquainted since childhood with *O what their joy and their glory must be*, and as to the words, treading in the steps of Watts and Cameron's *How bright those glorious spirits shine* (from Rev 7) I counted this a great honour. From its first appearance this has been the most requested of all my hymns. It has featured in a world mission pack from the Evangelical Missionary Alliance; in Operation Mobilisation's 1982 'World Wide Praise'; in the American Hymn Society's opening Festival 'Let Justice Roll' at Toronto 1993; at St Paul's Cathedral on Advent Sunday 1995 before Michael Saward's sermon; in Reformed and Mennonite books in North America, and more. Now that Alan Gaunt has revisited Peter Abelard's hymn with *What of those sabbaths? what glory! what grandeur!* (to O QUANTA QUALIA) this may be the time for Agnes Tang's tune, named after her home neighbourhood, to prove a worthy successor. But the real honour belongs to God, who inspired John to set down some of the sights and sounds of heaven itself from his exile on the island of Patmos.

Revelation 11.15
Heaven's open door: love's final victory

193 COME AND SEE THE SHINING HOPE THAT CHRIST'S APOSTLE SAW

Come and see the shining hope that Christ's apostle saw:
on the earth, confusion, but in heaven an open door,
where the living creatures praise the Lamb for evermore;
love has the victory for ever!
Amen, he comes! to bring his own reward;
Amen, praise God! for justice now restored.
Kingdoms of the world become the kingdom of the Lord:
love has the victory for ever.

All the gifts you send us, Lord, are faithful, good and true;
holiness and righteousness are shown in all you do:
who can see your greatest Gift and fail to worship you?
love has the victory for ever! *Amen, he comes!...*

Power and salvation all belong to God on high:
so the mighty multitudes of heaven make their cry,
singing Hallelujah where the echoes never die;
love has the victory for ever! *Amen, he comes!...*

Tune: MARCHING THROUGH GEORGIA

Scriptures: Rev 4-5; 11.15; 12.10; 15.3-4; 16.6; 19.1-6; 22.12 Isa 40.2; 62.11 Matt 4.8-10 Lk 4.5-8 Jn 1.29-36 2 Cor 9.15 Jas 1.17

Written: Poplar, 1975

First published: *Hymns for Today's Church* (Hodder & Stoughton) 1982

'Wherever the Old Testament speaks of the victory of the Messiah or the overthrow of the enemies of God, we are to recognise that the gospel recognises no other way of achieving these ends than the way of the cross'; so George B Caird in his *Revelation* commentary (A & C Black 1966). The Fellowship of Reconciliation has held since 1914 'that Love, as revealed and interpreted in the life and death of Jesus Christ, involves more than we have yet seen; that it is the only power by which evil can be overcome and the only sufficient basis of human society' (FoR basis, 1). That is what this text is about. Stirred by the welcome for *Psalm Praise* (see Nos. 192 and 198), and by someone asking about this tune, I introduced this at our final Advent service at St Matthias' Poplar: 30 Nov 1975. Second only for a time to No.192 above, it has often been broadcast, sung at 'Prom Praise', and quoted; from the RC *The Universe* to Nottingham's Cornerstone Evangelical Church, from Mission Praise to Romsey Abbey, and in Richard Bewes' *The Church Overcomes* (Mowbray 1984). Adopting military music to nobler ends, it is stirring to hear a thousand voices with orchestra launch into a Christian pacifist song.

Light upon the River

Revelation 12.1-10
God of the changing centuries: one

194 ETERNITY ONCE ENTERED TIME

Eternity once entered time,
and when the bells of Christmas chime
the earth itself remembers yet
that night the stars cannot forget.

And some two thousand years have spun,
two thousand circuits round the sun,
since God was seen in human form
so still and sleepy, small and warm.

If we could keep the date exact
and measure every inch of fact
and mark the moment God was born,
or put on trial, or crowned with thorn:

Or if we knew the years to be
before creation is set free,
or even count our span of days:
would we grow wise, or mend our ways?

For many a woman, man and child
has since been hunted, tried, defiled,
or stripped and tortured, hung to die,
while poison stains the very sky.

God grant us to repent, believe,
reflect the love that we receive
and, stunned by joy, have eyes to see
when time shall touch eternity.

LM Tune: SOLOTHURN; or EISENACH

Scriptures: Rev 12.1-10 Dan 2.20-23 Matt 1.25; 26.57ff; 27.11,29 Lk 2.6-7; 22.68; 23.1 Jn 1.14 Phil 2.6-8 Rom 8.18-22 Psa 39, 90 Acts 20.21

Written: Peckham, 24 June 1997

1997 provided many nudges towards writing for the next millennium, being celebrated (early) not least in SE London; our home is a short bus ride from the Greenwich meridian 'where it all starts'. The local and national build-up announced 'It's About Time!'; in *News of Hymnody* Ruth Day wrote about millennium hymns; Gavin Reid (Bishop of Maidstone) was leading the churches' involvement with millennium events, Colin Buchanan (Bishop of Woolwich) planning liturgies and Michael Saward (St Paul's Cathedral) a hymn competition. Phillip Jensen (of Sydney) was saying that '2000' meant nothing, and 'AD' everything. This was my first attempt to help things along. It did not start with Revelation; but this book revels in symbolic numbers. Chapter 12 (among others) has strong images of both pain and joy for the church and the world; as God had the first word, so he has the last.

Light upon the River

Revelation 12.1-10
God of the changing centuries: two

195 A WORLD IN PAIN, A BABY'S CRY

A world in pain, a baby's cry;
one dazzling night from times gone by
that gives us Anno Domini:
   Year of our Lord!

A world enslaved, a baby's cry:
the child who spans the earth and sky:
the very man to crucify!
   Such love; such woe.

A world of grief, a baby's cry,
so deep our tears, our joy so high:
these things stay with us till we die;
   Where is our God?

A world at war, a baby's cry;
the worst, the best, the question Why;
what is our hope, and our reply?
   Jesus is Lord!

A world of sin, a baby's cry,
bad news and good, none can deny;
God with us—God we glorify,
   Hallelujah!

888.4 Tune needed

Scriptures: Rev 12.1-10 Matt 1.23,25; 27.31 Lk 2.6-7, 34-35; 23.33 Psa 8.2; 42   1 Cor 12.3
Written: Peckham, July 1997

A baby's cry has everything: life, shock, need, hope, joy, pain, response... so it must have been when Jesus was born and the first 'Year of our Lord' dawned—only to be measured much later, and then inaccurately! This was another attempt at a 'Millennium' text (see No.194 above) which if singable at all might last beyond AD2000, and does not include that date. It would fit some standard tunes but probably needs a new one. The 20th century has not been very sympathetic to its infants, healthy or sick, east or west, born or unborn; our hope is not in the world, but in One who once cried as a baby.

Light upon the River

Revelation 15.3-4
The Song of Moses and the Lamb: evening Canticle

196 GREAT AND WONDERFUL YOUR DEEDS

Great and wonderful your deeds,
God from whom all power proceeds;
true and right are all your ways -
who shall not give thanks and praise?
 to your name be glory!

King of nations, take your crown!
Every race shall soon bow down;
holy God and Lord alone,
justice in your deeds is shown:
 all have seen your glory.

To the one almighty God,
to the Lamb who shed his blood,
to the Spirit now be given
by the hosts of earth and heaven
 love and praise and glory!

77.77.6 Tune: NASSAU (= WURTEMBURG)

Scriptures: Rev 1.5-6; 5.9-14; 15.3-4 Jn 1.14; 17.24 Acts 7.2,55 Psa 145 Isa 6.3 Ezek 1.28

Written: Limehouse, 1977

First published: *Church Family Worship* (Hodder & Stoughton) 1986

The canticle 'Great and wonderful' (*Magna et memorabilia*) was already much used before the *Alternative Service Book 1980* brought it into wider circulation. When still in its 'Series 3' status in the long process of liturgical revision, I wanted to make it friendlier for congregational singing.

Revelation 19.1-9
Citizens of heaven

197 THE VICTORY OF OUR GOD IS WON

The victory of our God is won
and all creation sings!
Four living creatures round the throne
acclaim the King of kings;
the elders bring their crowns to him
in worship day and night,
while cherubim and seraphim
sing praise in burning light.

Then all believers in the Lord
combine in perfect praise;
the patriarchs who know their God
with saints of ancient days:
the twelve apostles of the Lamb,
the prophets in their place,
the white-robed martyrs praise his name
and glory in his grace.

The Christians of these latter years
shall not be missing there;
the pastors and the pioneers
who wrestled with despair;
the churches where ten thousand pray,
the groups of two or three -
the angels hear them sing that day
how Jesus set them free.

All glory to the Lamb who died
and rescued us by blood,
the Saviour who was crucified
to bring the world to God!
Let all who witness to his word
from every tribe and tongue
sing 'Holy, holy, holy, Lord'
in everlasting song.

DCM Tune: LADYWELL

Scriptures: Rev 1.5-6; 4-5; 6.9-11; 7.9; 19.1-9; 21.14 Ezek 1.10 Isa 6.1-3 Psa 80.1; 99.1 Matt 8.11; 18.20 Lk 13.28-30 2 Kgs 2.11-12 2 Cor 6.4-10 1 Pet 1.12 Phil 3.20

Written: Limehouse, June 1980

First published: *Hymns with the New Lectionary* (Grove Books) 1980

Who is actually there? I found myself asking this at Limehouse while preparing a sermon on heaven. I looked for evidence in the Bible, of which the verses listed give some idea; my hymn text puts it into a singing mode, with a tune surely appropriate for such a theme. Five years later it fitted our 6.30 service on 20 Oct 1985, the 'Last Sunday after Pentecost' in the Calendar we then observed. Its theme was 'Citizens of heaven', a phrase first applied to Christians on earth (at Philippi) but under which it appeared in Robin Leaver's 1980 guide to Lectionary-linked hymns. That version has been both corrected and revised, and has since found a place in the *Evangelical Times* of June 1988. Anglicans and others may also spot echoes of *Te Deum Laudamus*, soon to reappear below at No.200.

Light upon the River

Revelation 21-22
All things new

198 THEN I SAW A NEW HEAVEN AND EARTH

Then I saw a new heaven and earth
for the first had passed away,
and the holy city, come down from God,
like a bride on her wedding day.
And I know how he loves his own,
for I heard his great voice tell
they would be his people, and he their God,
and among them he came to dwell.

He will wipe away every tear,
even death shall die at last:
there'll be no more sorrow or grief or pain;
they belong to the world that's past.
And the One on the throne said 'Look!
I am making all things new';
He is A and Z, he is First and Last,
and his words are exact and true.

So the thirsty can drink their fill
at the fountain giving life;
but the gates are shut on all evil things,
on deceit and decay and strife.
With foundations and walls and towers
like a jewel the city shines,
with its streets of gold and its gates of pearl
in a glory where each combines.

As they measured its length and breadth
I could see no temple there,
for its only temple is God the Lord
and the Lamb, in that city fair.
And it needs neither sun nor moon
in a place which knows no night,
for the city's lamp is the Lamb himself
and the glory of God its light.

And I saw by the sacred stream
flowing water, crystal clear,
and the tree of life with its healing stream
and its fruit growing all the year.
So the worshippers of the Lamb
bear his name, and see his face;
and they reign and serve and for ever live
to the praise of his glorious grace.

8.7.10.8.D Tune: NEW HEAVEN by Norman Warren

Scriptures: Rev 1.8,17; 2.8; 3.12; 21-22 Isa 25.8; 52.1-2; 54.11-12; 60.19-20; 65.17-19; 66.22 Lev 26.11-12 Ezek 37.27; 47.1-12; 48.30-35 Zech 13.1; 14.8 Gen 2.9-10; 3.22-24 Eph 1.6
Written: Poplar, 1972   **First published:** *Psalm Praise* (Falcon) 1973

The No.15 bus to Poplar swung round from Aldgate into the Commercial Road. Sitting upstairs, I was leafing through the latest stack of papers from our central London meeting of the *Psalm Praise* team, and came across Norman Warren's tune for my draft words from Revelation. Like No.192 above, they had been prompted by Eddie Shirras's comment (which he has forgotten) about this book as a source for new writing; at first unrhymed, they had gone into the file awaiting new music. Even my non-musical eyes spotted a winner here—I could hardly wait to get to the piano—and such it proved as our book was launched a few months later. This was one of the last entries, and even then underwent some eleventh hour improvements from the group. These final chapters of the Bible are rich in resonance with other Scriptures; my text echoes John Donne in verse 2, and is quoted by Richard Bewes in *The Church Overcomes* (Mowbray 1984). It has appeared in several British, American and Asian books, and one recognisable line in the Afrikaans edition reads 'Die Alfa and die Omega is Ek, die Begin en die Verste Verskiet'.

Revelation 22.12-22
The last promise; the final prayer

199 CHRIST IS SURELY COMING

Christ is surely coming bringing his reward,
Alpha and Omega, First and Last and Lord:
Root and Stem of David, brilliant Morning Star;
meet your Judge and Saviour, nations near and far!

See the holy city! There they enter in,
all by Christ made holy, washed from every sin:
thirsty ones, desiring all he loves to give,
come for living water, freely drink, and live!

Grace be with God's people! Praise his holy name!
Father, Son and Spirit, evermore the same;
hear the certain promise from the eternal home:
'Surely I come quickly! Come, Lord Jesus, come!'

11.11.11.11 Tune: LAND OF HOPE AND GLORY; or EVELYNS

Scriptures: Rev 1.8,17; 2.8,28; 5.5; 22.12-21 Isa 11.1; 33.22; 40.10; 45.21; 55.1-2; 62.11 Jer 23.5; 33.15 Num 24.17 Zech 8.1-8 Jn 4.14 Eccles 12.5

Written: Poplar, May 1975

First published: *Songs of Worship* (Scripture Union) 1980

Like No.191 above, this was an attempt to set Biblical words to a strong and famous tune; when Elgar's music is used, each fourth line is repeated. The second line has sometimes reversed Alpha and Omega for the sake of stress, but this is the original and preferred text. It was first published to CUDDESDON for music copyright reasons. It was broadcast from Birmingham, sung at the Baptist Union's Annual Assembly (both in 1981) and a decade later featured on the 'Walk of 1000 men' across England, led by evangelist Daniel Cozens. So the Bible's final words perfectly match its opening ones.

Light upon the River

Revelation 22.21
Grace: praise and prayer in the 'Te Deum'

200 GOD, WE PRAISE YOU! GOD, WE BLESS YOU!

God, we praise you! God, we bless you!
God, we name you sovereign Lord!
Mighty King whom angels worship,
Father, by your church adored;
all creation shows your glory,
heaven and earth draw near your throne
singing Holy Holy Holy,
Lord of hosts and God alone.

True apostles, faithful prophets
saints who set the world ablaze,
martyrs, once unknown, unheeded,
join one growing song of praise,
while your church on earth confesses
one majestic Trinity:
Father, Son and Holy Spirit,
God, our hope eternally.

Jesus Christ, the King of glory,
everlasting Son of God,
humble was your virgin mother,
hard the lonely path you trod.
By your cross is sin defeated,
hell confronted face to face,
heaven opened to believers,
sinners justified by grace.

Christ, at God's right hand victorious,
you will judge the world you made;
Lord, in mercy help your servants
for whose freedom you have paid.
Raise us up from dust to glory,
guard us from all sin today;
King enthroned above all praises,
save your people, God, we pray!

87.87.D Tune: LLANBAGLAN by D Afan Thomas;
ILA by Rusty Edwards; LUX EOI; or RUSTINGTON

Scriptures: Gen 1.1 Rev 4-5; 22.21 Psa 19.12-13; 22.3; 24.7-10; 28.9; 71.5; 96.13; 98.9; 103.20-22; 148.2 Heb 1.6 Isa 6.1-5 1 Sam 1.11 Eph 2.20; 3.5; 4.11 1 Tim 1.1; 3.14-16 Tit 2.2; 3.7 Jn 17.1-5 Matt 1.21-23 Lk 1.34-35 Mk 10.32,45 Acts 7.55 Col 2.15 Rom 3.24 Dan 12.2

Written: Meols, near Hoylake, Cheshire, Aug 1978

First published: *Hymns for Today's Church* (Hodder & Stoughton) 1982

Perhaps the greatest Christian hymn outside the Holy Scriptures, *Te Deum Laudamus* has been variously dated and ascribed (c.400AD? Bishop Niceta of Remesiana?) and has nurtured the rhythm of Christian worship since the early centuries. For many English-speakers it has been the classic and definitive Canticle since the Reformation, in its Book of Common Prayer form *We praise thee, O God: we acknowledge thee to be the Lord*. No modern version rivals this one, which musicians have continued to enrich, and metrical paraphrasers to attempt, from Charles Wesley's *Infinite God, to thee we raise* to Timothy Dudley Smith's 1970 *God of gods, we sound his praises*. Do we need any more? No.200 in this collection seems a fit conclusion to a journey through the Bible, since it distils so many texts, not least from Scripture's final verses, while also introducing the Psalms. To these, it is an obvious partner in the same tradition of daily prayer and praise as has nourished believers

Light upon the River

from temple, synagogue and now Christian congregation, in all times and places. I had for some time wanted to try for a version which was contemporary, which addressed the Godhead directly, and which embodied the essentials of this ancient hymn. Then in 1978 I had surgery at Moorfields Eye Hospital in London, which providentially preceded a holiday arranged earlier. We stayed in the parental home of a Limehouse church member, Margaret Watts, on the Wirral near Liverpool, and while I took things gently and could not bear direct sunlight, I drafted this version; LUX EOI soon seemed a natural partner, so I crafted the words to that exultant tune. The beginning is no more sudden , I trust, than the BCP Whitsunday Collect, 'God, who as at this time didst teach the hearts of thy faithful people...'; the end embraces a conclusion which was added later, but which for many has always been part of the canticle; here it takes us from 'God, we praise' to 'God, we pray'. This version was sung in 1979 at a clergy conference at Ely, and at our Whitsunday Family Service at Limehouse. 1998 saw it included in that year's 'Spring Harvest' selection, and in the Hymn Society's Act of Praise at Norwich. Many tunes have been set to it; my original preference remains, but its continuing appearances make it the most requested text of mine which does not lean too heavily on a single tune. It simply leans on a magnificent outpouring of adoration which is the birthright of all the church of Christ on earth, and which helps us to keep in touch with heaven.

FROM THE BOOK OF PSALMS
Versions and selections

As a form of writing and singing the praise of God, the rendering of the Hebrew Psalms into English verse is nearly six centuries old. In our language it can claim to be a more ancient craft than hymnwriting; some would say, a more Scriptural one. The Psalms come at the heart of the Bible, as a treasury of public and private devotion, and (as the ministry of Jesus and the apostles shows) a constant source of teaching, prophecy and gospel preaching. But not even the most meticulously faithful of the older metrical versions can truly claim to be 'Psalms' in the way that is true of the original text and an accurate translation, since they are inevitably constrained by metre, stanza and (usually) rhyme. But we often refer to a version like the Scottish *The Lord's my shepherd* as 'the 23rd Psalm'; in that sense I use the title in those which follow.

However, when my own text is a freer paraphrase, a shorter section, or a Psalm-based hymn, I use the heading 'From Psalm 100' (etc) to show a difference. As the dates of writing indicate, this section runs parallel to the first one; but many of the Psalms come in small time-clusters. In the early 1970s I wrote for what, under Michael Baughen's chairmanship, became *Psalm Praise*; in the mid-1980s I contributed to David Preston's selection *The Book of Praises*, and then to Michael Perry's twin projects (with others), *Psalms for Today* and *Songs from the Psalms*.

In the late 1990s much of my work was that requested by Jim Sayers, with Tim Grass, for the Psalm section of *Praise!*. This book, due in 1999, links the Grace Baptist Churches with FIEC (Fellowship of Independent Evangelical Churches); some versions were due to appear first in this major hymnal. I am grateful for the willingness of Brian Edwards (chairman) and the Editorial Board for them to be included here. I have greatly benefited from the fellowship and teamwork which have been part of all the projects, and from the scholarly and godly commentators on the Psalms in many generations—as well our many predecessors in the art of such writing. We stand, and sing, in an honoured tradition; we venture to write, and compose, because we do not best honour our past by trying to live in it. I share with fellow writers and editors a desire to see the Psalms rediscovered, reclaimed and restored for all our varied churches; some signs are hopeful, but there is still far to go. I pray that some of these texts may speed the process, for the glory of God.

As King David, or Asaph and his friends, might have said: *Selah!*

Light upon the River

Psalm 3
Taunting and trusting: sleeping and waking

201 HOW MANY ARE AGAINST ME, LORD

How many are against me, Lord,
how many fierce attacks rise up!
They say, 'God will not come to help'
and people taunt, 'There is no hope'.

But you are round me, Lord, my shield;
but you, my glory, lift my head!
You hear me from your holy hill
and answer when I cry aloud.

I go to rest, and sleep in peace;
I wake again; God keeps me safe:
ten thousand shall not make me fear,
for all their threats to take my life.

Arise, O Lord, to rescue me;
arise and save me, O my God!
You silence all my enemies
till scorn and spite are all destroyed.

Your blessings, Father, grant to us;
your help, O Saviour, still be ours;
O Holy Spirit, fill our lives:
to God be glory, love and praise!

LM Tune: AQUINAS by Keith Landis; or DEEP HARMONY

Scriptures: Psa 3; 4.8; 8.2; 127.2 2 Sam 15.13ff Acts 4.29
Written: Limehouse, May-Oct 1983
First published: *Psalms for Today* (Hodder & Stoughton) 1990

Would this section begin more fittingly with the searching, agenda-setting Psalm 1; or the dramatic, messianic Psalm 2? Many others have laboured in those fields; they have never been assigned to me! The desperate, highly personal start to the third of the Bible Psalms makes it less known than most, but if it is short on praise (for which Psalms are most noted) it is deep in trust. My text was prompted, not by any persecution remotely like David's when Absalom rebelled (the tradition seen in the Psalm title) but by a desire to sing a version for today. For many believers, these threats can still be deadly. The 2nd and 4th lines 'chime' rather than rhyme, with different vowel-sounds but the same consonants. I include a Trinitarian doxology, a point at issue between 17th century Anglicans and Puritans which can excite their successors. Sometimes a brief *Gloria*, as in the Prayer Book, seems an appropriate conclusion; sometimes (as in Psalm 4 below) not. The texts which follow will show varying practice.

Light upon the River

Psalm 4
Priorities: an evening prayer

202 O GOD, DEFENDER OF THE POOR

O God, defender of the poor,
have mercy when I pray;
you listened to my prayer before:
Lord, hear my prayer today!

How long will people choose vain things,
love empty words and wrong?
They scorn to serve the King of kings:
O living God, how long?

The saints, O Lord, you set apart
by grace to be your own;
let sinners tremble, search their hearts,
and bow before your throne.

While many pray that you will bless
and bring them all they need,
unless they long for holiness
their prayers are vain indeed.

Your light, O Lord, let us receive,
your face within us shine:
far richer is the joy you give
than all their corn and wine.

And even when I turn to sleep
your blessings still increase,
for you alone, O Lord, will keep
your child in perfect peace.

CM Tune: CHINE by Cathy Bridge;
LIVERPOOL (arr. John Barnard); SALZBURG; or ALBANO

Scriptures: Psa 4; 3.5; 127.2 Rom 11.1 Eph 2.8 Matt 5.6, 31-33 Heb 12.14 2 Cor 4.6
Written: Limehouse, 1978
First published: *The Book of Praises* (Carey Publications) 1987

'Then sleep easy', says the fictional Brother Cadfael, 'for God is awake'. My own opening line here does not come directly from the Psalm but reflects our experience of the Lord who defends his needy people. The Prayer Book (Coverdale) version has become familiar to many through the late night service of Compline, now in various revised forms since Cadfael's time. Verse 5 of my text makes clearer, I hope, its word about 'their corn and wine and oil'; Americans will sing 'grain' for 'corn'. My text appeared in *Word & Music* Sep-Oct 1984, before some revisions including verse 5.

Psalm 11
True security

203 I TRUST THE LORD FOR SAFETY

I trust the Lord for safety;
how can I run away
or seek my refuge in the hills
like birds at close of day?
My enemies attack me;
they shoot to pierce my heart:
how can I stay in safety here
when goodness falls apart?

The Lord is in his temple;
on high his mighty throne:
his eyes watch over us in love,
to God our ways are known.
The Lord is true and faithful;
he guards us by his grace:
and all who trust his righteousness
shall live to see his face.

76.86.D Tune: ST VICTOR; or CHRISTUS DER IST MEIN LEBEN

Scriptures: Psa 11 Isa 6.1 1 Pet 3.12 Rev 19.11; 21.5; 22.4
Written: Limehouse, 1978
First published: *The Book of Praises* (Carey Publications) 1987

'Panic and stability' is the title given to Psalm 11 in Derek Kidner's succinctly wise commentary on the Psalms (Tyndale Press 1975). The desire to run away to seemingly problem-free greener pastures, hilly or not, afflicts many of us, Christian workers and pastors included; there may this time be a personal element in my text. As so often, Michael Perry and David Preston offered valued criticisms; on its first public appearance it was printed as four 4-line stanzas, but I still see it as two of 8 lines each.

Light upon the River

Psalm 13
From despair to joy

204 HOW LONG WILL YOU FORGET ME, LORD

How long will you forget me, Lord,
and hide your face away?
How long shall evils tear my heart
and troubles fill my day?

Look on my need, O Lord my God
who grants my every breath;
give light that I may see your light
nor sleep the sleep of death.

Look on their threats and hear my cry,
and answer when I call;
or they will claim the victory
who long to see me fall.

Lord, in your mercy is my trust;
I shall be glad and free:
then shall I sing with all my heart
how you have dealt with me.

CM Tune: BANGOR

Scriptures: Psa 13; 36.9 1 Sam 2.1 Hab 1.2 Acts 4.29

Written: Limehouse, Nov 1977

First published: *Church Family Worship* (Hodder & Stoughton) 1986

'How long, O Lord?' is the aching question of the Psalms, prophets (including Isaiah at the time of his vision) and more recent times. Some striking versions of Psalm 13 are available, notably Michael Saward's *Forgotten for eternity*. But in searching for a congregational text, I thought it needed that question as its starting point. It was originally set to ST HUGH and placed under Passiontide. Michael Perry then queried a single word, which led to wholesale revision—except for line one! In 1996 in preparation for *Praise!* I was asked to reconsider verse 4; from several suggestions this was the text finally accepted. Like the Biblical Psalm it uses repetition in pairs of words in order to intensify first the bleakness, then the joy.

Light upon the River

from Psalm 18
Overwhelmed

205 I LOVE YOU, O LORD, YOU ALONE

I love you, O Lord, you alone,
my refuge on whom I depend;
my Maker, my Saviour, my own,
my hope and my trust without end.
The Lord is my strength and my song,
defender and guide of my ways;
my Master to whom I belong,
my God who shall have all my praise.

The dangers of death gathered round,
the waves of destruction came near;
but in my despairing I found
the Lord who released me from fear.
I called for his help in my pain,
to God my salvation I cried;
he brought me his comfort again,
I live by the strength he supplied.

The earth and the elements shake
with thunder and lightning and hail;
the cliffs and the mountaintops break
and mortals are feeble and pale.
God's justice is full and complete,
his mercy to us has no end;
the clouds are a path for his feet,
he comes on the wings of the wind.

My hope is the promise he gives,
my life is secure in his hand;
I shall not be lost, for he lives!
He comes to my side—I shall stand!
Lord God, you are powerful to save;
your Spirit will spur me to pray;
your Son has defeated the grave:
I trust and I praise you today.

88.88.D anapaestic Tune: JANE by David Peacock; or TREWEN

Scriptures: Psa 18 Ex 15.2 Isa 12.2; 63.1 Acts 27.23 Rom 8.26 1 Cor 15.17-20
Written: Limehouse, 1977
First published: *Hymns for Today's Church* (Hodder & Stoughton) 1982

A *Jubilate* words group meeting, and a scribbled note from Kenneth Habershon enlarges on his spoken comment: 'We need more words of emotion and response of heart and will, rather than mind and understanding'. He quoted from my work, stronger on objective teaching than adoring love or surrendered feeling. I searched my heart, my hymns, and the Scriptures; the eventual fruit was this text, and now I wonder how I can ever sing it. It points to a distinction between Psalms and songs; the former can articulate the praise of the believing community we belong to, even if I cannot claim every line (of distress or exultation) at that moment's experience. So the church sings *Magnificat* with Mary, *Nunc dimittis* with Simeon, and Psalm 18 with David. Another David gave wings to my words; David Peacock's JANE, named after his wife, brought the text into many books and hearts. In Sept 1997, after a long illness, Jane died in Torquay aged 46. At her Funeral at Upton Vale Baptist Church, one verse was sung by Geraldine Latty; then the full Psalm by everyone. I could not be there, but it had a relevance which was not in my mind or David's when we first wrote the text and tune. Perhaps that justifies the Christian enrichment of King David (verse 4) in the spirit of Isaac Watts. Even this text, which is not complete, sometimes proves too long, and verse 3 is often omitted. But seen and heard in full, says Weiser, 'Like the two spires of a cathedral the two parts of this mighty hymn soar to heaven'.

Psalm 19
Glory and grace: one

206 HOW CLEAR AND TRUE THE SKIES SING OUT GOD'S PRAISE

How clear and true the skies sing out God's praise,
how plainly they pronounce what he has done!
Each day declares as each tomorrow learns,
each passing night tells each succeeding one.

No voice is heard, no language we can trace;
God speaks, and his creation echoes back:
the sky his tent, his champion the sun,
who runs his daily race on heaven's track.

God's perfect law revives the human soul,
his faithful precepts make the simple wise;
his firm decrees bring joy to troubled hearts,
his clear commands give light to darkened eyes.

To be desired far more than treasured gold;
more sweet than honey are the words of God:
and by their truth am I, your servant, warned;
to keep them is to find a great reward.

So keep me free from every open sin;
against all secret failings be my guard:
my words and thoughts be such as make you glad,
my Rock, my strong Redeemer, and my God.

10.10.10.10 Tune: WILLARD by Keith Landis; or WOODLANDS

Scriptures: Psa 19; 119.14ff Rom 1.20; 7.12-22; 10.17-18 Ezek 3.1-3
Written: Poplar 1974

Psalm 19 uniquely celebrates, as a pair, the works and words of God (creation and revelation; in Derek Kidner's phrase, 'The skies, the Scriptures'). Notable predecessors among English versions include Joseph Addison's *The spacious firmament on high* (1712) and Timothy Dudley-Smith's *The stars declare his glory* (1970); recent successors are David Preston's *The heavens declare God's glory* (1986) and Carl Daw's *God's glory fills the heaven with hymns* (1988). The field seems even more crowded than usual, not to mention the WOODLANDS. I wrote this when most available versions gave trouble with either text or tune; we sang it at Limehouse on 23 Mar 1980. See also No.207 below.

Light upon the River

from Psalm 19
Glory and grace: two

207   GLORY AND PRAISE TO GOD

    Glory and praise to God!
    All the skies sing praise;
    songs from the sun and moon,
    from the nights and days.
        No human voice is there,
        no mortal speech is heard;
        still through the depths of space
        speeds the sounding word.
    Up comes the morning sun
    for his mighty race;
    and the Lord shines on us
    with his truth and grace.

    Glory and praise to God
    for his perfect law,
    making the simple wise
    and the waverer sure!
        Sweeter than honeycomb,
        richer than purest gold;
        praise for redemption's plan
        which the words unfold!
    Lord, keep my heart from sin,
    you have set me free;
    be my life and my light -
    Jesus, shine on me!

    65.65 triple (distinctive) Tune: WATER END

Scriptures: Psa 19; 119.103ff; 148.1-6 Jn 1.4-5, 14 Ezek 3.1-3
Written: Limehouse, June 1980
First published: *Psalms for Today* (Hodder & Stoughton) 1990

In 1980 the *Jubilate* musicians prepared a list of tunes needing new words; WATER END was one. Composed by Geoffrey Shaw for *Glad that I live am I*, it was seen by Percy Dearmer as 'a bright, unaffected tune'; he included it in *Songs of Praise* (1925). The word 'sky' may have drawn me back to Psalm 19, while my last line seems to have been before its time. The text should be printed either as here (the complete tune comes twice) or with clear space between the two halves if 4-line stanzas are preferred; otherwise, unworkable 65.65 tunes may be tried. This newer pairing of words and music features in a Langham Arts recording *The Glory of the Psalms*. In my comments on Scripture throughout these notes, I have not pointed to every critical theory of its supposed original source or shape. For example, those who choose to split this Psalm into two separate lyrics seem to lack not merely respect for the integrity of the text, but any imaginative appreciation of its artistry and strength.

Light upon the River

Psalm 20
Bad news for the arms trade

208 IN THE DAY OF NEED

In the day of need may your answer be the Lord;
may the God of Jacob strengthen you:
may he send you help from his high and holy place,
and support you for the glory of his name.

May the Lord God give you success in all your plans;
may he give you all your heart's desire:
may we sing for joy when we see the battle won,
when the Lord has heard and answered every prayer.

Now I know that God will encourage those he loves;
he will hear and answer from on high;
not a word shall fail of the promise he has made,
nor the works of his victorious right hand.

There are some who boast of the weapons of the world,
but the power of God is all our pride;
those who arm for war shall one day collapse and fall,
but God's people stand and in their King prevail.

12.9.12.11 Tune: SAMSON by Norman Warren

Scriptures: Psa 20; 37.4 Ezek 36.22-23 2 Cor 10.3-4 Matt 5.18
Written: Peckham, 1969
First published: *Psalm Praise* (Falcon) 1973

This was an early text submitted for what was to become *Psalm Praise*; see No.247. Our initial aim was to produce fresh versions of selected Psalms in a wide range of styles, not restricted by rhyme or traditional metres. Each writer of words was allotted several Psalms; No.20 fell to me. Although Norman Warren's new tune conveyed a different mood from what I had in mind, it has been appreciated (with the text) in at least two American hymnals. The final stanza still speaks to our own weapon-stuffed, war-crazed world; as often, King David spoke more truly than he knew, or behaved.

Light upon the River

Psalm 21
The coming King

209 LORD, TO YOU WE LIFT OUR VOICES

Lord, to you we lift our voices,
sing to praise your glorious might;
see, the anointed King rejoices!
In your strength is his delight:
　heart's desires, heartfelt praises,
he finds favour in your sight.

Lord, you welcomed him with blessing,
purest gold his head has crowned;
life for ever, days unceasing,
in your presence joys abound:
　his the glory, his the victory,
for in him true faith is found.

So this King will not be shaken,
held in love by God Most High;
by your hand your foes are taken,
at your coming they shall die:
　fire consuming all their scheming,
all their hopes you will destroy.

In your strength, O Lord, uplifted,
you will rid this earth of wrongs.
With your wealth your King is gifted:
take the praises of our songs:
　Son of David, high ascended,
every power to Christ belongs!

87.87.87 Tune: VOICES LIFTED by Eric Lewis

Scriptures: Psa 21 Heb 12.29 Rom 1.3 Eph 4.10

Written: Peckham, 15 Nov 1997

We move here from one of my first Peckham paraphrases to one of my latest in the very next Psalm, with 28 years (and half a mile) between them. Like No.208 above, this too was allocated to me for a Psalm collection; this time, for *Praise!* I had recently met Eric Lewis and his music at a conference, and matched my draft to his tune. I have taken the glorious King to be one greater than David.

Psalm 23
The one, good, great and chief Shepherd

210 THE LORD MY SHEPHERD RULES MY LIFE

The Lord my shepherd rules my life
and gives me all I need:
he leads me to refreshing streams;
in pastures green I feed.

The Lord revives my failing strength,
he makes my joy complete;
and in right paths, for his name's sake,
he guides my faltering feet.

Though in a valley dark as death,
no evil makes me fear;
your shepherd's staff protects my way,
for you are with me there.

While all my enemies look on
you spread a royal feast;
you fill my cup, anoint my head,
and treat me as your guest.

Your goodness and your gracious love
pursue me all my days:
your house, O Lord, shall be my home;
your name, my endless praise.

To Father, Son, and Spirit, praise!
To God whom we adore
be worship, glory, power and love
both now and evermore!

CM Tune: SHEPHERD PSALM by Christopher Hayward; RULER by Kenneth Sagar; BEDFORDSHIRE MAY DAY CAROL; BROTHER JAMES' AIR; or CRIMOND

Scriptures: Psa 23; 95.7; 100.1-4; 119.176 Jer 23.3 Ezek 34.11-16 Jn 10.11-15 Heb 13.20 1 Pet 5.4 Rev 7.17

Written: Limehouse, 1977

First published: *Jesus Praise* (Scripture Union) 1982

If some Psalms are over-stocked with English versions, what can be said of the 23rd? The text here has been both much published and much criticised; attacks have come mainly from those who take it as a 'revision' of the Rous/Whittingham *The Lord's my shepherd,* and become belated admirers of its phraseology. Whatever its origins or success, the much-rewritten 17th century Scots version did not reach a full edition of 'Hymns Ancient and Modern' until 1983, nor 'The English Hymnal' until the 1986 NEH. The 'Anglican Hymn Book' chose it in 1965, as it had been popular across the UK (notably at weddings and funerals) since the British royal wedding in 1947. Words and phrases of the Psalm inevitably overlap between various versions, but my text is a new one with a doxology which should make it readily distinct. The opening line raised the first question; one option was 'The Lord my shepherd knows my name' (cf Jn 10.3), but the *Jubilate* words group preferred my other choice, happily reflecting the Latin *Dominus regit me* of its Prayer Book heading. In the Bible, a shepherd may be a despised outsider, or a leader like Moses, David, or the God of Israel.

Light upon the River

from Psalm 24
The King of glory: responses

211 THIS EARTH BELONGS TO GOD

This earth belongs to God,
the world, its wealth, and all its people;
he formed the waters wide
and fashioned every sea and shore.

A Who may go up the hill of the Lord
   and stand in the place of holiness?
B Only the one whose heart is pure,
   whose hands and lips are clean.

Lift high your heads, you gates,
rise up, you everlasting doors, as
here now the King of glory
enters into full command.

A Who is the King, this King of glory,
   where is the throne he comes to claim?
B Christ is the King, the Lord of glory,
   fresh from his victory.

Lift high your heads, you gates,
and fling wide open the ancient doors, for
here comes the King of glory
taking universal power.

A Who is the King, this King of glory,
   what is the power by which he reigns?
B Christ is the King, his cross his glory,
   and by love he rules.

All glory be to God
the Father, Son, and Holy Spirit;
from ages past it was,
is now, and evermore shall be.

Tune: TRUMPET VOLUNTARY by Jeremiah Clarke

Scriptures: Psa 24; 15.1-3 Gen 1.1-10 Hag 2.6-9 Matt 5.8 1 Cor 2.8 Jas 2.1 Jn 13.31-32; 17.1-5

Written: Poplar, 1975

First published: *Songs of Worship* (Scripture Union) 1980

Given the opportunity to sing the *Trumpet Voluntary*, what theme could match such music? Asking that of myself, I was soon turning to Psalm 24 as heralding the coming King; in Christian terms, here is a song for Palm Sunday or the Ascension. Like the 23rd Psalm (No.210 above) my freer version of the 24th has been well used but firmly criticised, the music being the crux. Some dislike omitting a whole section of Jeremiah Clarke's tune (which is beyond voice-range); others, to any use of it in this way. I sympathise with both; but I still hope to go on singing. Robin Sheldon was the first to arrange the music for the text; Roy Castle, the trumpeter and entertainer who died prematurely in 1994, often accompanied it at Gold Hill Baptist Church, Buckinghamshire. It was sung at St Matthias' Poplar on Palm Sunday 23 Mar 1975, and from 1980 onwards featured in 'Prom Praise' at All Souls Langham Place, the Barbican Centre and the Royal Albert Hall. It began the Thanksgiving Service at the new centre for OMF International (Overseas Missionary Fellowship) and AEF (Africa Evangelical Fellowship) near Sevenoaks, Kent, in 1997. The 'questions and answers' marked A and B are best sung responsively without dividing men from women! It is as vital to see the global dimensions of praise (since the earth, not just our group, is the Lord's) as to know that Christ triumphs by love, at the cross. This may save our meetings or teachings from becoming mere power-trips; see also No.193.

Light upon the River

Psalm 27
Dominus Illuminatio Mea

212 LIGHT AND SALVATION IS THE LORD FOR ME

Light and salvation is the Lord for me
  whom shall I fear?
Stronghold and fortress of my life is he;
  what harm comes near?
When powers of evil try to take control
  they cannot thrive;
though deadly war breaks out against my soul
  I stay alive!

One thing I ask: in God's most holy place
  to spend my days,
live in his light, and on his glorious face
  direct my gaze.
Then he will keep me safe and raise me high
  within his care;
God is my music, my delight and joy,
  my praise, my prayer.

So when I call to you and seek your face
  and when I pray,
my Saviour God, do not withhold your grace
  nor turn away.
Father and mother may leave me alone;
  the Lord is here!
Guide me, O Lord, and let your path be shown
  secure and clear.

Save me, O God, when enemies arise
  who plot my death;
violence is in their hearts, their threats and lies,
  their very breath.
My eyes shall see the goodness of the Lord;
  I trust his word.
Wait for him still, with heart and strength restored;
  wait for the Lord!

10.4.10.4.D Tune: OLDHAM by Agnes Tang

Scriptures: Psa 27; 23.6; 34.4-6; 84.1-4; 121.7; 130.5-6 Jn 8.12; 12.35-36 1 Jn 1.5-7; 2.10 Rev 22.4   **Written:** Peckham, 1 Dec 1997

This text marks the end of a varied span of writing. Having tried to rescue a nobly archaic version of Psalm 27, and seen others which lacked its distinctive opening, I drafted this, the most recent in the book. It has had no 'trial period', but I was glad to make the attempt; its first three words in Latin (as printed in the Book of Common Prayer) are the motto of the University of Oxford. That institution flourishes best when its members recall both these and the words following, in whatever tongue

Light upon the River

Psalm 28

Anxiety and trust

213 O LORD MY ROCK, TO YOU I CRY ALOUD

O Lord my Rock, to you I cry aloud
    to hear my plea;
I shall be lost, if you stay silent now
    and deaf to me.
I lift my hands to your most holy place;
do not withhold your mercy, love and grace!

Do not, I pray, drag me off with the vile,
    with souls perverse;
smooth is their speech, but hidden in their hearts
    a silent curse.
For all the Lord has done, they show disdain,
but once torn down, they shall not rise again.

Praise to the Lord, who is my strength and shield;
    he hears my cry!
God is my help; my heart will give him thanks
    and leap for joy.
Strength of his people, fortress for his king;
our Shepherd, save us! All your praise we sing.

10.4.10.4.10.10 Tune: SANDON

Scriptures: Psa 28 Deut 32.4 Jas 3.9-10 Gen 15.1 Jn 10.11

Written: Peckham, Oct 1996

Unlike No.212 above, this version was requested by the Psalms team for *Praise!*, and the advice of its members taken in assessing some varied options. The tune, once agreed, helped to shape particular phrases; a good new one may be found, but would need to enhance the emphases as SANDON does. The fear of being finally lost (which has afflicted some fine Christians) can lead to some desperately bitter prayers, but this text stops marginally short of desiring punishment for our oppressors.

Light upon the River

Psalm 31
Past, present and future needs are met

214 IN YOU, O LORD, I FIND MY REFUGE

In you, O Lord, I find my refuge;
never let me be put to shame:
my rock, my fortress, help me, guide me;
come for the sake of your great name!
Into your hands I trust my spirit,
Lord God of truth, redeeming me:
from falsehood and from fears you save me;
you gave me space, and I was free.

Now once again show me your mercy;
these heavy years are filled with grief:
friend, foe and neighbour all discard me,
leave me for dead, with no relief.
I hear the whispering tongues of many;
fears lie in wait on every side:
they have been plotting all together;
threats to my life are multiplied.

But as for me, I trust in you, Lord;
I said that you, O God, are mine:
my times are in your hands; O save me
from all their hands, by grace divine!
O let your face shine on your servant!
Save me by your unfailing love:
let me not share the fate of liars;
come with your goodness from above.

For those who fear you, such great mercies,
your treasured blessings, are outpoured;
in your safe dwelling you protect me
from wounds and words—I praise you, Lord!
He showed his love within the city,
guarding his people, judging wrong:
love him, all you who trust his mercy;
take heart, and in the Lord be strong!

98.98.D Tune: RENDEZ A DIEU

Scriptures: Psa 31; 18.19; 122.3-5 Deut 32.4 Lk 23.46 Neh 6.1-14 Jer 11.18-20; 18.18-23; 38.1-13 Acts 23.12-22 Num 6.25 1 Jn 2.4,22; 4.20 Rev 21.8 Eph 6.10

Written: Peckham, 6 June 1996

This was an earlier assignment for *Praise!*, which began as six stanzas, was reduced to five, and finally squeezed into four, while I tried to keep it faithful to the complete Psalm. Its Bible original is a milder form of the kind of imprecation found in Psalm 28 and elsewhere. Many writers, C S Lewis not the least, have discussed the understanding of God involved here, and how such anger can ever be used in the church. But we often disagree on which passages are unacceptable as they stand, as the variously bracketed verses in different Psalters show. It is no use having strictly accurate Hebrew curses (which some clearly are) which no Christian congregation will sing. Most paraphrases turn prayers for vengeance into warnings of divine judgement and calls to repent. Clearly we are judges neither of our own enemies nor yet of David (and others) whose dangers and terrors we seldom share.

Psalm 32
Sin, forgiveness, restoration

215 HAPPY ARE THOSE WHOSE OFFENCE IS FORGIVEN

Happy are those whose offence is forgiven,
whose sin is covered by God;
happy are those whom the Lord reckons righteous,
whose heart is free from deceit.

While I kept silent about my wrongdoing
my strength was ebbing away:
daytime and night-time your hand was upon me;
its weight was crushing my life.

Then I admitted the sin that defiled me
and hid it from you no more;
when I resolved to confess it with sorrow
then you remitted my guilt.

So let God's people discover his goodness
and pray to him in their need;
he is my refuge when floods swirl around me,
my guard, protector and guide.

I will instruct you and lovingly teach you
the road that you should pursue;
horses need bridles and lack understanding,
but you can find the right path.

Trust him, and his steadfast love will surround you;
refuse, and great is your grief:
sing and be glad in the Lord, all believers,
and shout for joy in his name!

11.7.11.7 Tune: FELICITER by David Wilson

Scriptures: Psa 32 Rom 4.6-8 Lk 18.9-14

Written: Peckham, 1970

First published: *Psalm Praise* (Falcon) 1973

One Psalm on, we are back with an assignment from the earlier book, with no rhyme and a distinctive metre, for one of the classic penitential songs of David (cf. Nos. 257, 258 and 262 below). Up to 1987 it was 'Happy is he...', but since the apostle Paul sets an example in his Romans 4 quotation, it can now be gender-inclusive. Something always changes in the process, as the variations in Psalm 1 bear witness; the individual experience merges with that of the community. If this text survives, I would prefer a more searching 6/8 tune; but can any tune change its mood so decisively as the Psalm does? It is easier to switch chants in mid-stream than hymn tunes.

Light upon the River

Psalm 35
Facing enemies; facing God

216 CONTEND, O LORD WITH THOSE

Contend, O Lord, with those
who will contend with me;
be foe to all my foes,
my strong salvation be.
Sly and unjust, they hunt me down;
let them be blown away like dust!

The angel of the Lord
shall drive them far away
with his pursuing sword,
in total disarray,
to be surprised by their own nets
and fall in pits that they devised.

Then shall my heart with joy
delight in God anew,
and all my being cry
'O Lord, who is like you?'
From that strong mob the poor are saved,
no more enslaved by those who rob.

My kindness they condemn;
with spite I am repaid,
although I cared for them
and for their health I prayed.
But when I fall, they join in glee
to slander me; Lord, judge them all!

Lord, come to my defence!
How long will you look on?
Break down their violence
or I shall soon be gone.
For no just cause, with cunning eyes
they spread their lies and wage their wars.

Lord, all this you have seen;
do not be far away!
With justice intervene;
contend for me, I pray,
and vindicate me, lest they think
to make me sink ingloriously.

Lord, put to lasting shame
such inhumanity;
let them exalt your name
who share my victory!
Your righteousness shall fill my song,
and on my tongue be all your praise.

66.66.88 (66.66.44.44) Tune: MAELOR; CHRISTCHURCH; or CROFT'S 136th

Scriptures: Psa 35; 69.4; 71.19; 89.9 2 Kgs 19.35 2 Chron 32.21 Isa 37.36 Prov 6.12-15; 10.10 Jn 15.25

Written: Peckham, Feb 1997

Unlike No.214 (Psalm 31) above, this *Praise!* assignment grew from six stanzas to seven, from Oct 1996 to Feb 1997. It originally began 'Lord, plead my cause with those...', but I agreed with the team, who preferred the stronger 'Contend...'; the NIV had edged out the AV (King James) and Coverdale. A full treatment of this sometimes desperate Psalm was requested, which may sharpen the difference between churches wanting full value from their Psalter, and those content with less. Of its author, Artur Weiser says we are justified 'in ranking him with such men as Hosea and Jeremiah' in the effect on him of 'the ruthless gloating and venomous scorn of his former friends' (*The Psalms*, SCM 1962, trans. Herbert Hartwell). This too is matter for bringing before the Lord.

Psalm 36
Villains, vigilance, vision

217 NO FEAR OF GOD BEFORE THE EYES

No fear of God before the eyes,
    no penitence within:
such is the one no longer wise,
whose words are treachery and lies,
    who never grieves for sin.

Your love, O Lord, shall never sleep,
    nor shall your mercy cease;
your truth is like the mighty deep,
and like the rocky mountain steep
    your steadfast righteousness.

Beneath the shadow of your wings
    our refuge is most sure;
refreshed by your reviving springs
and all the joy your mercy brings
    our future is secure.

Continue, Lord, your love to me,
    for you are all my trust;
grant us the light we need, to see
how good you are, and still shall be
    to those you count as just.

86.886 Tune: SHERINGTON by Paul Edwards; REST (Maker); or BINNEY'S

Scriptures: Psa 36; 91.4; 121.4 Ruth 2.12 Gen 15.6 Rom 3.18; 4.3, 22-24 Gal 3.6

Written: Limehouse, 1980

First published: *Psalms for Today* (Hodder & Stoughton) 1980

This Psalm still has power to startle. A sombre opening suddenly turns to soaring praise for God's mercy, faithfulness and righteousness—in terms of Coverdale's (BCP) version. Originally my first stanza referred to 'the man' and 'his eyes'; in 1987 I decided that wickedness was no more limited to males than is the 'blessedness' of Psalm 1. Like *Eternal light, eternal light*, which suggests BINNEY'S, this needs a tune for all moods; in 1988 Paul Edwards sent me SHERINGTON ('begun 3.11.83, completed 1.1.87') which, he said, 'John Barnard has been helping me to get right over a long period!'

Light upon the River

from Psalm 37
The prosperity of the wicked

218 WHEN LAWLESS PEOPLE THRIVE

When lawless people thrive
and wrong suppresses right,
remember they will fade away
and wither overnight.
Commit your life to God,
and trust the Lord to make
the wisdom of your righteous cause
shine clear for his name's sake.

Be still before the Lord;
in patience learn to wait
and never fret if crime succeeds
and some grow rich and great.
For jealous discontent
tends only to destroy;
the meek who look to God their Lord
a kingdom shall enjoy.

The godless borrows much
and cannot then pay back;
the righteous give, and give again,
are blessed, and have no lack.
The saints whose lives are true
can turn away from wrong;
God's word is hidden in their heart,
God's wisdom guides their tongue.

I've seen a boasting thief
grow like a weed apace;
but when I passed that way again
I looked, but found no trace.
My steps are from the Lord
who helps my feet to stand;
I stumble but I do not fall;
my God shall hold my hand.

Salvation is from God
in times of blatant wrong,
and all who seek his shelter find
a refuge safe and strong.
So fully trust the Lord;
shun evil, follow right:
God gives you all your heart's desire
when he is your delight.

DSM Tune: COMMITMENT by Norman Warren;
CHALVEY; or NEARER HOME

Scriptures: Psa 37; 46.10; 73.1-14; 119.11 Job 21.7-13   1 Jn 3.4 Jas 5.8-9 Matt 5.3,5,42 Lk 6.30,38 Prov 22.7   1 Cor 10.12 Jonah 2.9   1 Pet 3.11

Written: Peckham, 1971   **First published:** *Psalm Praise* (Falcon) 1973

Why does God let the bad people win? This reverse of the coin of the 'problem of evil' (why do good people lose?) is explored most fully in this, one of my longer 'Psalm Praise' assignments. Hoping to match faithfulness with usefulness I rearranged some of the original order; for example, the 'heart's desire' of v.4 is delayed until my final couplet. Originally it began 'When lawless men succeed' and stanza 4 read 'I've seen an evil man firm as a massive tree, but when I passed that way again I looked—but where was he?'. The Prayer Book has, 'I went by, and lo, he was gone: I sought him, but his place could no where be found'; some have regretted my 1987 revision at such points. Michael Ball quotes the full earlier text in 'Singing to the Lord' (Bible Reading Fellowship 1979) and Stephen Layfield recorded it to his own music in 'He to whom wonders belong' (1993). One pirate version in print shows how not to make texts inclusive by starting 'When evil people sin'. The problem is not that they sin (which is hardly surprising) but that they so often seem to win. For a fuller answer to the root question we must look beyond the Psalms; even beyond Job.

Light upon the River

from Psalms 42 and 43
Longings: one

219 WILD CREATURES LONG TO COOL THEIR TONGUES

Wild creatures long to cool their tongues
where flowing streams run clear;
so now for God my spirit longs:
but how may I draw near?
With singing crowds that surged along
I gladly took my part;
but now when I recall their song,
my God, it breaks my heart.

In exile from the house of God
I hear the waters roll,
but they are like the swelling flood
in which he drowns my soul.
Has God consigned me to my death?
My enemies surround
to mock his name, destroy my faith,
and crush me to the ground.

Why does such grief weigh down my soul?
Why such despair and pain?
I hope in God who makes me whole
and praise him once again.

Why does such grief... (etc)

My God, defend my cause, I pray,
against their rage and spite.
You will not cast your child away;
send out your truth and light
to guide me to that holy place
where true delight belongs,
with music to set forth your grace
and worship you with songs.

Why does such grief... (etc)

Triple CM Tunes: verse IRISH, refrain CHORUS ANGELORUM;
or verse METZLER'S REDHEAD, refrain ST FULBERT

Scriptures: Psa 42; 43; 63.1 Jer 14.1-6 Joel 1.20 Jonah 2.3-7 Matt 5.6 Rev 22.17

Written: Poplar, 1975

Whatever the original link between Psalms 42 and 43, their common refrain (three times in all) prompted this text and No.220 below. The *Psalter Hymnal* of the Christian Reformed Church in N America (1987) includes *As a deer in want of water,* which in six stanzas also combines both Psalms. If congregations have problems in singing about past fellowship and present loneliness, that is inherent in our source; we are placed temporarily with outsiders who for varied reasons are unable to join in. They may also hesitate to mix their music; I have sung both *Eternal Light, eternal Light* and *Through the night of doubt and sorrow* to a pair of tunes each, chosen respectively to express the right mood and sustain the flagging spirits. I resort to it here to fill a gap in Triple CM tunes; but see also No.229 below. Tate and Brady's *As pants the hart* (Psa 42) has survived from the 1696 'New Version' into some recent books, alongside their less problematic *Through all the changing scenes* (Psa 34).

Light upon the River

from Psalms 42 and 43
Longings: two

220 GOD OF MY LIFE, TO YOU I PRAY

God of my life, to you I pray;
Spirit of life, fill me today;
Christ be my life, my truth, my way:
    glory to God, my God!

God of my strength when I am weak,
prize and reward of all who seek:
open my mouth, that I may speak
    glory to God, my God!

God of my joy, be my delight,
music by day and songs at night!
lead me to walk as in your sight:
    glory to God, my God!

888.6 Tune: LITTLE STANMORE by John Barnard; or SAFFRON WALDEN

Scriptures: Psa 42; 43; 51.15 Rom 8.2 Jn 14.6 2 Cor 12.9-10 Phil 3.14 Gen 15.1 Jer 1.9

Written: Oakley, April 1995

In regularly using the Psalms from the *Book of Common Prayer*, I was struck by a pattern of phrases in Coverdale's version in addition to the triple refrain noted in No.219 above: 'God of my life' (42.10), 'God of my strength' (42.11; 43.2), and 'God of my joy' (43.4; elsewhere the verses are numbered differently). And if 'my soul' is a constant concern, 'my God' is the eternal reality (42.8,15; 43.4,6). This was the basis of one of my last 'Suffolk' texts; meanwhile John Barnard's tune for Timothy Dudley-Smith's *Spirit of faith, by faith be mine* was proving popular. But while Timothy's words were complete, some thought the tune worth singing more than twice. Among them was Christopher Hayward, who introduced this at St Andrew the Great Cambridge on 12 Jan 1997.

Light upon the River

from Psalm 48
The city of God

221 GREAT IS THE LORD; HIS PRAISE IS GREAT

Great is the Lord; his praise is great
on Zion's mount, his holy place;
the royal city crowns the earth
and shines on all with radiant grace.

God is the Tower whose strength was shown
when Satan's armies threatened harm;
they gathered round, and looked, and ran
like boats before the driving storm.

Our ears have heard, our eyes have seen
what God the Lord of hosts has done;
within these walls we celebrate
his steadfast love, his ageless throne.

God is the Judge whose mighty name
across the world with praise shall ring;
for his resplendent victories
let Zion shout and Judah sing.

God is the King whose kingdom's power
we see built up on every side;
we tell our children of our God
who will for ever be our guide.

LM Tune: LA CORBIERE by Norman Warren; SIMEON; TRURO; or BIRLING

Scriptures: Psa 48; 46.1-9; 78.1-7 Isa 26.1 Matt 5.14,35 Ex 13.14-16 Deut 6.20-25
Written: Peckham, 1970
First published: *Psalm Praise* (Falcon) 1973

'Walk about Sion, and go round about her: and tell the towers thereof. Mark well her bulwarks...' David Sheppard, our bishop at the time my text was written, used to relate the end of Psalm 48 (in its vivid Prayer Book version) to his joy at seeing Zion's towers and walls rise in many places, where the true King is acknowledged across the globe. In retirement after 28 years as a bishop, he says 'My picture of the Body of Christ has grown larger and richer than I ever thought... I mean the whole Christian body, made up of Christ's people with the great variety of gifts the Holy Spirit gives. We can take great encouragement from "marking well her bulwarks"'. That is one detail of this song of God's city; not all of its riches could squeeze into my stanzas, but they try to capture some of the spirit of their source. They were part of a move from various unrhymed metres back to more traditional forms as 'Psalm Praise' took shape. Stanza 3 used to match the rest: 'God is the Lord of hosts, whose work we heard and saw, and made it known...'; discussion in the group led to its present text. Any tune still needs to start on a strong beat. Stanza 2 echoes Caesar's 'Veni, vidi, vici; I came, I saw, I conquered', but here it is the attacker who is routed. Later I found that Charles Wesley (of course) had got there first from this Psalm: 'Lo! their boast is turned to shame! Struck with sore amaze and dread, marching towards her walls they came; they came, they saw, they fled!' Sometimes the armies in my text become 'hostile'; but 'Satan's' shows that this is spiritual warfare, with the armour of God, for the eternal city.

Light upon the River

Psalm 50
God speaks: God comes

222 GOD THE LORD, THE KING ALMIGHTY

God the Lord, the King almighty,
calls the earth from east to west;
shining out from Zion's splendour,
city loveliest and best,
comes our God! He breaks the silence,
robed in burning majesty:
'Gather all my covenant people,
bound by sacrifice to me'.

'Hear me testify against you;
listen, Israel, as I speak:
I do not require your offerings,
sacrifice I do not seek.
Mountain birds and meadow creatures,
cattle on a thousand hills,
all the beasts are my possession,
moving as their maker wills'.

God who owns the whole creation
needs no gift, no food, no house:
bring to him your heart's thanksgiving;
God most high will hear your vows.
Trust him in the day of trouble,
call to him who will redeem;
God will be your strong deliverer,
his renown your daily theme.

Lies increase and evil prospers;
God is silent while men say,
'He has gone; let us forget him!'—
thinking he is false as they.
But his word will judge or save us;
let us come before his throne
giving thanks, receiving mercy:
God's salvation now made known.

87.87.D Tune: IN MEMORIAM (Roberts); BETHANY (Smart);
or ABBOT'S LEIGH

Scriptures: Psa 50; 48.1-2; 51.16-17; 104.10-18; 140.7 Isa 1.11;
21.10-17 Amos 5.21-27 Mic 6.6-8 1 Chron 29.11,14 Acts 17.25
Gen 1.24-25; 2.19-20; 14.18-20 Jer 50.34 Jn 12.47-50

Written: Limehouse, 1978

First published: *The Book of Praises* (Carey Publications) 1987

This is one of many texts to benefit from David Preston's care in spotting weaknesses and suggesting alternatives; it appeared in *Reformation Today* (Jan-Feb 1981) to illustrate his feature on Psalmody. Some phrases seem almost indispensible, so we may still sing of the 'cattle upon a thousand hills' in a context of both wonder and confrontation. It was hard to keep ABBOT'S LEIGH out of my mind, but another tune should be preferred. Those who reject all the traditional pronouns used of the Godhead, let alone (his) kingly power, will have to move on. 'What a God he must be whom the whole world obeys and who uses the whole world as the background of his actions!' (Weiser).

from Psalm 63
The thirsty soul

223 O GOD ETERNAL, YOU ARE MY GOD

O God eternal, you are my God!
For you I long in body and soul;
as in a dry and waterless land
I search, I thirst, I faint for you.

On holy ground your glory I saw;
your steadfast love is better than life:
I'll bless your name as long as I live
and lift my hands to you in prayer.

You feed my soul as if with a feast:
I'll sing your praise with jubilant lips:
upon my bed I call you to mind
and meditate on you at night.

For you have been the help of my life;
you take and keep me under your wing:
I cling to you, and find your support -
O God my joy, you are my God!

999.8 Tune: O GOD ETERNAL by Norman Warren

Scriptures: Psa 63; 42.1-2 Gen 17.7-8 Ex 3.5 Acts 20.24 1 Tim 2.8 Deut 10.20-21 Ruth 1.14-18; 2.12

Written: Peckham, 1970

First published: *Psalm Praise* (Falcon) 1973

'O God, you are my God'; the height and depth of that simple opening can hardly be expressed in a standard hymn tune or by a metrically regular paraphrase. It was an early text for 'Psalm Praise'; my own melody was rightly replaced by the haunting folk-quality of Norman Warren's. This has proved very effective for solo voice or woodwind instrument; the words were marginally tidied to match the flow of the music. Verses 9-11 of the original were specifically excluded from my brief; writing now, I might try to reflect their sense of danger and justice. But these four stanzas seem complete as they are. 'Steadfast love' is the covenant 'mercy' of God (Hebrew *hesed*) as in Nos.215,221 and others; this translation is an enduring gift of the Revised Standard Version to our language.

Light upon the River

from Psalm 66
Good reasons for praise

224 PRAISE OUR GOD WITH SHOUTS OF JOY

Praise our God with shouts of joy;
sing the glory of his name:
join to lift his praises high;
through the world his love proclaim!

Come and see what God has done
by the power of his right hand;
see the battles he has won
by his word of swift command!

God has tamed the raging seas,
carved a highway through the tide;
paid the cost of our release,
come himself to be our guide.

God has put us to the test,
bringing us through flood and fire
into freedom, peace and rest,
for our good is his desire.

He has not despised my prayer,
nor kept back his love from me;
he has raised me from despair:
to our God all glory be!

77.77 Tune: PRAISE OUR GOD by David Peacock;
HARTS; or DROOPING SOULS

Scriptures: Psa 66 Num 23.23 Ex 14.21-22 Josh 3.14-17 Deut 26.8 Mk 10.45 Isa 43.1-4 Dan 3.27 1 Pet 4.12 Jer 29.11-12; 32.38-41

Written: Limehouse, 1978

First published: *Psalms for Today* (Hodder & Stoughton) 1990

This is a *Jubilate Deo* in the good company of Psalm 100. Stanza 3 originally had 'paid in blood for our release'; I was persuaded to change it, but if the text retains a hint of the cross, this is exactly what Christians see prefigured in the first Exodus. Again, my version selects highlights from the full Psalm. David Peacock's tune is one of my favourites from *Hymns for the People* (Marshall Pickering 1993).

Light upon the River

from Psalm 68
Victory procession

225 LET GOD ARISE! HIS ENEMIES, BE GONE

Let God arise! His enemies, be gone
and melt like wax before the Holy One.

Make known the Lord, and sound his name aloud
to praise the king who rides upon the cloud.

Father and judge, he gave the world his law
with freedom, love, and justice for the poor.

God marched ahead, strong shepherd of his flock;
the heavens opened, earth in terror shook.

God spoke the word, and faithful was the band
of those who took the truth to every land.

See God ascend, with captives as his prize,
and gifts for all who shall in him arise.

Bless day by day the living God who saves,
who raises up his people from their graves.

Draw near the throne; musicians, lead our song!
All nations, tribes and races join the throng.

All strength is his! The rebels reign no more;
he scatters all who take delight in war.

God rules on high, and mighty is his voice;
to God be praise; in God we shall rejoice.

Glory to God, Creator, Saviour, Friend
whose greatness, love and wisdom never end.

10.10 Tune: SONG 46

Scriptures: Psa 68 Num 10.35 2 Sam 6.2 1 Chron 13.8; 15.16ff Ex 19.16-19; 20.1-21 Deut 5.1-22; 6.1-9; 15.7-11; 33.26 Mk 10.32 Jdg 5.4-5 Hab 3.3 Heb 12.25-29 Eph 4.7-13 Ezek 37.1-14 Jn 5.28-29
Written: Limehouse, 15 Sept 1983
First published: *Psalms for Today* (Hodder & Stoughton) 1990

The first four notes of SONG 46 match the opening syllables of Psalm 68 in most English translations; this seemed a natural way to begin a metrical version which rises to capture its stirring mood. While not covering every detail (and regrettably omitting Ethiopia) it finds room for the Christian implications brought out in Ephesians 4. It was sung first at Limehouse on Ascension Day, 16 May 1985, with verses shared alternately between the two halves of our evening congregation. If, as then, each verse begins as the one before finishes (on the same note) the momentum is kept up and the repetition appreciated. In many ways the Psalm prefigures Pentecost; the Old Testament texts referred to here indicate its earlier associations with the Ark of God containing the tablets of the law. Derek Kidner calls it 'This rushing cataract of a Psalm...boisterous and exhilarating'; let it be so sung!

Light upon the River

from Psalm 77
Has God forgotten?

226 GOD, I CRY ALOUD FOR HELP

God, I cry aloud for help:
set my spirit free from pain!
In troubled days and nights of worry,
O when will you take pity again?

Does your mercy still hold true?
Can I still your promise prove?
Or is your goodness gone for ever?
Have you, my God, forgotten to love?

I remember all you have done:
wonderful your ways of old!
No god, no saviour strong as you,
no work so great can ever be told.

None the love that matches yours,
none so grieved and none so good;
and no more holy human body
than his who once was nailed to the wood.

Burdened lives still groan for peace,
aching, anxious, bleeding, bowed;
so when despair and darkness come,
to you, my God, I cry aloud.

77.99 Tune: SCARBOROUGH FAIR

Scriptures: Psa 77; 22.1-5 Gen 37.35 2 Sam 12.15-17 Job 3; 19.5-6; 24.1 Mk 15.25,34 Heb 5.7 Hos 13.4

Written: Poplar, 1975

At a time when the search for new approaches to the Psalms went hand in hand with a wide range of musical styles, our sons (then at St Matthias' Primary School Poplar) recommended SCARBOROUGH FAIR which they had learned there. The sad melody seemed to fit a Psalm starting bleakly enough, but anyone who is still singing must have some seeds of hope; our longing is for something and someone who is actually there. Memory is crucial; Christians have good reason not to treat despair as either easily overcome, or permanently engulfing. Another wistful recommendation comes at No.258.

Psalm 78
The best of times, the worst of times

227 LISTEN, MY FRIENDS, TO EACH WORD

PART 1

1. Listen, my friends, to each word;
let my teaching be faithfully heard:
parables hidden of old
our parents have told.
> So let us not hide them, but speak in our turn
> God's wonders, so that our children can learn
> the truth we are eager to tell,
> the law he gave Israel;
> then children yet to be
> will pass on their faith to their family
> so they will trust in him
> and not let the memory dim.

2. Some have rejected God's law,
turned their backs on the wonders they saw,
miracles done by his hand
in old Egypt's land.
> He cut through the sea and let none of them fall,
> the waters he made stand up like a wall;
> the cloud was a guide in their flight
> the fire a pillar by night:
> he split rocks in the drought -
> abundance of water came flowing out;
> the streams came from the stone
> and rivers of water poured down.

3. God and his word they defy,
become rebels against the Most High,
treating their Lord as a slave,
demand what they crave.
> Can God give us food like this drink from the earth?
> A table, spread to supply all our dearth?
> He gave us a river indeed,
> but bread is what people need!
> Then God broke out in flame
> when they did not trust in his holy name;
> the Lord's command was given
> to open the windows of heaven.

Light upon the River

PART 2

4   God gave them manna like rain
    and from heaven provided their grain;
    bread of the angels to eat
    till they were replete.
        The wind he set free from the skies in the east,
        the south wind blew to replenish their feast
        with food till they needed no more
        and quails like sand on the shore:
        their camp was covered round
        among all their tents and across the ground;
        but God was moved to wrath
        young men were cut down in their path.

5   Spurning the gifts they received
    they refused to repent and believe,
    ending their days full of fears,
    in weakness their years.
        While still under judgement they cried in their pain
        'God help us!' to their Redeemer again
        and though all the prayers they said
        arose from hearts that were dead,
        the Lord forgave them all;
        in mercy he listened and heard their call,
        those creatures of a day,
        a breath that is passing away!

6   Time and again they rebelled,
    their devotion and trust they withheld,
    putting their God to the test
    and losing their rest.
        The rivers of Egypt had turned into blood,
        frogs jumping everywhere, gnats like a flood,
        came flies and the plague, boils and hail,
        and locusts, darkness prevailed;
        and then, each firstborn son
        struck down on the Passover night, each one;
        but God's flock safely led,
        protected and guided and fed.

Light upon the River

PART 3

7   Up to the hill he had bought,
to the holy land which they had sought,
God saw the tribes safely come
and gave them their home.
> But just as their fathers had done long before
> disloyal, faithless, they sinned even more,
> they tested and flouted his rule
> served idols and played the fool:
> the true God gave them up,
> removing their sanctuary and their hope;
> the ark passed from the land
> and into the enemy's hand.

8   Death came to men young and strong
and the maidens had no marriage song;
people and priest to the sword
by word from the Lord!
> Until once again as from sleep he awoke,
> he rose up, enemy power he broke,
> took Judah, the tribe of his love,
> Mount Zion, towering above,
> and David, from the sheep,
> to shepherd his people, to guard and keep;
> for God's word will not break,
> his flock he will never forsake.

Tune: GOD'S SPIRIT IS IN MY HEART (= GO, TELL EVERYONE)

Suggestions for singing: Use one or two parts only, but include verse 1; or select verses which make sense consecutively (1,2,4,6 or 1,4,7,8 etc); or divide into two groups to sing verses alternately.

Scriptures: Psa 78; 44.1-3; 95.7-11; 114; 136.10-16 Ex 7.14-17.7; 20.1-21; 40.36-38 Num 9.15-23; 11; 20.1-13 Job 14.1-2 Josh 3.14-17; 11.16-23 Zech 2.12 Jdg 2.10-15 1 Sam 4; 16.1-13; 26.21 2 Sam 7.8 Rom 1.24,26,28 Jn 6.31; 10.27-28,35 Lk 12.32

Written: Peckham, Jan-June 1996

I have often left Highbury with mixed feelings. But after meeting Tim Grass and Jim Sayers at the Baptist Chapel in Highbury Grove (London N5) early in 1996, I was excited at the thought of tackling a paraphrase of Psalm 78. With its 72 verses this is second only to the 119th in length, and may not instantly appeal to congregations. Tate and Brady's 'New Version' (1696) had 60 four-line stanzas; the Scots in 1650 took 65. A century earlier, Thomas Sternhold did it in 66, all in the same Common Metre; if this was one of John Hopkins' contributions (an old Prayer Book of mine marks it 'JH') I may be the first Suffolk clergyman since the 1550s to try it. I thought the text should look like Psalm 78; the Baptists wanted something substantial for this folk recitation of history-for-a-purpose. So it also had to be brisk; helped by a currently popular tune with an Israeli flavour to it, I produced my only hymn with 96 lines. The first group to sing it, revised after comments from Tim and Jim, was the Editorial Board of *Praise!*, meeting at Carey Baptist Church, Reading; its first appearance was to be in that book, and I am grateful for their belief that this was possible.

Light upon the River

Psalm 79
Devastation

228 O GOD, THE HEATHEN HAVE ATTACKED

O God, the heathen have attacked
your holy land, your house of prayer;
your city they have left a wreck,
your servants dead and dying there,
as if we had no God to help,
no king's defence, no father's care.

Lord, will your anger never cease?
It overwhelms us like a flood,
while unbelieving nations round
deride our tears, our pain and blood.
But will you let them mock your name
and taunt us: 'Now where is your God?'?

Lord, listen to the prisoners' groans,
set free the slaves condemned to die;
bring justice to this tortured world,
and when you hear your people's cry
we shall for ever give you thanks
and sing your glory, God most high!

88.88.88 Tune: DAS NEUGEBORNE KINDELEIN; or NEUMARK (= BREMEN)

Scriptures: Psa 79; 42.3,10; 74.1-10 2 Kgs 25.8-10 2 Chron 36.15-19 Jer 52.12-14 Zech 2.12 Isa 56.7 Matt 21.13 Mk 11.17 Lk 19.46 Gen 14.18-20

Written: Limehouse, 1978

First published: *The Book of Praises* (Carey Publications) 1987

Like many inner-city church buildings, St Anne's Limehouse suffered periodic vandalism. Once before, on Good Friday 1850, much of it was burned down; in 1978 history was nearly repeated. Part of the story comes in Marjorie's 'Joy in the City'; quick work by a neighbour and the Fire Brigade prevented far worse destruction. Even so, two fires burning for an hour did great damage, and the process of recovery was hard. I wrote this text later that year, to fill a gap in our material by putting a stark and questioning Psalm into contemporary form; but our own experience lent force to the process. The disasters told in such Scriptures were far worse than ours (which leads some to ask if this would ever be sung) but in many places today, Christians can all too easily identify with the anguish of the Psalm.

Light upon the River

Psalm 80
More pain, more prayer

229 ISRAEL'S SHEPHERD, HEAR OUR PRAYER

Israel's Shepherd, hear our prayer,
leading Joseph by your care,
throned between the cherubim,
light for us, as once for him:
waken all your mighty powers;
Israel's Shepherd, Lord, be ours!

Restore us now, O God, we pray
and make your face shine on our ways:
restore us, that we may be saved!

God of hosts, O Lord, how long
will your wrath be burning strong?
You were angered by our prayers,
feeding us the bread of tears;
to our neighbours we bring strife
while our foes deride our life.

Restore us, God of hosts, we pray
and make your face shine on our way:
restore us, that we may be saved!

Out of Egypt's land you brought
one choice vine, and set apart,
planted it and cleared the ground,
kept it till it filled the land:
mountains nestled in its shade,
coast to coast its branches spread.

Lord, why now destroy her hedge?
Strangers strip her foliage,
forest animals make free -
God of hosts, look down and see!
Bless from heaven this chosen root;
as a father, guard its fruit!

Now your vine is cut and burned
like the flock your wrath has spurned;
touch again your chosen son,
firstborn, raised for you alone,
that we turn not back to shame,
but for life we plead your name.

Revive, restore, Lord God of hosts:
shine on us, so we are not lost
and save us to the uttermost!

77.77.77, chorus 888   Tunes: WELLS and BE STILL AND KNOW

Scriptures: Psa 80; 42.3; 99.1 Gen 48.15; 49.22 Ex 4.22; 25.10-22 Num 6.25 Isa 5.1-7 Jer 2.21 Ezek 15 Hos 10.1 Mk 12.1 Jn 15.1-8

Written: Peckham, 1996

First published: *Praise! Preview* (Praise Trust) 1998

This Psalm was assigned during work on *Praise!* and earlier drafts were adjusted, with help. It is rich in imagery used throughout the Bible, notably the shepherd, cherubim, vine, and firstborn son, sometimes closely and boldly interwoven. We might love to know its original music, 'The Lilies of the Covenant' (so NIV); meanwhile our two C major tunes have contrasting dates but a strangely similar structure. The triple 'chorus' (not after each stanza) varies to represent the intensifying of 'God', 'God of hosts', 'Lord God of hosts'; on double tunes, see also No. 219 above. From the 8th century BC fall of Samaria, the Psalm foreshadows the New Testament 'vine' and speaks for many believers today. I first sang it at the April 1998 conference of Church Society, as part of a double presentation, 'Sing Old: Sing New'.

Light upon the River

Psalm 81
Clear voice, closed ears?

230 TO GOD OUR STRENGTH COME, SING ALOUD

To God our strength come, sing aloud
and shout for joy to Jacob's God!
Come, play the timbrel as you sing,
make harp and lyre with music ring:
at new moon, let the trumpet blow,
full moon and feast, his praises grow!

This is the law that Israel heard,
the God of Jacob's binding word;
a witness given to Joseph's tribes,
established, spoken, and transcribed:
when God has passed through Egypt's land
they heard, but did not understand.

'I freed your shoulders from their load,
your hands from clay and straw and wood;
in your distress you called to me,
I answered, and I set you free,
in thunder spoke the words of life
and proved you at the streams of Strife.

Then hear, my people, this command;
O Israel, listen, and be warned:
with you shall no new god be found,
to no strange god shall you be bound:
from Egypt I have brought you out;
ask me—you shall not go without!

But when my people closed their ears,
and Israel refused to hear,
I gave them over, heart and mind,
to go the way their mood inclined:
if only Israel would obey,
my people follow in my way!

I then would crush their enemies
and break these old hostilities,
while those whom hate and fear consume
would meet their long-awaited doom:
I would have given them finest wheat,
with honey from the rock to eat.'

88.88.88 Tune: SUSSEX CAROL or/and SURREY

Scriptures: Psa 81; 95.1-2,7-8 Gen 28.20-22 Num 10.10; 20.1-13 Ex 2.23-25; 17.1-7; 19.16-19; 20.1-21 Deut 5.4-7, 29; 31.9-13; 32.13 Rom 1.24,26,28

Written: Peckham, June 1996

This was also an assignment from the *Praise!* group, which went through several revisions. The striking repetition in the Psalm of 'Israel' and 'my people' has been kept here. The trumpet greeted the 'new moon' of the seventh month; the Day of Atonement came on the 10th day and the Feast of Tabernacles at full moon on the 15th, when every seventh year the Law was ceremonially read. Here is another possible combination of tunes by which to vary a substantial Psalm.

Light upon the River

Psalm 83
Many names: plans for genocide

231　O GOD, DO NOT KEEP SILENT

O God, do not keep silent;
see how they rage and storm!
Against your cherished people
your foes begin to swarm;
    they plan for total war!
They plot to kill a nation,
that we may be no more.

They range themselves against you;
one legion, many names.
Old grudges join with new ones,
all with their threats and claims,
    our neighbours, great and small.
Of old we know their hatred;
Lord God, you know them all!

Come, rule them with your justice,
subdue them with your rod,
as when they vainly threatened
the pasture lands of God;
    with fire and wind draw near!
As flame among the mountains
so rout them with your fear.

Pursue them, Lord, with judgement
and cover them with shame,
that all their pride may perish
and nations seek your name;
    O let that name be known -
the Lord most high, most glorious
in all the earth alone!

76.76.676 Tune: ES IST EIN' ROS ENTSPRUNGEN

Scriptures: Psa 83; 2.1-2,9 Jdg 7 2 Chron 20.1-30
Written: Peckham, Feb 1997

Reciting lists of enemies gives a certain mouthwatering satisfaction; it may also be a healthy discipline in prayer. It is harder for us to get tongues and minds round the nations catalogued in this Psalm—from the localised Hagrites (Hagarenes) to the conquering Assyrians, from the old enemy Amalek to the nearby cousins Edom (Esau). Many of them feature in the chapters noted; they become familiar to any who use the Psalter daily, and the older metrical versions faithfully name them. Stanza two of my text takes a different approach, and the fourth sounds a note of hope even in judgement. The original v.16, says Derek Kidner, 'comes to the brink of praying for the enemy's conversion'.

Light upon the River

Psalm 85
Revival: prayer for church and nation

232 WHEN THIS LAND KNEW GOD'S GRACIOUS LOVE OUTPOURED

When this land knew God's gracious love outpoured
guilt was removed and captive lives restored;
then was drawn back the anger of the Lord
    his people pardoned, their sins forgiven.

But now where wrong so flagrantly has trod
will you for ever punish with your rod?
Once more revive us! Give us life, O God!
    give joy for anguish; for wrath, salvation.

O let me hear God's word of sweet command:
Peace to his saints, salvation is at hand.
Peace to his people, glory in our land
    for those who fear him, who turn and worship.

That day draws near when truth will join with grace;
justice and peace will meet in love's embrace;
faith on the earth, and from his holy place
    he comes in glory, the righteous Saviour.

10.10.10.5 Tune: BIGGIN HILL by Michael Baughen;
GREAT OXENDEN by Paul Edwards; or SINE NOMINE

Scriptures: Psa 85 Lk 18.8 Ezra 9.6-15 Hab 3.2 Hag 2.6-9
Written: Poplar, 1972
First published: *Psalm Praise* (Falcon) 1973

Traditionally this Psalm is appointed for Christmas Day. Most congregations have other songs for that morning, but the link remains through its heightened expectations of glory, peace and salvation. Like Nos.192 and 198 in this book, it marked a transition in my work for *Psalm Praise* as I realised the possibilities of rhyme and a familiar tune; my first draft was rhymeless. Not for the last time, I took advantage of a refrain (the 'Alleluias' in *For all the saints*) to complete the text. We sang it at St Matthias' Poplar on 3 Sept 1972; small changes have been made since, and Stephen Layfield has recorded it to his own music (1993). Michael Baughen's tune, which accompanied its first appearance in print, was called WEYMOUTH STREET until that name was used elsewhere. One question sometimes raised about the first line is, Which land? The 'Sons of Korah' to whom it is credited would have had little doubt; some prefer to sing 'his land'. I hope that every nation can look back on years of God's outstanding blessings; for many of us, the Reformation and the 18th century evangelical revival were such times. But the Psalm also looks ahead with great confidence in the Saviour.

Light upon the River

Psalm 89
Lord, who is like you?

233 FOR EVER, LORD, I'LL SING YOUR LOVE

For ever, Lord, I'll sing your love,
your faithfulness make known;
all generations shall be told
your king is on the throne,
your covenant with David stands
for ever as your own:
> All praise from the angels on high,
> wonderful God!
> For who can compare with the Lord?

You rule the surging ocean tides
and calm the crashing waves,
you crushed the dragons of the deep
and sent them to their graves,
so heaven and earth which you have made
shall bless the God who saves:
> and praise from the north and the south,
> mountain and hill;
> your hand and your arm have prevailed.

As righteousness and justice are
foundations for your reign;
as faithfulness and love march on
and shall with you remain;
so none who learn to walk with you
will ever trust in vain:
> so praise be to God from his saints,
> people and prince,
> for you are their glory and strength.

In visions once you spoke to us,
'My gift of strength I bring;
my servant David I have found,
anointed him as king;
my hand will give him victory,
my praises he will sing':
> Loud praise from the ends of the earth;
> enemies fall
> and rebels will perish and die.

'His hand I set above the sea,
the rivers he shall guide;
he calls me Father, God my Rock,
I call him to my side,
appointing him as my Firstborn,
supremely glorified':
> High praise for the promise of God -
> covenant-love,
> eternally true and secure!

And if his sons forsake my law,
despising my decrees,
then I shall use my rod of power
to bring them to their knees;
yet never shall I change my mind
or break my guarantees':
> We praise for the throne that endures
> longer than time,
> more firm than the moon or the sun.

But, Lord, on your anointed one
your wrath has now come down;
the covenant is set aside
and fallen is the crown;
his wars are lost, his walls destroyed,
and gone is his renown:
> Our praise has been turned into shame,
> glory to grief;
> the days of his splendour are past.

How long, O Lord? Is it for ever
you have turned away?
How brief and empty are our lives
that blossom for a day!
Remember, Lord, your promised love
for David's sake, we pray!
> Then praise be to God for his grace,
> keeping his word
> for ever and ever: Amen!

86.86.86 with refrain Tune: GOD REST YE MERRY

Light upon the River

Suggestion: take verses 1-6 briskly, then slower until final 3 lines
Scriptures: Psa 89; 72.17-19; 78.1-7; 79.5; 80.4; 93.3-4; 132.10-12; 148.2 Isa 40.18, 25; 46.5 Gen 5.22-24 1 Sam 16.1-13 2 Sam 7.12-16 1 Chron 17.11-14 Acts 2.30 Rev 1.5
Written: Peckham, 18 Nov 1997

From Christmas words we move to Christmas music; having been asked by the *Praise!* team to try a full version of this Psalm (see No.227 above) I settled on music with enough speed and syllables for the task, enlisting its chorus for the same purpose as in No.232. It is another text for Psalm enthusiasts, needing some variation in speed to cope with the classic highs and lows of Israel's story. Like Psalm 72 but from a more questioning perspective, it celebrates the idealised reign of David, looks beyond it, and closes one of the five 'books' of the Psalms with its own doxology and loud Amen

Light upon the River

Psalm 90
God our eternal home

234 ETERNAL FATHER, GOD OF GRACE

Eternal Father, God of grace,
   as generations come and go
   for ever you have been our home;
before the mountains came to be,
   before the universe was born
   you are the Lord, you are our God
from everlasting and for evermore.

You turn us back into the dust,
   for in your sight a thousand years
   like yesterday are quickly gone.
You sweep us up as withered grass,
   our secret sins are known to you
   and in your light our lives are judged,
as under sentence all our days decline.

Our span of life is seventy years,
   or eighty if we have the strength,
   but soon they pass and are no more;
But who considers all your wrath?
   and who will feel a godly fear?
   so teach us how to count our days
that we may gain a heart renewed and wise.

Return, we pray: O Lord, how long?
   And when you come, and morning breaks,
   O meet us with your steadfast love!
Then we shall balance evil days
   with days of joy when we can see
   your favour shine upon our work
and let our children see your majesty!

888.888.10 Tune: ETERNAL FATHER by Christopher Seaman

Scriptures: Psa 90; 4.2; 89.46 Deut 32.36 Isa 40.6-8 1 Pet 5.10 Gen 2.7; 3.17-19 Job 10.9 Eccles 3.20 2 Pet 1.19; 3.8 Acts 2.43;

Written: Peckham, 1969-1970

First published: *Psalm Praise* (Falcon) 1973

Two historical factors have confirmed the unique place held by Psalm 90 ('a prayer of Moses the man of God') in the English-speaking church. Miles Coverdale's version is one of two Psalms appointed for the Burial of the Dead: 'Lord, thou hast been our refuge from one generation to another... the days of our age are threescore years and ten...O satisfy us with thy mercy, and that soon...'. And Isaac Watts' *Our God, our help in ages past* became a national hymn for great occasions, notably since its delayed marriage to the tune ST ANNE in 1861. Such was the background to this item in my first 'Psalm Praise' assignment. The metre is regular but rare; the tune first composed for it has not proved easy. Few other Scriptures (let alone paraphrases) have the scope of the original Psalm; the Watts hymn is more searching than may seem from the edited selection of stanzas which are usually sung.

Light upon the River

Psalm 92
For the Sabbath Day: soaring praise to the living God

235 MAKE MUSIC TO THE LORD MOST HIGH

Make music to the Lord most high
whose praise is our delight;
as day begins we sing your love,
your faithfulness by night.

Lord, when we see what you have done
our songs of joy resound;
your handiwork, how vast it is,
your counsels, how profound!

The godless mind will never know -
because its sense is void -
that though the wicked spread like grass
they all shall be destroyed.

For ever, Lord, you are supreme;
your throne remains on high
while rebels meet eternal doom
and evildoers die.

But like the cedar and the palm
the righteous stand serene;
they flourish in the house of God,
their leaves are fresh and green

To fruitful age they still proclaim
the Lord who makes them new;
our God, in whom there is no wrong,
my Rock, for ever true.

CM Tune: KILMARNOCK; BISHOPTHORPE; or RODMELL

Scriptures: Psa 92; 8.3 Eph 5.19-20 Col 3.16 Lam 3.22-23 Lk 2.25-38 Isa 40.29-31 Deut 32.4,13,15,18,31
Written: Limehouse, 1981
First published: *The Book of Praises* (Carey Publications) 1987

Music is specifically encouraged in this 'Sabbath Song'; so is regularity and testimony. It is more assured than many Psalms, but we are still conscious of the godless rebels. Here is a terrible warning that their end is as certain as their minds are closed. The option of godliness remains open, and the song ends joyfully for the senior members of the congregation. I wrote this text to meet the need of a new version; *Sweet is the work, my God, my King* is still enjoyed, but needs some gentle revision. So did mine in 1987-8, with the usual help. It was included in the 1988 Greenock Psalmody Festival.

Light upon the River

Psalm 95
Venite!

236 COME WITH ALL JOY TO SING TO GOD

Come with all joy to sing to God
our saving Rock, the living Lord;
in glad thanksgiving seek his face
with songs of victory and grace.

In holiness and light arrayed
above all gods that we have made,
he is the one almighty King,
and his the glory that we sing.

The earth is his from east to west,
from ocean-floor to mountain-crest;
he made the sea and formed the lands,
he shaped the islands by his hands.

Come near to worship! Come with faith;
bow down to God who gives us breath:
God is our Shepherd, God alone;
we are his people, all his own.

But if you hear his voice today
do not reject what he will say;
when Israel wandered from God's path
they suffered forty years of wrath.

That generation went astray;
they did not want to know his way:
they put their Saviour to the test,
and saw his power, but lost their rest.

So to the God of earth and heaven,
the Father, Spirit, Son, be given
praise now, as praise has ever been
and ever shall be praise—Amen!

LM Tune: VOATES by Agnes Tang; or FULDA

Scriptures: Psa 95; 100.1-2 Gen 1.1-10 Ex 17.1-7 Num 14.20-23; 20.1-13 Deut 1.34-36; 12.8-10 Heb 3.7-4.11 Matt 11.28-30

Written: Limehouse, 1978

First published: *Hymns for Today's Church* (Hodder & Stoughton) 1982

With its double requirement of bowing down and listening to God, Psalm 95 has a unique place in the Hebrew Psalter, the New Testament, and the Prayer Book service of Morning Prayer, as the *Venite, exultemus Domino*. The *Psalm Praise* compilers remained dissatisfied with the versions which opened that 1973 book; a metrical alternative seemed desirable, not least when the liturgical revisers of that period cut out the very words which originally won it a place in the service and which are judged most vital in Hebrews 3 and 4. Michael Perry and David Preston were separately assembling Psalm versions and helped to finalise this one; others which have appeared since suggest a continuing need here. Like its source, this text leads up to the crucial word 'rest'; unlike most others it has a doxology, which I am sorry to see occasionally omitted.

Light upon the River

Psalm 96

Patterns of praise: heaven and nature sing

237 SING, SING, SING TO THE LORD

Sing, sing, sing to the Lord,
sing, every land, your own new song;
sing of your Saviour each day!
   Let all the nations
   hear of his glory,
   victories, wonders,
   tell them the story -
praising the Lord with heart and tongue,
praising the Lord with heart and tongue.

Great, great, great is the Lord,
great and most worthy of our love,
great above all other gods.
   They are but nothings,
   God is all-glorious,
   splendid, majestic,
   strong and victorious,
Maker of earth and heaven above,
Maker of earth and heaven above.

Bring, bring, bring to the Lord,
bring to his name the worship due,
bring your best gift to his throne:
   God is all-holy,
   tremble before him;
   clothed in his beauty,
   come to adore him -
tell what the Lord has done for you,
tell what the Lord has done for you.

Joy, joy, joy in the heavens,
joy for the life of sea and earth,
joy in the field and the wood!
   Welcome his kingdom,
   praise his salvation;
   now he is coming,
   Lord of creation,
judging the peoples with his truth,
judging the peoples with his truth.

687.5555.88 Tune: BOW COMMON LANE by Stephen James

Scriptures: Psa 96; 29.1-2; 72.10-11; 95.3; 98.1,2,9; 99.3,5,9
1 Chron 16.23-33 Gen 1.1; 2.1,4 Rom 8.19-21 Isa 61.10-11
Rev 22.7,20

Written: Glenfinnan, Scotland, Aug 1982

First published: *Worship Songs Ancient and Modern* (Canterbury Press Norwich) 1992

Stephen James reckoned that it must have been the scenery. Our last holiday as a full family of six was spent in the spectacular setting of the Western Highlands, thanks to Kenneth and Mary Habershon. That was the summer of our revised *God save our gracious queen;* but I was also trying to do justice to the soaring beauty of this Psalm with its patterns of triple repetition. Steve was then living near us in Bow Common Lane, London E14; this seemed a better name for his lyrical music than a first suggestion, 'Sing sing'. His ministry was then at St Helen's Bishopsgate where Dick Lucas was Rector. It was Dick who first invited me to go into print about today's hymn-scene; more important, countless pastors and preachers thank God for the recent story of St Helen's and its wide-ranging initiatives such as the Proclamation Trust. The words were modified to match the tune, and later to avoid ambiguity. We sang them at Limehouse on Sept 18 1983, at a Commissioning service for Lydia Pownall (later Lydia Hurle) before she began her work in East Asia.

Light upon the River

Psalm 97
The true King

238 THE LORD IS KING! LET EARTH BE GLAD

> The Lord is king! Let earth be glad,
> let coasts and islands all rejoice;
> > cloud and mist enfold him;
> > righteousness and justice
> make firm foundations for his throne;
> his enemies are all consumed.
>
> The mountains melt at his approach
> for he is Master of the world;
> > earth beneath his lightning
> > shines and shakes and trembles.
> The heavens announce his righteousness,
> all nations see his majesty.
>
> Let those who follow worthless cults
> be put to shame before the Lord!
> > Gods and superstitions
> > bow down low before him!
> For God Most High rules all the earth
> and every power submits to him.
>
> Hate evil, you who love the Lord!
> He keeps his loyal servants safe,
> > frees them from the wicked,.
> > shines on them, delights them;
> you righteous, in the Lord rejoice:
> give glory to his holy name!

88.66.88 Tunes in 'Psalm Praise' by Ivor Keys and Norman Warren

Scriptures: Psa 97; 96.4-6,10; 98.9 Ex 19.16-19 Jdg 5.4-5 Heb 12.29 Matt 24.30 Acts 14.11-15; 19.17-20 Gen 14.18-20

Written: Peckham, 1970

First published: *Psalm Praise* (Falcon) 1973

This was one of the first texts prepared for *Psalm Praise* from the portion allotted to me. It attracted two tunes, both of which are published there but need some hard work by singers and musicians. It appeared on the album issued at the time, *Psalm Praise: Sing a New Song* for which Marjorie was in the choir. The Psalm is graphic in picturing God's judgements, and like others must be used wisely.

Light upon the River

from Psalm 100
Jubilate Deo!

239 SHOUT FOR JOY TO THE LORD, ALL THE EARTH

Shout for joy to the Lord, all the earth!
Serve the Lord with the gladness of praise;
come before him with songs full of joy.

Know that he is the Lord—he is God!
He has made us, and we are his own;
all his people, the flock in his care.

So with thanksgiving enter his gates,
and come into his courts with your praise;
give him thanks, and give praise to his name.

For the Lord of the earth, he is good;
and his love will for ever endure,
and his faithfulness last evermore.

999 anapaestic Tune needed

Scriptures: Psa 100; 95.1-2,6-7 Acts 3.1 Ezra 3.11 Jer 33.11
Written: Limehouse, 1982

This brief Psalm has a vast theme and a long history. Its structure is of grand simplicity: a double call to come before God, and a double reason for coming. The 'Old Hundredth' is one of our noblest Reformation tunes, adopted for Isaac Watts' *Before Jehovah's aweful throne* and kept most regularly for *All people that on earth do dwell*; in total contrast is the familiar *Jubilate* of Anglican chant (a Morning Prayer option from the BCP), or Michael Perry's *Jubilate everybody* which others have 'borrowed'. I was invited to try a different approach, but the novel metre sounds like an emergency call for help, to which no musician has yet responded. Avoiders of masculine pronouns may have almost as much trouble here, I fear, as with *He's got the whole world in his hands*. My final stanza (verse 5 in the Bible) is the refrain from many Scriptures, including several other Psalms.

Light upon the River

from Psalm 104
Creation and salvation

240 I'LL SING A NEW HYMN TO MY GOD

I'll sing a new hymn to my God
of glory majestic and free,
unconquered in splendour, the Lord
who spoke, and all worlds came to be.
His Spirit was sent to create;
no mortal can silence his word:
creation declares, God is great,
and quakes when his music is heard.

High mountain and deep ocean floor
will melt, for their Maker will come,
and nations opposing his law
are judged by his thundering doom.
No offering or work of our hands,
no service our hearts can perform,
can match what his justice demands
or shelter our lives from his storm.

But now full of hope we come near,
for all are rewarded who seek;
we find you, the God whom we fear,
in Jesus, the Word that you speak.
In him all our payment is made
and we are created anew;
no longer condemned or afraid,
but safe in your love, we love you!

8888.D anapaestic Tune: TREWEN

Scriptures: Psa 104; 33.9; 148.1-6 Gen 1.1-2,14-18 2 Pet 3.5 Rom 3.19-26; 8.1 Heb 1.2; 4.16; 7.19; 10.22 Jas 4.8 Deut 4.29 Isa 55.6-7 Lam 3.25 Hos 10.12 Amos 5.4-6 1 Jn 4.9-19 Jn 21.15-17

Written: Poplar, 1976

Uniquely in this section, this text did not arise from a Psalm; but its close affinities with the 104th give it a place here. Its original prompting was ch.16 of the book of Judith in the Apocrypha, with its fine Psalm-like verses to which I have given a full Christian perspective. Unlike No.205 above, it holds back the final offering of love until the final line.

Light upon the River

Psalm 108
Morning songs for our Maker and Saviour

241 MY HEART IS READY, O MY GOD

My heart is ready, O my God;
let songs of joy be born,
let music sound from strings and voice:
I will awake the dawn!

Across the continents I sing,
and growing praise shall rise;
for your great love spans earth and heaven,
your truth surmounts the skies.

O God, be praised above the heavens;
let glory fill the earth,
and help and save with your right hand
the race you brought to birth.

God speaks from his pure sanctuary
to claim both west and east:
'The mountains and the plains are mine,
the greatest and the least'.

'My people are my battle-dress,
my sceptre, helm and sword,
and rebel nations have become
a footstool for the Lord!'

Who else can give us victory
and break the strongholds down?
O God, if you reject us now
we cannot fight alone.

How useless is all human help
when fighting stubborn wrong!
But we shall triumph in the Lord,
and God shall be our song.

CM Tune: HORSELL by Gareth Green; WARWICK (Stanley); SAN ROCCO, or TIVERTON

Scriptures: Psa 108; 36.5; 57.7-11; 60.5-12 Isa 6.3 Matt 12.29 Mk 3.27 2 Cor 10.3-4
Written: Limehouse, 1981
First published: *The Book of Praises* (Carey Publications) 1982

This Psalm combines the endings of two earlier ones (57 and 60) which, says Derek Kidner, begin under stress but end strongly, though David is hunted in one and defeated in the other. It is the latter borrowings which, like Psalm 83, give us names to sing: 'Gilead is mine, and Manasses is mine: Ephraim also is the strength of my head. Judah is my lawgiver, Moab is my washpot: over Edom will I cast out my shoe, upon Philistia will I triumph' (etc). As in No.231 above, this text loses the names but tries in stanzas 4 and 5 to express their significance; the last line links with the first to express its unity. I wrote it when *Symphony* magazine (see No.1) invited new Psalm versions; this appeared in issue No.12 (Autumn-Winter 1981-2). The present revision, including direct speech, dates from 1988.

Light upon the River

Psalm 111
Praise God for his gifts, and for himself

242 HALLELUJAH, PRAISE THE LORD

Hallelujah, praise the Lord!
Where the people love his name,
where my Saviour is adored,
thanks and praise shall be my theme.
All his works are just and great;
here we find our chief delight:
good it is to meditate
all his everlasting right.

We recall what he has done,
tender mercies, firm and sure;
he is God, the holy One,
all his promises endure.
God provides our daily bread,
he defends his people's cause,
life and home and all we need
by his everlasting laws.

Rich in his redeeming grace,
keeping covenant he came;
see the glory in his face:
holy, holy is his name!
Fear him—that is wisdom's way;
here begin our happiest days:
trust him—thus we shall obey
God our everlasting praise.

77.77.D Tune: TENDER MERCIES by Christopher Norton; SALZBURG (Hintze); or SYRIA

Scriptures: Psa 111 Rev 15.3-4 Matt 6.11 Lk 11.3 Eph 1.7 Deut 7.9 2 Cor 4.6 Lev 22.32-33 Job 28.28 Prov 1.7; 9.10 Eccles 12.13

Written: Glenfinnan and Limehouse, Aug 1982

First published: *The Book of Praises* (Carey Publications) 1987

This is another text from Glenfinnan Lodge (see No.237), completed at home on Jonathan's 17th birthday. The Psalm had been on my list 'to be tackled some time'. Normally I cannot insist on one spelling of 'Hallelujah', since books, languages, and traditions vary. For the sake of tracing first lines, I have settled for the 'H' word in these texts. David Preston has assisted my struggle with other phrases; on the word 'praise', Erik Routley is eloquent in *Hymns and the Faith* (John Murray, 1955) pp.2-3.

Light upon the River

Psalm 113
More praise, more reasons

243 PRAISE THE LORD, HALLELUJAH

Praise the Lord, Hallelujah!
Servants of God, sing praise to his name!
Let his name be uplifted, worshipped now and evermore.
    From the sunrise to its setting
      let the name of the Lord be praised:
God is highly exalted over all.

Who is like him in glory,
over the nations, ruling the world?
Our God rules over heaven, yet stoops down to see the earth.
    He lifts up the poor and needy
      from their ashes to a royal throne:
God gives joy to the family—praise the Lord!

Tune: OVERTON by Stephen James

Scriptures: Psa 113; 50.1 Mal 1.11 Gen 11.5 1 Sam 2.8 Lk 1.52
Written: Limehouse, 1981

If some resemblance between this and the previous text is noticed, it is partly because together with Psalm 112 (not represented here) they make up a trio of songs beginning 'Hallelujah'. This one, like Psalms 146 to 150, ends in the same way, and I am sorry when in translation we lose this international word which has flagged up the kingdom of God wherever the Gospel takes root. For these verses, the tune came first; Steve James offered it for a new text, and together they appeared in the Songbook of St Helen's Bishopsgate (see No.237 above) where he was then working.

Light upon the River

Psalm 114
Exodus and Easter

244 WHEN ISRAEL FLED FROM EGYPT

When Israel fled from Egypt
and Jacob's people left that foreign land,
then Judah was God's temple
and Israel was the treasure in his hand.

The Red Sea looked, and wondered;
the Jordan halted in its winding way.
The mountains danced in gladness,
the hills began to skip like lambs for joy.

O sea, why did you falter?
And why, O river, did you turn around?
You hills and mountains, tell us,
why with your dancing did you shake the ground?

You lands and waters, tremble!
The Lord, the God of Jacob, has come near;
he turns the rocks to rivers
and from the stones the living streams appear.

All glory to the Father
and to the risen Saviour, Christ the Lord,
and to the Holy Spirit:
one God, your name be ceaselessly adored.

7.10.7.10 Tune: DANCING HILLS by Noël Tredinnick;
IN EXITU by David Preston; or ACH BLEIB BEI UNS

Scriptures: Psa 114; 136.10-16 Ex 12.51; 14.21-22; 15.16-17; 17.1-7; 19.5 Num 20.1-13 Josh 3.14-17 Ezek 11.16 1 Pet 2.9

Written: Limehouse, 1978

First published: *The Book of Praises* (Carey Publications) 1987

Like the greatest and simplest of Easter hymns, *Jesus Christ is risen today*, the Anglican chant for Psalm 114 is anonymous. So, come to that, are the words; hymn and Psalm together make a powerful impact as we celebrate the fulfilment of the Hebrew Passover in the risen Christ. But like the hundredth, this Psalm can be approached in varied ways; Noël Tredinnick and David Preston have both written tunes for this distinctive metre.

from Psalm 116
Saved from death and worse

245 I LOVE MY GREAT LORD

I love my great Lord
whose mercy has heard
and answered my cry;
to God I will call till
   the day that I die.

The shackles of death
had pulled me beneath
and close to the grave;
but then I cried out to the Lord
   who can save.

My soul, take your rest!
The Lord had so blessed
and granted to you
protection and confidence,
   timely and true.

From death and its fears,
from stumbling and tears,
O Lord, you saved me
to live, and to walk with you,
   faithful and free.

How can I repay
what God gives today
for me and for all?
Your cup I shall welcome,
   your name I will call.

My praises I will
in public fulfil;
whatever shall come
your service is freedom,
   your presence is home.

Lord God, I shall raise
thankofferings of praise
your love to acclaim:
O sing Hallelujah,
   and bow to the name!

All praise now be given
to the Father in heaven,
all praise through the Son,
all praise in the Spirit:
   praise God, everyone!

555.11 Tune: ARDWICK

Scriptures: Psa 116; 40.1-3 Jonah 2.1-10 Jer 38.1-13 Heb 13.15
Written: Limehouse, May 1983

This metre was used to marvellous effect by Charles Wesley in such hymns as *Away with our fears* and *Come, let us anew our journey pursue*, whose lines are usually set out as here. The Psalm always brings to mind a lay preacher at Redland Parish Church Bristol (where we belonged, 1963-65) who recited it by heart as his own testimony, before filling in the details personal to him. This text is an attempt to wed a springing metre with a bold, exuberant Psalm. Revisions in 1986-87 took a different path to those of No.205. There I varied 2nd and 3rd person lines; here I aimed at inclusive language.

Light upon the River

Psalm 117
Great God, global worship, few words

246 PRAISE THE LORD, ALL NATIONS, PRAISE

Praise the Lord, all nations, praise!
Worship him, all humankind:
Hallelujah, praise the Lord!
Mighty is your love for us,
firm for ever is your truth:
Hallelujah, praise the Lord!

777.D Tune: VENI SANCTE SPIRITUS

Scriptures: Psa 117 Rom 15.11

Written: Limehouse, 1978

First published: *Psalms for Today* (Hodder & Stoughton) 1990

Short 'worship songs' do not have to be trivial. In this, the smallest of all Psalms, together with the 134th, we possess a model for such brief offerings of praise. Both are God-centred and outward looking, and give the best of reasons for singing. But it is often the simpler items which I find hardest to get right, and the number of adjustments I have made to this one is alarming; they spanned nearly a decade. We have valued the two-stanza Isaac Watts version *From all that dwell below the skies*, and the Psalm mattered enough for the apostle Paul to use its evidence in his greatest epistle.

Light upon the River

from Psalm 118
This is the day: one

247 PRAISE TO THE LORD, FOR THE LORD IS GOOD

Praise to the Lord, for the Lord is good;
thank him for his everlasting love:
this was the song of the Israelites,
this was the song of the priests of old;
this is the song we can sing today,
all who will worship and fear the Lord:
    give thanks in Jesus' name;
    his love remains the same.

Out of my need, to the Lord I called;
he answered me, and he set me free.
I'm not afraid; he is on my side:
what can my enemies do to me?
Far better trust in the Lord my God
than to depend on the lords of earth:
    take refuge in the Lord;
    rely upon his word.

Christ is the stone banished by the builders;
chief cornerstone he has now become.
This is the miracle God has done,
wonderful, marvellous, in our eyes;
this is the day which the Lord has made,
we'll sing Hosanna to celebrate:
    save us, O Lord, we pray
    this resurrection day!

Blessings be yours in the house of God;
blessings be yours in the name of Christ!
He is the Lord and he lights our life,
he is the Saviour to whom we sing,
praise to the Lord, for the Lord is good,
thank him for his everlasting love:
    this day and all our days
    transform with thankful praise

99.99.99.66 Tune: PRAISE TO THE LORD by Norman Warren

Scriptures: Psa 118 1 Chron 16.34 2 Chron 5.13; 7.3 Ezra 3.11 Jer 33.11 Heb 13.6 Matt 21.9,42 Mk 11.7-10; 12.10 Jn 12.13 Acts 4.11 1 Pet 2.7

Written: Peckham, 1970

First published: *Psalm Praise* (Falcon) 1973

This was the first Psalm version I wrote, and the first to reach Michael Baughen in response to the team assignments for what became 'Psalm Praise'. My first delight was to find I had been allotted this pivotal Psalm, repeatedly quoted in the New Testament and treasured by Christians as prophetic of the Lord Jesus Christ. Here are his life, death, resurrection, special day and special praises; the favourite Psalm of Martin Luther among others: 'This is my psalm, my chosen psalm. I love them all; I love all holy Scripture, which is my consolation and my life. But this psalm is nearest my heart, and I have a familiar right to call it mine. It has saved me from many a pressing danger... It is my friend, dearer to me than all the honour and power of the earth.' My own small danger was different; I should not have gone to work with such speed. The result is a text which I include for the sake of completeness. It has been sung in Cornwall and Australia, put into Danish, featured in Suffolk's 'Unity Choir' concerts in the 1990s, and is quoted in full in Michael Ball's 'Singing to the Lord' (BRF 1979); yet in spite of Norman Warren's tune, the long lines and stanzas do not quite work, or do justice to its great theme. As a small early milestone on a writing, singing journey, it has its own place in the picture. But now...

Light upon the River

from Psalm 118
This is the day: two

248 GIVE THANKS TO GOD, FOR HE IS GOOD

Give thanks to God, for he is good,
the everlasting Giver:
let all his people praise the Lord
whose love endures for ever.
For his right hand has made me strong;
I am his new creation:
he is my God, he is my song,
my strength and my salvation.

When troubles loomed on every side
and nameless fears surrounded,
to God my Lord I quickly cried
and soon his help abounded.
For God has heard my desperate plea
and seen my pain and sadness;
he came to me and set me free
in paths of peace and gladness.

We trust in God, in him alone;
the stone that was rejected
has now become the cornerstone
that God has resurrected.
The day is his, the first of days,
to celebrate with singing;
rejoice in God, and give him praise,
our best hosannas bringing.

The Lord has made his light to shine
on all our dark depression;
from east to west, believers join
his victory procession.
O save us, Lord: give us success!
Your gifts flow like a river;
O bless us, God whose name we bless!
Your love endures for ever.

87.87.D iambic Tune: SOMERSET by Michael Saward;
GOLDEN SHEAVES; or MEGERRAN

Scriptures: Psa 118   1 Chron 16.34   2 Chron 5.13; 7.3 Ezra 3.11
Jer 33.11 2 Cor 5.17 Ex 15.2 Isa 12.2 Matt 21.9,42 Mk 11.9-10;
12.10 Jn 12.13 Acts 4.11   1 Pet 2.7

Written: Limehouse, Aug 1980

Like No.247, this text springs from the most exhilarating of Bible Psalms, found between the shortest and the longest. The 118th gives us the word 'Hosanna' ('Save us, we pray!') and Isaac Watts' *This is the day the Lord has made*; ideally it needs responsive or antiphonal voices, and is the natural choice for a Palm Sunday celebrated in the light of Good Friday and Easter to come. My first paraphrase was something of an experiment, and this second attempt has a familiar metre. Michael Saward's tune is in *Psalm Praise* to his own *I thank you, Lord, with all my heart* (from Psalm 111).

Light upon the River

from Psalm 119
Delight in the law of God

249 ALL YOUR COMMANDMENTS, FATHER ALMIGHTY

All your commandments, Father almighty,
Bring to your children healing and blessing;
Christians who keep them find here their comfort.

Daily instruct us as your disciples:
Each of your statutes stands firm for ever;
Faithful your promise, free your forgiveness.

God of all mercy, grant me your guidance;
How can a young man keep his way holy?
I have found treasure in your instruction.

Joy comes to nations knowing your judgements;
Keeping them brings us close to your kingdom—
Laws that spell freedom, true liberation.

My heart is listening for you each morning;
Never desert me; speak in the night-time;
Open my eyes, Lord, then lead me onwards.

Put right my passions by your clear precepts:
Quell my rebellions, rescue me quickly:
Raise and restore me, mighty Redeemer.

Saviour whose Spirit gave us the Scriptures,
Train me to trust them when I am tempted;
Unless you helped me, I would go under.

Vain are my own ways; yours is the victory;
Wonderful Counsellor, you are my wisdom:
Your word shall teach me; I will obey you.

10.10.10 Tune: SOMERTON B by Mervyn Horder; PROMISES by Christopher Norton; or ALL YOUR COMMANDMENTS by Norman Warren

Scriptures: Psa 119 (selected); 1.2; 19.7-14 Lk 24.32,45 Rom 15.4 Eph 2.4 Mk 12.34 Jas 1.15 1 Sam 3.1-14 Dan 2.19-22 Acts 16.9-10 2 Tim 3.15-17 2 Pet 1.21 Isa 9.6
Written: Limehouse, 1980
First published: *Songs from the Psalms* (Hodder & Stoughton) 1990

Unlike Psalms 78 and 89 (the 2nd and 3rd longest) the 119th was not presented to me with a request for a full version! Its 22 sections correspond to the Hebrew alphabet, with the eight verses in each part all starting with the same letter. When it is sung by a congregation, only fragments of the whole are normally used. Ronald Knox's translation reflects this alphabetical plan; some recent readers find the Hebrew device impossibly artificial, while others feel the same about rhyme in English. (Psalms 25, 34, 111 and 112 are also 'acrostic'.) But many through history have memorised the Psalm and nourished themselves on the riches it offers, among them Augustine of Hippo, the Puritans, William Wilberforce, John Ruskin and Henry Martyn. Clarence P Walhout's *Blessed are those who heed the law of God* (1980) has 22 six-line stanzas, on the faithful pattern of the older metrical Psalters; other writers have been content with extracts, or with dwelling on the different titles for the word of God (law, commands, precepts etc) as in the original. My own version uses the alphabet at the beginning and end of each line; metrical enjoyment need not hinder meditation, but can actually help it.

Light upon the River

Psalm 121
Finding security in God

250 I TO THE HILLS LIFT UP MY EYES

I to the hills lift up my eyes;
from where shall help be given?
My help comes only from the Lord
who made the earth and heaven.

He will not let your foot be moved;
guard over you he keeps:
he watches over Israel
and slumbers not, nor sleeps.

Strong is the Lord, your shield and shade;
safe are you in his sight:
sun shall not hurt your life by day
nor shall the moon by night.

So shall the Lord keep you from harm;
he will keep safe and sure
your going out, your coming in
from now, for evermore.

CM Tune: BEN MORE by Mervyn Horder

Scriptures: Psa 121; 91.5,6,12; 126.6 Jude 24 Lk 21.18-19 Num 27.15-17

Written: Oakley and Peckham, 1994-95

'This Psalm has a place in the feelings of ordinary people somewhere near Ps 23...It is abundantly worthwhile to try and repack it for today': thus Mervyn Horder, Oct 1994, in the course of a detailed correspondence. He had composed a tune for the Scots version of 1850, but saw the need for clearer words. Mine were modelled on his music, but proved to be one text we could not agree on. We each made concessions; but he wanted a soon/moon rhyme; I was unwilling to give up the key question- mark in line 2! So we can share responsibility for the limitations of the result, and be grateful for the Scriptural gem which stirred us both. The hills are 'enigmatic' (so Kidner: are they a menace or a refuge?). But so is the moon; Michael Wilcock suggests that the Lord guards us not only from real and known dangers (the sun) but also from those which are unknown, hidden, or even imaginary.

Light upon the River

Psalm 122
The city of God; the house of the Lord; the glad congregation

251 JERUSALEM! HOW GLAD I WAS

Jerusalem! How glad I was
when they invited me
to climb with them the mount of prayer,
the place of majesty.
Jerusalem! Within your gates
our willing feet have stood,
and there we raised our voices high
to fill the house of God.

Jerusalem! A city built
compact and walled around;
the sacred tribes ascended here
and made their psalms resound.
Let us, like Israel, go up
to pay the Lord our dues,
to hear the judgements of the law,
the joy of God's good news.

Jerusalem! May you have peace,
your people long endure;
may all your citizens be safe,
your towers and streets secure.
For brothers, sisters, friends, I pray
let peace return again:
O Lord our God, meet us in grace;
in glory come to reign!

DCM Tune: DURROW; TOTARA; or HAYDN

Scriptures: Psa 122; 125.5; 128.5; 137.5 Matt 21.13; 23.57 Lk 19.41-42 Heb 10.19-24; 12.22-24

Written: Glenfinnan, Scotland, Aug 1982

First published: *Psalms for Today* (Hodder & Stoughton) 1990

This was the third of my 'Glenfinnan Psalms', fruit of our Scottish family holiday: see Nos.237 and 242. Again I walk on holy ground in many ways. Isaac Watts has enriched three centuries with *How pleased and blest was I*; thousands of years earlier, pilgrims sang this 'Song of Ascents' in the sacred city. There is nothing on earth like the wonder of prayer, praise and listening together, and very little as effective as the personal invitation, 'Let us go!'. Our task as ever is to transpose the songs of David (who made Mount Zion his throne) for an age when 'neither on this mountain nor in Jerusalem will you worship the Father' (Jn 4.21-24). My first draft began 'Jerusalem, how glad I am that they invited me...'; other changes before publication brought it closer to the Psalm.

Psalm 123
In simple trust: the mercy of God

252 I LIFT MY EYES TO YOU

I lift my eyes to you,
to heaven your royal throne;
as servants watch their master's hand
we look to you alone

Have mercy, Lord, we pray,
and hear your people's cries;
until your mercy reaches us
on you we fix our eyes.

The proud have mocked us long;
their scorn we have endured:
our days are filled with their contempt;
we look to you, O Lord.

SM Tune: ST MICHAEL; or SWABIA

Scriptures: Psa 123 Matt 5.34; 8.9; 24.45-46 Heb 12.2 Lk 18.7 Acts 5.41

Written: Limehouse, Feb 1981

First published: *The Book of Praises* (Carey Publications) 1987

This text in Short Metre (rare for me) was written to fill a gap in versions of an exquisitely simple Psalm, which expresses in its four verses both the depths of endurance and the heights of longing. Psalm 121 began by looking to the hills; this next 'Song of Ascents' simply looks to God.

Light upon the River

Psalm 125
Faith in the city

253 THOSE WHO RELY ON THE LORD ARE UNSHAKEABLE

Those who rely on the Lord are unshakeable,
firm as Mount Zion, supremely assured;
just as the mountains encircle Jerusalem,
round us for ever is standing the Lord.

Evil shall not always trample on righteousness;
God's time will come when oppression shall cease.
Lord, bless the righteous, restrain the impenitent:
grant to your people the gift of your peace.

12.10.12.10 Tune: WAS LEBET, WAS SCHWEBET; or SANCTISSIMUS

Scriptures: Psa 125; 122.6-8 Jn 14.27

Written: Limehouse, 1980

First published: *The Book of Praises* (Carey Publications) 1987

'As the mountains are round about Jerusalem, so the LORD is round his people from henceforth even for ever.' That text from Psalm 125 adorned the hallway of the Vicarage at Ulpha beside the river Duddon, where Roy Greenwood was our host for both youth weekends and family holidays from Barrow in Furness. Ulpha, itself among the Cumbrian fells, is one of many places where those words have been treasured in special ways. My first draft began 'Trust in the Lord'; David Preston worked with me to give the two stanzas their present shape. We had problems with the penultimate line; what exactly are we praying for the impenitent? We hope this text is both true to the Psalm, and fit to sing.

Light upon the River

Psalm 127
City, home and family

254 IF GOD DOES NOT BUILD UP OUR HOUSE

If God does not build up our house,
in vain the builders' hands;
if God does not protect the town,
in vain the watchman stands.

In vain we rise at early dawn
or night's late vigil keep
in worry for our daily bread:
God loves, and grants us sleep.

Our sons and daughters are a gift,
a blessing from the Lord;
like arrows from a warrior's bow
they bring a rich reward.

How blessed are they in God their Lord
whose children bless that name,
who stand assured before the world
and are not put to shame!

To God who made us, God who saves,
and God who is our friend,
one God, be glory, blessing, praise
for love that has no end.

CM Tune: ST BOTOLPH; or THIS ENDRIS NYGHT

Scriptures: Psa 127 Matt 6.11 Lk 11.3 Prov 31.28

Written: Limehouse, 1987

An early draft for this 'family Psalm' was under discussion in 1981; it began 'Unless the Lord builds up our house'. I then found that Mollie Knight's version had an almost identical opening; still wanting to persevere with mine, I changed the first line—and then so much more that it became almost a new text. The man and his sons, I felt, could fairly be made inclusive, while the persons on watch (stanza 1) were probably men! Such questions face anyone who wishes to versify for today even a Psalm so basic as this, while retaining its original purpose. Home and neighbourhood security, sleeplessness and over-work, parenting and young adulthood, are always relevant; so is the building and blessing of God.

from Psalm 128
Family blessings: one

255 BLESSED ARE THOSE WHO FEAR THE LORD

Blessed are those who fear the Lord,
walking in God's perfect ways:
all they do shall bring reward;
love enriches all their days.

Blessings greet the husband, wife,
parents, children, old and young;
fruits of faith be theirs for life,
joy in songs together sung.

Bless us, Lord! Your kingdom come:
childrens children shouting praise,
prayer in nation, church and home,
peace in Christ to crown our days.

77.77 Tune: INNOCENTS; or CULBACH

Scriptures: Psa 128; 127.3-5; 144.12 Gen 6.9 Job 1.8; 2.3; 42.12-16 Matt 6.10; 21.15-16 Lk 11.2 Col 3.15-16 Gal 6.16

Written: Limehouse, 1981

First published: *The Wedding Book* (Marshall Pickering) 1989

After 'Psalm Praise' some of us began work on metrical versions of Psalms not included there; this was one. It was a natural choice for Family Services, but lacked a credible paraphrase. My draft included the faithfully pictorial 'Husband, like a sturdy tree; wife, a vine of choicest fruits: gathered round, the family, growing up like olive shoots', which Michael Perry persuaded me to change in time. 'Husband' and 'wife seem increasingly valuable words to retain; a later, freer approach follows at No.256.

Light upon the River

from Psalm 128
Family blessings: two

256 TO SET THEIR HEARTS ON GOD

To set their hearts on God,
to walk in holy ways:
in making such a start as this
all blessings shall be theirs.

The bridegroom and the bride,
the husband and the wife,
the growing circle of their home:
here is the happy life!

Around the table, joy;
in every room be peace:
at going out and coming in
give love the pride of place.

God grant to young and old
faith's riches, wisdom's health;
for you and yours, and us and ours,
long fruitfulness, true wealth.

All praises be to God!
From God all mercies flow;
all blessings Nazareth once knew
let every family know!

SM Tune: SANDYS

Scriptures: Psa 128; 121.8 Eph 5.21-25 Col 3.14 Jas 1.5,17; 2.5; 3.17 Matt 2.23 Lk 1.26; 2.39-40, 51-52

Written: Limehouse, 20 Jan 1988

First published: *The Wedding Book* (Marshall Pickering) 1989

In 1987 Michael Perry was working on new Psalm versions and a 'Wedding Book' with its own selection of hymns. He asked me to adapt my existing text of this Psalm (No.255 above) for a marriage. I had to ask 'Is this a psalm or a hymn?', but eventually offered a revised version. Meanwhile, influenced partly by the fresh approach of other writers, I wrote this new text as a specific wedding item, still rooted in the Psalm. Like its forerunner (and the Bible?) this one centres on the nuclear family but extends to a much wider, inclusive circle. Both versions appeared in print together.

Light upon the River

Psalm 130
From the depths: one

257 OUT OF THE DEPTHS I CRY TO YOU

Out of the depths I cry to you:
O Lord, hear my voice!
Let your ears be attentive
when I for mercy plead.

If you recorded every sin,
O Lord, who could stand?
But with you is forgiveness,
and therefore you are feared.

Eagerly waiting for the Lord
I hope in his word;
watchmen look for the morning,
but my soul looks for God.

Great is his power to set us free;
his love never fails.
He alone will redeem us;
O Israel, hope in God!

85.75 Tune needed

Scriptures: Psa 130; 40.1-3; 69.1-3,13-18; 131.3 Lk 2.25,38 1 Cor 13.8 Gal 6.16 1 Tim 5.5

Written: Poplar, 1972

I have never been quite satisfied with metrical versions (including mine) of this humbling Psalm, vast and simple as it is: De profundis. Maybe Luther's German is better; but alongside the Scripture itself, or the 'Parish Psalter' setting of the Prayer Book words with their double chant, they seem almost trivial. This text was not accepted for *Psalm Praise* but I kept it on file, hoping one day for a tune. The 'depths' are uncertain; being unspecified (unlike some other desperate Psalms) they are of universal scope. The 'morning' is certain; so is the mercy of God, and the redemption of his people.

Light upon the River

Psalm 130
From the depths: two

258   UP FROM THE DEPTHS I CRY TO GOD

Up from the depths I cry to God:
O listen, Lord, to me!
O hear my voice in this distress,
this mire of misery.

I wait for God with all my heart,
my hope is in his word;
and more than watchmen for the dawn
Im longing for the Lord.

If you, my God, should measure guilt,
who then could ever stand?
But those who fear your name will find
forgiveness from your hand.

I wait for God... (etc)

O Israel, set your hope on God
whose mercy is supreme!
the nation mourning for its sin
he surely will redeem.

I wait for God...(etc)

CM with refrain Tune: MACPHERSON'S FAREWELL

Scriptures: Psa 130; 40.1-3; 69.1-3,13-18; 131.3 Rom 15.4 Acts 28.20 Ezra 9 Neh 9 Dan 9.1-19 Matt 1.21; 5.4 Tit 2.14

Written: Poplar, Mar 1975

First published: *Psalms for Today* (Hodder & Stoughton) 1990

This second text for a great penitential Psalm (see No.257 above) stands or falls by its tune. The tragic MACPHERSON'S FAREWELL was learned by our sons at St Matthias Primary School in Poplar; they commended the tune to me (see also No.226) and these words proved printable. 1996 found the text in use at Grove Chapel Camberwell, not far from our home, and in at least two Canadian hymnals. But the relationship between fear and forgiveness is more complex than my stanzas allow for.

Light upon the River

Psalm 131
At rest

259 LORD, YOU HAVE WEANED MY HEART FROM PRIDE

Lord, you have weaned my heart from pride,
my eyes from scorn are free;
no longer am I occupied
with thoughts too high for me.

Contented now, and reconciled,
secure from all alarms,
my heart is quiet as a child
safe in its mother's arms.

O set your hope on Israel's God,
all you that know his name;
now and for ever trust the Lord,
eternally the same.

CM Tune: ST BOTOLPH

Scriptures: Psa 131; 9.10; 130.7-8 Deut 29.29 Eccles 5.2 Jer 45 Matt 18.1-4 Acts 28.20 Mal 3.6 Heb 13.8
Written: Limehouse, 1978
First published: *The Book of Praises* (Carey Publications) 1978

'My heart is not proud, O Lord' (NIV); 'Lord, I am not high minded' (BCP); how can such transparently personal words transfer to a congregation? My original version for this began 'Lord, let me learn...'; among his other suggestions, David Preston moved me closer to the Psalm's unaffected opening confession. The childlike spirit of its author suggests that he had gained a true maturity.

Light upon the River

Psalm 134
Evening blessings

260 COME, PRAISE THE LORD, ALL YOU HIS SERVANTS

Come, praise the Lord, all you his servants
who stand within his house by night:
Come, lift your hands and hearts in worship;
God be your praise and your delight.

Come, bless the Lord, all those who love him,
who serve within the holy place;
may God who made both earth and heaven
grant us the blessings of his grace.

98.98 Tune: MARYDENE by David Preston; or SPIRITUS VITAE

Scriptures: Psa 134   1 Chron 9.33; 23.30   1 Tim 2.8 Lk 24.50-53
Written: Limehouse, May 1978
First published: *Church Family Worship* (Hodder & Stoughton) 1986

As this Psalm was coming into wide use in the revision of Evening Prayer in the Church of England, I wrote without knowing that Timothy Dudley-Smith was also engaging with it. *Bless the Lord as day departs* was completed in August 1978 and published in his *Lift Every Heart* (Collins/Hope) in 1984, where the notes are apposite also to this text. My own first draft yielded to some of the varying advice from other friends; *Psalms for Today* (1990) set the words to the grand LES COMMANDEMENS, but I might have written differently with that tune in mind. The reciprocal (if unequal) 'blessing' is a striking feature of the Psalm, and the grace of God as creator is vital to its construction and thought.

Light upon the River

from Psalm 139
God omniscient, omnipresent, all-holy—and love!

261 LORD ALL-KNOWING, YOU HAVE FOUND ME

Lord all-knowing, you have found me;
every secret thought and word,
all my actions, all my longings,
you have seen and you have heard.

Lord almighty, you have made me,
fashioned me to keep your laws;
your design and your creation,
every part of me is yours.

Lord all-holy, you have judged me
by a standard true and right;
all the best I have to offer
withers in your burning light.

Lord all-loving, you have saved me
in supreme and mighty grace,
by your Son's triumphant mercy,
suffering, dying, in my place.

Lord all-glorious, you will take me
where your ransomed servants sing;
you have spoken, rescued, conquered,
Christ, our prophet, priest and king—Hallelujah! -
Christ, our prophet, priest and king.

87.87 Tune ALTON by Patrick Appleford

Scriptures: Psa 139 Job 42.1-6 Jn 1.47-49; 2.24-25 Acts 1.24; 3.22; 7.37 Heb 1.2; 3.1; 4.12-13 Gal 2.20; 3.21-22 Rev 5.9; 17.14

Written: Barrow in Furness, 1967

First published: *Church Family Worship* (Hodder & Stoughton) 1986

Patrick Applefords tune ALTON appeared in 1960, set to *Firmly I believe and truly*. I considered the tune worth borrowing for some Bible-based words, and wrote (and sang) this during my first curacy at St Mark's Barrow. Although after many years the hymn has now been broadcast and widely published, the words have never yet, I think, been set to the tune they were designed for, with its clear change of mood in the middle stanza. They do not claim to do justice to the profound majesty of the Psalm, but do aspire to the same sense of wonder in the presence and character of God, seen supremely in Christ.

Light upon the River

Psalm 143
Penitence and hope

262 O GOD OF JUSTICE, ANSWER ME

O God of justice, answer me:
most True, most Holy, hear my plea,
and judge me not; for in your sight
no living soul is in the right.

My enemy has brought me down;
my shame and weakness have been shown.
I know your help from days gone by;
for your reviving strength I cry.

From lowest depths of my despair
I lift my hands to you in prayer:
save me from sinking to the dead;
refresh my heart and raise my head.

Each morning let me know your love
and all my faithlessness remove:
destroy the powers that bring me low;
in grace and wisdom let me grow.

You are my Lord; teach me your will
and in your goodness guide me still:
I am your servant; set me free
to be what you would have me be.

LM Tune: AQUINAS by Keith Landis; or BRESLAU

Scriptures: Psa 143; 114.3 Eccles 7.20 Rom 3.20 Gal 2.16 Matt 13.28   1 Pet 5.8   1 Tim 2.8 Lam 3.22-23 Lk 1.38; 2.40 Heb 13.21
Written: Limehouse, 1978

'Enter not into judgement with thy servant, O Lord; for in thy sight shall no man living be justified'. So runs one of eleven possible sentences which open the Prayer Book services of Morning and Evening Prayer. Five are from the Psalms; this one, from Psalm 143. Here is another profound heartcry, and a classic statement of need and conviction combined with confidence in the mercy of God. I felt that such a Psalm needed a new metrical version; my original 2nd line was 'in mercy hear a prisoner's plea'.

Light upon the River

Psalm 145
A general thanksgiving

263 I WILL EXALT YOU, GOD, MY KING

I will exalt you, God, my King,
for ever praise, for ever sing
all glory to your treasured name:
all praise, all love our hearts proclaim!

As parents to their children tell
how always God does all things well,
so I delight to meditate
how just you are, how good, how great.

Believers trust and pray and prove
the glories of your mighty love:
our streets shall sing, our cities bloom,
your everlasting kingdom come!

In every promise God keeps faith;
you raise us, Lord, from sin and death:
you help the strugglers in the race -
redeemed, sustained, and crowned by grace.

By truth that shines in all your ways
you guide your people all their days;
your loving care for humankind
ensures that all who seek shall find.

How happy those who come to know
your love so full, your wrath so slow!
You give us life and health and food:
to all, so near; for all, so good.

As generations take their turn
and saints in each your glory learn,
your name be praised, and praised again,
and praised for evermore: Amen!

Tune: MAGNIFICAT NOW by Peter Lewis; LANCING; or GALILEE

Scriptures: Psa 145 Zech 8.4-5 Rev 22.1-3 Dan 4.3,34; 6.26; 7.14 Matt 6.10; 7.7-8 Lk 11.2 2 Tim 2.11-13 Jn 5.21 Rom 6.4-6,13 Eph 2.4-6 Jer 29.13 Acts 14.17; 17.25-27

Written: Poplar, 1974

There is a time for questioning, wondering, for desperate cries for help; there is also a time for the outpouring of grateful praise. The Book of Psalms is rich in both categories of song, and this last of those with David's name attached (and last of the alphabetical or acrostic Psalms; see No.249) is from the second group. It forms a grand launching-pad for the final group of five 'Hallelujah' Psalms. The word 'all', which I deliberately repeat here, is reminiscent of the 'everything' of Genesis 1, and characteristic of the Psalm. My text was much revised to meet the demands of two editorial groups, but so far has proved a 'near miss' for publication. 'Final' adjustments were made in 1988 and 1998.

Light upon the River

In the spirit of Psalm 150
God all-blessed and all-praised

264 BLESS THE LORD IN PSALM AND CHORUS

Bless the Lord in psalm and chorus,
children, parents, old and young;
as they joined in praise before us,
let new praises now be sung.
    Praise and sing with holy wonder
    God unseen but not unknown;
    bless the Silence, bless the Thunder,
    fragile Love upon the throne!

Bless the One for every creature,
deepest fin or loftiest wing;
highest, lowest, praise Gods nature,
servants' slave yet highest King.
    Praise the Darkness and the Mystery,
    dreams and marvels yet concealed;
    then by place and name and history
    bless the Word of truth revealed.

Bless the Star of Israel's story,
cloud by day and flame at night;
praise the Fire whose mighty glory
fills the shrine with smoke and light.
    Praise the Father, Son and Spirit:
    freed to worship, love, adore,
    earth and heaven, learn Gods merit,
    bless your God for evermore!

Bless our guide and Friend and Lover;
praise our Water, Rock, and Sun;
Praise with joy and bless for ever
God our Saviour, everyone!
    Praise our Evening and our Morning,
    bless the Coming one, who came;
    bless our Hope whose day is dawning,
    praise one holy, living Name!

Blessings full and praise eternal
sing for wood and nails and blood;
Everlasting, Universal,
praise and bless the Lord our God.
    Blessings, crowning all our praises,
    highest, deepest, furthest, free,
    bless the Christ, all praise to Jesus:
    praises, blessings, glory be!

Light upon the River

87.87.D Tune: ALLELUIA; IN BABILONE; or NEW PRAISES by Eric Lewis

Scriptures: Psa 150? But rather than fill half a page with more Bible references, I leave it to the reader who has reached this far, or who opens the book at this point, to enjoy exploring your own list!

Written: Limehouse, Oct 1987

Here is a text which, to quote Tolkien, 'grew in the telling'. Being dissatisfied with No.45 in this collection, I began on a different version of the canticle which was more inclusive, not only in gender terms but also in our reasons for praising God. Psalm 150 gives no reasons at all, since they have come in the previous 149! In spirit my purpose is the same, though the word 'psalm' entered the first line mainly to avoid confusion with a similar one. The resulting 'psalm and chorus' is the first of several balancing or contrasting pairs of words here, built around the foundational 'bless' and 'praise'. Many of them are titles or descriptions of God, with roots (if not explicit names) in Scripture, and the Trinity at the centre rather than the end. While not always following Brian Wren's approaches to language, I appreciate his exploration of phrases that break the mould and sharpen our appreciation of God and one another; recently I had heard him plead (at Finchley) for positive images of 'darkness' and 'night', which are not always bad in the Bible. The last line of my first verse echoes W H Vanstone's book (and poem/hymn) *Love's endeavour, Love's expense*; but I have kept the name and title of Jesus Christ until the completion of the hymn. its length requires a tune which keeps us moving; I have not managed to close my 'Psalter' as succinctly as Scripture does. But 'let everything that has breath praise the Lord!' Amen.

LOCAL AND SPECIAL:
texts requested or offered for particular congregations

Although many of the texts in the earlier parts of this book grew from specific places and situations (Nos.24 and 25 being adjacent but contrasting examples) these final fifteen hymns and songs come in a slightly different group. As before, the notes below each one identify the seeds from which the plants have borne fruit; they nearly all relate to churches or communities that we have belonged to for a while. This time the order is chronological, not exactly by date of writing, but generally by our own changing scenes and stories. Some of these texts have been, or can be, adapted for wider use; where that is possible, the 'general' options are found in the margin. As can be seen, seven of them belong to Suffolk, but do not quite match the seven villages we served there. I did not set out to write for each in turn; in any case, not all were equally keen on new hymns! Some verses for churches not named here ended up as poems rather than hymns; all are included implicitly in Nos. 268, 270, and 274. Since we left Suffolk Simon Baynes, an old friend who is Vicar of Winkfield (Berkshire) has produced a book of poems about his own church and parish which makes me wish I had started earlier, with at least some portion of his spirit: 'St Mary's, Keep The Vision', available from the author. But my own texts were meant to be, and have been, sung. They are offered not as models but as mementoes; small 'Thank You' cards to those who in these places have kept the vision—without which, as we know, the people perish. And as a large 'Thank You' to God for the privilege of living and working among such people and scenes. As is fitting, we open this last section with the hymn providing the book with its title.

The Diocese of Southwark

265 AS THE LIGHT UPON THE RIVER

As the light upon the river
at the rising of the sun,
shine, O Lord, upon our city;
here on earth, your will be done:
here we meet in glad thanksgiving,
worship, praise and prayer we bring,
grief for sin and joy for mercy -
all for you, O Christ our King.

Light upon the River

Crucified and risen Saviour,
God incarnate, First and Last,
yours the city of the future,
yours the pilgrims of the past:
Lord, revive your weary people!
Let your voice again be heard;
rid your church of all excuses
for our deafness to your word.

From our failure and our blindness,
bound by debts we cannot pay,
God of Jubilee, release us -
O renew us all, we pray!
In a world exhausted, restless,
still oppressing and oppressed,
Lord of Sabbath, bring us freedom,
resurrection, life, and rest.

Strengthen us to love our neighbours -
welcome strangers at our door,
find the lost and reach the lonely
so that they shall weep no more:
in our homes, our crowded journeys,
work or leisure, calm or noise,
come to satisfy our longings,
Christ the Joy of all our joys!

As the rain upon the garden
as the water from the spring,
pour on us your Holy Spirit,
gifts to use and songs to sing:
as the light upon the river
at the rising of the sun,
shine, O Lord, upon our city -
as in heaven, your will be done.

87.87.D Tune: LIGHT UPON THE RIVER by Norman Warren; EXALTED NAME by David Ashley White; LUX EOI; or ABBOTS LEIGH

Scriptures: 2 Sam 3.3-4 Jer 29.7 Matt 6.10; 12.8 Rev 1.17-18; 2.8; 21.12 Heb 11.10,13-16; 13.2 Psa 43.4; 95.7 Lk 1.77-79; 6.5; 7.41-42 Lev 19.18; 25.8-55 Mk 2.28 Neh 8.10 Gen 2.9-10 Jn 7.37-39 1 Cor 12.4 Eph 5.18-19

Written: Limehouse, 16 Jan 1980

First published: Southwark Diocesan services 1980; *The Hymn* (Hymn Society of America) 1984

'What will you miss most from London?', I was asked when being interviewed at Palgrave for a ministry in rural Suffolk. Entirely off the cuff I said 'The river Thames'. Someone said, 'We've got the Waveney!' Today I would still give the same answer. All rivers great and small can be envisaged in this text, but it was the Thames I had in mind; the varied dawn skies and changing riverscapes seen from embankment and walkway are a jogger's delight. The Church of England has 43 Dioceses, each with a bishop, a cathedral, and (usually) hundreds of parishes. Southwark Diocese, formed in 1905, includes London south of the Thames and the mainly suburban areas beyond; 1980 saw its 75th anniversary, and in a competition this was chosen as the 'Jubilee Hymn'. By then we had been north of the river for a while; but Southwark Diocese was the scene of my schooling, our courtship, much travelling, and (up to the present) some six years' residence and nine of work. Here Marcus, our youngest, was born, and Tim, our eldest, was to return. The hymn (for me, the first of its kind) includes Biblical and local allusions; Canterbury pilgrims (verse 2) travelled from Southwark where today (verse 3) crowded buses and trains move in and out. Further out are more gardens (verse 4). 'God incarnate' is a reminder of some notorious denials o   at doctrine, while the remission of debt in the Jubilee year has become a key issue with N．．nnium links. Racism, though perhaps better understood, is not yet dead among us. On our return to Peckham in 1995 the hymn was still around in places; it had been widely sung in 1980, from the Cathedral to Wimbledon's centre court, and has featured in Church Urban Fund material and broadcasts from Greenwich tied in with the year 2000.

Light upon the River

Limehouse Parish Church (St Anne's)

266 TOWERING OVER ROAD AND RIVER

Towering over road and river
stands this house of prayer,
witnessing to God the Giver
who in Christ draws near:
    Lord, you plan our history's pages
    through all ages—bless us here!

If these stones could tell the story
of our joys and fears
they would sing 'To God be glory!'
till the Lord appears:
    walls and pillars, bell and tower,
    tell your power through the years.

Wars may rage, and fire, and trouble;
still your people stand:
love divine is measured double,
faith and hope regained:
    we are tried, but not forsaken,
    never shaken from your hand.

Here all races are united,
west is joined with east;
all are welcome, all invited
to the Gospel feast:
    each succeeding generation
    finds salvation here in Christ.

So your church shall praise for ever
our Redeemer's fame,
Jesus Christ, our risen Saviour -
glory to his name!
    Songs of worship and thanksgiving
    shall our living Lord proclaim.

85.85.87 Tune: ANGEL VOICES

Light upon the River

Scriptures: 2 Cor 5.19 Lk 1.50; 14.15-24;19.40 Rom 16.27 Psa 66.12 Heb 13.5 Jn 10.27-28 Isa 47.4; 55.1-2; 63.16 Matt 8.11 Rev 19.9 Acts 4.12 1 Thess 5.9

Written: Limehouse, 31 Dec 1979

The river in this text is the same as in the last one; they were written close together. But when in 1971 we were about to cross the Thames from Peckham to Poplar, I first met John Pearce. He was then a vicar in Homerton in the Borough of Hackney; he told me, 'Keep your eyes on Limehouse; the future is there!' By an extraordinary sequence of opportunities, impossibilities, providences and prayers, I became Rector of Limehouse five years later, and in 1989 John succeeded me. The parish was carved out of Stepney in the 18th century, and St Anne's designed by Nicholas Hawksmoor (see No.267 below) and opened in 1730. So in 1980 we were due for a series of birthday celebrations, and one way to start was a new hymn to a familiar, soaring tune. I left it a bit late, but the text was ready just in time for our Watch Night service to begin the 250th anniversary year. It was sung at our main Festival Service on 14 Sept when Bishop Maurice Wood preached, and several times since, being printed in the parish magazine and the church's Song Book. It has been quoted elsewhere, and used by at least one other church whose Vicar said it suited them too! Local allusions include the tower, still a noble signpost by land or water for miles around; the Portland stone, now restored to white from dirty grey; the wars which hit East London but spared St Anne's; and the fire which in 1850 spared only part of it. In 1978 we (and the magnificent organ) were mercifully saved from a similar disaster; see No.228 above. The fourth verse reflects the cosmopolitan parish whose names recall the docks, the sea, and Chinatown; and whose recent residents include those from Europe, Africa, the Caribbean and Vietnam; Christ is for us all, and the Limehouse congregation is a microcosm of his kingdom.

Light upon the River

Christ Church Spitalfields

267 CHRIST'S CHURCH SHALL GLORY IN HIS POWER

Christ's church shall glory in his power:
his people are the pillars;
Christ is the stone, the door, the tower,
and Christ the life to fill us.
   So by his skilful hand
   the church of Christ shall stand;
   the Master-weavers plan
   he works, as he began,
and brings it to perfection.

and grow to his perfection;
he is our rock, our mighty tower,
our life, our resurrection.
   the master-builders plan
   he works, as he began,
and soon will crown with splendour.

Christ's people serve his wayward world:
the native and the stranger,
the strong, the weak, the young, the old;
we share his joy, his danger.
   Though sin brings all men low,
   the church of Christ shall grow;
   his cross our greatest need,
   his word the living seed
that brings a fruitful harvest.

Christ's people serve his wayward world
to whom he seems a stranger;
he knows its welcome from of old,
he shares our joy, our danger.
   So strong, and yet so weak,
   the church of Christ shall speak;
   his cross our greatest need,
   his word the vital seed
that brings a fruitful harvest.

This lamp of Christ shall brightly burn,
and to our earthly city
forgotten beauty shall return,
and purity, and pity.
   To give the oppressed their right
   the church of Christ shall fight,
   and though the years seem long,
   Christ is our strength and song,
and he is our salvation.

Christ's living lamp shall brightly burn,

   God is our strength and song,
and God is our salvation.

Christs body triumphs in his name:
one Father, sovereign Giver,
one Spirit, with his love aflame,
one Lord, the same for ever.
   To you, O God our prize,
   the church of Christ shall rise
   beyond all measured height
   to that eternal light
where Christ shall reign all-holy.

87.87.66667 Tune: EIN'FESTE BURG

Light upon the River

Scriptures (one or both versions): Rev 1.20;3.12; 11.15   1 Pet 2.4 Jn 10.7-9 Prov 18.10 Ex 15.2;35.35 Eph 1.7,11; 4.13; 5.27; 6.12 Phil 1.6; 3.14,20 Isa 53.6; 58.6-12 Mk 10.45 Rom 3.23; 5.5 Lk 8.11,15 Jer 29.7   1 Tim 6.17   1 Thess 4.16-17

Written: Limehouse, June 1979

Revised text first published: *Hymns for Todays Church* (Hodder & Stoughton) 1982

The Spitalfields hymn preceded the Limehouse one by six months and paved the way for it. Christ Church's consecration preceded that of St Anne's by a year, so its 250th Birthday came in 1979. Sited between east London and the City of banks and business, this too is a Hawksmoor design; probably the masterpiece among his churches. Eddy Stride, who features in the notes to some 'Genesis' hymns (including Nos.3, 4 and 9) was Rector there for most of our Poplar and Limehouse years, and after a service where the music specially enhanced the architecture, the idea of a topical hymn was born. Still rather overwhelmed by the stonework, spaces, lighting, bells, and people, on the bus home I began to put some thoughts together. The original text was sung later that year, printed with notes in the church magazine, and (in September) revised for more general use. The Church Urban Fund has used this hymn as well as No.265, in cathedrals and elsewhere. Every local church is 'Christ's church', but the primary words related to Spitalfields. Some of the immigrants, before Jewish and Asian people arrived, were Huguenot Protestants escaping continental persecution; their tall weavers' houses still survive (see verse 1) among the newer tower blocks. Seed and harvest (verse 2) are reminders of the fruit and vegetable market, now gone from its historic Commercial Street site. The steady restoration of the church building reclaimed some beauty for a neighbourhood often starved of it (verse 3) and the same stanza recalls Eddys battles against corruption in church and state, on the side of those whose lives were being wrecked by racism, alcohol, pornography, gambling, or abortion, or by chronic unbelief. And the west front of Christ Church's great tower and spire 'carries the eye ever upwards' (verse 4); so, crucially, does the Gospel for which the church has stood from its first foundation.

Light upon the River

**North Hartismere Benefice, Suffolk: one
The villages of Brome, Burgate, Oakley, Palgrave, Stuston,
Thrandeston, and Wortham**

268 FOR ALL OUR SEVEN CHURCHES

For all our seven churches
that grew from God's good seed,
each planted, watered, nurtured,
for life and health we plead:
where songs of Christ's arising
with joy begin the week,
our God of gifts surprising
is found by all who seek.

The stars and skies and seasons,
the rainbow, cloud and sun,
provide a million reasons
to worship God alone:
the winding roads invite us
by farm and field and stream;
one Way alone will light us
safe home, set free, redeemed.

Our heritage of history:
grey towers among green trees
where we declare Gods mystery
in sacrifice of praise;
we tell in great thanksgiving
where miracles begin,
how Christ the ever-living
once died to bear our sin.

The centuries behind us -
two thousand years of grace -
their very stones remind us
to seek the Saviour's face.
The saints now raised in glory,
the toil of God's own poor:
he shares the struggling story
of all who went before.

The treasures we inherit,
our name, our need he knows,
and pours on us his Spirit
from whom all loving flows:
let us, his precious purchase,
out witness here record:
among his seven churches
the risen Christ is Lord.

Alternatives for general use
1.1 For all our village churches
(or *chosen* churches)
5.7 among his living churches

76.76.D Tune: ST THEODULPH, starting with 2nd half of the tune

Scriptures: Lk 8.11,15; 6.20 1 Cor 3.6; 6.19-20; 15.42-43 Jn 10.10; 14.6 Jer 29.13 Gen 1.8,16; 8.22; 9.13 Deut 6.13 Rom 1.20; 5.5 Heb 9.28;13.15 Psa 27.1,8 Ex 15.16-17 Acts 20.28 Eph 1.14 Rev 1.12-13,20; 2.1ff

Written: Oakley, 21 April 1989

Modified version first published: *Country Way,* 1992

On moving to 'high Suffolk', it was natural to connect the seven churches of the new Benefice of North Hartismere with those in Revelation 2-3; not in close parallels but in the presence of the Lord who 'walks among the seven golden lampstands'. They featured in my opening sermons, and soon the idea of a hymn began to form. The first couplet (which became the last) came to me as I walked home down the path from Morning Prayer; more was written after breakfast; the rest, following a funeral that day and a visit to Timothy Dudley-Smith at Bramerton in Norfolk. Marjorie suggested the tune, and on 29 Oct we sang it at Wortham in a service for all the churches. Alan Durand of Oakley accompanied it at least once on his 'home' organ; in time he got to know all seven. Later the words appeared in the first issue of the quarterly *Country Way* with some unplanned changes; preferred options are suggested here. The more specific allusions are, in verse 1: especially 'watered', as our first months had plentiful rain. Verse 2: stars and skies were spectacular after London's lights and towers; rainbows spanning the fields were a special and frequent blessing, and 'light us', since we needed torches for excursions after dark. Verse 3; each village had its ancient, much-loved parish church; the 'mystery' of Christ is now made plain in both word and sacrament. Verse 4: Stones crumble like our own mortality; some monuments have telling inscriptions, while the folly of others may also make us pause. Richard Cobbold, Rector of Wortham 1825-77, is one of the special saints; he lovingly chronicled 'the toil of God's own poor' in his illustrated parish account written in 1860, published 1977, and given to me at my first service there.

Light upon the River

North Hartismere Benefice, Suffolk: two

269 PRAISE THE LORD WITH THE PEOPLE OF PALGRAVE

Praise the Lord with the people of Palgrave,
sing from Stuston and Thrandeston too;
boys and girls, young and old, big and little,
praising Jesus who loves me and you.
    Hallelujah, God our Father!
    Hallelujah, Christ our Friend!
    Hallelujah, Holy Spirit!
    Sing together to the end.

For the years, all the hundred and fifty,
of the school by the church on the green;
for the people who lived in our village
when no cars or computers were seen.
    Singing praises in the present,
    saying Thank You for the past,
    staying faithful in the future
    from the first day to the last.

For the scholars and teachers and parents,
all who help, phone and type, clean and care;
every class, every game, every journey;
all we learn, as we grow, all we share.
    Being grateful for the good things,
    being sorry when were wrong;
    showing kindness to our neighbours,
    let us praise God in our song.

Praise the Lord for his friend Simon Peter
and the places we call by his name;
for disciples today who are trusting
in the Friend who is always the same.
    God be with us night and morning,
    God be with us through the day;
    God be with us to the evening,
    and for ever, Lord, we pray.

Alternatives for general use
4.1-2: Praise the Lord for his friends and disciples
       who were glad at the sound of his name;

Tune: FOR I'M BUILDING A PEOPLE OF POWER

Light upon the River

Scriptures: Gal 2.20 Jn 15.15 Psa 106.1 Lk 18.13 Mk 12.28-31 Matt 28.20

Written: Oakley, 1990

In its original foundation, the Church of England Primary School in Palgrave dates from 1841. In 1990, my second year as Rector and therefore also a school governor, the staff began to plan for its 150th anniversary. Janice Mortlock, herself a parent, governor, and classroom assistant, married to Michael, asked if I could write a song or hymn for the occasion. Once I hit on a tune (which had appeared in *Mission Praise*) the words came more quickly than usual, as I tried to weave in as much of school life as I could; the school's catchment area included Stuston and Thrandeston, so covered three of the seven villages. It did not mention swimming or the nature reserve, but I hoped verse 3 was fairly inclusive. So I filed it, and nearly forgot it until Janice reminded me the following Spring; in that celebration year it was then copied, vetted, learned and practised. We sang it on various occasions, notably at the main Anniversary Service at St Peter's Church on the same patch of green (verses 1 and 3) on 23 June, with the biggest Sunday congregation (over 200) we saw in Suffolk. The words appeared in the Newsletter of the Palgrave Society, circulating among those of that surname; verse 2 marked another 'first' as it was printed, with drawings of and by the children, on a commemorative tea-cloth! It was sung again at the Leavers' Services of 1992 and 1993, the latter by request of Head Teacher Bob Perrett who retired that day, and was chosen for Thrandeston's *Songs of Praise*, in Aug 1993. This was its first airing outside Palgrave, verse 4 being adapted as above. With wider changes it may be usable by others.

Light upon the River

North Hartismere Benefice, Suffolk: three

270 WHERE IS THE ROCK, AND WHERE IS THE RIVER

Where is the rock, and where is the river of life everlasting,
flowing for ever—and where is our God?

High on the water was Noah borne up;
judgement had fallen but safe was the ark.
High rose the mountains, but sure was their hope
as the creatures set foot on the welcoming rock.
 God is our Rock, and God is our River of life everlasting,
 flowing for ever: all glory to God!

Jacob and Moses, Elijah and John
found at the river a merciful flood;
deep through the waters came Jesus the Son
and the glory of Calvary brings us to God.
 Christ is our Rock, and Christ is our River of life everlasting,
 flowing for ever: all glory to God!

Suffolk's slow waters flow down to the sea,
Waveney river and pools of the Dove;
here in its valley let all be set free
by the rock of Gods truth and the streams of his love.

 Here is our Rock, and here is our River of life everlasting,
 flowing for ever: all glory to God!

Tune: MULL OF KINTYRE

Scriptures: Gen 6-8; 32.22-32 Psa 18.2 Ex 2.1-10 1 Kgs 17.2-6 Mk 1.4-5,9-11; 10.38-39 1 Pet 3.18 1 Cor 10.4 Jn 7.37-39
Written: Oakley, 1990

'Weve got the Waveney!'; see No.265. So here it is. This once navigable stream formed the northern edge, more or less, of our Benefice, Diocese and County. We could cross its bridges, explore its banks, and trace its variable source in Redgrave Fen, depending on the seasonal rainfall. Its tributary the Dove flowed through the eastern corner of the Benefice, near our Oakley home. In 1990 John Mortlock, farmer and churchwarden at Thrandeston and brother of Michael, asked if I could put new words to the MULL OF KINTYRE tune popularised by Paul McCartney with his No.1 hit (as 'Wings') in 1977. Listening to his tape I felt the watery flow of the music, so I used some of the Bible's water/river/sea imagery in the episodes referred to. Verse 3 with its local names could be omitted for general use, though its reception was more muted than that for No.269. The first suitable occasion for it came on 24 Feb 1991 (Lent 2) when our theme at Thrandeston's Family Service was the story of Noah. A dozen of us sang it then; mainly Mortlocks, and with Marjorie at the organ.

Light upon the River

All Saints' Stuston, and others

271 ALL THE SAINTS WHO SERVE IN HEAVEN

All the saints who serve in heaven,
all the saints who serve on earth:
only God has made them holy;
they are saints by Gods new birth.
Some are shy and some are famous,
some have pain and death to face;
but they all have faith in Jesus
and he saves them by his grace.
   O when the saints (O when the saints)
   go marching in (go marching in)
   O when the saints go marching in,
   I want to be in that number,
   when the saints go marching in.

All the saints who walked and witnessed
on the roads of Galilee,
all the saints who followed after,
all the saints who yet shall be.
All the saints in Rome and Corinth,
Athens, Egypt. Crete, Judaea,
they are one in work and worship
with the saints of Hartismere.
   (alt: with the saints who live right here!)
   O when the saints...(etc)

As in Christ we come together
so in us his light shall shine;
sing out Holy, Holy Holy
to the Majesty divine.
As the Lord of love and wisdom
never sleeps or fails or faints,
sing out Glory, Glory, Glory,
to the God of all the saints.
   O when the saints...(etc)

Tune: WHEN THE SAINTS GO MARCHING IN

Scriptures: Rev 14.12; 22.3 1 Pet 1.3 Heb 11.32-40 Eph 2.4-10 Rom 1.7   1 Cor 1.2   2 Cor 1.1 Acts 9.31; 17.32-34 Psa 68.31; 121.4 Tit 1.5 Matt 5.14-16 Zeph 3.5 Isa 40.28
Written: Oakley, 1992

Saints are always plural, all created by God, not all famous, not all dead; all Christians are saints! These Biblical convictions, self-evident to some but revolutionary to many, gave a text written for a united event but then attached to Stuston through the dedication of its church as 'All Saints'. Early in 1992 Peter and Christine Brooks, who co-ordinated childrens work in the Hartismere Deanery (two dozen churches in five benefices) asked me to adapt *When the saints go marching in* for local use. All Saints Day, 1 Nov, would be celebrated that year in a childrens and youth service at the parish church of Eye—the one town in the area. It seemed clear that the chorus must be kept; the tune for the less-known verses of this classic jazz march might help. It was not possible, as I had hoped, to get different voices to sing out the place names in verse 2, nor to find an authentic musician to play; but our small group did its best in an 'All Saints' service which was enjoyably lively and untidily educational. This hardly rivals Fred Pratt Green's *Rejoice in God's saints*, but may serve a similar purpose. On the evening of the same day, with churchwarden Joyce Beale's blessing, we sang it rather less riotously in a 'Songs of Praise' at All Saints Stuston, the smallest of our 'grey towers among green trees' and the one with the most Scriptural name. The reading was Hebrews 11.32—12.3.

Light upon the River

Thrandeston, Suffolk

272 WELCOME, WELCOME EVERY GUEST

Welcome, welcome every guest,
Welcome Jesus in our midst,
Welcome him who welcomes us
by the mercy of his cross:

Hallelujah!
Hallelujah!

Hallelujah, hallelujah, hallelujah!

Holy, holy, holy Lord,
welcome Christ with every chord:
all who find this place of prayer,
come to God and find him near:

Every member taking part
with the music of our heart;
with a psalm and hymn and song
let our praise be loud and long:

Let new pipes and notes resound,
ancient walls ring out with sound;
God be praised in every key,
every note and harmony:

Glory be to God on high,
glory, all his people cry;
Father, Son and Spirit true:
praise to God for ever new!

77.77 with Hallelujahs   Tune: CHISLEHURST

Scriptures: Matt 18.20 Rom 15.7 Isa 6.3 Acts 17.27 Psa 150 Eph 4.19 Col 3.15-16 Jn 14.17
Written: Oakley, Nov-Dec 1991

The 15th century church in the village of Thrandeston (St Margaret's; see no.271!) never had a pipe organ. In the 1970s its harmonium was replaced by a Hammond organ which served well until Harvest 1991. During the *Nunc Dimittis* on Friday evening, which I missed, smoke was seen and smelt, and the churchwardens bundled the instrument out of the chancel door to let off steam in the churchyard. Guest preacher Sam Read from Earsham commented on the first lesson which concerned burnt offerings. After some heartsearching we bought a small pipe organ, formerly used at Christ Church Highbury, from Bishops' in Ipswich. Two small pews were moved to make room for it in the north aisle, with the necessary legal faculty, and it was duly installed. When something similar happened at Wingate (Lancashire) in 1861, a song was born; Pott's words and Monk's music gave us *Angel voices* as the most famous hymn written to welcome a new organ. If Wingate, why not Thrandeston? From Marjorie's short list of possible tunes, I picked Sydney Nicholson's lyrical CHISLEHURST (borrowed from *Hail the day that sees him rise*, which had two tunes already) and wrote this text. We sang it when the organ was dedicated on 29 March 1992; a Mothering Sunday Communion service which began with *Angel voices*, ended with coffee, and drew more than thirty people. The words stress the blend of old and new (relevant if not original) and verse 2 hints at the trouble some have in finding God, or Thrandeston. One resident said 'When we first arrived they kept moving our house!'; a visitor complained about a locked church, but later discovered he was in the wrong village. If the hymn proved transferable, other tunes are not so hard to find; but Marjorie and I often met in Chislehurst.

Light upon the River

Wortham, Suffolk

273 PRAISE GOD FOR WINDOWS! GREET THE DAY

Praise God for windows! Greet the day
that fills our Wortham skies with light!
Each colour moves some heart to pray
and thank God for his gift of sight.

When darkness comes, we meet again
as light shines out beyond the trees,
across the field and farm and lane
to point to higher things than these.

These sculptured pews, this patterned flint,
the tower's strength, the organ's tones:
let each convey some telling hint
of God, to all who tread these stones.

What names, what lives recorded here,
of faith and work from earlier days!
What memories we have to share,
of those who heard and sang God praise!

Our kith and kin, our foe or friend,
the neighbour, stranger, rich or poor:
here were they born, or found their end,
came in and out by that same door.

Some may have stumbled, some have strayed
but found God's grace to pardon sin;
we mark the tracks that they have made
and as they finish, we begin.

God grant that we may lift our eyes
beyond the past or present view;
for all that shall be, let us rise
with Christ, the light that makes us new.

LM Tune: TRURO

Scriptures: Gen 8.6   1 Thess 1.3 Heb 12.1   1 Sam 7.22 Isa 53.6 Lk 21.28 Eph 5.14
Written: Oakley, 1990; Peckham Dec 1995

'Have you seen the window?' said churchwarden Audrie Hancock one Sunday, in my early months as Rector. Each of 'our seven churches' has its special features. Wortham most recalled Thomas Gray and his elegy (hence some of these Long Metre thoughts) and was notable for being off the beaten track, open day and night, joined to its dark tower, but bright with its clear windows. Still fresh from London, I wondered at first which one had been smashed. But no; this week the new 'Ling window' had been installed—a simple, clear design of the four seasons in memory of a local farmer, with the text: 'To everything there is a season'. Several new windows were installed over the next few years, often to replace older, much-buckled glass; some commemorated people I had known and buried, Mrs Hancock among them. In that time, Wortham lost through death a third of its regular congregation. I had sometimes thought about a 'window hymn'; traditional hymns took in walls and fonts, foundations and bells, but no windows that I knew of. But time passed, and we moved; I was able to look at scraps of unfinished writing, This was one, and three months after leaving Suffolk a text came together at last; line 2 read 'which floods our world, our church, with light'. I sent a draft to Maureen Ling, daughter-in-law of the late 'Billy' Ling of the window; she suggested some small improvements and conferred with Beryl Rice, the organist, over tunes. It was sung at a Family Service in Feb 1996. The fields (verse 2) adjoin the churchyard; the lane leads up to its small side gate, and opposite is the Rash family farm, with its own place in Wortham's history. The dark wooden pews (verse 3) are carved with creatures and texts from Psalm 104; the medieval flint is patterned diagonally at clerestory level; the roofless tower is the widest round church tower in Britain. Village feuds are not unknown; but one of the saints whose grave is now cared for was my Victorian predecessor Richard Cobbold. He wrote the highly readable novel 'Margaret Catchpole'; but his smaller masterpiece (see No.268) opens with a prayer for God to bless all who came after his time. So I echo the prayers which have blessed me here.

Light upon the River

The Diocese of St Edmundsbury and Ipswich

274 HOLY SPIRIT, HEAVEN'S BREATH

THE CORE HYMN

Holy Spirit, heaven's Breath,
blow wherever now is death:
safe and sound, or lone and lost,
bring us life at Pentecost!

Wind that races from the sea
causing future things to be,
from our chaos make anew
minds to love and worship you.

Wind that blows through farm and field
tiny seed for mighty yield,
sow the word of life in us;
plant the tree they call the cross.

Wind that shreds the cloudy sky,
gale for making wet or dry,
move the guilty soul to tears,
then remove the mourner's fears.

Wind that fans into a flame
sparks of faith in Jesus' name,
come in judgement and in love;
burn in us till mountains move!

Praise the Spirit, earth and heaven,
praise to Jesus Christ be given:
Suffolk sings from fen to shore
God our glory evermore!

ADDITIONAL VERSES
Coastal:
Wind that whips the grassy dunes,
gives the salty waves their tunes,
make fresh music, rhythm, rhyme;
make your people move in time!
Countryside:
Wind that bends the shaking trees
bringing woodlands to their knees,
break our hearts, to mend again,
self to die, and love remain.
Town:
Wind that eddies through the town
gusting up the streets and down,
drive our dirt and dross away,
make us clean this holy day.
Music:
Wind that sounds through pipe and reed
treble, bass, in turn to lead;
harmonise your church's voice
that in truth we shall rejoice.
Bells:
Wind that shakes the steeple's bell,
echoes round the towers that tell
God has given his church a tongue;
let his changes here be rung!
Living creatures:
Wind that cattle must endure,
breeze where gulls and geese can soar;
breath by which creation sings,
make us rise on eagles' wings!

(for general use: verse 6 line 3: praises sing from every shore:)

77.77 Tune: CARYL by Donald Webster; HARTS; or NORTHAMPTON

Light upon the River

Scriptures: Ezek 36.24-30; 37.1-14 Acts 2.1-21; 5.30-31 Gen 1.1-10 Matt 5.4; 13.23; 17.20; 21.21 Mk 4.20; 11.23 Lk 6.21; 7.15 Isa 42.3 Psa 29.9 Ex 19.4

Written: Oakley, 18-19 May 1994

First published: St Edmundsbury and Ipswich Diocesan services, 1995

Coming back to the Rectory from a singing session at Palgrave Primary School, I found a note: 'Ring Keith Jones'. He was an Ipswich Vicar involved in planning Suffolk's Festival of Faith for the year after; the mid-point of the 'Decade of Evangelism'. He wanted suggestions for suitable hymns; and by the way, if I might like to write something with a local flavour...! Later I suggested 2 classics and 5 moderns; but that day I felt an unusually strong urge to get something on paper straight away. My twin points of reference were the Day of Pentecost in Acts 2 with its 'sound of a rushing mighty wind', and our five years (so far) in Suffolk with its strong patterns of wind and weather. A hectic hour was slotted in before visits and Bible-study; late at night and the next day I was tidying this and changing that, with much conjugal help. It seemed useful to have a 'Core Hymn' for all to sing, with other verses to choose from, suiting varied needs and areas. HARTS was a brisk enough tune to carry the theme along. When the completed 'pack' for the Festival appeared, the hymn was sung across the county and diocese, sometimes to NORTHAMPTON. David Boyes, formerly of Suffolk, was the first to request its use beyond; in Cambridgeshire the penultimate line could be 'praises sing from fen to shore', but remoter congregations may prefer the option above. Some of our years in East Anglia saw hurricane-style, tree-uprooting winds; its churches generally preferred something less alarming.

Light upon the River

Peckham Park Baptist Church, London SE15

275 WHAT IS OUR MISSION IN THIS PLACE

What is our mission in this place,
our vision for these days?
The Park alive with love for God
and Peckham filled with praise!
The church a true community
to serve our neighbourhood;
friends gathered round by Jesus Christ
at work for all, for good.

To welcome everyone in need
with free, affirming care;
to hear Gods word, to teach his truth,
his justice find and share:
to send, and to be sent ourselves
and look for opening doors
along the street, or London-wide,
or far beyond our shores.

To build in partnership with Christ,
to pray 'Your kingdom come',
that he who changed us at his cross
will heal this place, our home.
O Holy Spirit, move our hearts;
mend us and make us one,
in beautiful variety
our heaven on earth begun!

Alternatives for general use
1.3 Our homes alive with love for God
1.4 our cities filled with praise!
2.7 along the street, or nationwide,

DCM Tune: ELLACOMBE

Light upon the River

Scriptures: Matt 6.10; 10.10-16 Mk 3.13-19; 31-35 Lk 8.1-3; 9.1-6; 10.1-9; 15.1-2 Jn 17.6-26;20.19-23 Acts 14.27 1 Cor 16.9 2 Cor 2.12 Rev 3.8 2 Chron 7.14 Eph 4.3

Written: Peckham, 24-29 Mar 1996

On our return to London in Sept 1995 we had no employment and, for the first time in over thirty years, no church to which we belonged. For some weeks we attended as visitors a wide variety of churches, most within walking distance. By Christmas we resolved to settle at Peckham Park Baptist Church, which was warmly welcoming, culturally diverse, lively, evangelical—and about 3 minutes from our door! We were soon committed without becoming actual members, and in March our minister Simon Jones introduced 'A first draft Mission Statement for The Park' (its popular name). The main statement prepared by the leadership team read: 'The Park seeks to be a community gathered around Jesus Christ, committed to serving our neighbourhood by providing unconditional welcome to all, practical care and Christian teaching. Through these activities, with God's help, we believe Peckham can be changed for the better.' Beside that basis were six 'boxes' which explained some of its phrases. 'Practical care' involved sharing in employment preparation offered by PECAN, whose adult literacy work Marjorie was soon training for; among overseas links (in the 'neighbourhood' box) were Simon and Esther Clift, Tim's new neighbours in Dodoma (Tanzania) whom we were soon to visit. We pondered the Statement, and next Sunday (24 Mar) I began to see a possible hymn lurking there. That week it gradually took shape with Marjorie's help on stacks of rough paper; the tune moved from BRISTOL (Common Metre) via KINGSFOLD (DCM) to ELLACOMBE. It was kindly received, and Stephen Carrick-Davies launched it in church that summer. Steve worked for a time for the Church Urban Fund, and next year an adapted text it found its way into a mailing for supporting churches. The Mission Statement, meanwhile, was finalised and distributed under the guidance of Geoff Donaldson, Simon's colleague who succeeded him as pastor.

Light upon the River

St Michael and All Angels, Southfields, London SW18

276 BEFORE THE ROADS OR RAILWAYS CAME

Before the roads or railways came
or buildings rose so high,
great Michael won his princely fame
and angels rode the sky;
as once above the fields they told
of glory, and a King,
so may their music heard of old
tune all our tongues to sing.

And long before south London fields
or fruitful orchards grew,
a cross, a garden, once revealed
what angels hardly knew:
so here as homes and gardens spread
a living church was born,
whose lofty roof and bricks of red
saw nineteen-hundred dawn.

In reach of river, city, trees,
of common land and heath,
it spans the turning centuries
and speaks of life and death:
and as our schools and shops arrived,
with parks and leisure space,
so lives are changed and souls revived -
salvation by Gods grace!

As men and women teach or write
or travel, rule, or build,
for rich and poor, for black and white,
Gods promise is fulfilled:
as we survey these hundred years
or mark two thousand gone,
we find a path through joys and tears
and, one in Christ, move on.

Not every tongue has called him Lord
nor every knee bowed down;
let young and old, in deed and word,
know him and make him known:
our strong Foundation, sinners' Friend,
whom angel hosts obey,
Redeemer, Jesus, come! Extend
your kingdom here today!

DCM Tune: ELLACOMBE

Light upon the River

Scriptures: Dan 10.13,21; 12.1 Jude 9 Rev 12.7; 22.20 Lk 2.8-14; 7.34 Psa 19.7; 148.2 Jn 5.21-25; 19.41-42   1 Pet 1.12; 2.6 Eph 2.8 2 Cor 1.20 Gal 3.28 Rom 14.11; 15.20 Phil 2.10-11; 3.10   1 Cor 3.11 Matt 11.19 Heb 1.6-7,14 Acts 15.11; 28.31

Written: Peckham, Mar-Apr 1997

A return to London gave time to explore some family roots. At St Jude's E Brixton I found myself between the two homes of my parents before they married, at Tulse Hill and Herne Hill respectively; when at St Luke's W Norwood, I disovered my grandparents' grave. I also had a strange (for me) gap with no preaching, which ended at Southfields after 5 months when David Casiot invited me to share in that churchs 'rolling centenary'. They were marking a hundred years of many key events, from plans to consecration. But here too I traced my origins; my father grew up near St Michael and All Angels church, when that and London's southern expansion were still new. The centenary sparked the hymn; primed by David (a friend since 1960) and an exhibition of local history, I again filled many sides of A4 with notes and scribbled lines. They started on Maundy Thursday 1997, our second visit, and were complete a month later after another walk around the parish. ELLACOMBE again proved useful (see the previous hymn) but the two churches may meet only in these pages! We sang it with the Southfields congregation on 30 April 1998, the anniversary of the church's consecration; also featured were hymns by Tony Coombe, a previous vicar, and by Richard Augustus Dobson, the first. Among the local features in mind are (verse 1) Wimbledon Park Road, the District Line, and the church's dedication: (verse 2) orchards and market gardens in the 'south...fields': (verse 3) the nearby Thames and Westminster; the greener Richmond, Kew, or Wandsworth Common; much sport around Wimbledon and its parks; the church school, and my Dad's: (verse 4) teacher/churchwarden David Neil-Smith, sometime resident Ms George Eliot, the princely Teck family, more recent African members and Rwandan links, the new millennium: (verse 5) local Muslims and others, new space for CYPECs (youth and childrens) groups, and the 1897 foundation stone laid 'to the glory of God and the extension of the Redeemer's kingdom'. My one regret is to not have room for the east window commemorating Queen Victoria's dentist.

Light upon the River

Highfields Evangelical Free Church, Cardiff: one

277 COME, HEAR THE GOSPEL WORD

Come, hear the Gospel word,
the truth of God made plain;
sing Hallelujah, praise the Lord!
Dry bones are risen again!

By field and tent and inn
God brings his plans to be,
and makes a stable, hall, or mine
fulfil his sure decree.

And God who makes things new
has given this open door;
a time to build, a time to grow
and trust our Saviour more.

Come, wonder at the Tree;
no leaf it bears, nor fruit,
but carries our iniquity
in Christ, our substitute.

Come, tremble by his grave;
the stone is rolled away!
He came to serve, he died to save;
raised up, he lives today.

Come, meet the Saviour here,
for he will not condemn;
repent, believe, in faith and fear,
and learn to love his name.

Enjoy this meeting-place,
and do not count it strange
if God who gives unchanging grace
requires his church to change.

Lord God, this house is yours;
may we your people be
renewed in Christ with all our powers
for Christ eternally.

SM Tune: MAES-YR-HAF by Geraint Fielder

Scriptures: Ezek 37.1-14 Lk 2.7-8; 24.2 Gen 18.1ff Acts 14.27; 19.9 Job 28.1ff Eccles 3.1-3 1 Cor 3.10 Gal 3.13 Isa 53.6 Mk 1.15; 10.45; 16.4 Jn 8.11 Psa 5.11

Written: Peckham, July 1997

With this text and the next, we move from Southfields to Highfields, from England to Wales, and from a place with personal links to one unknown to me—the only two hymns I have tried for a church I have never met. But we did know Rob Fielder, who joined Christ Church Old Kent Road soon after us; in July 1997 his father Geraint (known by name from long ago) asked me for a hymn for his church. Further letters and papers sketched the history of Highfields Evangelical Free Church, soon to open a new home in buildings dating from the Welsh 'Forward Movement' around 1900. Highfields Church, whose history included the places I later listed in verse 2, kept outgrowing its premises; in September they would start at Monthermer Road. Lord Tonypandy (formerly George Thomas MP, Speaker of the House of Commons) had exclaimed 'Hallelujah for the resurrection of the preaching of the Gospel there!'. I had just read his biography 'Order, order!' (by Ramon Hunston) and seen the huge part the coal mines played in the story of his family, and this community. Geraint had himself written three tunes; could I use any of them? This first text was matched to one, and revised by the end of July after some useful comments from the composer. The tune title means 'Summer field', named after the house where it was written. But there was more to come.

Light upon the River

Highfields Evangelical Free Church, Cardiff: two

278 COME AND BELIEVE IT! SEE WHAT GOD IS DOING

Come and believe it! See what God is doing -
people and places, all in Christ renewing:
heaven draws nearer, death and hell subduing,
    lift hearts and voices high!

God gives our past and future celebration,
evening and morning, old and new creation,
now is the day of favour and salvation:
    now let us turn to Christ!

What shall our prayer be at this day's arrival?
Come, Holy Spirit, with your true revival!
Christ filling all things, Master with no rival,
    Jesus is Lord of all!

Learn from the Saviour, mighty in his meekness;
here we have proved that strength is found through weakness
if we hold fast his cross, and his uniqueness:
    glory to God on high!

God of new openings, blending with tradition,
show new horizons for your urgent mission;
sowing or reaping, bringing to fruition,
    grant us to walk with Christ.

Praise for the word and witness we inherit -
raised from the dead in Christ, our only merit:
praise to the Father, Son and Holy Spirit,
    one God, our All-in-all!

11.11.11.6 Tune: HIGHFIELDS by Geraint Fielder

Scriptures: Psa 126.3 Rev 1.18 Gen 1.1-5 Lk 4.16-21 2 Cor 6.1-2; 9.6; 11.30; 12.9-10 Eph 1.23; 4.10 Acts 4.12; 10.36 Jn 4.36-38 Gal 6.8-9 1 Cor 15.28 **Written:** Peckham, July 1997

Having drafted No.277 (above) I thought that a grand occasion needed something altogether larger than Short Metre. Using another of Geraint Fielder's tunes, and using more ideas from his historical notes and current magazines, I devised this second text without at first realising that both began with 'Come!'. But I wanted to use the words of the Minister, Peter Baker, in that month's Newsletter, 'Part of what God is doing in bringing the Christian Gospel back to the community... our willingness to be caught up in what God is doing...'. The refurbished building was first established through the earlier Welsh revival; hence verse 3. Among perceptions of a multi-faith culture, Christ's uniqueness must be clearly shown (verse 4). And I wanted to use 'tradition' in a positive way, since much of it is good if well-used (verse 5). The 4th line of each verse, in repeated sequence high/Christ/all, matches the rising music at this point. Both hymns were sung at the September services; David Jackman preached, but for George Thomas heaven had truly drawn nearer. Before the new beginnings in Cardiff, he went to be for ever with his Lord.

Light upon the River

Christ Church, Old Kent Road: London SE15

279 HOW OLD THE ROAD, WHERE PILGRIMS WENT

How old the road, where pilgrims went
from Southwark streets to fields of Kent!
How many travellers today
will find the new and living Way?

And who among them briefly sees,
by shops and flats and businesses,
one different tower of brick and stone
which stands for Christ as Lord alone?

While road and railway thunder on
and stores and shows have come and gone,
the church of Christ still points on high
to show what money cannot buy.

And many live, and buy and sell,
from Peckham through to Camberwell:
and some receive the Gift unpriced;
they hear God's word, and turn to Christ.

From many cultures, children play;
there's none too young to learn to pray!
For ripening age, let it be told,
there can be praise in growing old!

So let God's people, like their tower,
point firmly, clearly, to his power;
and walk, where his true pilgrims trod,
the way of Christ, the road to God.

LM Tune: OLD KENT by Agnes Tang; or MORNING HYMN

Light upon the River

Scriptures: Heb 10.19-24; 11.13 1 Pet 1.18-19; 2.11 Isa 24.2; 55.1-2, 6-7 Lk 17.28 Ezek 7.12; 37.4   2 Cor 9.15 1 Thess 1.9-10 Zech 8.4-5 Psa 148.12-13 Prov 18.10 Jn 14.6

Written: Peckham, Easter (Mar-Apr) 1997

It seems good to close this collection at the point where we are now; to come, if not quite full circle, at least back to where some of the earlier texts, like our sons, had their infancy—Nos. 208 and 247 among them. As I complete these notes eight days before Easter, I have this week led assemblies at Pilgrim's Way Primary School in our parish of Christ Church, telling the story of the cross to some who had never heard it. Timothy and Jonathan started school here—one of many places along the Old Kent Road to use the 'pilgrim' theme in their names. Whatever the original Canterbury pilgrims believed, their route is now noisier, busier, and less human; cars continue their relentless destruction in Southwark as in Suffolk. But in Easter 1997 I decided that if other churches have hymns to their names, so at least should ours. Standing in North Peckham, the one surviving church building on the Old Kent Road, it remains officially 'Christ Church Camberwell', having been carved from the old Camberwell parish in the 19th century as was Limehouse from Stepney in the 18th. Its first building was on the opposite side; the Gas Board which replaced it provided some iron gas pipes to form unique church pillars. Another century and half have brought many changes, but the tower (all but its topmost pyramid) remains a landmark even among its new neighbours. We resumed our own regular commitment there at the start of 1997. John Beasley points out in his *Peckham and Nunhead Churches* (South Riding Press, 1995) that Christ Church is the oldest still used in its original tradition, the Church of England. During its time the vast Astoria cinema has come and gone, and many homes and workplaces besides; new stores and new Christian groups have mushroomed between our two Peckham periods, and more recently still. Buying and selling remain local enthusiasms (often found in the Bible with warnings attached!); nearby Rye Lane is as busy as ever. Toddlers' groups and playgrounds are visible growth points; care for the elderly is more hidden; my stanza 5. Our church organist Agnes Tang provides the tune for this final text, which unlike some will not easily transpose to other places. But although (Heb 13.14) we have 'no continuing city' those who find the true Way through it can join with all the other travellers who appreciate what Psalm 119.54 declares. In its Prayer Book version: 'Thy statutes have been my songs: in the house of my pilgrimage'.

INDEX OF SCRIPTURE TEXTS

Hymns in **bold numbers** correspond with the Scripture texts *above* the hymns in the main body of the book; except for the final section (Nos. 265-279) these are the main Bible references by which the hymns are arranged and located. These are usually limited to one reference (verse or section) for each hymn. The other references are those alluded to or reflected in the hymns, or which illustrate them, as listed *below* each one; there they are normally given in the order in which they come in the hymn, except that references to the same book of the Bible are usually placed together.

Text	Hymn no						
Genesis		17.7-8	223	**Leviticus**		31.9-13	230
1.1	200 237	17.7-11	9	19.18	265	32.1-47	**16**
1.1-3	71 240	18.1ff	6 277	22.32-33	242	32.4	213 214
1.1-5	**1** 278	18.23-33	7	25.8-55	138 265		235
1.1-10	211 236	22.17	9	26.11-12	198	32.13	230 235
	274	24.12	8	27.17-24	138	32.15,18	235
1.3-5	186	28.10-22	**10 11**			33.27	168
1.6-10	**2**	28.20-22	230	**Numbers**		32.31	235
1.6-26	151	31.42,53	12	1–2	**14**	32.36	234
1.8	268	32.22-32	270	6.25	214 229		
1.14-18	240	34.28	67	9.15-23	14 227	**Joshua**	
1.16	34 268	37.35	226	10.10	230	1.1-9	**17**
1.16-17, 20-25	4	39.20-23	155	10.35	225	3.14-17	223 227
1.20-28	**3**	41.14	155	11	227		244
1.24-25	222	48.15	229	13.27	14	11.16-23	227
1.25	**4**	48.15-16	**12**	14.20-23	236	24.12-24	**18**
1.26-27	127 144	49.22	229	14.30,38	14		
1.28	177	**Exodus**		16	14	**Judges**	
2.1,4	237	2–4	173	20.1-13	227 230	2.10-15	227
2.4-6	25	2.1-10	270		236 244	5.4-5	235 238
2.4-15	**2**	2.23-25	230	20.22-29	14	7	231
2.7	234	3.1-17	170	21.4-9	14		
2.9-10	198 265	3.5	39 223	22.21-35	14	**Ruth**	
2.15	177	4.22	229	23.23	41 224	1.14-18	223
2.19-20	**4** 222	7.14-17.7	227	24.5-6	14	2.12	217 223
2.24	129	12.51	244	24.17	14 85		
3.17	71	13.14-16	221		198	**1 Samuel**	
3.17-19	177 234	14.21-22	224 244	25	14	1.11	200
3.22-24	198	15.1-18	**13**	27.1-11	14	2.1	204
5.22-24	233	15.2	119 205	27.15-17	250	2.1-10	**19 20** 83
6–8	**4** 270		248 267	36.1-12	14	2.8	243
6.9	255	15.16-17	244 268			3.1	26
8.1-5	118	15.22	6	**Deuteronomy**		3.1-14	249
8.6	273	15.26	178	1.34-36	236	4	227
8.22	268	17.1-7	230 236	4.29	240	7.22	273
9.1-7	177		244	5.1-22	225	16.1-13	227 233
9.12-17	137	19.1-6	180	5.4-7,29	230	26.21	227
9.13	268	19.4	274	6.5	32		
11.1-9	**5**	19.5	244	6.13	32 268	**2 Samuel**	
11.5	243	19.16-19	225 230	6.20-25	221	2.26-38	**21**
12.1-9	**6 7** 173		238	7.9	242	3.3-4	265
13.3-4	6	20.1-21	225 227	8.2	132	5.13ff	202
14.18-20	222 227		230	8.3	121	6.2	225
	239	25.10-22	229	8.6	169	6.12,17	**22**
15.1	213 220	35.35	267	10.12-21	**15**	7.8	227
15.1-6	**8 9**	40.36-38	227	10.20-21	223	7.12-16	22 233
15.6	7 217			12.8-10	236	8.13	174
17.4	7			26.8	224	12.1-14	174
				29.29	259	12.15-17	226

- 310 -

23.1	174	**Nehemiah**		27.8	268	79.5	233
23.1-7	**22**	6.1-14	214	28	**213**	80	**229**
23.3-6	**23**	8.10	265	28.9	200	80.1	197
		9	258	29.1-2	237	80.4	233
1 Kings				29.9	274	81	**230**
4.32	174	**Job**		31	**214**	83	**231**
8.27-30	**24**	1.8	255	31.15	150	84.1-4	212
8.35-36	**25**	2.3	255	32	**215**	85	**232**
8.56-57	24	3	226	33.9	240	85.6	152
17.1	174	9.1-10	68	34.1	150	87.1-3	5
17.2-6	270	10.9	234	34.4-6	93 212	89	**233**
17—18	**26**	14.1-2	227	34.8	101 131	89.9	216
18.16-21	174	19.5-6	226	35	**216**	89.46	234
18.41-46	118	19.25	135	36	**217**	90	194 **234**
19.1-14	46	21.7-13	218	36.5	241	90.1-2	100 176
19.7-18	27	22.29	183	36.5-9	127	91.4	217
19.11-13	**27**	24.1	226	36.9	204	91.5-6,12	250
21.17-29	174	28	**32**	37	**218**	92	**235**
		28.1ff	277	37.4	208	93.3-4	233
2 Kings		28.12-28	36	39	194	95	**236**
1.15-17	174	28.28	242	40.1-3	245 257	95.1-2	230 239
2.7-14	28	35.10	62		258	95.3	237
2.11-12	197	38.1-38	**33**	42	195 **219**	95.6-7	239
2.13	**28**	38.7	**34**		**220**	95.7	210 265
2.19-22	28	42.1-6	261	42.1-2	223	95.7-8	171 230
4	28	42.12-16	255	42.3	228 229	95.7-11	227
5.1-14	28			42.10	228	96	**237**
. 6	28	**Psalms**		43	**219 220**	96.4-6,10	238
19.35	216	1.2	249	43.4	265	96.13	200
20.9-11	1	2.1-2,9	231	44.1-3	227	97	**238**
22.5-10	29	3	**201**	45.1	141	98.1-2	237
25.8-10	228	3.5	202	46.1-9	221	98.9	200 237
28.2-3	29	4	**202**	46.10	218		239
		4.2	234	47.2	141	99.1	45 197
1 Chronicles		4.7	159	48.1-2	222		229
9.33	260	4.8	165 201	48	5 **221**	99.3,5,9	237
13.8	225	5.11	277	48.14	30	100	**239**
15.16ff	225	8.2	195 201	50	**222**	100.1-2	236
16.23-33	237	8.3	235	50.1	243	103.1-2	45
16.34	247 248	9.10	259	51.1-4, 14-15	93	103.1-4	93 178
17.11-14	233	11	**203**	51.15	220		210
22.5-10	**29**	13	**204**	51.16-17	222	103.20-21	187
23.30	260	14.1	5	57.7-11	241	103.20-22	45 200
28.2-3	29	15.1-3	211	60.1	45	104	**240**
29.11	222	18	**205**	60.5-12	241	104.1-4, 19-24	33
29.14	122 222	18.2	270	62.8	150	104.10-16	25
		18.19	214	63	**223**	104.24	2
2 Chronicles		19	36 **206**	63.1	219	104.29	4
5.13	247 248		**207**	66	**224**	105.16-22	155
5.13-14	**30**	19.1-3	137	66.12	266	106.1	269
6.26-27	25	19.7	276	68	**225**	106.2	33
6.32	30	19.7-14	249	68.31	271	107.10-16	155
7.1-10	30	19.12-13	200	69.1-3	257 258	107.20	178
7.3	247 248	19.14	183	69.4	216	108	**241**
7.14	275	20	**208**	69.13-18	257 258	111	**242**
20.1-30	231	21	**209**	71.5	200	111.10	32
20.7	12	21.4	159	71.19	216	113	**243**
32.21	216	22.1-5	226	72.10-11	237	113.3	1
33.10-20	**31**	22.3	200	72.17-19	233	114	227 **244**
36.15-19	227	23	**210**	73.1-14	218	114.3	262
		23.1	161	73.23-26	159	115.1	50
Ezra		23.1-3	29 192	73.25	99	116	**245**
3.11	239 247	23.6	118 212	74.1-10	228	117	73 **246**
	248	24	**211**	77	**226**	118	**247 248**
7.10	170	24.7-10	200	77.6	62	118.22-24	115 189
9	258	25.11	1	78	**227**	118.27	62
9.6-15	232	27	**212**	78.1-7	221 233	119	126 **249**
		27.1	186 268	79	**228**	119.11	218

Scripture Index

119.14ff	206	20.27	36	40.29-31	165 183	37—38	155
119.46,78,80	126	22.7	218		235	38.1-13	214 245
119.89	135	23.7	160	40.30-31	54 156	45	170 259
119.103ff	207	23.11	69 183	41.8	8 12 16	50.34	222
119.105	169	30.7-9	129	42.3	274	52.12-14	228
119.176	210	31.28	254	43.1-4	224		
121	**250**			43.5-7	46	**Lamentations**	
121.3-7	165	**Ecclesiastes**		45.21	199	3.22-23	235 262
121.4	217 271	1—2	158	46.5	233	3.25	240
121.7	212	1.17	50	47.4	266		
121.8	92 256	2.8-11	50	49.10	192	**Ezekiel**	
122	**251**	3.1-3	277	49.26	12	1–2	**54**
122.3-5	214	3.1-8	150	52.1-2	69	1.10	197
122.6-8	253	3.20	234	52.1-10	**46**	1.28	196
123	**252**	5.2	259	52.7	112	3.1-3	206 207
125	**253**	7.20	262	53	**47**	3.1-9	170 174
125.5	251	12	**37**	53.1	128	7.12	279
126.3	278	12.5	199	53.3	64	11.16	244
126.6	250	12.11	169	53.4-6	185	11.19	122
127	**254**	12.13	242	53.6	267 273	15	229
127.2	165 178				277	34.11-16	210
	201 202	**Song of Songs**		53.7	182	34.23	192
127.3-5	255	2.8	69	53.7-9	181	36.22-23	208
128	**255 256**	2.10-13	**38** 118	54.11-12	198	36.24-30	274
128.5	251	8.14	38	55.1-2	199 266	36.26	122
130	**257 258**	4.16	69		279	37.1-14	168 225
130.5-6	212	5.4,16	69	55.6-7	39 240		274 277
130.7-8	259				279	37.4	279
131	**259**	**Isaiah**		56.7	228	37.27	198
131.3	257 258	1.2-3	**39**	57.15	40 127	47.1-12	198
132.10-12	233	1.11	222		191	48.30-35	198
133.3	176	2.1-5	59	58.6-12	267		
134	**260**	5.1-7	229	60.1-3	87	**Daniel**	
134.1	1 96	6.1	203	60.1-6	**48**	2.19	190 191
136.10-16	227 244	6.1-3	149 197	60.15-22	**49**	2.19-22	249
137.5	251	6.1-5	200	60.16	12	2.20-23	**34 55**
139	**261**	6.1-8	**40** 54	61.1-2	89		194
139.1-9	33	6.3	124 196	61.3-6	46	2.24-47	174
139.11-12	55 186		241 272	61.10-11	46 237	3.8-30	174
140.7	66 222	6.8ff	121 170	62.11	199	3.27	224
143	**262**		174	63.1	205	4.3,34	263
144.12	255	9.6	87 167	63.16	266	5.15-31	174
145	196 **263**		249	65.17-19	198	6	174
145.7	177	11.1	199	66.22	198	6.26	263
148.1-2	187	11.2	151			7.14	263
148.1-6	33 128	11.6-7	4	**Jeremiah**		9.1-19	258
	207 240	12	41 187	1.4-10	127 170	10.13,21	276
148.2	73 200	12.2	183 205	1.5	6	12.1	276
	233 276		248	1.9-10	174 220	12.2	200
148.7,10	4	13.10	68	2.21	229		
148.12-13	279	21.10-17	222	9.23-24	**50 51**	**Hosea**	
150	264 272	24.2	279	11.18-20	214	10.1	229
150.4-6	69	25.6-9	**42**	14.1-6	219	10.12	240
150.6	128	25.8	192 198	18.18-23	214	11.1-4	**56**
		26.1	221	23.3	210	11.3-4	96
Proverbs		32.1	117	23.5	117 199	11.8-9,12	**56**
1.7	32 242	33.22	199	23.29	169	13.4	226
3.1-18	159	35.1-7	**43**	29.7	265 267	14.1-8	**57**
3.5-6	160	35	**44**	29.11-12	224	14.2	103
8	35 168	35.10	69 187	29.13	263 268		
8.12-36	**36**	37.14-17	**45**	31.7-14	46	**Joel**	
9.1	92	37.36	216	31.31-37	**52**	1.20	219
9.10	32 242	40.6-8	135 234	31.33-34	**53**	2.10	68
15.6,15,17	92	40.10	199	32.38-41	224		
17.1	92	40.12-31	127	33.11	239 247	**Amos**	
18.10	143 267	40.18,25	233		248	3.4-6	58
	279	40.28	271	33.15	199	4.13	**58**

Light upon the River

5.4-6	240	5.5-6	43	21.9	247 248	6.4	188
5.8	58	5.6	202	21.13	228 251	6.14-29	155 174
5.21-27	222	5.8	211	21.15-16	255	6.30-34	77 100
9.5-6	58	5.9	129	21.21	98 274	7.37	28
		5.14	221	21.42	247 248	8.12	26
Jonah		5.14-16	271	22.37-38	159	8.21	39
2.1-10	245	5.17	91 170	23.5-12	78	8.31	67
2.3-7	219	5.31-33	202	23.27	251	8.34-37	102
2.9	218	5.34	252	23.34	139	8.38	103 126
		5.35	221	24.21	192	9.2-8	91 184
Micah		5.38-39	166	24.29-46	**68**	9.19	39
4.1-5	**59**	5.38-48	181	24.30	238	10.32	200 225
4.4	92	5.42	218	24.45.46	252	10.38-39	29 270
5.5	87	5.45	25	25.1-10	**69**	10.42-44	111
6.6-8	222	6	**64**	25.6	1	10.42-45	**78**
		6.9	146	25.13	68	10.45	66 200
Habakkuk		6.10	255 263	25.31	104		224 267
1.2	204		265 275	26.26-28	131 133		277
2.4	173	6.11	242 254	26.30	**70** 80	10.52	112
3.2	232	6.12	165	26.36—28.10	94	11—16	**79**
3.3	225	6.13	178	26.51-52	21 78	11.7-10	22 97
		6.30	119	26.57ff	109 194		247 248
Zephaniah		6.31-33	60	27.11	194	11.17	228
3.5	271	6.33	159 161	27.29	**71** 175	11.23	98 274
3.14-20	46	7.7-8	55 263		194	12.1	229
		7.9-11	146	27.31	195	12.10	247 248
Haggai		7.24-25	134	27.45-50	182	12.28-31	67 269
1.6	**60**	7.24-27	**65**	27.46	137	12.34	249
2.4-9	60	7.28-29	**63**	27.50-61	**72**	13.19	192
2.6-9	211 232	8.9	252	28.1	189	13.24-37	68
		8.11	197 266	28.6-7	133	13.26-27	85
Zechariah		8.14-27	185	28.1-10	**73** 110	13.32-37	69 123
2.12	227 228	8.23-27	**66**		137		138
4.4	92	9.22	137	28.18	134 135	14.22-25	131 133
8.1-8	199	9.36	100		148	14.26	70 **80**
8.4-5	92 263	9.38	89	28.18-20	**72 74**	14.32-39	172
	279	10.1-4	67	28.20	17 63	14.32—16.8	94
13.1	198	10.1-10	89		269	14.36	97
14.8	198	10.10-16	275			14.53ff	109
		10.29	4	**Mark**		15.15	97
Malachi		10.33	167	1.1	104 149	15.17	71 97
1.11	243	10.34	182	1.1-13	**75**		175
3.6	259	11.2-6	44	1.4-5,9-11	270	15.25	97 226
4.2	1	11.19	276	1.12-13	172	15.25-37	**81**
		11.25-30	102	1.14-20	**76**	15.33	39
Matthew		11.27	128	1.15	138 277	15.34	97 226
1.18-21	82	11.28-30	165 236	1.21	63	15.38-39	72
1.20-25	**61** 141	12.8	265	1.32-39	**77**	15.46	97
1.21	258	12.28	89	1.45	77	16.1-8	110
1.21-23	200	12.29	241	2.1-2,13	77	16.2	189
1.23	17 77	12.37	103	2.21-22	48	16.4	277
	195	12.38-40	128	2.23	77		
1.25	194 195	13.3	137	2.28	265	**Luke**	
2.1	185	13.17	28	3.7,13	77	1.19	34
2.1-12	**48 62**	13.23	274	3.13-19	76 275	1.26	256
2.2	84	13.28	262	3.27	241	1.26-35	**82** 144
2.23	92 256	16.24-26	102 181	3.31-35	275	1.34-35	200
3.13-17	28	17.1-8	91 184	3.32	77	1.38	262
3.13-4.11	75	17.20	98 274	4.1-2	77 170	1.46-55	19 20 **83**
4.4	121	18.1-4	259	4.1-20	103	1.50	266
4.8-10	193	18.20	72 197	4.7,19	119	1.51	5
4.18-22	76		272	4.20	274	1.52	243
4.23	63	18.23-37	31	4.35-41	66	1.68	58
5.1-2	**63**	20.25-26	111	5.6	219	1.77-79	58 265
5.3	137 218	20.25-28	78	5.21,24	77	2.4-7	**84**
5.4	258 274	20.28	66 182	6.1-4	77	2.4-16	61
5.5	129 218	21—28	79	6.3	65 97	2.6-7	3 194

Scripture Index

	195	11.2-3	64	24.15	80			185
2.7	97 122	11.3	242 254	24.15-32	132	6.38-40		88 121
	128 188	11.4	165	24.28-31	92	6.41		104
2.7-8	100 277	11.11-13	146	24.32	186 249	6.62		108
2.8-14	85 276	11.20-22	26	24.34	135	6.63		103
2.8-20	**86**	12.9	167	24.36-40	85	6.66		117
2.11	35	12.32	106 117	24.36-52	108	6.68		103
2.13-14	87		119 227	24.38	182	6.65		102
2.14	108 190	12.35-37	69	24.40-43	97	7.37		**102**
	191	12.50	75	24.42	97	7.37-39		43 115
2.23	188	13.28-30	197	24.44-49	72 98			187 265
2.25	257	13.29	48		115			270
2.25-38	**87** 235	14.15-24	266	24.45	249	7.46		63 **103**
2.32	184	14.28-30	102	24.49	107	8.11		277
2.33	86	15.1-2	93 275	24.50-53	260	8.12		1 102
2.34-35	195	15.1-24	76					**104** 149
2.38	257	15.4	136	**John**				186
2.39	92	15.8	136	1.1	54 91	8.31-35		142
2.39-40	256	15.17-21	**93**	1.1-9	36 162	8.32		78
2.40	262	15.22-24	46	1.1-14	35 **99**	8.39		9
2.41-42	**88**	17.17	67	1.4-5	168 184	8.56		8 9
2.51	86	17.28	279		207	8.58		7
2.51-52	92 256	18.7	252	1.4-9	149	9.5		104 186
3.21-22	75	18.8	152 232	1.10-14	**88 100**	9.25		141
4.1	90	18.9-14	215	1.12	128	10.7-9		102 155
4.1-2	140	18.13	269	1.14	54 77 91			267
4.1-13	75	18.42	87		144 169	10.10		64 268
4.4	121	19.5-6	92		194 196	10.11		213
4.5-8	193	19.10	5 44 76		207	10.11-15		210
4.14	90		78 93	1.14-18	184	10.27-28		227 266
4.14-15	128		121 132	1.18	167 190	10.35		17 134
4.16-21	**89** 278	19.28—24.53	79	1.29	3 190			227
4.18	142 183	19.35	3		191 192	11.25		**104** 105
4.21	185	19.40	266		193			134
4.28-30	100	19.41-42	251	1.29-36	75 193	12—21		79
4.31	63	19.46	228	1.36	190 191	12.13		247 248
5.1-11	76	20.9-18	115		192 193	12.13-15		22
5.5	156	21.18-19	250	1.47-49	261	12.26		159
6.5	265	21.27-33	68	1.49-51	10 11	12.31		176
6.13	67	21.28	114 138	2.1-11	**48 101**	12.36		166
6.20	268		273	2.6	67	12.46		184
6.20-21	140	21.33	132 135	2.18-22	24 88	12.47-50		103 222
6.21	274	21.36	138	2.24-25	261	13.1		38 70
6.27-38	140 181	22.14-20	131 133	3.3-8	180			102 156
6.30,38	218	22.16	70	3.14-15	14 182			182
6.46-49	65	22.20	52	3.14-16	9 81	13.31-32		211
7.11-17	90	22.37	47	3.16	84 121	14.2		**106**
7.15	274	22.39-44	**94**	3.16-18	188	14.6		102 160
7.34	276	22.39—24.8	94	3.19	110 165			220 268
7.41-42	265	22.66ff	109		184			279
8.1-3	140 275	22.68	194	3.21	10	14.15		159
8.11,15	98 267	23.1	194	4.6	188	14.16-17		127 151
	268	23.18-25	100	4.10-14	28 187	14.18		26
8.46	90	23.26	85	4.14	199	14.21		159
9.1-6	275	23.32-46	47	4.19	188	14.26		**107**
9.12-17	140	23.33	128 185	4.36-38	278	14.27		49 253
9.28-36	184		195	4.42	66 191	15.1-8		229
9.51-53	100	23.33-34	140	5.21	263	15.15		131 142
9.57-58	64 140	23.46	214	5.21-25	105 108			188 269
10.1-4	89	23.50-53	47		168 276	15.16		107 111
10.1-9	275	23.53	122	5.28-29	225	15.18-19		110
10.20	67 106	24.1	189	6.9	67	15.26		107 151
10.28-36	**91**	24.1-8	85 185	6.27	60 159	16.7-15		107
10.38-42	92 159	24.1-10	**95** 110	6.31	227	16.13-15		127
11.1	26	24.2	277	6.35	104	16.28		**108**
11.2	146 255	24.6-7	133	6.37	102	16.33		99
	263	24.13-35	**96**	6.38	90 182	17.1-5		200 211

- 314 -

17.1—20.18	94		151	4.3ff	9 217	13.14	184
17.6-26	275	10.38-40	128	4.6-8	215	14.9	184
17.8	103	11.18	57 81	4.16	6 180	14.11	276
17.24	196	12.1-19	155	4.16-24	7	14.12	73
18.18—19-30	109	13.29	94	4.22-24	217	14.19	129
19.1-5	71 99	13.38-52	**117**	5.1	52 133	15.4	249 258
	175	14.11-15	238		182	15.7	272
19.11	5 97	14.17	118 263	5.5	71 267	15.11	73 246
19.30	81 97	14.27	275 277		268	15.13	178
	182	15.11	276	5.6-8	144	15.17-19	27
19.41-42	128 276	15.25-26	**119**	5.9-11	41	15.20	276
20.1	128 189	15.36	115	5.10	153	16.25-27	**124**
20.1-18	95 **110**	16.5-15	**120**	5.12-17	105	16.27	266
20.19	189	16.6-10	**121**	5.17	9 131		
20.19-23	107 275	16.9-10	249	6.1-14	**119 125**	**1 Corinthians**	
20.30-31	110	16.12-15	153	6.4-6	109 263	1.2	271
21.6	156	16.16-40	155	6.5	167	1.18	98 99
21.15-17	159 240	16.22-25	153	6.8-9	105	1.18-25	6
21.28	144	17.18	114	6.10-11	130	1.23	164
		17.24-29	**122**	6.13	263	1.24	35
Acts		17.24-31	127	6.19-22	126 148	1.26-31	51 117
1.1	63	17.25	222	7.12-22	206	1.27	99
1.4-8	107	17.25-27	263	8.1	41 109	1.30-31	35 62
1.8	72	17.26	16		240	2.8	104 116
1.9	167	17.27	272	8.2	220		149 211
1.12-26	111 112	17.27-28	5	8.11	185	3.6	268
1.24	261	17.30-31	**123**	8.13	163	3.9-17	65
2.1-11	**113**	17.32-34	99 117	8.15	9	3.10	277
2.1-21	274		271	8.15-21	127	3.11	276
2.3	71	18.23	113	8.17-28	3	3.16-17	24
2.23-33	114	19.9	277	8.18	173	3.22	156
2.28-39	9	19.17-20	238	8.18-22	138 194	4.7	122
2.29-32	31	20.7	189	8.18-27	37 113	5.7-8	**130**
2.30	233	20.7-8	149	8.19-21	237	5.18-19	41
2.39	83	20.21	98 194	8.19-23	44	6.19-20	24 30
2.43	234	20.24	223	8.22	128		136 148
3.15	114	20.28	268	8.26	205		156 268
3.17-26	188	22.1-21	116	8.29	9 122	7.14	9
3.19	165	23.12-22	214		188	7.22	153
3.22	261	25.19	86	8.29-34	163	7.22-23	136
4.1-31	115	26	174	8.32	82 84	8.5-6	117
4.2	**114**	26.1-23	116	9.5	55	8.29	137
4.7-20	**115**	26.18	186	9.8	9	9.1	111
4.10	114	26.28	139	9.33	126	9.24-27	175
4.11	247 248	27.23	26 205	10.1	76	10.4	270
4.12	98 266	28.20	258 259	10.9	128	10.12	218
	278	28.31	276	10.9-11	**126**	10.16-17	70 131
4.29	201 204			10.13-14	74 93	11.23-26	42 96
5.30	94 114	**Romans**		10.14-15	40		**131**
5.30-32	40 151	1.1-7	**124**	10.17	164	11.23-32	**132 133**
	274	1.3	209	10.17-18	206	12.3	195
5.31	57 81	1.4	107 149	11.1	202	12.4	265
5.41	252	1.5	9	11.15	87	12.4-7	147 179
7.1-38	173	1.7	271	11.26-27	66	12.4-13	107
7.2	196	1.16	126	11.33-36	33 **127**	12.12-13	131 166
7.37	261	1.20	206 268		128 144		147
7.55	196 200	1.24,26,28	227 230	11.36	150	12.27	166
8.2	135	1.25	16	12	**129**	13.8	96 257
8.4	170	2.4	177	12.1	70	13.13	96 164
8.32-33	47	2.12,16	163	12.2	92 160	14.47	10
9.1-31	**116**	3.18	217	12.4-8	147 148	15.1-4	110
9.31	271	3.19-26	109 144	12.5	166	15.1-28	134
10.19	94		240	12.15	178	15.12-20	135
10.33	170	3.20	262	12.17	166	15.17-20	205
10.34-41	113	3.23	267	13.6-10	142	15.20	173
10.36	278	3.24	200	13.11-12	87 132	15.20-22	130
10.36-43	75 112	3.27	102		165 166	15.20-26	114

- 315 -

Scripture Index

15.26	90	4.26	46 487	4.30	143	4.4-5	166
15.28	278	4.28	9	5.1-2	145	4.4-9	**160**
15.42-43	105 268	5.1	**142**	5.6-13	165	4.7	113 152
15.54-57	105 114	5.11	164	5.8	186	4.10-11	177
	187	5.13	166	5.8-14	**149** 163	4.10-14	157
15.57	15	5.13-14	142		166	4.11-13	129 156
16.2	189	5.22	75	5.14	186 273		**161**
16.9	275	5.22-25	107	5.15-17	150	4.13	152
		6.8-9	278	5.16	1	4.19-20	**161**
2 Corinthians		6.14	51	5.18	142	4.21-22	153
1.1	271	6.16	255 257	5.18-19	265	4.23	157
1.3-4	178			5.19-20	**151** 235		
1.20	82 86	**Ephesians**		5.21-25	256	**Colossians**	
	276	1	**143**	5.25-27	179	1.9-12	146
1.22	143	1.3-8	117 **144**	5.27	267	1.9-19	143
2.12	275	1.4	163	5.29-30	147	1.10	159
2.14	15	1.6	198	5.30	148	1.12-20	**162**
3.18	122 137	1.7	55 96	6.10	214	1.13	96
	163 184		121 242	6.10-13	145	1.15	91
4.4	**136**		267	6.12	267	1.15-19	54 188
4.4-6	**137**	1.9-10	113 162	6.19-20	154	1.15-20	3 108
4.6	149 168	1.10	108 188	6.23-24	143	1.18	9 116
	185 202	1.11	163 267				147 148
	242	1.11-12	116	**Philippians**			172
4.7-11	139	1.14	268	1—2	152 153	1.19-20	113
4.8-10	76	1.17	151	1.1-6	120	1.20	29 182
5.13	139	1.17-18	145	1.5-6	**154**	2.2-3	35
5.14-20	153	1.17-23	124	1.6	156 179	2.5	160
5.17	116 173	1.18	55 **145**		267	2.6	93 159
	248	1.19-20	125 163	1.7	157	2.9	54
5.19	31 266	1.19-23	108 162	1.12-14	154 **155**	2.9-10	148 162
6.1	6 121	1.22-23	147	1.20	126	2.9-12	9
6.1-2	138 278	1.23	278	1.20-21	**156**	2.12	125
6.2	73 176	2.1	90	1.20-24	121	2.13-15	109
6.4-10	**139** 197	2.1-10	56 144	1.21	105	2.15	15 162
6.7	96	2.4	249	1.27	154		200
6.16	24	2.4-6	103 105	2.2	188	2.19	116
7.6	183		263	2.2-5	157	3.1	95 114
8.9-15	161	2.4-10	271	2.4-5	**157**	3.1-2	145
8.9	140	2.8	202 276	2.5	188	3.1-10	125
9.6	278	2.14	21 87	2.5-11	117 128	3.1-14	**163**
9.8-15	161	2.14-17	76 162		144 154	3.2	160
9.11	166	2.19-22	65 88	2.6	162	3.9-14	184
9.15	193 279	2.20	200	2.6-8	194	3.10	122
10.3-4	208 241	3.14-21	**146**	2.9	172	3.11	59
11.16-30	139	3.16-17	61	2.10-11	276	3.14	256
11.26-27	120	3.17	21 122	2.11	42 74	3.15	23
11.30	278	3.17-19	139		157	3.15-16	255 272
11.31	55	3.18	40	2.13	171	3.16	235
12.5-10	139	3.20	101 127	2.21	157	3.17	150
12.9-10	119 148		128	2.23	106	4.2-4	139
	183 220	3.20-21	113	2.25-30	119	4.5	150
	278	4.1-6	124	3.4-11	158 159	4.12	148
		4.3	275	3.7-11	121 173	4.18	155
Galatians		4.4-16	147	3.8	152 157		
1.16	127	4.7-13	225		168	**1 Thessalonians**	
2.16	262	4.7-16	**148**	3.10	154 276	1	**164**
2.20	38 **141**	4.8-9	105	3.10-11	156 167	1.3	273
	156 261	4.9-10	117	3.12-14	175	1.5-10	154
	269	4.10	172 209	3.14	35 76	1.9	57
3.6-8	9 217		278		188 220	1.9-10	279
3.13	94 277	4.12-13	146		267	2.2	154
3.21-22	261	4.13	267	3.18-20	153	4.11-12	150
3.27	125	4.13-15	145 176	3.20	164 197	4.13	61
3.28	59 153	4.15-16	116 131		267	4.13-14	135
	276	4.19	272	4.2	153	4.16-17	123 267
4.4-5	84	4.21-32	163	4.3	154	5.4-11	**165**

- 316 -

Light upon the River

5.5-24	**166**	3.7—4.11	236	2.1	211		234	
5.9	266	3.15	171	2.5	146 256			
		4.6-9	128	2.14-17	64	**2 Peter**		
2 Thessalonians		4.7	171	2.15-16	140 157	1.1-19	**184**	
3.1	**155**	4.12-13	134 136	2.18	80	1.16-19	91	
3.6-13	150 **166**		171 261	2.23	6 7 8 12	1.19	234	
		4.14-16	78 **172**		175	1.21	168 **185**	
1 Timothy		4.16	133 240	3.9	137		249	
1.1	200	5.1-10	188	3.9-10	213	3.1-13	49	
1.15	84	6.18-20	172	3.17	80 256	3.5	240	
2.5	128	6.19	168	4.8	240	3.8	234	
2.8	223 260	7.19	240	4.1-10	21	3.9	144	
	262	7.25	172	4.14-15	134	3.18	104 184	
3.14-16	144 200	8.1	190 191	4.15	105			
3.16	128 **167**	8.6-13	52	5.1-6	83 **177**	**1 John**		
4.8	114	9.11-15	52	5.7	25	1.1	119	
5.5	257	9.12	29 74	5.8-9	218	1.1-2	99	
6.13-16	127 **168**	9.26	185	5.13-16	**178**	1.1-3	91 182	
6.15-16	34 128	9.27-28	1 123			1.5-7	**186** 212	
	149 162	9.28	73 141	**1 Peter**		1.7	129 182	
	167		268	1.1-5	143 163		192	
6.17	267	10.12	185 190	1.2	**179**	2.1	172	
			191	1.3	110 152	2.2	109	
2 Timothy		10.19-24	251 279		180 271	2.4	214	
1.8-12	126	10.22	240	1.3-4	146 168	2.8	186	
1.10	110 176	11	**173**	1.9-10	9	2.10	212	
2.9	155	11.8-19	7 9	1.12	33 197	2.15-17	159	
2.11	119	11.10	5 265		276	2.22	214	
2.11-13	144 167	11.13-16	265 279	1.13-15	160	2.28	126	
	263	11.32-40	271	1.18-19	110 136	3.2	1 106	
2.15	126	12.1	273		279	3.2-3	184	
3.15-17	134 **168**	12.1-2	53 158	1.19	4 192	3.4	172 218	
	249		175	1.23	180	3.16-18	64 140	
4.1	163	12.1-3	173	1.25	135	3.17	157	
4.6-8	175	12.2	145 155	2.3	101	4.1	166	
			172 190	2.4	267	4.7-10	136	
Titus			191 252	2.4-5	65 179	4.8	30	
1.5	271	12.7-10	56	2.6	276	4.9-10	38 39	
2.2	200	12.10	209	2.7	247 248		109	
2.13	144 154	12.12-13	44	2.9	186 244	4.9-19	121 240	
	184	12.14	202	2.9-10	**180**	4.14	66	
2.14	258	12.22-24	46 252	2.11	279	4.16	30	
3.3-8	76 103	12.24	52	2.16	142	4.18	71	
3.6	125	12.25	56	2.21	76	4.19	98 145	
3.7	200	12.25-26	27	2.21-25	47 **181**		164	
		12.25-29	225		**182**	4.20	214	
Hebrews		12.29	238	2.22	172	5.1-2	100	
1.1-2	7 61 134	13.2	265	2.24	61 70 81	5.5	99	
1.2	77 240	13.3	155		94 109	5.11	114	
	261	13.5	46 56		132 166	5.21	164	
1.1-3	6		226 266	3.8-9	166			
1.3	54 149	13.6	247	3.10-12	123	**Jude**		
	162 163	13.8	176 259	3.11	133 218	3	154	
	172 188	13.15	30 245	3.12	203	9	276	
	191		268	3.18	182 270	14	39	
1.4	74	13.20	53 210	3.20	67	24	250	
1.6	200	13.21	89 262	3.21-22	125	24-25	166	
1.6-7	276			3.22	108 163			
1.8	82 117	**James**		4.7	160	**Revelation**		
1.13	34	1.5	256	4.8-11	129	1.4-20	**187**	
1.14	276	1.11	50	4.10	134	1.5	13 233	
2.1-4	27	1.12	71	4.12	224	1.5-6	188 196	
2.5-9	114	1.15	249	4.14-16	126		197	
2.9	44	1.17	2 34 98	5.4	210	1.5-7	68	
2.14-18	78		186 193	5.6-11	**183**	1.7	182	
3.1	179 261		256	5.8	44 262	1.8	198 199	
3.7	171	1.17-18	48 177	5.10	9 139	1.10	34 **189**	

- 317 -

Theme Index

1.12-13	268	4.2-8	187	12.11	131	21.8	214		
1.15-16	182	4.6-9	69	14.3	138	21.10-21	69		
1.16	67 69	4.8	124	14.12	271	21.12	187 265		
1.16-18	42	4.12	35	15.3-4	193 **196**	21.14	197		
1.17	198 199	5.5	199		242	21.22-26	60		
1.17-18	188 265	5.6	106	16.6	193	21.23	49		
1.18	28 86 96	5.8-14	69	17.14	148 261	22.1-3	43 263		
	189 278	5.9	58 138	19.1	73 192	22.1-4	106		
1.20	268		149 261	19.1-6	73 193	22.3	271		
2.1	182	5.9-10	66	19.1-9	**197**	22.4	118 168		
2.1ff	268	5.9-14	131 196	19.4	192		182 203		
2.8	188 198	5.11-14	106 187	19.6-9	46		212		
	199 265	5.12	149	19.9	266	22.7	237		
2.10	71 155	5.12-14	75 192	19.11	203	22.12	193		
2.28	1 69 199	6.9-11	197	19.13	169	22.12-21	**199**		
3.7	155	6.12-14	68	19.16	148	22.16	69 85		
3.8	275	7.9	175 197	20.6	114	22.17	102 219		
3.12	198	7.9-17	192	20.12-13	163	22.20	98 121		
3.14	188	7.11-12	35	21—22	88 **198**		141 237		
3.20	168	7.17	210	21.1	113 121		276		
4	54	10.17-18	206	21.2-3	69	22.21	**200**		
4—5	**190 191**	11.15	185 **193**	21.2-4	46				
	193 197	12.1-10	**194 195**	21.4	117				
	200	12.7	276	21.4-5	59 106				
4.1	81 200	12.10	109 193	21.5	203				

INDEX OF TUNES

Tunes needed	50 65 79 118 155	BARBARA ALLEN	71	CHINE	202
167 195 239 257		BATTLE HYMN OF		CHISLEHURST	272
A GAELIC BLESSING	186	THE REPUBLIC	185	CHORUS ANGELORUM	219
ABBOT'S LEIGH	222 265	BE STILL AND KNOW	229	CHOSEN JUDGE	123
ABRAHAM	8	BEATITUDO	12 155	CHRIST THE LIGHT	104
ABRIDGE	92	BEDFORDSHIRE MAY		CHRISTCHURCH	216
ACH BLEIB BEI UNS	244	DAY CAROL	210	CHRISTE SANCTORUM	20
ACLE	75	BEN LOMOND	168	CHRISTIAN	160
ADORAMUS	2	BEN MORE	250	CHRISTMAS GREETINGS	84
ADVENT	138	BENSON	46	CHRISTUS DER	
ADVENT PSALM	68	BERGERS see FRAGRANCE		IST MEIN LEBEN	203
ALBANO	202	BEST GIFT	101	CHURCH TRIUMPHANT	14 115
ALFORD	58	BETHANY (Smart)	222	CLARLI	109
ALIREB	36	BIGGIN HILL	232	COME PRAISE THE NAME	184
ALL FOR JESUS	17	BINNEY'S	137 217	COMMITMENT	218
ALL SAINTS	24 172	BIRLING	221	COVENANT SONG	53
ALL YOUR		BISHOPTHORPE	235	CREDITON	126
COMMANDMENTS	249	BLAENWERN	129	CRIMOND	210
ALLELUIA	264	BLOW THE WIND		CROFT'S 136th	179 216
ALTON	261	SOUTHERLY	107	CROSS OF JESUS	61
ANDREW MARK	83	BOW COMMON LANE	237	CRUCIFER	41
ANELLEN	86	BREMEN see NEUMARK		CRUDWELL	192
ANGEL VOICES	266	BRESLAU	133 262	CRUGER	144 160
ANGELS' SONG	96 111	BRISTOL	157	CUDDESDON	191
Anon	38 238	BROADHEATH	17	CULBACH	255
AQUINAS	201 262	BROTHER JAMES' AIR	210	CWM RHONDDA	13
ARDWICK	245	BRUNSWICK	31	DANCING HILLS	244
ARMAGEDDON	18 116	BUNESSAN	85	DARMSTADT	59
ASCALON	130	BUSHILL	113	DARTMEET	42
ASCENDED	108	CARLISLE	57	DARWALL'S 148th	148 171
ASHLAND	159	CARYL	274	DAS NEUGEBORNE	
ASKHAM BRYAN	34	CELESTE	2	KINDELEIN	228
AURELIA	160	CHALVEY	218	DEEP HARMONY	201
AVE VIRGO		CHARITY	102	DEVA	125
see GAUDEAMUS PARITER		CHARLES WESLEY	47	DIADEMATA	105
BANGOR	204	CHELWOOD	21		

Light upon the River

DINE HENDER ER FULLE AV BLOMSTER	95	HELEPETE	46	MARCHING THROUGH GEORGIA	193
DOMINICA	72	HERMAS	116	MARLEE	109
DOMINUS REGIT ME	71 132	HERONGATE	168	MARYDENE	260
DROOPING SOULS	42 224	HESLINGTON	39	MAUTBY	81
DUMPTON GAP	134	HIGHFIELDS	278	MEGERRAN	248
DUNDEE	29 37	HIGHWOOD	121	MELCOMBE	96
DUNFERMLINE	7	HOLIFIELD	169	MELITA	81
DURROW	251	HORSELL	241	MELLING	86
EBENEZER (=TON-Y-BOTEL)	108	HOSEA	56	MEN OF HARLECH	173
EDELWEISS	141	HOUGHTON	166	MENDIP	157
EDWIN	64	IBSTONE	145	MERRITT	168
EIN' FESTE BURG	267	ILA	200	MERTON	51
EISENACH	194	IN BABILONE	264	METZLER'S REDHEAD	219
ELIJAH	26	IN EXITU	244	MONKLAND	84
ELISHA	28	IN MEMORIAM (Roberts)	222	MORNING	85
ELLACOMBE	275 276	IN SILENCE MY SOUL IS WAITING	56	MORNING HYMN	159 279
EPHESIANS	145	IN SILENT PAIN	182	MORNING STAR	192
EPIPHANY HYMN	169	INNOCENTS	255	MOWSLEY	66
ERLESTOKE	88	IRISH	219	MULL OF KINTYRE	270
ERPINGHAM	43	ISHMAEL	120	MUNSLOW	100
ES IST EIN' ROS ENTSPRUNGEN	231	JACOB	168	NASSAU see WURTEMBURG	
ETERNAL FATHER	234	JANE	205	NATIVITY	117 143
EVELYNS	131 199	JERICHO	120	NEANDER see UNSER HERRSCHER	
EVINGTON	122	JOHN HENRY	97	NEARER HOME	16 218
EXALTED NAME	265	KELVINGROVE	94	NEUMARK (=BREMEN)	62 228
EXOUSIA	74	KIEV	170	NEW CROSS	192
FARMBOROUGH	190	KILMARNOCK	235	NEW HEAVEN	198
FARRANCE STREET	149	KING'S LYNN	6 55	NEW PRAISES	264
FELICITER	215	KING'S WESTON	131	NIDDLEDALE	101
FENNY STRATFORD	187	KINGSFOLD	15 119	NORICUM	36
FESTUS	163	KOCHER	49	NORTH COATES	70 124
FLIGHT OF THE EARLS	11	KREMSER	33	NORTHAMPTON	274
FOR I'M BUILDING A PEOPLE OF POWER	269	LA CORBIERE	221	NORWOOD	87
FRAGRANCE (=BERGERS)	40	LADYWELL	197	NUN DANKET	59
FRIARMERE VICARAGE	33	LANCING	263	NYLAND	55
FROM STRENGTH TO STRENGTH	142	LAND OF HOPE & GLORY	191 199	O GOD ETERNAL	223
FRY	168	LAUDATE DOMINUM	98 166	O QUANTA QUALIA	192
FULDA	163 236	LAUS DEO (Redhead)	43 164	O STRENGTH AND STAY	93
GALILEE	263	LAUS DEO (Bach)	52	OAKLEY	13 14
GAUDEAMUS PARITER (=AVE VIRGO)	44	LAVENDON	146	OFFERTORIUM	9
GOD REST YE MERRY	233	LIEBSTER IMMANUEL	169	OLD KENT	279
GOD'S SPIRIT IS IN MY HEART	227	LIGHT UPON THE RIVER	265	OLDHAM	212
GOLDEN SHEAVES	248	LINGWOOD	113	OMBERSLEY	1 168
GONFALON ROYAL	90 187	LITTLE HEATH	4 47	ONE-O-ONE	59
GRANBY	168	LITTLE STANMORE	220	ORIENTIS PARTIBUS	42 45
GREAT OXENDEN	232	LIVERPOOL	202	ORMESBY	77 154 188
GREEN GROW THE RUSHES-O	67	LIVING WORD	169	OUR CALLING	181
GRIDLEY	145 177	LLAN	63	OUR GREAT HIGH PRIEST	172
GROWING	145	LLANBAGLAN	200	OVERTON	243
GUDS ORD	169	LLANSANNAN	103	PARKSTONE	14 145
HA DVAR	71	LONDON NEW	7	PASSONS	163
HAGGAI	60	LONDON ROAD	81	PENLAN	55 144
HALLELUJAH	73	LOVE DIVINE	39	PLATT'S LANE	122
HALTON HOLGATE	61 164	LOVE UNKNOWN	140	POPLAR	24
HAND ME DOWN MY SILVER TRUMPET, GABRIEL	89	LUCERNA LAUDONIAE	36	PRAISE OUR GOD	224
HARROW WEALD	128	LUDHAM	25	PRAISE TO GOD	86
HARTS	224 274	LUTHER'S HYMN	52	PRAISE TO THE LORD	247
HAYDN	351	LUX EOI	200 265	PROMISES	249
HE CAN BREAK EVERY FETTER	189	MACPHERSON'S FAREWELL	258	PURPOSE	46
		MAELOR	216	QUEM PASTORES	149
		MAES-YR-HAF	277	RATISBON	35
		MAGNIFICAT NOW	263	REALITY	182
		MAKROLINE	80	RE'EMI	99
		MANE OG SOL	151	REGENT SQUARE	101 104
		MARCHING	170	RENDEZ A DIEU	214

Theme Index

REPTON	10 48	SANDOWN	136	TERRYL	179		
REST (Maker)	217	SANDYS	256	TERSANCTUS	162		
RESTORATION	127	SARAH RACHEL	168	THAXTED	178		
REVELATION	54	SAVANNAH	42 86	THE FIRST NOWELL	110		
RIDLINGTON	80 132	SCARBOROUGH FAIR	226	THIS ENDRIS NYGHT	156 254		
RINKART	59	SCRIABIN	82	THRANDESTON	157		
RODMELL	235	SEVEN SEAS	168	THRICE BLEST	71		
RULER	210	SHEPHERD PSALM	210	TIVERTON	241		
RUSTINGTON	200	SHERINGTON	217	TON-Y-BOTEL see EBENEZER			
SAFFRON WALDEN	220	SHONA	59	TOTARA	251		
ST ALBINUS	66	SHOREHAM	180	TREWEN	205 240		
ST BERNARD	112	SIMEON	150 221	TRIMINGHAM	148		
ST BOTOLPH	254 259	SINE NOMINE	232	TRUMPET VOLUNTARY	211		
ST CATHERINE'S COURT	33	SING GLORY, GLORY	114	TRURO	221 273		
ST CECILIA	177	SLEEPERS WAKE		TWO SAMUEL	22		
ST CHRYSOSTOM	81	see WACHET AUF		UNFOLDING	176		
ST COLUMBA	80	SOLOTHURN	106 194	UNSER HERRSCHER			
ST DENIO	127	SOMERSET	248	(=NEANDER)	13 74		
ST EDMUND	4	SOMERTON A	140	VENI SANCTE SPIRITUS	246		
ST ETHELWALD	174	SOMERTON B	249	VENICE	174		
ST FLAVIAN	126	SOMMERLEID	122	VOATES	236		
ST FRANCIS XAVIER	152	SONG 46	88 225	VOICES LIFTED	209		
ST FULBERT	19 219	SONGS OF PRAISE	183	VOX DILECTI	75 135		
ST GEORGE	64 99	SPIRIT OF HOLINESS	107	WACHET AUF			
ST GEORGE'S WINDSOR	139	SPIRITUS VITAE	260	(=SLEEPERS WAKE)	69		
ST GERTRUDE	116	SPLENDOUR	78	WARWICK (Stanley)	241		
ST HELEN	113	STALHAM	5	WAS LEBET, WAS SCHWEBET	253		
ST HELENS	162	STENKA RAZIN	76	WATER END	207		
ST HUGH	152	STEVENAJ	2	WELLS	229		
ST JOHN	109	STREETS OF LAREDO	33 147	WESTMINSTER	29 156		
ST LEONARD	24 175	STUTTGART	27	WHEN I FEEL THE TOUCH	161		
ST MATTHIAS	91	SUMMERCOURT	3	WHEN THE SAINTS			
ST MICHAEL	252	SUMMERVILLE	188	GO MARCHING IN	271		
ST NICHOLAS	101	SURREY	165 230	WILFORD	71		
ST STEPHEN	23 158	SURSUM CORDA	100	WILLARD	146 206		
ST THEODULPH	268	SUSSEX	21	WINCHESTER NEW	3 26		
ST THOMAS	120	SUSSEX CAROL	230	WINTERTON	187		
ST VICTOR	203	SWABIA	252	WIR PFLUGEN	32		
SAINTS IN CHRIST	153	SYRIA	242	WOLVERCOTE	9 49		
SALZBURG	202 242	TANYMARIAN	108	WOODLANDS	146 206		
SAMSON	208	TEDCRICK	184	WORTHAM	101		
SAN ROCCO	241	TEMPUS ADEST FLORIDUM	44	WURTEMBURG (=NASSAU)	30 196		
SANCTISSIMUS	253	TENHEAD	122	YANWORTH	153		
SANDON	213	TENDER MERCIES	242	YVONNE	169		

INDEX OF SELECTED THEMES

i.e. distinctive or dominant topics

Theme	Hymn No.				
Aaron	14		39 43 54 58 79 219	Bethlehem	35 39 62 85 87 185
Abraham	6 7 8 9 12 83 120		222 229 274	Bible: see Scripture	
	173	Annunciation	82	Birds	3 4 16 38 54 118
Adam	4 130	Apostles	67 111 112 116 131		203 222 227 274
Adoption	103		147 197 200	Building	65 92 266 267 276
Advent	44 46 66 68 69 85	Ascension	74 105 108 111 148		277
	104 114 123 132		167 172 175 211	Caleb	14
	138 199 211 232		225	Cana	48 101
	237	Athens	271	Change	5 12 24 134 266
Age	235	Atonement: see Cross			269 274 276 277
All Saints	271	Baptism	5 9 116 119 120		279
Angels	10 11 31 33 34 35		125 147 270	Cherubim	45 197 229
	61 68 69 73 74 85	Baptism of Jesus	75 270	Children	12 14 56 83 84 221
	86 87 110 123 131	Beauty	16 33 34 38 160 184		234 254 255 256
	167 187 197 216		267		263 264 269 279
	276	Bells	266 274	Christmas	61 82 84 85 86 87
Animals, living creatures	3 4 14 25	Bethany	79		97 138 194 232
		Bethel	6	Church	5 6 24 26 34 72 98

– 320 –

Light upon the River

	107 116 135 146	Ezekiel	54		275
	147 148 152 162	Faith	6 7 8 9 70 72 90 101	Hunger	64 83 157 161 192
	164 166 179 180		152 156 158 164	Idols, idolatry	16 18 26 57 117 127
	197 200 265 266		172 173 174 175		140 164 227 237
	267 268 275 279		205 266 274	Image of God	122 137 144 163
Cities	5 24 87 116 214 263	Faithfulness	107 167 177 193		184
	265 267 275 276		233 235 239 249	Incarnation	5 35 54 77 78 82 84
City of God	46 106 198 199 221		263		88 97 99 100 127
	228 251	Families	10 12 18 146 243		128 137 140 141
Cleansing	28 274		254 255 256 263		144 167 185
Clothes	140	Farms, farming	25 60 268 273 274		194 195
Comfort	41 140	Fasting	140	Invitation	102
Commands, see Law of God		Fear	7 11 12 17 27 31 37	Isaac	12
Conservation	3 177		41 44 46 59 103 105	Jacob	10 11 12 14 16 208
Contentment	156 157 160		205 234 245 248		230 244 270
	161 177 218 259	Flood	4 67 270	Jerusalem	46 69 79 87 187 251
Conversion	116 136 155	Food and drink, feasting 42 46 60			253
Corinth	271		64 69 92 130 140	John the Baptist	75 111 112 270
Countryside	268 269 270 273		210 228	Jordan	28 75 244 270
	274	Forgiveness	31 52 53 55 58 103	Joseph (OT)	229 230
Covenant	6 9 49 51 52 53 87		165 178 215 227	Joshua	14 17 18
	96 133 222 233 242		232 249 257 258	Journeys, travel	6 7 9 10 11 13 17 18
Creation, nature	1 2 3 4 14 24 25 31	Freedom	13 44 66 89 109 125		62 77 92 96 120 132
	33 34 36 38 43 44		142 155 174 183		140 188 250 265
	55 58 118 122 143		200 207 215 224		276 279
	151 162 177		245 249 257	Joy	42 44 46 48 160 164
	194 200 205 206	Friends, friendship	5 129 155 159		166 194 213 215
	207 211 222 236		269 273 275		216 220 223 224
	237 239 240 250	Galilee	66 87 271		235 236 237 239
	260 261 268 274	Garden	95 110 128 265		249 265 279
Crete	271	Gethsemane	94	Jubilee	138 265
Cross (specific)	29 39 40 47 51 61	Gifts	80 101 107 122 129	Judaea	271
	71 72 78 81 94 97		133 146 147 148	Judah	221 227 244
	99 117 131 181 182		150 179 193 227	Judas Iscariot	111 112
	185		248 265 268	Judgement	13 19 20 27 41 79
Cults	238	Glory (specific)	40 190 191 196 207		123 163 176 200
Damascus	116	Good Friday	47 79 81 94 181 182		209 219 221 227
Daniel	55	Gospel	74 89 102 115 120		228 229 231 232
David	22 29 82 199 209		134 135 152 154		234 235 236 237
	227 228 233		266 277		261 262 270
Death	5 14 37 64 72 79 90	Government	5 23 60 159	Justice	23 193 196 216 225
	105 135 152 155	Guidance	10 11 120 134 215		231 238 240 262
	156 178 204 205		249 262 263		267
	227 228 229 234	Guilt	31 47 81 109 191	Land	13 16 23 43 44 49
	235 245		215 232 258		227 232
Disciples, discipleship	66 67 70	Hannah	19 20	Last Supper	70 79 80
	76 80 101 111 112	Haran	6	Law of God	15 17 52 53 67 71
	249	Harvest	14 16 60 267		142 148 206 227
Earth: see Land, World		Healing, health	12 28 37 103 106		230 249
Easter	13 42 67 73 79 95		178 185 263	Leadership	5 23 26 78 111 112
	96 97 110 114 130	Heaven	81 102 106 131 132		152
	135 138 163		138 172 184 192	Light (specific)	104 149 168 186
	185 187 247 248		193 197 198 200		212
Egypt	56 173 227 229 230		271 275	Lord's Day	79 189 247 248
	244 271	Hell: see Judgement		Lord's Supper: see Holy Communion
Elderly	235 264 279	History	16 24 174 176 188	Love	15 38 56 67 71 72
Election	6 143		227 234 266 268		78 102 108 124 129
Elijah	26 28 91 270		269 271 273 276		142 143 146 163
Elisha	28		277 278		164 172 184
Emmanuel	61	Holy Communion	70 79 80 92 96		192 194 205 210
Emmaus	96		131 132 133 178		211 217 223 226
Enemies	153 201 203 204	Holy Spirit (specific)	89 107 274		233 239 240 241
	209 210 212 213	Home	12 19 65 92 100 120		246 247 261 266
	214 215 216 217		122 129 140 157		270
	219 225 229 230		254 255 256	Lydia	120
	231 238 247 262	Hope	164 168 172 178	Mamre	6
Epiphany	48 62		183 193 205 240	Manasseh	31
Evangelism	96 102 120 147 154		257 258 259 266	Manna	228
	235	Hospitality	92 129	Marriage	69 38 101 129 255
Evening	1 149 165 202	Humanity	16 36 113 128 261		256

- 321 -

Scripture Index

Martha	79	Prayer	7 27 29 55 79 93 94		67 68 182 194 268
Martyrs	131 139 155 173		146 164 166 178	Suffering	119 172 181 192
	174 192 197 200		202 205 208 212		194 195
Mary (mother of Jesus) 82 83 86 144			213 223 224 228	Sunday: see Lord's Day	
	188 200		229 262	Superstition	26 238
Mary (sister of Martha) 79		Preaching, preachers 40 116 139 153		Teaching	63 65 74 77 79 103
Mary Magdalene 95 110			154 164 170 174		137 147 269
Matthias	111 112	Priesthood	172 179 180	Tarsus	116
Maundy Thursday:		Prison, prisoners	42 84 109 119 153	Temple	24 29 30 65 79 88
see Holy Communion			155 157 161 173		192 198 203 219
Mercy	28 31 40 55 87 103		174 228		228 244 251
	118 131 190 191	Promises	6 10 82 83 86 87	Temptation	75 172 249
	205 213 214 217		242 249	Thanksgiving	151 160 166 236
	249 252 258 261	Protection	11 14 201 202 203		239 245 265 266
	265		210 214 215 218		268
Michael	276		250 254	Time	1 136 138 150 156
Mind	145 160 163 188	Prophets	6 54 59 131 139 147		176 194 195 234
Miracles	4 9 13 14 27 28 44		170 197 200		273 276
	48 67 89 90 101 155	Providence	16	Transfiguration 91 184	
	185 224 227 268	Railways	276 279	Travel: see Journeys	
Miriam	14	Rain	23 25 26 33 43 57	Trees	6 14 22 25 38 43 44
Mission	74 76 98 102 115		118 265		49 57 58 94 97 106
	121 176 180 274	Red Sea	244		137 198 229 235
	275 278	Repentance	31 57 81 93 123 138		268 273 274
Money	60 79 89 279		144 152 170 194		276
Moreh	6		277	Trial, trials	109 139 145 172
Morning	235 241 249 257	Return of Christ: see Advent			192 224
	262 265	Revival	229 232 265 278	Trinity	24 45 71 113 124
Moses	6 13 14 16 91 173	Resurrection	7 16 24 72 73 79 85		127 149 151 179
	270		90 95 96 97 104 105		187 190 191 200
Mountains	32 38 44 58 59 91		110 114 130 134		205 211 220 264
	98 205 221 231 238		135 143 151		267
	240 241 244 251		163 185 189 247	Trouble	226 228 248 258
	253		248 268 277	Trust	19 156 205 214 215
Music	22 30 69 159 212	Risk	119 134 156		222 252 259
	219 220 225 230	Rivers	14 25 28 44 75 118	Villages	77 268 269 273
	235 241 272 273		120 198 210 219	Violence	21 29 194 216
	274		227 244 265 266	Vision	54
Naaman	28		270 276	War	21 22 29 59 64 182
Nain	90	Rome	271		195 208 225 231
Nation	14 23 24 26 49 60	Rulers	5		266
	232 255 258	Sabbath	79 120 138 265	Wealth	5 19 28 49 50 51 52
Nations	13 48 74 87 98 116	Saints	34 119 153 173 174		60 62 121 218
	196 228 231 237		175 271	Wedding: see Marriage	
	238 241 243 246	Salvation	41 47 247 248	Welcome	19 100 103 131 272
Nazareth	115 256	Scripture	14 17 26 27 91 134	Whitsunday	107 274
Neighbours	5 59 64 65 67 126		169 170 171 185	Wind	33 274
	129 157 164 214		249	Windows	273
	265 269 273 275	School	269 276	Wisdom	32 33 35 36 48 50
Noah	270	Sea	13 31 32 120 211		51 52 55 62 71 87
Obedience	6 15 17 18 63 93		224 233 236 244		88 103 151 218 242
	134 170 171 249		270 274		249
Palm Sunday	22 79 97 211 247	Seasons	43 55 268	Wise men (Magi) 48 62	
	248	Second Coming: see Advent		Word of God	26 28 49 58 98 99
Passover	91 130 227 228	Security	119 179 201 203		121 166 168 169
Paul (Saul)	116 120		212 250 253		170 206 225 233
Peace	21 22 23 29 49 59	Seraphim	40 89 149 197		236 247 249 257
	251 253	Service	15 18 68 78 111 112		258
Pentecost	107 113 225 274		116 121 139 147	Words	77 103
Persecution	116 119 139 155		154 166 169 239	World	15 64 98 100 113
	173 192 216		245 252 260		121 140 177 195
Peter	111 269	Shame	126 175 177 216		211 228 231 243
Philippi	120	Silence	27 109		267
Pilgrimage	62 140 265 279	Sin	31 47 93 182 194	Work	60 65 92 97 150 159
Poverty	5 15 19 20 28 83 89		195 215 217 227		164 166 254 269
	121 140 243		257 258		276
Praise	30 41 45 117 162	Sleep	10 11 165 178 201	Wrath: see Judgement	
	184 190 191 200		202 254	Youth	37 249 269
	210 213 224 246	Sport	159 269	Zion, Mount Zion 22 44 69 221	
	260 264 272	Stars	9 31 32 33 34 58 62		222 227 253

Light upon the River

INDEX OF HYMN TEXTS
including Psalm versions

	Hymn number
A world in pain, a baby's cry	195
Abraham's faith	8
All authority and power	74
All glory be to God on high	190
All the brown and bare horizons	43
All the law your God has given	17
All the saints who serve in heaven	271
All your commandments, Father almighty	249
Almighty God, the Fountain-head	31
Almighty Lord, the Holy One	165
And did you risk yourself, O Christ	119
Angels are bringing news in the morning	85
Arise and shine! Your light has come	48
As Jacob travelled far along	10
As once for you, Lord Christ, there was no room	100
As sons of the day and daughters of light	166
As the light upon the river	265
Ascended Christ	148
At the supper's ending	70
Attend, all heaven and earth	16
Baptized into Christ Jesus	125
Before the roads and railways came	276
Before they leave the upper room	80
Bless the Lord in psalm and chorus	264
Bless the Lord, our fathers' God	45
Blessed are those who fear the Lord	255
Cattle know their master's manger	39
Christ has prepared for us a place	106
Christ is all the world's good news	102
Christ is going to the Father	108
Christ is surely coming	199
Christ once was sacrificed	130
Christ the Light who shines unfading	104
Christ the Lord who calls us	131
Christ's church shall glory in his power	267
Christmas greetings, Christmas joy	84
City of God, Jerusalem	46
Come and believe it! See what God is doing	278
Come and see the shining hope	193
Come and tread the pathway	77
Come, hear the Gospel word	277
Come, Lord, to make yourself at home	92
Come, praise the Lord, all you his servants	260
Come, praise the name of Jesus	184
Come, see the winter is past	38
Come to a world of need	105
Come with all joy to sing to God	236
Contend, O Lord, with those	216
Creator God, with whom we share	3
Dark is all the world below him	61
Downtrodden Christ	81
Eternal Father, God of grace	234
Eternal light, shine in my heart	168
Eternity once entered time	194
Exult, creation round God's throne	187
Far greater than great	127

Father and God, from whom our world derives	146
Father of our Lord Jesus Christ	143
First and Best-beloved	188
For all our seven churches	268
For ever, Lord, I'll sing your love	233
Freedom and life are ours	142
Friends of God whose faith abounded	175
Give praise for famous men	174
Give thanks for the gifts	147
Give thanks to God, for he is good	248
Glory and praise to God	207
Glory in the highest to the God of heaven	191
Glory to God, the source of all our mission	121
(God brings us comfort) Praise God today	41
God has been gracious	82
God, I cry aloud for help	226
God of all human history	176
God of every tribe and nation	113
God of hope and Lord of healing	178
God of Israel's names and numbers	14
God of my life, to you I pray	220
God of the world's great cities	5
God our Father and Creator	24
God the Lord, the King almighty	222
God, we praise you! God, we bless you!	200
God's word to God's world	98
Grace and peace be ours for ever	164
Great and wonderful your deeds	196
Great is the Lord; his praise is great	221
Great the wonder, great the mystery	167
Hallelujah: Christ is king	73
Hallelujah, praise the Lord	242
Happy are those whose offence is forgiven	215
He stood before the court	109
Here from all nations	192
His Father's house	88
Holy Lord and Father	124
Holy Spirit, heaven's breath	274
How can scholars boast of wisdom	51
How clear and true the skies sing out	206
How good is life, and length of days	159
How long will you forget me, Lord	204
How many are against me, Lord	201
How old the road, where pilgrims went	279
How shall the wise be proud of their wisdom	50
How sure the Scriptures are	171
I lift my eyes to you	252
I love my great Lord	245
I love you, O Lord, you alone	205
I never looked for Jesus	136
I to the hills lift up my eyes	250
I trust the Lord for safety	203
I will exalt you, God, my King	263
I will sing the Lord's high triumph	13
I'll sing a new hymn to my God	240
If Christ had not been raised from death	135
If God does not build up our house	254
If God has chosen a nation	180

Hymn Index

If the Spirit of God is moving us now	89
If we are raised to life with Christ	163
In God the Father's plan	179
In God the Lord my heart is strong	19
In life or death, Lord Jesus Christ	156
In silent pain the eternal Son	182
In the day of need	208
In you, O Lord, I find my refuge	214
Into our darkness once you came	1
Is your harvest less than you had hoped	60
Israel's Shepherd, hear our prayer	229
It was no empty dreamer	49
It was on Sunday morning	189
Jerusalem! How glad I was	251
Jesus, come, for we invite you	101
Jesus, most generous Lord	140
Jesus, Saviour of the world	66
Jesus whose glory, name and praise	117
Jordan's waters part in two	28
King David was a man of war	29
Let God arise! His enemies, be gone	225
Life-giving Christ, our hope and head	90
Light and salvation is the Lord to me	212
Light of gladness, Lord of glory	149
Listen, my friends, to each word	227
Listen! Wisdom cries aloud	35
Long before the reign of kings	4
Lord all-knowing, you have found me	261
Lord God who blessed our fathers here	12
Lord most high	141
Lord of our time	150
Lord of the heights, we sing your glory	40
Lord, show us how to live	177
Lord, teach us to rejoice in you	157
Lord, teach your children how to build	65
Lord, to you we lift our voices	209
Lord, you chose your first disciples	76
Lord, you have seen your church's needs	152
Lord, you have weaned my heart from pride	259
Lord, you need no house	122
Lord, you sometimes speak in wonders	27
Make music to the Lord most high	235
Make us, O God, ashamed of sin	126
Master, by your word of welcome	103
Master, what love is here	72
Mercy and peace from heaven's King	87
Moon and bright sun	151
Must the sword devour for ever	21
My heart is ready, O my God	241
My heart rejoices and my strength is kindled	20
My Lord of light who made the worlds	71
My Lord, you wore no royal crown	78
My soul proclaims the greatness of the Lord	83
No fear of God before the eyes	217
Now in view of all God's mercies	129
Now is the time, the time of God's favour	138
Now let us learn of Christ	145
Now praise the Protector of heaven	2
O God, defender of the poor	202
O God, do not keep silent	231
O God eternal, you are my God	223
O God of justice, answer me	262
O God, the heathen have attacked	228
O Lord my Rock, to you I cry aloud	213
O Lord whose love designed this day	96
O when Jesus lay there in the manger	97
O where shall peace be found	59
One beyond all	128
Our God has made his covenant new	52
Our God, supreme and good	64
Out of the depths I cry to you	257
Partners in the Gospel	154
Powerful in making us wise to salvation	169
Praise God for windows	273
Praise God today: his glories never end	41
Praise our God with shouts of joy	224
Praise the Lord, all nations, praise	246
Praise the Lord, Hallelujah	243
Praise the Lord with the people of Palgrave	269
Praise to God and peace on earth	86
Praise to God the Father	162
Praise to the Lord, for the Lord is good	247
Preachers of the God of grace	139
Rain on the earth by heaven's blessing	25
Remember your Creator now	37
Return to face your God	57
Saul of Tarsus planned it	116
See Christ who on the river's shore	75
See the feast our God prepares	42
See your hands overflowing with flowers	95
Serve the Lord God only	18
Shout for joy to the Lord, all the earth	239
Since our great High Priest, Christ Jesus	172
Sing glory, glory, Hallelujah	114
Sing, sing, sing to the Lord	237
Sing when the rain is coming	118
Spirit of holiness	107
Strong in Christ, our great salvation	173
Sunday was the day when he came to Jerusalem	79
Teach me, Lord Jesus, all I need to know	63
The countless stars of heaven	9
The dance of the stars in burning glory	34
The glorious God of heaven	55
The God who spoke at Haran	6
The land is dry	26
The Lord has said that he will be our God	53
The Lord is here, the darkness gone	110
The Lord is King! Let earth be glad	238
The Lord my shepherd rules my life	210
The Lord who made the mountains	58
The saints in Christ are one in every place	153
The Spirit led by day	120
The sun went down on Jacob's grief	11
The victory of our God is won	197
The vision of the living God	54
The wonder of salvation	144
The Word was very God	99
The works of the Lord are created in wisdom	33
Then I saw a new heaven and earth	198
This earth belongs to God	211
This world has great rewards to give	158
Those who rely on the Lord are unshakeable	253
Through all the world let Christ be known	115
To Christ who once this supper made	133
To everyone whom God has made	123
To God our strength come, sing aloud	230
To know God's mind and do his will	112
To set their hearts on God	256
To this we have been called	181
To walk the way of Abraham	7
Towering over road and river	266
True light, blazing in the darkest place	186
Twelve for the twelve apostles	67
Up from the depths I cry to God	258

Light upon the River

Wake, O wake, and sleep no longer	69	When prison walls extend their reach	155
We have done wrong, and only God can save us	93	When rulers judge in righteousness	23
We heard Christ's word, and looking back	132	When the King shall come again	44
We meet together in the name	134	When the sun is darkened	68
Welcome, welcome every guest	272	When this land knew God's gracious love	232
What does the Lord our God require	15	When we are down you raise us up	183
What is our mission in this place	275	When we are in want	161
Whatever things are lovely	160	When you prayed beneath the trees	94
When at first the word was spoken	170	Where is the glory of our God	137
When David found his rest	22	Where is the one our God will choose	111
When holy men of old	185	Where is the rock, and where is the river	270
When Israel fled from Egypt	244	Who believes what we have heard	47
When Israel was young, you loved him	56	Who can measure heaven and earth	36
When Jesus led his chosen three	91	Wild creatures long to cool their tongues	219
When lawless people thrive	218	Wise men, they came to look for wisdom	62
When mines are dug for silver	32	With one voice they joined their praise	30

A Prayer about the ambiguities, temptations and satisfactions of putting things on paper for ourselves and others and for the glory of God: to be sung (in the mind) to GRIFFIN'S BROOK. These lines were included in a collection presented in 1991 by members of the Hymn Society of Great Britain and Ireland to that tune's composer—see Nos. 5 and 135 of these texts. That is, to John Wilson: hymnologist, musician, teacher, editor, treasurer, wit, and friend. Born in 1905, he died in July 1992, mourned and appreciated by hymn-lovers on both sides of the Atlantic.

*Christ who worked to full perfection
by a route that led uphill,
in your love, your strength, your pattern,
help me find your will.*

*When the signs you send to guide me
seem to point in different ways,
help me see and think more clearly
which way brings your praise.*

*When the things I thought completed
all my planning have outgrown,
grant me strength of mind to finish,
or to lay them down.*

*When the choicest work I offer
stays unknown or set aside,
show me how to dodge self-pity,
how to pounce on pride.*

*When my lesser gifts are welcomed
and applauded, for a while,
help us see their true proportions;
give me grace to smile.*

*When, like you, I'm interrupted,
pulled by slowness or by speed,
then remind me that you give me
all the time I need.*

*Teach me yet again, dear Master,
since your prize was won through pain,
that in you my work is valued
and is not in vain.*

NOTES

NOTES